Praise for *A Long Journey*

WINNER · Atlantic Book Award for Scholarly Writing, 2021
WINNER · Clio Prize (Atlantic Region), 2021
WINNER · Peter Cashin Prize, 2021
SHORTLISTED · BMO Winterset Award, 2021

. . . . . .

"*A Long Journey* is a compelling, necessary read."
— Joan Sullivan, *The Telegram*

"Procter delivers the most thorough examination of its kind."
— Jenn Thornhill Verma, *Atlantic Books Today*

"Andrea Procter's compelling and comprehensive book amplifies and balances the personal and scholarly to provide a compassionate and measured depiction of the impacts felt by northern residents as a result of Moravian Mission and International Grenfell Association schools. Procter's collaborative and intimate approach, at the behest of Indigenous community members, is also exemplary of meaningful and consensual allyship."
— *Jury, BMO Winterset Award*

"Andrea Procter's remarkable book…is a model of engaged collaborative scholarship with the Inuit, NunatuKavut, and Innu nations of Labrador. While specifically about residential schools in Labrador and Newfoundland, this book is also evocative depiction of the Indigenous peoples of the province, particularly in their homelands in Labrador, and deserves a wider readership for the stories it tells and the nuances it expresses. It can also serve as an example for others who are committed to respectful collaborations that enable Indigenous peoples, in this case with diverse cultural perspectives, to convey their understandings of their own lives in a way that models rigorous collaborative scholarship."
— *Jury, Clio Prize (Atlantic Region)*

A LONG JOURNEY

Residential Schools in Labrador and Newfoundland

Andrea Procter

ISER Books

LIBRARY AND ARCHIVES CANADA CATALOGUING IN PUBLICATION
Title: A long journey : residential schools in Labrador and Newfoundland / Andrea Procter.
Names: Procter, Andrea H., 1974- author.
Series: Social and economic studies (St. John's, N.L.) ; no. 86.
Description: Series statement: Social and economic studies ; no. 86 | Includes bibliographical references and index.
Identifiers: Canadiana (print) 20200168398 | Canadiana (ebook) 20200168436 | ISBN 9781894725644 (softcover) | ISBN 9781894725668 (EPUB) | ISBN 9781894725675 (Kindle) | ISBN 9781894725651 (PDF)
Subjects: LCSH: Boarding schools—Newfoundland and Labrador—History. | CSH: Native peoples—Residential schools—Newfoundland and Labrador—History. | CSH: Native students—Newfoundland and Labrador—History.
Classification: LCC E96.5 .P76 2020 | DDC 371.829/970718—dc23

Cover image: Lizzie Lucy at the St. Anthony orphanage, ca.1932 (courtesy of The Rooms)
Cover design: Alison Carr
Page design and typesetting: Alison Carr
Copy editing: Richard Tallman

Published by ISER Books, an imprint of Memorial University Press
Institute of Social and Economic Research
Memorial University of Newfoundland
PO Box 4200
St. John's, NL A1C 5S7
www.memorialuniversitypress.ca

Printed in Canada
26 25 24 23 22 21 2 3 4 5 6 7 8

CONTENTS

FOREWORD

A Long Journey as a Healing and Commemoration Legacy Component

Serendipity, or happy coincidence, played a large part in Andrea Procter coming to write this scholarly work on education in Labrador. After several unsuccessful attempts to engage prominent writers who were known to the Indigenous community in Labrador, my friend Dr. Hans Rollmann gave me Andrea's name as someone who was knowledgeable in Labrador's Indigenous culture and who had a track record of a good working relationship within the community. As each of the potential candidates presented good reasons why scheduling, personal circumstances, and geography — among other things — would not allow them to complete this work, our good fortune found Andrea at a stage of her academic and working career to enthusiastically accept the concept of the Healing and Commemoration process we laid out to her.

As the lengthy class action lawsuit that had proceeded through the Newfoundland and Labrador Supreme Court came to an abrupt close with the proactive actions of the Trudeau Liberals in 2016, the western Canadian law firm of Ahlstrom Wright Oliver and Cooper LLP, led by the ebullient Steven Cooper and represented in this province by the firm run by John Crosbie, Q.C. acting on behalf of the plaintiff students, reached a negotiated Settlement Agreement with Canada alone; the other defendants — the province of Newfoundland and Labrador, The International Grenfell Association, and the Moravian Church — were all absolved of liability through the settlement process. No doubt these parties breathed a sigh of relief from the lifting of the potential for financial burden or a negative impact on their corporate image. For the students, this simply meant some additional worry as the opportunity to hear acknowledgement and apologies from Newfoundland, the IGA, and the Moravian Church hierarchy was swept away by the stroke of a pen.

Canada and Cooper proceeded in a Settlement Agreement process to ask the Indigenous leaders of the Inuit, NunatuKavut people, and Innu Nation to select representatives as the preliminary step in a consultation process to breathe life into the Agreement. From there, the law firm selected plaintiff Toby Obed; the Innu Nation chose Helen Andrew; NunatuKavut Community Council selected Kirk Lethbridge; and the Nunatsiavut government chose me. We held a preliminary meeting in Ottawa in June 2017, and among other decisions made then, I was appointed as Ministerial Special Representative to partner with federal government colleagues in a project of Healing and Commemoration activities to honour the group of some 950 students.

Our small advisory panel listened to the lawyers and federal government officials, who presented a list of potential ideas to discuss and make additional comments upon, and while the Healing and Commemoration Advisory Panel, as we were called, generally liked the negotiated agreements mentioned, we, as Indigenous people, balked at being the voice for all the students without further consultation with the larger student group back home. We thought a further meeting in a Labrador location with a sample of students might give everyone a better chance to hear a clearer, expanded, and inclusive list of reconciliation activities.

The next meeting did indeed have strong support for a priority list of activities: a personal visit to Labrador by Prime Minister Justin Trudeau with a formal apology to representative students and Indigenous officials; artists and craftspersons contracted to produce lasting and meaningful pieces for everyone to celebrate; community visits to hear students' personal experiences in the schools; a permanent sound and visual record of digitally produced vignettes; and, finally and importantly, a recounting of the history of education in Labrador with an emphasis on how the delivery of education evolved to become our piece of the Canadian jigsaw puzzle of federal and provincial policies, imposed on the Indigenous population, that served to demonstrate the colonial influences so representative of an era that perpetuated insidious bigotry and a dismissive attitude of any cultural norms not held as Christian or Eurocentric.

Thus began a year and a half journey to work towards the goal of commemoration of the resilience of the students, and to employ the healing benefits of talking within a respectful, safe, comforting setting with trained professionals who were willing to act as mentors, supports, sounding boards, confidants, and, in many cases, friends to anyone who wanted to speak about any aspect of school life, personal mental growth, challenges, aspirations, and reflections. The interventions, we were told in these sessions, allowed many to find a sense of lightheartedness or of a load being lifted from one's shoulders as they recounted their experiences. Finally, someone was listening to their personal stories of childhood pain, shame, and loss, tempered with growth and resilience as they reflected on these times as adults.

Andrea Procter agreed to join us in these sessions. She knew many students intimately, and her understanding of the histories of the communities in the context of schooling made everyone appreciate her presence. She joins an impressive group of scholars and historians who are expanding our knowledge of the Indigenous peoples of Labrador and their relationships with the provincial and federal governments and their numerous agents of assimilating forces. Following in the footsteps of Carol Brice-Bennett in *Our Footprints Are Everywhere*, Maura Hanrahan in *The Lasting Breach: The Omission of Aboriginal People from the Terms of Union between Newfoundland and Canada and Its Ongoing Impacts*, and Martha MacDonald in *Inside Stories: Agency and Identity through Language Loss Narratives in Nunatsiavut*, and others, Dr. Procter has gathered a fascinating account of the recorded annals, books, archives, and personal stories to provide an up-to-date and comprehensive appreciation of the Labrador experience. She chronicles how the experiences of

Indigenous children in Labrador shifted from a family-centred, culturally relevant immersion in life to the worldwide phenomenon of Christian-based norms and values that combined with subtle and overt colonialist attitudes to drive a wedge between these children and their families and distinctive culture.

As my role as Ministerial Special Representative developed, our priority was to test the willingness of the Canadian government to have Prime Minister Trudeau come to Labrador and offer an apology. Andrea has captured the essence of that event in this book, so I need not say any more about it. However, the morning after the event, I had the task of being a shuttle driver for students and any others who needed to get to the airport, and my first early morning run was to have CBC parliamentary reporter David Cochrane as a passenger. He made a comment that has stayed with me since it spoke to the impacts of the residential schools as a stark reminder of how nature and nurture work to mould a person in this country. He said that what struck him the most, when Toby Obed went on the stage and shook his good hand with Prime Minister Trudeau and gave him a celebratory hug, was that the two men *were the same age.* Mr. Obed's life challenges arose even before he was born, when his family and all Inuit of Hebron in northern Labrador were forcefully relocated in the late 1950s to more southern Labrador communities. Personal and family cohesion was gone; hunting grounds were gone; self-esteem as male and female providers was gone; church affiliations were gone. The fast spiral downward destroyed Toby's family and any chance that this quick-witted, funny, intelligent, and resourceful guy could aspire to much beyond survival. But what did survive was an iconic man who cared deeply that an apology be delivered to the surviving students. As we all watched Toby and held our collective breath, he wrestled with his emotions to accept the apology on behalf of all the students, putting aside his personal and private hurt for the good of others and demonstrating how far he had come in personal growth and resilience. At that moment, in the eyes of all the students, his acceptance was as fine and sincere an acceptance as was the prime minister's apology, and the emotional impact — on those present and the many others who could not be in the auditorium — was profound.

The story Andrea tells — of good-intentioned peoples and groups, churches, and governments wearing the robe of patriarchal authority but blind to the very people they hope to advance — is still being played out in many spheres. We learn from Andrea's book that histories need reporting, need explanation, and that the harsh light of scholarly examination needs to shine in all the corners of Canada to prevent bad decisions from being perpetuated through seemingly good intentions.

In the course of the Healing and Commemoration sessions we heard the stories of students who have been scarred by the residential school experience, and we also were told forcefully by others of the value of and appreciation for the education they received. We heard how the resilient youth of the dorm days allowed great friendships to be fostered, romances to grow, the hopes and dreams for a peaceful adulthood to be achieved. Some of these stories — the bad and the good — are central in the broader historical narrative that Andrea Procter offers in this book. The common denominator for positive change is, as always, the youth who defy old norms, who are fearless in demanding new relationships, and whose spirit has every Indigenous group in Labrador exchanging family and cultural ties, where before, people stuck to their own lives and communities to the exclusion of the rest of Labrador. So also it is with Newfoundlanders who embrace Labrador life and people, and who are now developing the accepting values of understanding and breaking the old barriers of bigotry. Because of the youth and their willingness to bend their beliefs, Indigenous people in Labrador are more self-confident, self-assured, and willing to share the pride in their Indigenous culture.

Andrea's book is a testament to the good outcomes of hard work and scholarly effort, which allow us to look at ourselves in a way we had not considered because the whole picture was too big to grasp until someone could clarify it for us.

I hope our efforts to emphasize commemoration and healing and Andrea's capturing of this fascinating story will encourage Prime Minister Trudeau's words to ring true: "All Canadians possess the ability to learn from the past and shape the future."

James Igloliorte
Ministerial Special Representative, Newfoundland and Labrador
Residential Schools Healing and Commemoration Project, 2016–19

ACKNOWLEDGEMENTS

To all the children who attended these boarding schools, and to the adults they became, I hope you can see yourselves reflected in these pages. Your voices and your silences have been my constant companions as I wrote this book. I hope I have done you justice.

To all the former students who shared stories, thank you for your courage and your strength. I hope your grandchildren will hear those stories and better understand how your experiences continue to shape their lives. I also hope that other Indigenous and Labrador voices will add to this conversation about our shared history and our shared responsibilities.

In doing this work, I am building on the efforts of many before me. Evelyn Winters developed the Nunatsiavut government's program for residential school healing, and Darlene Wall worked tirelessly with the NunatuKavut Community Council to help former students. Thank you, Evelyn and Darlene, for all your work on this issue, and for your patience in helping me understand the impacts of the boarding schools.

I am grateful to the many former students and other experts who helped to direct me on the right path. Thank you to Shirley Flowers, Michelle Kinney, Reta Crane Saunders, Fran Williams, Helen Andrews, Amy Hudson, Carolyn Michelin, Michele Wood, Fiona Andersen, Peggy Andersen, Navarana Igloliorte, Tim Borlase, Ron Sparkes, Bob Hopcroft, Keating Hagmann, Ossie Michelin, Jodie Lane, Charlotte Wolfrey, Hilda Dyson, Rutie Dicker, Rutie Lampe, Edna Winters, Sophie Pamak, Marjorie Flowers, and Toby Obed for talking with me about your experiences and for guiding my thinking throughout this process.

Other former students and their family members read through multiple versions of these chapters and provided me with critical and thoughtful advice. Thank you, Eva Luther, Joan Andersen, Sharon Edmunds, Jim Igloliorte, and Tracey Doherty for sharing so much of your time and your wisdom in reviewing drafts and suggesting changes. Thank you to Bertha Holeiter, Beatrice Hope, Joan Andersen, and the members of the Moravian Church of Newfoundland and Labrador board for offering your thoughts on the work. Thank you also to Labrador historians Greg Mitchell, Martha MacDonald, Carolina Tytleman, and Hans Rollmann for your detailed edits and comments, and for providing kind encouragement.

I am especially indebted to historian and former boarding school student Patty Way, who must have used up a good few of her red markers in noting mistakes and corrections in my work. Patty's knowledge of Labrador and her leadership in researching its history are inspiring, and we are lucky to have her. Thank you, Patty, for everything you do.

Jim Igloliorte led the Newfoundland and Labrador Residential Schools Healing and Commemoration team through a year of community visits and intense conversations. He has my utmost respect and appreciation for his leadership, patience, and ability to bring humour to even the most challenging of situations.

Nancy Drozd, Lauren Peirce, Krista Robertson, and all the other staff at the federal department of Crown–Indigenous Relations were staunch supporters of the Healing and Commemoration project, and did everything they could to ensure that the legacy of the boarding schools in Labrador is one of reconciliation and hope. Thank you for your energy and for your belief in the importance of this work. Thank you to Crown–Indigenous Relations and Northern Affairs Canada for its financial support of this publication.

To all the archivists who helped me — Aimee Chaulk at Them Days, Melanie Tucker and Beverly Bennett at The Rooms, Lorraine Parsons at Moravian Church House in London, Linda White and Colleen Quigley at Memorial University, Tricia Logan at the National Centre for Truth and Reconciliation, and Joan Andersen at the White Elephant Museum in

Makkovik — thank you for pointing me in the right direction, and for being so generous with your advice. Thank you also to the wonderful Linda Mugford and Libby Dean, who helped search for archival materials in the collections at Them Days in Happy Valley–Goose Bay, Labrador, and at the Moravian Archives in Bethlehem, Pennsylvania.

Cynthia Rurak, my wonderfully thoughtful and thorough editor, helped me to craft a clearly written manuscript. Thank you, Cynthia, for all your guidance! Thank you also to the staff at ISER Books, especially Fiona Polack, Alison Carr, Diane Tye, Randy Drover, and Richard Tallman, for all your help in the publishing process and in recognizing the need to share the Labrador story. Sincere gratitude to Peter Ramsden as well for his precision and artistry in designing the maps.

Finally, thank you to my husband Jamie Skidmore for all your love and for making my world a brighter place. And to our daughter Leila, thank you for teaching me about being a mother. You helped me feel all the heartbreak of these boarding schools, but you also helped me understand the urgent need to create a better future. This book is dedicated to you and to all children, past and future.

INTRODUCTION

The Journey of Reconciliation

"By telling the story of Newfoundland and Labrador residential schools, we ensure that this history will never be forgotten."
— Prime Minister Justin Trudeau

"Do not let the mistakes of the past continue today."
— Wanda Lucy, Hopedale

A light snow was falling the day Prime Minister Justin Trudeau flew in to Happy Valley–Goose Bay. It was a Friday morning, 24 November 2017, and Trudeau had come to Labrador to apologize to the former boarding school students of the region.[1] Hundreds of people gathered to hear the prime minister deliver a heartfelt apology on behalf of the Canadian government. His words paid tribute to those students who had suffered harm while at one of the five boarding schools in Labrador and St. Anthony, Newfoundland, after 1949:

> To the survivors who experienced the indignity of abuse, neglect, hardship and discrimination by the individuals, institutions and system entrusted with your care, we are truly sorry for what you have endured.
>
> We are sorry for the lack of understanding of Indigenous societies and cultures that led to Indigenous children being sent

> away from their homes, families and communities and placed into residential schools.
>
> We are sorry for the misguided belief that Indigenous children could only be properly provided for, cared for, or educated if they were separated from the influence of their families, traditions, and cultures.[2]

For the surviving students, the apology was long overdue. Thousands of children had attended the boarding schools run by the Moravian Church and the International Grenfell Association in North West River, Cartwright, Makkovik, Nain, and St. Anthony. But they had been left out of the national apology and reconciliation process begun in 2008 by then Prime Minister Stephen Harper. The government of Canada at the time had argued that it was not accountable for the boarding schools because they had opened before Newfoundland and Labrador had become a part of Canada. In response, hundreds of the former students had launched a

Prime Minister Justin Trudeau delivers the federal government's apology in Happy Valley–Goose Bay, Labrador, on 24 November 2017 (courtesy of the Department of Crown–Indigenous Relations and Northern Affairs Canada).

class-action suit against the federal government. As Charlotte Wolfrey, an Inuit leader from Rigolet, Labrador, explained:

> The truth for us in Labrador has certainly been told over and over and over again, but it has fallen on deaf ears. It pains us, it hurts us, as Labrador people, as Inuit, and as Innu to not be believed. Our truth was not included in the apology or the settlement, and our only recourse is the courts of Canada.[3]

The former students wanted the federal government to acknowledge that it had failed in its responsibilities towards Indigenous peoples after Newfoundland and Labrador joined Canada in 1949. They wanted their stories to be heard, and to be recognized as part of the family of Indigenous residential school survivors across Canada. "The policies of the federal government and the decisions that they make continue to fragment and divide our people," argued Nunatsiavut Finance Minister Danny Pottle in 2011. "We need to be brought into this circle. Labrador Inuit have told the truth. Labrador Inuit want to be believed. Labrador Inuit want to begin the journey of reconciliation. But how can there be truly reconciliation when there are people left out of this process?"[4]

The class-action lawsuit went to court in 2015, and former students had to testify about their experiences — something that no other residential school survivor was forced to do in the other Canadian class-action lawsuits.[5] Fortunately, the case was relatively short-lived. In 2016, soon after Trudeau's Liberal Party came into power, the federal government assumed responsibility for the Newfoundland and Labrador schools. They moved to settle the case out of court. The settlement awarded $50 million to the legal team and the plaintiffs.[6] One-third of this went to lawyers' fees.[7] The remaining two-thirds were divided among the former students, based on how long they had attended the schools and how much physical and sexual abuse they had suffered. A committee of former students also asked for further actions from the federal government, including healing and commemoration activities and an official apology from the prime minister.[8]

While delivering his apology, Trudeau acknowledged the government's earlier failure to recognize the experiences of Inuit and Innu children in the boarding schools. He assured the former students:

> [W]hat happened in those five schools . . . is not a burden you have to carry alone anymore. It is my hope that today you can begin to heal — that you can finally put your inner child to rest. We share this burden with you by fully accepting our responsibilities — and our failings — as a government and as a country.[9]

The apology brings the former students in Labrador and northern Newfoundland into the circle of residential school survivors across Canada.[10] It acknowledges the similarities in their experiences and in the governance structure that created the schools. Although the Labrador and St. Anthony institutions were not part of the federally operated residential school system, they had much in common. As this book will show, the Moravian Church and International Grenfell Association staff modified their approach to running the boarding schools over time, but, like residential schools elsewhere, one goal remained constant: to dramatically change and transform the children.[11] In the beginning, the Moravian schools set out to convert children to Christianity. Later, both the Moravian Church and the International Grenfell Association aimed to "civilize" them. Finally, the schools planned to integrate the students into Canadian society and make them into wage-earning citizens. In all cases, the boarding schools tried to somehow "improve" the children by separating them from the influence of their families and communities. This separation often caused children to lose close connections with their culture, their language, and their family. It also made the children vulnerable to bullying and abuse.

The Nunatsiavut Inuit, NunatuKavut Inuit, and Innu students who experienced this "improvement" project are now demanding that we all, as Canadians, re-examine the motives behind the schools. As Shirley Flowers, a former student originally from Rigolet, argues, "The residential school was part of a bigger scheme of colonization. There was intent; the schools were there with the intent to change people, to make them like others and to make them not fit. And today, you know, we have to learn to decolonize."[12]

In his apology, Trudeau emphasized the need to heal and to move towards reconciliation. To do that, he said, the story of the Newfoundland and Labrador residential schools needs to be told: "All Canadians have much to learn from this story and we hope to hear you tell your stories — in your own way and in your own words — as this healing and commemoration process unfolds."[13] This book is an attempt to do just that: to examine the history of the Labrador and St. Anthony boarding schools and to listen to the stories of the students who attended them. Although the apology included only those who had attended the schools after 1949, many children went to the boarding schools long before this date. *A Long Journey* will therefore explore the entire history of these institutions, from their beginnings until they closed their doors for good.

A Snapshot of the Boarding Schools

The five boarding schools in Labrador and St. Anthony have a unique history. Two of the schools were founded by missionaries of the Moravian Church, one of the oldest Protestant denominations in the world. The International Grenfell Association (IGA), a charitable organization that provided medical and educational services in northern Newfoundland and Labrador, established the other three institutions. All five opened in the early 1900s.

In one significant way, the boarding schools differed from the residential schools in the rest of Canada: they were not operated or funded under the federal Indian Act.[14] The Moravian Church and the IGA ran the boarding schools themselves, with limited involvement of the Newfoundland government and, after 1949, the Canadian government. The IGA boarding schools and orphanage were not established exclusively for Indigenous children, although many of their residents were Inuit.

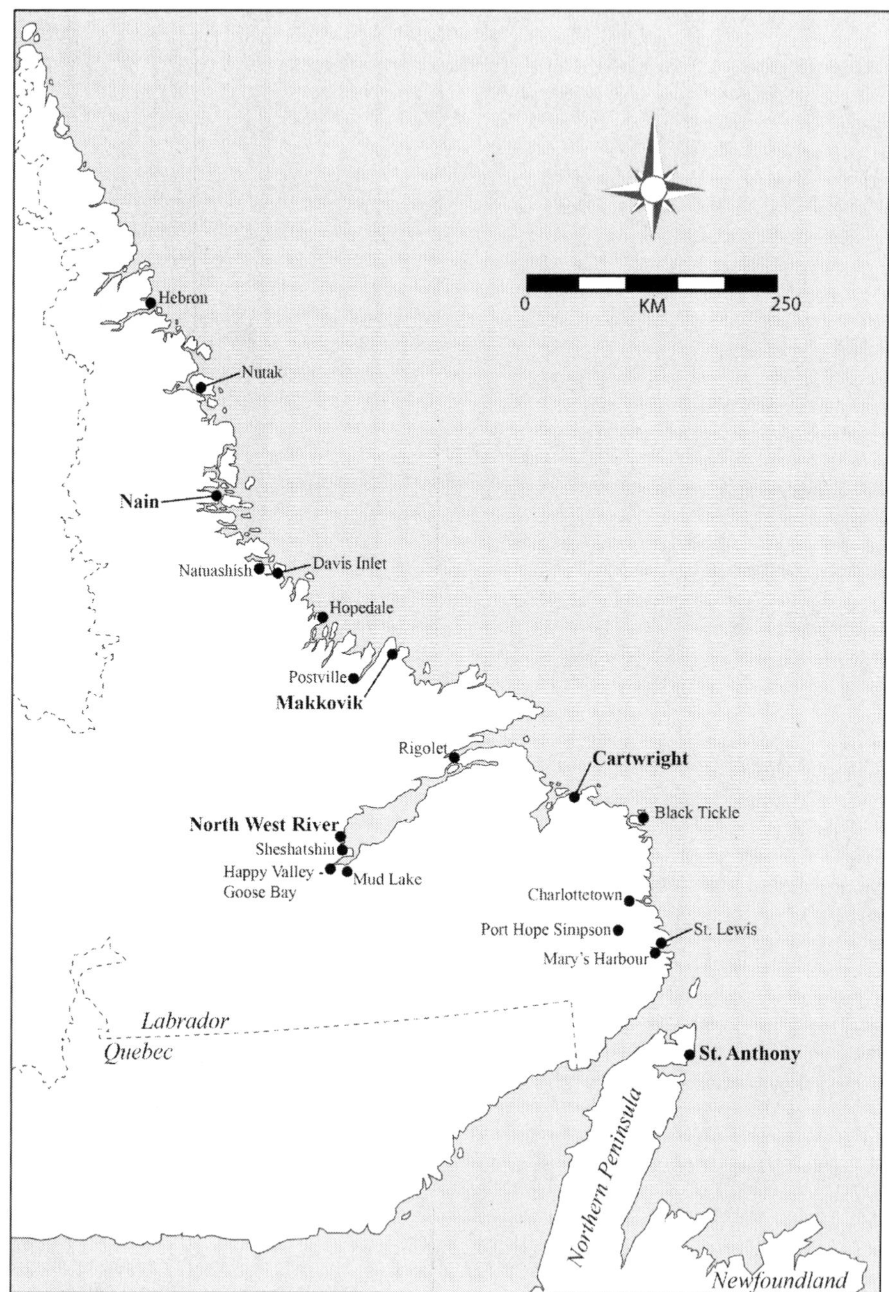

Map 1: Labrador and the Northern Peninsula of Newfoundland (map by Peter Ramsden).

However, as this book will illustrate, the history of the boarding schools in Labrador and St. Anthony reflects many of the same motives, practices, and student experiences of residential schools elsewhere.

The Moravian Church operated boarding schools at Makkovik (1914 to 1955) and Nain (1929 to 1972) for the Inuit and "Settler"/*Kablunângajuit* children of Labrador's north coast. The IGA established boarding schools in Labrador at Cartwright (1920 to 1964) and North West River (1926 to 1980) for the children of central, southern, and, later, northern Labrador, who were mainly Nunatsiavut and NunatuKavut Inuit. It also operated a small boarding school at St. Mary's River (now known as Mary's Harbour) from 1931 to 1938 that was not part of the court settlement because it closed before 1949. The IGA also founded an orphanage at St. Anthony (1906 to 1969) for children from the Northern Peninsula of Newfoundland and southern Labrador. As Chapter Eight outlines, the children in this orphanage from Newfoundland were mainly of European ancestry, and the children from Labrador were mainly of NunatuKavut Inuit ancestry. Over 2,000 children lived at these six institutions, and most ranged in age from five to sixteen.

The Moravian Church and the International Grenfell Association were non-governmental organizations. They had come to Labrador intending to change the region by introducing Christianity, medical services, and social development. Moravian missionaries arrived in the late eighteenth century from Europe to Christianize the Inuit.[15] Grenfell staff arrived in Labrador and northern Newfoundland in the late nineteenth century from Britain to provide medical services. Not long afterwards, the IGA expanded its scope to include social reform in the region.[16] At the time, Newfoundland and Labrador was a colony in the British Empire, and colonial officials in the capital of St. John's largely ignored Labrador. They saw it as a source of fish, but offered no funding for schools, justice, roads, health care, or political representation.[17] When first the Moravian Church and then the IGA volunteered to assume some of these responsibilities, the Newfoundland government gladly accepted the offer.

Both organizations saw education as an important part of their work in reshaping the lives of local residents. Educating children was a powerful way to effect change. Moravians felt that literacy was important in converting Inuit to the Christian faith.[18] Education could also convince children that their families' spiritual beliefs and cultural practices were immoral. Grenfell workers likewise aimed to transform local society. The IGA staff members were largely well-educated and wealthy Americans and Britons who wanted to improve local conditions by promoting new lifestyles and livelihoods.[19] Like missionaries everywhere, members of both organizations felt confident that they knew best.

As this book describes, the Moravian Church and the IGA established many of the first day schools in Labrador. At the time, very few children in rural areas of Newfoundland and Labrador had the opportunity to attend school. Where schools did exist, parents had to pay school fees, and children usually completed only a few years of school before they had to work for a living. Churches ran the schools under a denominational education system, in which the Newfoundland government gave grants to the churches and left them to organize the schooling.[20] Neither the Moravian Church nor the IGA fit under this system. Instead, the Moravians were allowed to develop their own schools and curriculum in northern Labrador, as long as they paid for their own expenses. Farther south, the IGA established non-denominational schools and summer programs, and it initially paid for many of the costs.

After establishing day schools or summer schools, the two organizations opened boarding schools, as we will see in Chapters Four to Eleven. In most cases, the boarding schools consisted of dormitories where children lived while they attended the day schools. Other children who lived with their families in the community also attended these day schools. Members of both organizations used the boarding schools to instill their values in the children under their care. Dormitory supervisors and teachers emphasized the need to obey authority and to live according to a strict schedule. They promoted European societal ideas of proper behaviour, teaching the children conformity, appropriate manners, housekeeping standards, and moral principles.

In every boarding school except for Nain, teachers taught in English. They did not encourage Indigenous children to speak their native language, Inuktitut or Innu-aimun. Children usually lived at the schools from September to June, and rarely saw their families. This time away from home prevented parents from teaching their children their language and cultural traditions. By separating children from their families for extended periods of time, the boarding schools also disrupted close family relationships and community connections. Yet despite its drawbacks, some families welcomed the education that the boarding schools provided. It was often the only schooling available, and parents hoped that the literacy skills and other training would benefit their children's future.

The boarding schools operated largely without government funding or oversight until the 1930s and 1940s. In the early years, the people who worked in the institutions were either underpaid staff or volunteers from Europe or the United States. Most of them dedicated years of their lives to the work. The organizations raised funds constantly to pay for the schools, to feed, clothe, and teach the children, and to maintain the buildings. Parents contributed through school fees and donations of country food and wood. Most of the money, books, clothing, and volunteer labour came from donors in the United States, Canada, and Britain.[21]

School attendance was voluntary until 1942 when the Newfoundland government passed the School Attendance Act.[22] All children from seven to fourteen then had to attend school if they lived within two miles of one.[23] But the law had no real impact in Labrador. Few schools existed, and there were almost no police officers around to enforce it. After 1949, however, mandatory school attendance was enforced when Newfoundland and Labrador joined Canada. Family allowance payments from the federal government were now available to families, but only if their children attended school.[24] With increased government involvement in their lives, parents had little choice but to send their children to school.

As the following chapters illustrate, children lived in the boarding schools and orphanage for a number of reasons. Some students came to attend school if they lived in small villages without access to schools or higher grades. Other children lived in the institutions because IGA or government staff decided that they should be removed from home conditions of poverty or neglect. Yet other children lived in the boarding schools because they or their family were receiving medical treatment at an IGA hospital.

Some of the institutions received federal support after Confederation. Newfoundland's decision to join Canada in 1949 resulted in a signed agreement with the federal government. These Terms of Union did not mention the Indigenous peoples in the province. Because Canada occupies lands and waters belonging to Indigenous peoples, the federal government promised in its Constitution to respect inherent Indigenous rights and to protect the well-being of Indigenous peoples. But the Terms of Union did not specify whether this duty applied to the Indigenous peoples of the new province. As a result, the federal government was slow to acknowledge its constitutional responsibilities towards Labrador Inuit and Innu.[25]

By the mid-1950s, the provincial government had taken over responsibility for all schools, although the Moravian Church and the IGA maintained control of the dormitories. Under the provincial education system, local school boards hired teachers with provincial monies and schools taught the prescribed Newfoundland curriculum.[26] In 1954, the provincial government pressured the federal government to accept its financial responsibilities for the Inuit and Innu in Labrador. Under a Canada–Newfoundland funding agreement, the federal government eventually agreed to pay some expenses for Indigenous health care, housing, and schools.[27]

Ten years later, Canada agreed to cover more expenses in communities it designated as "Native." These included only the Innu communities of Sheshatshiu and Davis Inlet, and the northern Inuit communities of Nain, Hopedale, Makkovik, and Postville. Rigolet was added to the list of Inuit communities in 1967, Black Tickle in 1972, and Mud Lake in 1975.[28] The 1964 Federal–Provincial Agreement stated that the federal government would pay for two-thirds of health, housing, and education expenses in Inuit communities and all of the expenses in Innu communities.[29]

According to the federal government, these percentages reflected the proportion of non-Indigenous people in the communities. Representatives from both governments decided how to spend the federal funds. Indigenous representatives were not involved in the decision-making until the early 1970s, when the two levels of government finally invited Indigenous members to join the committee.[30] Much of the direct federal funding for the boarding school system in Labrador came through this agreement. This federal funding also paid for the construction, expansion, and operation of day schools in central and northern Labrador.[31]

In the meantime, the Moravian Church and the IGA had begun closing their boarding schools, the first in 1955. The schools closed for a variety of reasons. In some cases, local people campaigned to shut them down. Students did not want to move away to attend boarding school, so they and their families pushed for day schools in their home communities instead. Some of these campaigns united with the Indigenous rights movement of the 1970s, which saw Indigenous leaders fight to regain control over their children's education.[32] In other cases, the provincial government pressured families to resettle in larger communities where children could attend day schools.[33] In still other cases, provincial child welfare policy shifted from placing children in institutions towards placing them with foster families.[34] The shift in policy meant that boarding schools no longer served as homes for children apprehended by social services. Taken together, these pressures closed all boarding schools by 1980.

How This Account Was Written

In 2017, the federal government appointed James Igloliorte to lead the healing and commemoration activities stemming from the class-action settlement.[35] A retired provincial court judge from Hopedale, James Igloliorte is a respected and well-known Inuit leader in Labrador. He is also a former student of the Moravian day school in Hopedale and the Yale School and dormitory in North West River. I was asked to research the history of the schools as an anthropologist with years of experience working in Labrador and on the recommendation of the NunatuKavut Community Council and the Nunatsiavut government.

Over the winter and spring of 2018, I joined James Igloliorte and a small team of Healing and Commemoration Project staff in visiting communities in Labrador, St. John's, and Ottawa. We spoke with former students at community healing events about their memories. For those who wished, we recorded their stories about the boarding schools. The Provincial Archives of Newfoundland and Labrador at The Rooms in St. John's (PANL) will preserve these stories until they can be transferred to Them Days Archive in Labrador for future generations.

Former students' stories about their experiences are at the heart of this historical account. For years, the story of the boarding schools has been told by the authorities who ran them. The Moravian Church and the IGA have published numerous books and periodicals about their efforts, and their voices have dominated the discussion. *A Long Journey* attempts to address this imbalance by listening to former students as well. Survivors shared their stories in interviews held during the healing and commemoration events, at the Truth and Reconciliation Commission sharing panels in 2011, in the 2010 Nunatsiavut government film, *Courage to Remember*, and for *Them Days* magazine and archive, which collects stories of Labrador. This book combines these interviews with historical material from archives at The Rooms in St. John's, Memorial University of Newfoundland, *Them Days* in Happy Valley–Goose Bay, and the White Elephant Museum in Makkovik. The Moravian Church also opened its archives for this research in Bethlehem, Pennsylvania, and London, England. Both the Moravian Church and the IGA kept extensive records of their activities in Labrador and issued many fundraising publications to support their work on the coast. Together, these archival records and interviews with former students tell the story of the boarding schools from a range of perspectives.

An advisory group of former students and other experts reviewed drafts of this book. They provided guidance on presenting the history in a way that respects the students' experiences and they contributed additional context and factual details as needed. With assistance from the federal government, we worked with Memorial University's ISER Books to publish this historical account in order to ensure that the stories of these boarding schools are shared and remembered.

A Long Journey

A Long Journey: Residential Schools in Labrador and Newfoundland is divided into four parts. Part One sets the stage for understanding the impact of the boarding schools on the students and their communities. It outlines a brief history of the encounter between Europeans and the Indigenous peoples of Labrador, and describes broad cultural differences between them. It also highlights Inuit and Innu approaches to raising and educating children, which were very different from how Moravian missionaries and International Grenfell Association staff taught and disciplined children in the boarding schools. Appreciating the history of the Indigenous–European relationship helps us to better understand how the Moravian Church and the IGA justified their involvement in Indigenous education. It also makes it easier to imagine how strange, uncomfortable, and isolating attending the boarding schools might have felt for the children.

Part Two introduces the Moravian Church and the boarding schools in Makkovik and Nain. It describes the Moravian missionaries' early efforts to teach children and adults how to read and write in Inuktitut. In the late 1800s and early 1900s, the Church started to offer English-language schooling as well, centred at its boarding school in Makkovik. The Nain boarding school opened in 1929 for students in both Inuktitut and English classes, and operated until the early 1970s. Part Two concludes with the story of a proposed boarding school in Okak Bay, north of Nain, which was planned but never built. The story is directly linked to the authorities' subsequent decision to forcibly relocate Inuit in Okak Bay and Hebron to communities farther south, where their children could attend day schools.

Part Three begins with a look at Wilfred Grenfell and his International Grenfell Association. It examines the orphanage at St. Anthony, the Cartwright area boarding schools of Muddy Bay and Lockwood, the St. Mary's River boarding school, and the Yale School and dormitories at North West River. The final chapter describes the increasing activism of students in Nain in the 1960s and 1970s. Frustrated that they were forced to move away to finish their education, the students refused to go to "the dorm" in North West River for high school. Their resistance eventually convinced the local school board to provide high school classes in north coast schools. The students' successful campaign helped to close the North West River dormitory, the last of the surviving boarding schools.

Part Four briefly explores the Innu experience with schools. While Roman Catholic priests started day schools for Innu children at Davis Inlet and Sheshatshiu in the 1950s, they did not build any boarding schools. Some Innu students attended the IGA boarding schools at North West River and St. Anthony while they received medical care. Other students moved to St. John's to attend Catholic schools there. After many traumatic experiences with schooling, the Innu have fought to regain control of their children's education.

A concluding chapter circles back to the healing and commemoration initiatives. It explores the reaction in Labrador to the prime minister's apology, and it outlines the other ways in which the story of the boarding schools is being commemorated. The chapter also reflects on the overall impact of the boarding schools and examines the state of Indigenous education in Labrador today. Finally, it looks forward to a future in which reconciliation between all Indigenous and non-Indigenous Canadians becomes a reality.

PART ONE

The Peoples of Labrador

CHAPTER ONE

The Peoples of Labrador: *Life Before the Boarding Schools*

> "It is the hardest thing . . . to make an Esquimaux understand how a man . . . in Europe, is expected to work early and late to gain a livelihood; their notion is, that the rich should support the poor, as indeed they are themselves willing to do, when they have abundance."
>
> — Moravian missionary in Nain, 1843

To understand the impact of the boarding schools on Labrador's Indigenous peoples, we need to look at the history of the Indigenous–European encounter. This relationship has been shaped by centuries of conflict over the land and resources of Labrador. The conflict highlighted cultural differences between Indigenous societies and European colonizers. These differences were then used to justify attempts to transform a people by educating their children.

The Indigenous peoples of Labrador — the Inuit and the Innu — lived throughout the Ungava Peninsula long before Europeans arrived. They forged links with other peoples through global trading networks, kinship, and political alliances, but they were sovereign nations. Independent and autonomous, they governed themselves, they thrived on their land, and they raised and taught their children according to their own traditions.

Inuit and Early Europeans

Before the sixteenth century, Inuit lived primarily by hunting marine life, especially seals and whales. They also traded iron and marine resources, such as whale blubber, baleen, walrus ivory, and sealskins.[1] Their trading partners included other Inuit in the eastern Arctic and Norse in Greenland, who had iron to trade. When Inuit expanded to the southern regions of Labrador to hunt for seals and whales, some archaeologists think they were also looking for other sources of iron.[2]

From the 1500s to the mid-1700s, Inuit in Labrador saw growing numbers of Europeans come to their region. Thousands of Basque, Portuguese, Dutch, French, and British fishermen and traders made seasonal trips to exploit the lucrative coastline of Labrador. They fished for cod, seals, and whales, making vast profits from the fish, pelts, whale oil, and baleen. In Europe, people burned whale oil in lamps and used baleen to shape women's corsets and hooped petticoats. The market for these products was huge. In the mid-1500s, Basque whalers would sail back to Spain each year from Labrador and the Gulf of St. Lawrence with cargo on up to 30 ships.[3] Each ship's cargo of whale oil would be worth about $5 million today.[4] But the industry killed over 20,000 whales between 1530 and 1580, and the right whale and bowhead whale populations plummeted.[5] With whales disappearing, the European whalers moved on to other species or other regions, robbing the Inuit, who were whalers themselves, of their main source of sustenance.

The European migratory fishery was harmful in other ways. Fishermen also spread infectious diseases like measles, typhoid, whooping cough, smallpox, and influenza, to which the previously unexposed Indigenous population had little immunity. It is difficult to know exactly how many Indigenous people died as a result of these diseases across Labrador and throughout North America, but their impact was devastating.[6] Even into the 1800s, when Moravians kept death records, Labrador Inuit faced startling mortality rates. A measles epidemic killed over 32 Inuit in 1827, for example, and almost 100 died in another epidemic in

1863–64.[7] Relentless illness plagued the coast in the following decades. Comparable death rates may well have affected Inuit and Innu in earlier centuries, as Europeans introduced these diseases to North America.

Relations between the Europeans and Inuit in Labrador became more combative as competition for the drastically diminishing resources intensified. By the early 1700s, many Europeans were afraid to venture north, where Inuit fiercely defended their territory against the intruders.[8] Inuit burned down stages, wharves, and outbuildings that the Europeans left behind over the winter, retrieving iron nails from the ashes, which they melted down to make other implements.[9] Violence and killings on both sides were common.

In 1763, the Treaty of Paris saw France cede control of coastal Labrador to Britain. English and American vessels replaced those of the French, and hostility between Inuit and the fishermen escalated.[10] While the French and Inuit had developed a trade language, the British newcomers could not communicate with the Inuit. Misunderstandings led to more violence. British rulers tried to quell the bloodshed. They hoped to develop a migratory cod fishery in Labrador, and to use the region as a training ground for potential recruits to the Royal Navy. The newly appointed governor of Newfoundland, Sir Hugh Palliser, issued a proclamation in 1764 urging friendly relations with the Inuit. A year later, he made a peace and friendship treaty with Inuit in Chateau Bay, southern Labrador.[11] But the violence continued. Between 1763 and 1767, Americans and British fishermen and soldiers massacred over 50 Inuit in southern Labrador. In one incident, crew on an American vessel murdered 18 Inuit. In another, Inuit killed three Englishmen at Cape Charles. British soldiers at Fort York in Chateau Bay retaliated by ambushing and killing 24 Inuit. They also captured nine others, including Mikak, a woman who would later become a famous Inuk leader.[12]

Inuit Life

By the mid-1700s, when our boarding school story begins, Inuit families had faced the impacts of European violence, overfishing, and epidemics for more than 200 years. Both Inuit and European societies had changed as result of their encounter in Labrador. But they remained very different from each other.

Inuit in Labrador lived along the coast, travelling each season to hunt, fish, trade, and forage. In the winter, small groups lived in single- or multi-family sod houses, built into the earth for warmth and protection against the elements.[13] In the summer, larger groups would congregate at good fishing and hunting places, where they lived in tents. Skilled male hunters often had more than one wife, a practice that would upset Moravian notions of sexual propriety. The conflict with Europeans killed many Inuit men in the mid-1700s, so there were likely more women than men. Some experts think that polygamy was even more common in Labrador at that time because of the high male death toll.[14]

Each group referred to themselves as "the people of . . ." by using the Inuktitut ending "-miut." The people of Napartok Bay, for instance, called themselves "Napartumiut." Within their respective territories, they planned seasonal travels around migratory or abundant foods: Arctic char, migratory birds, eggs, mussels, caribou, and seals in the spring; whales, fish, caribou, and seals in the summer; berries, seals, and migratory birds in the fall; and seals, fox, and caribou in the winter.[15] Inuit in northern Labrador also traded whale oil, baleen, and fur with Inuit in southern Labrador in exchange for European goods and boats.[16]

Inuit organized their society around values and practices that remain important today. Of these, generosity and individual independence were both fundamental. Inuit believed that sharing food, helping each other, and offering hospitality kept social connections strong within families and the larger community.[17] Unlike European society, which developed a capitalist ideology that emphasized the individual accumulation of wealth and justified the unequal distribution of resources, Inuit social practices ensured that everyone had enough food and support. In good times and bad, the community looked after itself by sharing labour, food, and supplies. Individuals gained prestige by sharing riches, not by hoarding them.[18]

At the same time, Inuit valued individual independence: they believed

Inuit sod house, Okak, c. 1900 (courtesy of Them Days Archive).

that people should make their own decisions without interference or coercion from others.[19] This respect for autonomy differed from the individualism and other cultural values of the Europeans who came to Labrador. In Europe, competition was valued. Society was hierarchical and based on force: some people had more power and wealth, and they used their power to control those with less. The Inuit approach, on the other hand, was non-authoritarian. Instead of using force, Inuit leaders relied on influence to convince others to follow their lead. People who tried to boss others around were shunned and ignored.[20]

Leadership in Inuit communities was therefore flexible. People followed those who had the most knowledge about a situation. If they did not agree, they moved away. Inuit society did not have hierarchical classes of people or central authorities who controlled others. When Europeans arrived in Labrador, they could not understand this flexible style of leadership.[21] They expected to see authoritative leaders similar to the rulers of Europe. Not seeing what they expected or understood, they dismissed Inuit leadership and means of self-governance as ineffectual and therefore replaceable.

Inuit flexibility and their non-interference ethic also extended to their relationship with the natural world. Because they knew they could not control the environment, Inuit sought to understand it. Survival in Labrador depended on extensive knowledge about how to read the weather, the animals, the plants, the ice, and the ocean. As they still do today, Inuit understood the need to adapt to changing situations and the importance of remaining flexible.[22]

Europeans, on the other hand, sought to control the world around them. By the mid-1700s, European society based on agriculture and engineering relied on modifying the environment and on maintaining strict control over the labourers who were needed to carry out the work. A police force and an army enforced the laws and punishments of a criminal justice system. Days were scheduled around work hours and meal times, signalled by the clock. Workers were encouraged to believe in ideas such as the Protestant work ethic, which emphasized discipline, hard work, and thrift.[23] Inuit families, on the other hand, were not tied to the clock. People did their work, ate, and travelled when conditions best suited.[24]

Inuit Ways of Teaching Children

When the Moravians arrived in Labrador, Inuit already had well-established ways of teaching children to become competent, knowledgeable, and responsible adults. Inuit society at the time placed a high value on the individual autonomy of both children and adults; attempts to directly control others were frowned upon. These values remain important today. The traditional practice of naming in Inuit culture demonstrates this respect for children and their autonomy. Inuit believed that, when a baby was born, it took on the soul of a relative who had recently died. The child was therefore given that person's name. Family members treated the child with the same courtesy they would have given her namesake. Because it would be inappropriate to discipline an Elder, it was just as inappropriate to command or yell at the child who was named after her.[25]

Children therefore learned through observation and participation rather than formal instruction. Families encouraged them to experiment and make their own mistakes. They gave children tasks to stretch their comfort levels and knowledge, such as making them responsible for a job or a navigation. By having to make the attempt, they learned by experience.[26] Unlike children in European societies, where obedience to established rules maintained social order, Inuit children enjoyed much more freedom. They did not live by a set schedule, so they could eat when they were hungry and sleep when tired. As long as they were in no danger, children were not strictly restrained in their actions.[27] When correction became necessary, they were disciplined through indirect social controls such as teasing, shaming, or social ostracism rather than by direct confrontation, spanking, or yelling.[28] As anthropologist Jean Briggs illustrates in her book, *Never in Anger*, parents also taught their children how to control their anger and frustration so they would become mature adults.[29] As a result, children learned to become self-reliant, to take initiative, and to solve problems.

Inuit children learned to understand the Inuit social world of relationships, language, and religion. They also acquired the enormous amount of environmental and practical expertise needed to thrive as adults in the demanding Labrador environment. Gender divisions were not strictly kept, but girls mainly learned how to prepare skins, sew, prepare food, and hunt and trap from their female relatives. Boys watched their male relatives to learn how to navigate, hunt, trap, and build kayaks, houses, and tools, among many other skills.[30] Through their Inuit education, children were taught to look after themselves and their family, to respect individual independence, and to value community solidarity.

Innu and Early Europeans

The Innu in Labrador had a different encounter with European colonizers. They likely first met Europeans who came to the north shore of the Gulf of St. Lawrence and the coast of Labrador in the 1500s. In 1720, a Dutch whaler wrote about meeting Innu in Groswater Bay. He reported that the group had French tools and clothing, spoke a few French words, and were obviously familiar with trading with Europeans.[31]

During the seventeenth-century fur-trade conflicts, Innu allied themselves with the Huron and the French in Quebec against the Iroquois. But when the Iroquois defeated the Huron in the mid-1600s, more Innu moved into their eastern territory near Mingan on the Lower North Shore of Quebec.[32] They maintained a close trading partnership with the French, but when France handed control of the Labrador coast to the British in 1763, most French trading posts closed. When Hudson's Bay Company traders arrived in the 1800s, their approach to trade with the Innu was ruthless. Throughout the nineteenth century, they tried to make the Innu dependent on them by encouraging them to trap for furs instead of hunting caribou for food and clothes. Traders provided Innu trappers with ammunition and goods at the beginning of the season, with the requirement that they repay the debt at the end. However, they offered very low prices for each pelt. This made it difficult for the Innu to repay the loan and often drove them further into debt. Even when epidemics and recurring famines from fluctuating animal populations decimated Innu families, the Hudson's Bay Company often refused to provide enough ammunition for them to hunt for their food.[33]

At the same time, more European settlers encroached on Innu lands on the north shore of the St. Lawrence River. In 1866, a Jesuit priest reported that European settlements had forced Innu to move farther from the coast.[34] For Innu living in central Labrador in the late 1800s and early 1900s, a similar pattern developed when non-Innu trappers extended their trap lines farther into the interior. Innu protested having to share the land, as the animals they relied on to survive were disappearing.[35]

Innu Life

In the nineteenth and early twentieth centuries, Innu lived by hunting caribou and trapping fur. They travelled each season between the bays and the interior. Families spent the winter in the interior, hunting caribou and trapping fox and other fur-bearing animals. In the spring, they came out to the coast to trade furs for supplies, visit friends, fish for Arctic char and salmon, and hunt seals. They would return to caribou hunting in the interior in the fall, travelling by foot, canoe, and dogsled.[36]

Innu family, 1940s (courtesy of The Rooms).

Several families would often travel together, with larger numbers of people gathering at the summer places. When animals were scarce, people divided into smaller groupings, but they would come together again when hunting large herds of caribou. Sharing products of the hunt remains a fundamental value in Innu life, and the *mukushan* feast celebrating a caribou hunt is still an important spiritual and social gathering.[37] By sharing with others, expert hunters and generous individuals gained prestige and leadership roles. But people were not tied to one leader. Like the Inuit, they respected each other's autonomy, and so were free to make their own decisions about where and with whom to hunt and travel.[38]

Innu Ways of Teaching Children

Respect for autonomy was a key element of Innu child-rearing and childhood education as well. Instead of rigid discipline, humiliation, or punishment, Innu relied on a child's interest and initiative to drive his or her education.[39] Children learned the skills and the knowledge they needed by watching and taking part in camp life. "In the old days," describes Tuamish, an Elder from the Davis Inlet area, "there was no such thing as school. We didn't learn our culture in school. We learned from our people.

We educated ourselves in our culture and traditions."[40] Elders describe their Innu education in pre-settlement days, when they lived in *nutshimit* (the land), as based on observation and experience:

> When a child was taught how to make things, they usually picked it up easily when she or he listened. We used to learn how to prepare for mukushan and how to respect nature. In nutshimit, we respected the water habitat, the fish. We always respected the animals. We would listen and learn.[41]

Nishet Penashue of Sheshatshiu remembers watching her mother. "I learned how to do things by observing my mother at work. She never ordered me to do things. For example, when my father killed a porcupine, my mother would singe it, and boil it, and I would watch her carefully to see how it was done."[42] Her mother found that observation was the best way for Nishet to learn. She told her once, "When I try to explain things to you, you make mistakes, but when you just observe, you do a good job."[43] Learning practical skills for surviving in *nutshimit* was important, as Davis Inlet Elder Kaniuekutat describes:

> There was always work to do for children. We were taught to make snowshoes, toboggans. There was a lot of things that we had to do when I was a child. I was told once that if I didn't make something, like snowshoes or how to set up a tent, I would never be in nutshimit and would not know how to survive. That's what my parents told me. Now I know I gained a lot of experience about how to survive in nutshimit. I know if you don't have skills, you will never use the land. I did many things in nutshimit that my father taught me. I still have those skills.[44]

Families taught their children practical skills, cultural wisdom, and environmental knowledge. Girls learned how to prepare skins, sew, cook, and make moccasins and snowshoes. Boys learned how to hunt, trap, navigate, and build and paddle canoes. Both were taught appropriate behaviour, spiritual values, Innu history, and a wealth of Innu stories and legends.[45]

The Colonial "Improvement" Project

As this chapter has described, early encounters between Indigenous people and Europeans in Labrador were often violent. But in some cases, European fishermen, trappers, and traders forged friendlier bonds with Inuit or Innu families. From them, the newcomers learned the skills needed to survive. They also relied on Inuit and Innu trappers and hunters to obtain the trade products their European companies wanted to export. When competition for Labrador's resources intensified, however, British colonial authorities strived to assert more control over the region. They sent in missionaries — so often one of the most effective agents of colonialism's assault on Indigenous peoples.[46] Moravian missionaries arrived to convert (and control) Inuit, and years later the Hudson's Bay Company invited Roman Catholic missionaries to Labrador to convert (and control) Innu.[47] When Grenfell Mission doctors and volunteers arrived in the region in the late 1800s, they represented a newer form of missionary — perhaps not as overtly religious, but just as intent on effecting social change.[48]

The Moravians, Catholics, and the IGA all brought their own assumptions and interests with them, but all relied on a sense of cultural superiority to justify their actions. Cultural differences between European and Indigenous societies became a focal point in their efforts. In the almost complete absence of colonial governance, but quietly supported by the authorities, the missionaries attempted to transform and "improve" Inuit and Innu societies by Christianizing and civilizing them, using education as a key tool. They used day schools and boarding schools to isolate children from their families and tried to instill their own cultural values in their students. However, they often found that Inuit and Innu cultural practices, governance, and ways of teaching children were firmly established. They quickly realized that they needed to negotiate with Indigenous families in order to succeed in their goals of social transformation. At every step, the colonial "improvement" project was challenged, confronted, and changed by its intended Inuit and Innu recipients.

PART TWO

The Moravian Mission Boarding Schools

CHAPTER TWO

The Moravian Church in Labrador

"[Jens] Haven has formed the laudable plan, not only of uniting the [Inuit] people with the English nation, but of instructing them in the Christian religion."
— Governor Hugh Palliser, 1764, in J.E. Hutton, *A History of Moravian Missions* (1922)

The eighteenth century marked the expansion of the colonial fishing industry in Newfoundland and Labrador. Seasonal European and American whalers, fishermen, and traders increasingly encroached on Inuit territories throughout the 1700s. Hostilities, mistrust, and violence between the groups became an almost unceasing occurrence. The violence increased when, in 1763, France ceded rights to the Labrador coast to Britain after the Seven Years' War. The new governor of Newfoundland, Sir Hugh Palliser, wanted to develop a ship fishery on the Labrador coast, but the British were afraid to venture into hostile Inuit territory. So when members of the Moravian Church approached Palliser about establishing a Christian mission among Inuit in Labrador, the governor agreed, hoping that the missionaries could help to pacify the coast.[1]

The Moravian Missionaries

The Moravian Church, or *Unitas Fratrum* (Unity of the Brethren), was an early Protestant church founded in 1457. It was active in Central Europe for nearly 200 years before persecution drove it underground.[2] In the eighteenth century, the Church was revived under the patronage of Count Zinzendorf, a Pietist nobleman in Saxony. In 1722, Zinzendorf took in refugees from Moravia and Bohemia fleeing persecution. They built the new community of Herrnhut, which became a haven for other Moravian refugees.[3]

The religious practices of the Moravian Church centred on community fellowship and simplicity in lifestyle and doctrine. Moravian doctrine was grounded in the literature of the Bible and catechism of the Moravian Church, and hymns and music played a central role in rituals and celebrations. Church leaders appointed a Council of Elders in Germany, who directed the Church and its activities around the world.[4]

Shortly after the Church's revival, Moravian brethren embarked on missionary work to spread the Gospel around the world. Acting under the direction of the Elders in Germany, the first missionaries were sent to the West Indies in 1732. A year later, Moravian missionaries arrived in Greenland where some, including Jens Haven and Christian Drachardt from Denmark, learned to speak some Inuktitut.[5]

The ability to speak with Inuit in their own language would prove to be essential in Labrador. In 1764, Jens Haven impressed Newfoundland Governor Palliser with his Inuktitut skills and with his proposal for a Labrador mission. Haven made an exploratory visit to the coast, where he met with Inuit on the Northern Peninsula of Newfoundland.[6] Palliser afterwards reported on Haven's expedition to the colonial authority, the Board of Trade. He suggested that the Inuktitut-speaking missionary might well be useful to the British in the region:

> The Moravian who I mentioned to your Lordships . . . was able to converse with them very well in their own Language to their great Astonishment and Satisfaction, having never before met with any European that could converse with them otherways than by Signes. . . . Measures may be taken for opening a friendly Communication with them, for gratifying them with what they

> want in the way of traffic [i.e., trade] and thereby provide a Security for our Fishers for Cod, Whale and Seal upon that Coast.[7]

The Brethren's Society for the Furtherance of the Gospel among the Heathen (SFG), the Moravian agency in London that oversaw missions in British colonies, lobbied for British support in establishing a mission and trading post in northern Labrador. Governor Palliser, harbouring his own political agenda, championed the idea. He hoped that a missionary presence could keep the Inuit away from the lucrative fishery developing in southern Labrador:

> I would recommend an advanced Post as far to the Northward as possible for a trucking [trading] place, where those Savages may be stopt from coming further Southward by supplying them there with what they want or will be most useful to them & we may procure what we want of them and thus keep the rest of the Coast open & free for our Adventurers to try whether it affords a fishery.[8]

The British government accepted the Moravians' proposal. In 1769, after much discussion, it granted the Moravian Church 100,000 acres of land in Labrador. The missionaries had argued that such a large piece of land was needed to keep Inuit distant from others.[9] The Mission could then build its stations and work undisturbed to "reclaim the converted from their vagabond way of life, . . . separate [them] from their heathen countrymen, and form [them] into societies."[10] This exclusive territory would also enable the Moravians to establish a trading monopoly with the Inuit.

Jens Haven was not the first Moravian to travel to Labrador. In 1752, the German missionary Johann Christian Erhardt had led an exploratory trade mission to the Makkovik area. The trip ended in disaster when Erhardt and six of the crew were killed by Inuit.[11] But Jens Haven was willing to risk another attempt. In the summer of 1770, he and other Inuktitut-speaking missionaries travelled to Labrador to find a suitable location for their new Mission station. Under the guidance of Mikak, an Inuit woman who had been kidnapped and brought to England, where she met with Haven, they decided on a place where hundreds of Inuit had gathered. They called their new Mission station Nain.[12]

The Mission Stations

The next year, in 1771, 14 Moravian brethren from Germany, Denmark, and England arrived at Nain. The group included Jens Haven, his wife, and two other married couples. Their first task was to construct a mission house. In case the Inuit turned hostile, they also surrounded the house with a stockade. Skilled in carpentry and other trades, the missionaries set up a smithy, planted a garden, fashioned tools, and built boats for trade.[13] They were expected to live off the land as much as possible, although this proved to be difficult. Gardening provided the Mission station with little produce, and hunting and fishing for food required skills that most missionaries never mastered. They largely depended on European foodstuffs, imported each year on the Mission supply ship, the *Harmony*.[14]

The Moravians also established a trading post to attract Inuit to the station and to generate profits for station expenses. Trade was initially kept separate from religious activities.[15] Missionaries who worked in the trading post did not preach, and the Mission tried to maintain fair trading practices. The Council of Elders in Germany instructed the station traders to offer reasonable rates of exchange for the sealskins, fur, ivory, and other materials that the Inuit offered. In return, the trading post supplied such things as fishhooks, fishing lines, needles, and knives.[16] Initially, the Elders also instructed that no guns or alcohol should be offered as trade goods, unlike the practices of other merchants.[17] No gifts should be given, and no food should be freely distributed. According to the missionaries, trade should teach the importance of reward for hard work and frugality. They insisted that Inuit offer items or do work in exchange for goods or food. Nothing should be given for free. But this trading approach conflicted with Inuit food-sharing practices and caused many misunderstandings and disagreements over the next 150 years. The Mission's interest in converting Inuit while at the same time making profits from trade created constant tension.[18]

Despite the Moravians' hopes for a large gathering at Nain, Inuit visitors to the new station were few. Only one family decided to live at Nain during its first winter.[19] Many others stopped by over the first few months to trade at the post and inspect the new arrivals, but their visits were brief. As it turned out, Nain was a poor location for year-round settlement. Although Inuit sometimes came to the area in the summer for the good trout fishing, the hunting and whaling possibilities were scarce. The missionaries encouraged Inuit to stay for longer so they could hear and embrace the Gospel, but few families obliged them.[20] They saw little reason to adjust their seasonal trips to the outer islands during the summer and to the bays and the interior during the fall and winter. Inuit families continued to live to the north and the south of the Mission station and to travel widely.[21]

Colonial authorities in Newfoundland also hoped the Moravians would attract more Inuit to their stations. They wanted to restrict the Inuit to the north in order to ensure that the British fishing industry could expand along the south coast of Labrador without Inuit interference. Shortly after the Nain station was started, the governor issued a new proclamation. It required "the Unitas Fratrum [Moravian Mission] to use every fair and gentle means in their power to prevent the said Esquimaux savages from going to the southward, without first obtaining their permission in writing for so doing."[22] But Inuit continued to travel, and in the 1770s more British came to the south coast and established peaceful trade with the Inuit. The English trader, George Cartwright, built a post in Sandwich Bay at the town that now bears his name. Seeing the profits to be made, other merchants followed. Inuit traded with the new arrivals, far distant from the Moravian station.[23] Despite British and Moravian efforts to contain them in the north, Inuit continued to live in southern Labrador (see Part Three of this book), and violence gradually diminished between Inuit and the Europeans and Americans.[24]

Moravian efforts to convert the Inuit at Nain were at first modest and disappointing. In his diary, the missionary Christian Drachardt recorded how Inuit responded to his initial attempts at religious discussions. He described how he asked them, "Do you know that the Saviour died for you?" Some told him they did not want to hear about it. Others suggested that they discuss something else. One man replied that he was not surprised that God loved him, as he had not killed any Kallunaat [white people]![25] But the missionaries were patient. Since the Inuit preferred to spend time where they could hunt food for themselves, the Moravians sought to build Mission stations in locations closer to Inuit hunting areas. The British government supported the extension of their efforts and again gave them 100,000-acre land grants. The Mission established two new stations on these pieces of land, one to the north of Nain, and one to the south. The station at Okak opened in 1776, and at Hopedale in 1782.[26]

In 1791, the Inuit faced serious food shortages for the first time. European whalers had long since decimated the right whale and bowhead whale populations, and the Inuit found themselves unable to catch any whales along the entire coast. The Moravian missionaries offered some relief during times of scarcity, and a number of Inuit turned to the stations for help, especially widows and others in precarious social positions.[27] It was largely these Inuit women who led the spiritual breakthrough for which the Moravians had long been hoping. Referred to as the "Great Awakening" of 1804–05, the movement saw many more northern Inuit converting to the Moravian faith.[28] Heartened by their success, the missionaries redoubled their efforts to attract Inuit by building stations at Hebron (1830–1959), and later at Zoar (1865–90), Ramah (1871–1907), Makkovik (1896), and Killinek (1904–24). By the mid-1800s, Nain, Okak, Hopedale, and Hebron had between 200 and 400 Inuit connected with each station.[29]

The Moravian stations consisted of a church, communal dwelling house, trading store, and other buildings. They were staffed by missionaries from Europe, their families, and a storekeeper. Missionaries reported to a superintendent stationed in Labrador, and corresponded regularly

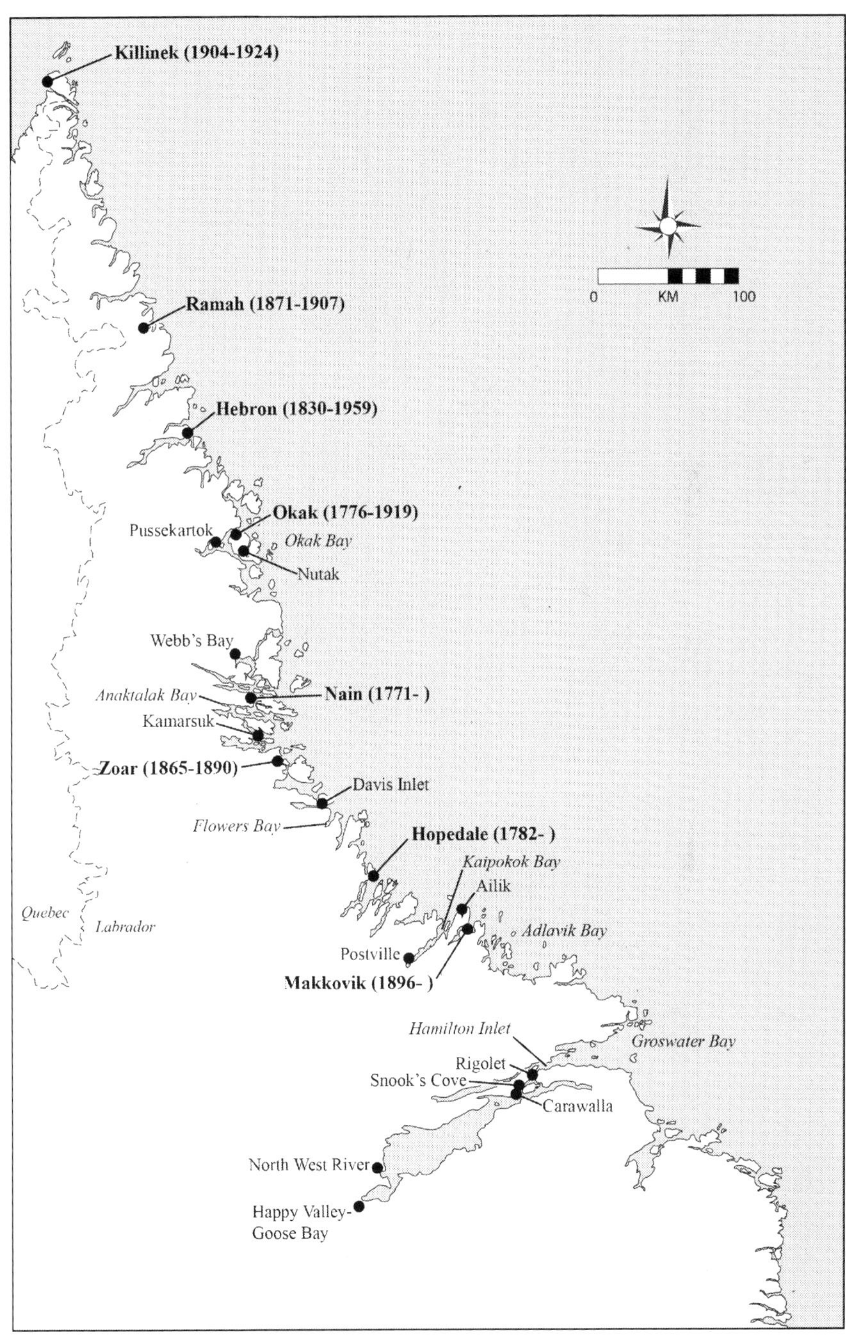

Map 2: Moravian stations and other communities in northern Labrador (map by Peter Ramsden).

with the Moravian Church and the SFG in Europe. Every year, the missionaries exported seal oil, sealskins, and fox pelts. After the mid-1800s, they also exported salt cod, char, and salmon to sell in London.[30]

Moravian Efforts to Change Inuit Life

The Moravian Mission carefully devised its plans for social change in Labrador. Missionaries aimed to transform some aspects of Inuit life, but not others. They wanted to convince Inuit to convert, to abandon some cultural practices, and to adopt new values. At the same time, they wanted to ensure that Inuit kept their language and remained as self-sufficient as possible.[31] A 1772 Moravian pamphlet described their goal as "trying to civilise and humanise [the Inuit] in some degree till they become Christians."[32] But while their goal may have been to change the Inuit "in some degree," the Mission's efforts in Labrador significantly transformed Inuit life.

Missionaries tried to undermine Inuit shamanism and spiritual practices. They banned drumming, throat-singing, and dancing, and dismissed Inuit intellectual culture as "too tedious to mention."[33] They sought to replace Inuit spiritual beliefs with Christian notions and their own ideals of order, diligence, and hard work. They attempted to direct and control Inuit behaviour towards their own moral standards of proper conduct. And they tried to organize the Inuit into communities in which people were industrious and disciplined.[34] Their "improvement" efforts focused on every aspect of Inuit life: family relations, sexual behaviour, morality, hunting and fishing practices, and ideas about private property, charity, and thrift.[35] They were especially keen to root out "drunkenness, adultery, whoredom, sorcery, theft, anger and revenge, and all other works of the flesh."[36] Disobedient Inuit converts were disciplined by exclusion from the church gatherings and even from living at the station.

The missionaries believed that one way to effect these changes was to keep converted Inuit away from harmful influences. However, it soon became obvious that Inuit could not live at the Mission stations year-round.

They could not support themselves if they settled at a station permanently, and the missionaries did not want to support an entire village. The Mission also lost vital income when Inuit did not hunt and trap for products to exchange at their store. The trade profits helped to fund missions around the world, in addition to subsidizing the Labrador venture.[37]

The Inuit who visited the Mission stations also continued to spend time in southern Labrador, where they traded with European and American traders and visited friends and relatives. In the south, they could access trade goods that the Moravians refused to stock in their stores, such as guns, European foodstuffs, and alcohol. Eventually, this competition forced the missionaries to adjust their approach and to offer a wider range of trade goods, including guns, food, and ammunition.[38]

The missionaries tried to find ways to encourage Inuit to live at the Mission stations for longer periods. In the nineteenth century, they developed commercial sealing and cod fishing industries as means to keep converts nearby.[39] Inuit had turned to seals as a main source of food in the early 1800s when whale populations were depleted. Seeing a commercial opportunity, the Mission supplied sealing nets to Inuit. Nets caught many more seals than the traditional harpoon method, but they were expensive and hard to maintain. Few Inuit owned them; instead, the Mission rented them in return for most of the catch. Inuit crews could keep some seal meat and a quarter to a third of the haul, but the Mission claimed the rest for the valuable sealskins and seal oil. The commercial sealing industry provided the Mission with a profitable trade. Critically, for this story, it also provided Inuit with enough food to remain at the stations between Christmas and Easter.[40]

The missionaries also encouraged Inuit to become commercial cod fishermen in the mid-1800s. The fishery kept Inuit near the stations in the summertime, instead of going inland to hunt caribou. Converted Inuit often met non-Moravian Inuit during the caribou hunt, and the missionaries complained of the heathen's corrupting influence on their congregation. The cod fishery tied Inuit to the coast, where they would fish intensively during the short summer season.[41]

Both the commercial seal and cod industries linked Inuit to the Mission stations and to the global market. The industries also allowed Inuit to sustain themselves if other animal populations plummeted. Inuit fishermen could trade fish and seals for shop goods that had become indispensable, such as ammunition, tools, and some European foodstuffs. Some individuals also earned income by working for the missionaries at the stations, if they needed the support or offered their services. Inuit rendered seal blubber into oil, cut wood, cleared snow, and provided domestic labour for the Mission.[42]

Mission station life also influenced changes in Inuit housing, clothing, and diet. Inuit from Nain and further south started to build wooden frame houses for themselves in the 1840s. Traditional sod houses were warmer in the winter, but some missionaries were concerned about "improper Christian sexual activity" in the multi-family homes.[43] European-style houses, however, were not ideal for northern Labrador. Sod houses needed only seal oil lamps to keep them warm. But the poorly insulated wooden houses needed firewood for fuel. It was difficult to gather enough

Moravian Mission buildings at Okak, ca. 1900 (courtesy of Them Days Archive).

wood to heat the new houses, especially in areas above the tree line or where forests had been depleted.[44]

Despite the drawbacks of wooden houses, some missionaries felt that the new style of housing had a positive influence. They lauded the effect of wooden houses on "domestic arrangements and increased attention to cleanliness, decency and comfort."[45] But European-style housing required Inuit women to spend a great deal of time at household tasks, such as cleaning wood floors, heating the home, and preparing the food. This work was even more intensive in the single-family homes. Instead of multiple women sharing in the work, all jobs fell to the female head of the household.[46]

Some Moravian Inuit also adopted the European style of clothing. Again, cleaning the clothes created more work for the women, but missionaries interpreted the Inuit attention to clean clothes as proof that they were becoming civilized and spiritually enlightened. In an 1844 letter to the SFG in London, the Okak missionaries wrote:

> You allude to the progress of our Esquimaux in civilization. . . . For when a rude heathen . . . attains to some degree of knowledge of himself and of Christ, his Saviour, he never fails to perceive the comfort and propriety of cleanliness. It often gives us pleasure, to see the Esquimaux women washing their own and their families' clothes in the neighbouring rivulet, which is generally effected, by treading them with their feet and wringing them with their hands; soap they seldom use. Most of our people are now accustomed to wear shirts and other under-garments.[47]

The diet of Moravian Inuit families also started to change in the early 1800s, despite the Mission's efforts to ensure that the Inuit did not become wholly dependent on European food. While they lived at the Mission stations, Inuit families consumed more salt fish, flour, sugar, garden vegetables, and tea, and they ate less meat and seal blubber.[48] Store-bought foods were easier to obtain than country foods in the villages, but they were not as nutritious, and the poorer diet contributed to a decline in health.

These various transformations in Inuit housing, clothing, and diet in the village allowed missionaries' wives to exhibit and impose their standards for cleanliness and housekeeping. They instructed Inuit women in housekeeping skills, cooking, sewing cloth, and European ideas of hygiene. They also taught Inuit girls these skills in the schools.[49] The missionaries' wives also tried to model European methods of child-rearing for the Inuit. The missionaries had relatively few children, however, and would send them back to Europe at the age of five or six to attend boarding school.[50]

Over the years, the Mission continued with its attempts to ensure Inuit remained at the stations for as long as possible. Despite these efforts, Inuit families continued to spend most of the year on the land. After a summer of fishing cod, the majority would spend the fall on the islands and in the bays trapping and hunting migratory birds, caribou, and seals. Families would return to the stations for Christmas and stay until after Easter. During that time, the church would host many religious celebrations

Harriet Dan carrying firewood, Nain, c.1910 (courtesy of Them Days Archive).

Inuit family, Okak, c. 1905 (courtesy of Them Days Archive).

and children would attend school. Most families would then leave for their cabins and camps for sealing at the floe edge.[51] Moravian Inuit maintained this seasonal life centred around fishing, hunting, and religious gatherings well into the twentieth century.[52]

The Moravian communities offered social, spiritual, and economic opportunities that were not available elsewhere. Many Moravian Inuit women enjoyed independence and social security through wage labour and female fellowship at the stations. Families survived difficult years of wildlife shortages, famine, and epidemics through Mission trade and social support.[53] Over time, the spiritual comforts of the church also became a major attraction, and one that continues for many Inuit today. But of all the changes caused by the Inuit encounter with the Moravian Mission, the schools would prove to be one of the most powerful tools of social transformation.

CHAPTER THREE

Early Moravian Schooling: *Teaching the Gospel of Christ*

"In the schools for the children, to which other young people, and particularly women come, the scholars showed much eagerness to learn. They easily comprehend what is explained to them."
— Hopedale missionaries, 1803

". . . we have the best hopes, that the good seed of the word sown in the hearts of the children, will bear fruit in due season."
— Hopedale missionaries, 1824

The Moravians placed a high value on the role of education in achieving Christian enlightenment. Early advocates for universal education, they believed that schooling should be available to all, regardless of race, class, gender, or intelligence.[1] Literacy, which offered the ability to understand religious texts, was important to the Moravian religious experience. Missionaries therefore encouraged converts to learn how to read by organizing classes.[2] Education also gave missionaries the opportunity to socialize children in Christian beliefs and behaviours. Literacy and schooling therefore played a key role in Moravian efforts to convert Inuit to Christianity in Labrador.

In 1780, Moravian missionaries established small day schools in Nain and Okak, and in Hopedale in 1783.[3] Building on the success of these schools, they eventually opened day schools at all Labrador Mission stations. The missionaries taught Inuit children in Inuktitut, using a written form of the language that uses the Roman alphabet instead of the syllabics used later in other parts of the Inuit homeland.[4] Pupils, aged about five to fourteen, learned how to read, write, and do basic arithmetic. They memorized hymns, passages from Scripture, the Ten Commandments, and the Lord's Prayer. After the 1840s, the schools introduced non-religious subjects such as geography.[5] The girls also learned household skills, such as sewing and knitting, and the missionaries tried to emphasize Christian ideas about household management:

> About the end of December the missionary sisters began their classes for instruction in various branches of women's work. . . . Every Eskimo girl learns the sewing required by the domestic circumstances of the people without any school teaching. Yet these classes offer an opportunity for giving the girls some idea of order and cleanliness, as well as frugality in the careful use of what might appear worthless.[6]

Schoolchildren with Inuk teacher, Okak (courtesy of Them Days Archive).

Inuit availability determined the school schedule. Children attended classes in Mission buildings for a few hours on weekdays between Christmas and Easter, when their families lived at the stations. Girls and boys usually learned together, and were sometimes joined by adults eager to learn to read.[7] In their reports to Europe, missionaries described with pleasure how children would read to their families at home, teaching what they had learned at school to their relatives.[8]

Initially, all teachers were Moravian missionaries. In the 1860s, church leaders suggested that they needed to encourage more Inuit involvement in church affairs, so the missionaries asked some Inuit to teach in the schools as well. They chose both male and female Inuit teachers from among the church's chapel servants, and gave them the younger classes to teach.[9] Most often, these Inuit teachers were senior or former students of Moravian schools themselves.

Literacy in the North

Moravian schooling was free and voluntary. The missionaries often expressed surprise at how enthusiastically Inuit embraced education. In an 1838 publication for Mission supporters, Hebron missionaries reported feeling encouraged by the Inuit response to their schools:

> Our premises being very near the Esquimaux houses, even children below the ordinary age have been able regularly to attend. On one occasion, when we had thought of omitting the school for the youngest children, in consequence of the extremely cold and stormy weather, the voices of some of these little ones were heard, under the teacher's window inquiring "Will the bell not ring this morning?" and he gladly found himself constrained to keep the school as usual.[10]

In 1824, a retiring missionary described people's interest in the schools at all Mission stations:

> The schools, which are held with both children and adults from November to April, are a most powerful means of forwarding their improvement in every thing good and profitable for them. Most of our people attend them with great diligence, and with an earnest desire to be soon able to read the New Testament for themselves. There are among the children, some of five and even four years of age, who read well. The severest punishment that can be inflicted on a child, is to keep him from school.[11]

Inuit enthusiasm for learning to read Inuktitut and the resulting high rates of literacy likely influenced the religious success of the Moravian Mission. Historian Hans Rollmann attributes the higher rates of conversion during the "Great Awakening" of 1804–05 to people's growing ability to read.[12] In the early 1800s, the Brethren issued newly translated Inuktitut versions of religious texts such as the Passion Narrative and the New Testament. They noted that many Inuit developed deeper spiritual insight through reading this literature.[13]

By the 1820s, Moravian Inuit also used their reading and writing abilities to communicate with one another. Missionaries were impressed with the number of letters Inuit sent to each other:

> The acquisition of the art of writing has afforded to many of them the means of intercourse with their friends in other settlements. Brother Kohlmeister says, that he has sometimes had nearly fifty short letters committed to his care by the Esquimaux, when, in his official capacity, he was proceeding from one settlement to the other. These letters contain information respecting the families and friends of the writers, and, not unfrequently, edifying remarks and meditations, on religious subjects, which may have been peculiarly impressed on their minds and hearts, with exhortations and encouragements to be faithful to their Saviour.[14]

Moravian Inuit also shared their knowledge of reading and writing with Inuit friends and relatives who lived in central Labrador, including at Snook's Cove and Carawalla, near Rigolet.[15] Individuals who had been educated in Moravian schools and later moved south taught their families and other fellow Inuit how to read. As a result, they often asked Inuit at the Moravian stations to send them Inuktitut Bibles and other religious texts.[16]

Nathaniel Illiniartitsijok, Inuk teacher, Nain, ca. 1905 (courtesy of Them Days Archive).

Many Inuit embraced the opportunity for schooling at Moravian stations. By the 1840s, almost all Moravian Inuit in northern Labrador knew how to read, according to historian Helge Kleivan.[17] In the early twentieth century, the educational achievements of the Moravian Inuit impressed many, including the philanthropist and education advocate Wilfred Grenfell. He admired both their literacy and their economic savvy:

> The best educated people in the country at present are the Eskimo. Almost without exception they can read and write. Many can play musical instruments, share in part singing, and are well able to keep accounts, and know the value of things. These accomplishments, entirely and solely due to the Moravian missionaries, have largely helped them to hold their own in trade, a faculty for want of which almost every aboriginal race is apt to suffer so severely. I have known an Eskimo called in to read and write a letter for a Newfoundland fisherman . . . .[18]

Approaches to Teaching and Control

The early Moravian schools were successful in teaching Inuit how to read and write in Inuktitut. But the missionaries worried that they were less successful in producing children who were firmly grounded in Christian values and behaviours.[19] From the Mission's perspective, the main focus of the schools was individual religious transformation through education.[20] While literacy was a large part of their teachings, the missionaries also wanted the schooling to influence Inuit children in adopting Christian attitudes, values, and beliefs. The Moravian schools were not unique in this aim, as all schooling in Newfoundland and Labrador during this period was religious education provided by Christian organizations.[21]

To achieve their goals of socialization, the Moravian missionaries considered starting "infant schools" for younger children so they could exert their influence at an earlier age. Inuit usually started school at the age of five, but in 1835 the SFG in London suggested that the Mission offer classes for three- and four-year-olds.[22] They hoped to maximize their impact while children were especially impressionable:

> The schools were a particular object of our attention, as we know what advantage attends early impressions of the value of the word of God, and what blessed fruits are often produced from the good seed sown in the tender hearts of children. . . . We are therefore the more anxious, to improve to the utmost the season of childhood, as a season of spiritual profit.[23]

In response to this suggestion, however, the missionaries in Labrador argued that an Infants' School would likely not have a profound effect. They reported that "occasionally infants of three or four years are taken thither [to school] by their mothers, though, as far as we can judge, hitherto to little purpose."[24] Nonetheless, they agreed that an early start with schooling helped to instill values in the children. They were "convinced that much is gained by their being early habituated to receive instruction, and to listen to what is told them of that Saviour who loves them so tenderly."[25]

Okak missionaries took a novel approach to child-rearing by starting an "orphan asylum" in 1865.[26] The home provided care for "for the poor children, who are frequently sadly neglected by their surviving relatives."[27] Inuit often used orphaned children as a source of labour, but the missionaries felt this to be a cruel practice. However, their congregation disagreed with the new institution. Inuit felt that the orphanage was "an infringement on their rights, as they are thereby deprived of the services of those whom they formerly employed without giving them the proper returns."[28] A clash of child-raising approaches was also evident. The Inuit parents who supervised the orphanage "have not the least idea of the Christian bringing-up of children," according to the Okak missionaries.[29] "Even the poor children are foolish enough to prefer a life . . . without any restraint, to that which is offered them amid the comparative comforts of the asylum."[30] Missionaries threatened families who took in runaway children from the orphanage with severe consequences, but "the congregation do not in general look on this arrangement as a benefit."[31] Without the support of Okak Inuit, the orphan asylum failed in its efforts. It closed seven years later in 1872.[32]

In all their attempts at schooling Inuit children, the missionaries found that they needed to refine their teaching methods to adapt to Inuit expectations about how to treat children. With the introduction of the schools, differences between the Inuit and European educational approaches had become apparent. Samuel Liebisch, one of the missionaries who started the first school in Nain in the winter of 1780, observed: "One cannot say any hard word to a flighty boy or girl, or even use a loud voice. That is against their way of raising [children]. If one forgets, they will be *kuvonok*, i.e., unhappy, and stay [away] from school two or three times."[33] Given Inuit disapproval of strict discipline, the Moravian teachers likely did not rely on the corporal punishment methods that were so common in other schools.[34] Instead, they had to adjust their teaching methods to attract pupils to their classes.

While Inuit found the European approach to teaching children too harsh, the missionaries criticized Inuit parenting as being too tolerant. A missionary in Hopedale in 1807 complained:

> The education of their children is most miserably managed by the parents, and harm must almost inevitably ensue from their very habits of living together. Even the very faithful among the parents, who sincerely desire to educate their children in the fear and admonition of the Lord, cannot keep them in proper order, so as to prevent seduction to evil.[35]

If "proper order" was not maintained, the Brethren argued, the children would become susceptible to harmful influences. They blamed Inuit housing practices, lenience, and family life for what the Mission saw as the children's imperfect education. But while the missionaries wished to exercise more control over Inuit children, they could not insist on complete authority. To do so would upset the delicate balance they maintained with the Inuit who chose to come to the stations.[36]

Teachers could also exert only a limited influence on the children because of the economic realities of Inuit life. The Moravian schools were initially day schools that children attended while their families lived at the Mission stations. From the start, missionaries were disappointed that the children could only stay for a few weeks before they left with their parents for their hunting and fishing places. The teachers voiced their concern about the impact on children of living for most of the year away from the Mission's influence. "As to the children," wrote Okak missionaries in 1809, "it is a great pity that, during the summer months, when they are absent with their parents, they too easily forget both what they have learned and felt the power of."[37] The same sentiment was echoed decades later:

> Our school children have in general afforded us satisfaction, particularly as we perceived among them a great desire to read and understand the word of God. The annual examination did

> great credit to their proficiency, and made us the more deeply regret the hard necessity, which compels them to accompany their parents to their provision-places during the summer months, and thus forego the benefit of Christian instruction for a considerable portion of the year.[38]

As much as the Mission regretted it, Inuit families needed to hunt, trap, and fish for most of the year to support themselves. Naturally, they took their children with them. Moravian missionaries recognized that the Inuit livelihood was not conducive to more intensive schooling. "The main hindrance to their [Inuit children] retaining better what they have heard and learned," they remarked in 1802, "is the roving life of the Eskimo, which being necessary for providing their maintenance, we cannot prevent."[39]

It was not until Inuit livelihoods changed in the early years of the twentieth century that the Mission gained more control over the education of Inuit children through its boarding school in Nain. Before this occurred, however, the Mission embraced the opportunity of providing boarding education to the children of people historically excluded from the Mission: the "Settlers," as the Moravians called them.

The "Settlers" and English Schooling

By the 1830s, the Moravian Mission had established stations as far north as Hebron and as far south as Hopedale. The missionaries wanted to bring more Inuit into the church while also isolating Moravian Inuit from other Inuit, Europeans, Americans, and Newfoundlanders in the region, but they had difficulties on both borders of their "territory." Many Inuit who lived north of Hebron had refused to convert to Christianity. Some would still visit the Mission stations periodically, as the Moravians were the only traders in the area. To the south of Hopedale lived other Inuit families who also refused to be drawn into the Moravian sphere of influence. Missionaries called these non-Moravian Inuit "Southlanders," and described their behaviour as "rude and unmannerly" and "far worse than that of the people of the North."[40]

The Brethren disapproved of the Southlander Inuit, and expressed their criticism loudly. Some of these non-Moravians were Inuit who had always refused to move north; some were dissenting Inuit who had disagreed with the missionaries and had moved south. In 1833, for example, a small group of Inuit left Okak after a conflict with the Mission. "They thought themselves qualified to propose to us various reforms in our rules and regulations," wrote a missionary in astonishment.[41]

The Southlanders' interactions with their Moravian Inuit relatives were a source of constant anxiety for the Mission. When they came to trade at the stations, Southlanders tried to draw baptized Inuit into what the Brethren saw as "hurtful and immoral practices."[42] They also spread malicious rumours and planted seeds of doubt among the Moravian Inuit about the Mission and Christianity. The missionaries, for their part, called the non-Moravians "degenerate Esquimaux" for adopting some aspects of European dress and diet. They fostered the notion that the only "real" Inuit were Moravian Inuit — a narrative that continues to impact the ways in which governments and fellow Labradorians regard descendants of non-Moravian Inuit in both Nunatsiavut and NunatuKavut today.[43]

As more European, Newfoundland, and American traders and fishermen moved into southern and central Labrador in the early to mid-1800s, some married into Inuit families. In doing so, they too became included in the Mission's "Southlander" category. By the 1830s, Moravian missionaries labelled any non-Moravian person who lived to the south of the Mission stations a Southlander.[44] They applied the label whether the person was of Inuit, European, or mixed ancestry. In the eyes of the Mission, Southlanders represented a threat to their efforts to keep the Moravian Inuit in the north and protect them from non-Christian and immoral influences.[45]

The Southlanders also represented a threat to the Moravian trade monopoly. European traders were gradually moving north, creating new trading networks with Inuit. The British company, Noble and Pinson, established trading posts in the 1770s and 1780s along the south coast, including at Cape Charles and Seal Islands; George Cartwright from England set up business in Sandwich Bay in 1775;[46] William Phippard and John Newhook became the first two Englishmen to settle in Groswater Bay in 1780;[47] and the Québécois trader, Pierre Marcoux, traded in Hamilton Inlet and at North West River in the 1780s.[48] By the 1830s, the Slade Company, Hunt and Henley, the Hudson's Bay Company, and many other traders were active on the Labrador coast.[49] The Moravian missionaries struggled to convince Moravian Inuit to stop trading with these other firms. By the 1840s, they realized that, in order to compete with the Southlanders, the Mission trade had to increase the prices it paid for fish, seals, and fur.[50]

The Mission Opens Its Doors

Some of the European and Canadian traders and fishermen who came to Labrador stayed and joined Inuit families. They married Inuit women, had families, and raised children. The children grew up exposed to both parents' cultural and linguistic backgrounds, and many families raised their children in bilingual households. These families benefited from Inuit knowledge of the land and kinship support networks as well as from European trading knowledge, and many became self-sufficient traders, fishers, and sealers. As pressure on resources in southern Labrador increased, more European-Inuit families moved farther north. When the Hudson's Bay Company established trading posts at Davis Inlet, Nachvak, and Rigolet in the mid-1800s, some of their employees also decided to stay in the region.[51] Because the newcomers and their families were not members of the Moravian Church, the Mission initially barred them from settling at the Mission stations.[52] But the missionaries often could not prevent them from establishing homesteads at rich fishing or sealing places in nearby bays.[53]

The Moravian missionaries referred to these families of mixed-ancestry who lived near their stations as "Settlers."[54] They initially saw them as a threat to the Mission trade and to their goal of "protecting"

Moravian Inuit from outside influences. In the 1850s, however, the missionaries' distrust of the Settlers in the Hopedale and Nain region faded.[55] Some historians suggest that the Mission's change of heart was due to the fact that the Settlers no longer threatened Mission trading interests.[56] Most families had given up trading, and instead supported themselves solely by fishing, trapping, and sealing from their isolated homesteads.

The missionaries also warmed to the Settlers' growing interest in the Moravian Church. They gradually allowed Settler families to take part in church festivals, and permitted them to build houses near the Mission complex in Hopedale, where they lived when they came to the station for church celebrations. In 1853, the church agreed to baptize its first Settler, John Reed. John was the son of William Reed, an Englishman, and Mary Reed, an Inuk woman from Groswater Bay. He was married to Johanne Reed, a non-Moravian Inuk.[57] John and Johanne were both baptized and

Settler (Kablunângajuit) family at Adlatok Bay. Back, l-r: Tilly Gear Mitchell, Mary Anne Mitchell, William Mitchell, Elizabeth Mitchell. Front, l-r: Marianne Ford Mitchell, Lea Mitchell, Edward Mitchell, Wilson Mitchell (courtesy of Them Days Archive).

then formally married in the Moravian Church. Following their lead — and often encouraged by the Inuit women in their families — more Settlers asked to become members of Moravian congregations in Labrador.[58]

The Mission began to see the Settlers as a new source of potential church followers. Given the high mortality rates among Inuit during the frequent epidemics of the mid-nineteenth century, missionaries wondered whether the future of their work in Labrador lay with the Settler population. As "their number is on the increase, while the Eskimoes are gradually, if slowly, dying out," they argued, "it becomes of no little importance in view of the future development of Christianity in Labrador."[59]

The Brethren slowly adapted to the needs and interests of their new church members. Most Settlers spoke English, but until the 1860s most Moravian missionaries spoke German, so they used Inuktitut to communicate with each other.[60] In 1865, Settlers near Hopedale asked for more accommodation of their needs:

> Other settlers . . . expressed a wish that an English Missionary might be appointed to take the spiritual charge of the settlers and instruct their children. We do not as yet see how this suggestion could be carried out, as the settlers' residences lie scattered over a considerable extent of country, but sincerely wish that something might be done for their spiritual benefit.[61]

More Settler families visited Hopedale and Nain for church festivities and became members of the congregation through the late 1800s, but none lived at the Mission stations permanently; instead, they lived several hours away from the villages, far enough from any neighbours to have enough space to be self-sufficient. To accommodate the changing composition of their congregation, the Mission hired English-speaking missionaries. And, for the first time, the Mission offered schooling in English for Settler children.[62]

New Souls in Need: The "Rising Generation" of Settler Children

Over the course of the nineteenth century, the Mission's approach towards those they considered as "non-Inuit" shifted significantly. The Moravian "policy of containment," as historian James Hiller describes it, originally aimed to isolate Moravian Inuit from others.[63] But as these others moved north and showed they posed no threat to the Church's interests, the Mission adapted. The Brethren now viewed the "once dreaded" Settlers as "a new and important sphere of labour," in which education again played a major role.[64] "It is a matter of the greatest importance for the future of Christianity in Labrador," missionaries wrote in the 1882 issue of the *Periodical Accounts of the Moravian Missions*, "that the rising generation [of Settler children] should be brought without delay under the influence of saving truth."[65]

Moravian schooling had until this point been offered solely in Inuktitut, scheduled for the weeks when Inuit families lived at the Mission stations during the winter. Students were taught to read and write in Inuktitut, using Biblical texts. They were also instructed in elementary arithmetic, church history, and geography. The missionaries encouraged Settlers to send their children to these free Inuktitut classes, but it proved difficult. The Settler families did not spend extended time at the stations in the winter, as they needed to support themselves from their homesteads in the bays. Above all, they wanted to have their children taught in English.[66]

In response, the missionaries made various early attempts to offer English-language schooling. In 1879, Brother Heinrich Ritter, an English-speaking missionary based in Hopedale, spent three weeks in Flounder's Bight (present-day Makkovik) teaching children in English on a trial basis.[67] The new school operated out of the home of Norwegian immigrant Torsten Kverna Andersen and his wife, Mary Ann Thomas. Torsten had first come to Labrador in the 1850s as an employee of the Hudson's Bay Company before leaving the company to set up his own small trading post. His wife, Mary, was the daughter of Samuel James Thomas, originally from England, and Mary Broomfield, an Inuk woman.[68]

The class consisted of six of the Andersen children plus three other students. They took classes with the missionary for four hours each morning, and did four hours of confirmation classes in the afternoon. Never having attended school before, the children "had to learn to sit still before other work could be taken in hand," but by the end of the three weeks Brother Ritter reported the experiment a success: "On March 6th we held an examination in reading, writing, arithmetic, and geography, with satisfactory results. All worked very well, and were very happy."[69]

The next year, in 1880, the Settlers' School, as it was called, was again held at Easter, this time in Hopedale. The children boarded in a Settler's house for the three-week term, as they had travelled far from home to attend. Two of their mothers acted as housemothers. The curriculum kept its emphasis on learning through religious texts, and Ritter's wife offered sewing and knitting classes for the girls.[70] Ritter describes Bible

Schoolchildren at Hopedale, 1903 (courtesy of Them Days Archive).

history as his "chief delight" of the classes, especially as Bertha Andersen, daughter of Torsten and Mary Andersen, "displayed great readiness and ability in repeating the narratives at the examination."[71]

The missionaries intended the Settler School to operate annually. They charged parents a fee of sixpence per day for schooling and board, although many found it difficult to pay. As a result, Ritter felt that a session of four weeks was the most that families could afford. Eventually, he hoped that the school would become self-sustaining, able to survive on the fees charged to parents and the occasional donation from supporters in Great Britain.[72]

Small English-language schools continued to run periodically in Hopedale after 1880, and at the Mission's newest station at Makkovik, established in 1896.[73] In the spring of 1909, a similar Settler school was started in Nain by the English missionary W.W. Perrett.[74] For the Settlers who lived around Nain, it was the first time the Mission had offered them any English-language schooling, as Rev. Perrett describes:

> I have just commenced school for the children of the settlers who belong to our Nain congregation, and who hitherto have had no opportunity whatever of attending school. They live scattered in the bays north and south of Nain, and have no one to help or urge them on a little. Some of the parents can read and write a little, and these do what they can for the children, but there are several lads and lasses who have reached 16 or 17 years of age who can hardly distinguish "b" from a bull's foot.[75]

The Settler schools operated separately from the Inuit schools in Nain and Hopedale, and were distinct in several ways. Children were segregated into separate classes, and the language of instruction was different, of course. Although the basic curriculum was similar, the texts that each school used were different. In the early years, the English-language teachers struggled to obtain enough books and resources for the students.[76] The Settler schools operated on an ad hoc basis, depending on when Settler families spent time in the community; the Inuktitut schools were scheduled more regularly.[77] The missionaries also offered the Inuit school classes for free, while they charged parents a nominal fee for the Settler school.[78] If a family did not have a house in the village, they also needed to organize boarding for the Settler children during the school term.[79]

The parental support for students and the teachers also differed. By the beginning of the 1900s, the Mission had schooled generations of Moravian Inuit, and parents could help their children with homework and off-season learning.[80] In Settler families, education had often not been available, so many parents did not know how to read or write.[81] Most teachers in the Settler school were therefore missionaries. In the Inuktitut-language schools, on the other hand, a number of teachers after the 1860s were Inuit who had gone through years of Moravian schooling.

There were two main complications in running the English-language schools: securing a place for Settler children to live, and finding the money to pay for their board. Settler families often solved the housing issue themselves by offering to take in and look after children in their houses

Makkovik school, 30 March 1904 (courtesy of Them Days Archive).

in the village. In 1910 and 1911, for instance, children at the Settler school in Nain boarded at the home of chapel servant George Voisey, while his wife acted as housemother.[82] The next year, a new schoolhouse was built with separate classrooms for Inuit and Settler children. The new building also included a room in which the children could stay while at the school.[83] The financial issue was more difficult to solve. Many Settlers could not afford to pay the fees, especially during difficult times, and the Mission did not provide enough funding to cover the costs. Families often decided to withdraw their children or not to send them at all. For these reasons, the majority of Settler children did not attend school, and their literacy rates remained low.[84]

The missionaries struggled to solve the schooling problems. By 1916, the Settler school in Hopedale had expanded from its original three-week term to nine weeks between February and April.[85] But without a resident teacher, a place for students to stay while their parents were away, and funding to pay for children's board, the Hopedale project soon became a drain on the missionaries' time and energy. On top of it all, the few weeks of school were too short a session for much to get accomplished.[86] The missionaries dreamed of a boarding school that would "collect as many children as possible . . . from the Makkovik, Hopedale, and Nain districts and keep them for 9 or 10 months, allowing them to return home for the summer."[87] Inuit children would also be able to attend such a school and take lessons in English, especially as some were "very eager" to learn the language.[88]

As the next chapter illustrates, the missionaries' dream for such a boarding school eventually became a reality at the new Mission station at Makkovik. Established to serve the local Settler population, the Makkovik boarding school would provide formal, long-term English education for children from more remote homesteads.

CHAPTER FOUR

The Makkovik Boarding School

"We gained a bit of education and we — I think I was a little tougher, but I do feel sorry for people that was treated worse than I was."
— Annie Evans, Makkovik, 2018

By the mid-1890s, the Moravian Mission decided to establish a new station for the Settlers (also called *Kablunângajuit*) living in the harbours and bays south of Hopedale. The missionaries chose to build where Torsten Andersen had settled at Makkovik. Brother Hermann Jannasch, an English-speaking German missionary, oversaw construction of the church and Mission complex. He envisioned a boarding school to soon follow:

> We hope, also, that the establishment of a [southern] station . . . will solve another problem, which has long baffled both our missionaries and the heads of these settler households. That is the education of their boys and girls, and there are about sixty baptized children in the outlying settler congregation of Hopedale. Repeated endeavours have been made to establish and maintain a school for them, but, after brave and strenuous efforts, have suffered shipwreck on one or another of the obstacles inevitable in such a land with such a climate. Suitable quarters could not be

> found for the children, or their parents could not expose the little ones to the perils and hardships of the long sledge journey.[1]

Starting in 1898, Jannasch and later his replacement, Rev. Walter Perrett, taught school at Makkovik during the winter. Students boarded in a local chapel servant's house or stayed in the Mission house during the term. In March 1899, 12 children came to the station for school; in 1901, 14 children attended classes for six weeks around Easter.[2] In 1912, the German Rev. Berthold Lenz served as the missionary for Makkovik. He was helped by his wife, Ingeborg Jannasch, the daughter of Hermann Jannasch.[3] Together, they championed Moravian schooling and created a much larger boarding school at the station. They felt that a boarding school was the only way to gather the children of the Makkovik region. In their view, bringing the children to live at a central school would have a beneficial impact on their future congregation:

> It is of special importance to get the children of these scattered families into our school, in order to awaken in them an understanding for all that the Mission and the church stand for, and above all things to make them early acquainted with the Bible and the Friend of children.[4]

In 1914, the Mission oversaw construction of a two-storey schoolhouse in Makkovik by local volunteers. Settlers/*Kablunângajuit* who lived in the outlying area worked on the building when they could. But few people lived at the station, and with a busy fishing season it was not easy for the men to take time away from their nets. Rev. Lenz recognized the challenges:

> It is more difficult at our stations than elsewhere to carry out work of this kind, since nearly all of our members live at a distance. We are very thankful that several of them have contributed liberally towards the cost of the materials, with the result that we now have practically all that we require.[5]

Makkovik school, ca. 1916, Rev. Lenz, wearing glasses, at left rear (courtesy of Them Days Archive).

It took nearly two years to complete the wooden schoolhouse. During construction, the boarding school continued in the Mission house. By the winter of 1914, Bertha Andersen was looking after the boarders for free. A former student herself, she had impressed the missionaries with her enthusiasm in recounting Bible stories to her teachers in 1879.[6] The new schoolhouse opened for the first time in the winter of 1916.[7] An American woman staying for the winter in Makkovik volunteered to teach the children.[8]

By 1920, with the school in Makkovik completed and staffed, the English-language schools in both Nain and Hopedale closed. "As the Makkovik School is now an accomplished fact and in full swing," announced a Hopedale missionary, "we have given up holding English school in Hopedale, preferring that the children shall take advantage of the much longer term and the much more efficient teaching in Makkovik."[9] Likewise, the Settler school in Nain ceased operating because "something much better is offered them now, in connection with the new school at Makkovik, than we could offer them."[10]

Makkovik, ca. 1920 (l-r: Schoolhouse, Moravian Mission house and church) (courtesy of Them Days Archive).

The missionaries along the coast encouraged parents to send their children to the Makkovik school if they wished them to take classes in English for the full school year. Several children from Hopedale attended the new school, but the interest from Nain families was at first muted. "Only one of our settlers has taken his children of school age down there," reported Rev. Paul Hettasch from Nain, "but we expect the children who return home from there will be the best advocates of the place over against those who are still holding back."[11]

In a few years, the number of children increased. With growing numbers, the Makkovik schoolhouse proved too small, and the boarding school moved back into the Mission building. The missionaries turned the original schoolhouse into a nursing station in 1925. But lack of use earned it the name "White Elephant."[12] The building still stands today as the Makkovik community museum.

The Mission house accommodated the teachers, the minister and his wife, students, and classrooms. Hilda Broomfield Dicker, who went to the boarding school from Hopedale, remembered the building:

> The teachers and the minister and his wife lived upstairs, and then the school, where the schoolchildren lived was downstairs. And there was three bedrooms, two for the boys and one big bedroom for the girls. And we all had double beds. All bunks, two on top and two down under.[13]

School Operations

The school in Makkovik housed between 25 to 35 boarding students each year in the 1920s and 1930s. Classes also included from seven to 12 day pupils from the local community. Two or three teachers taught all the students, most of whom came from Settler/*Kablunângajuit* families. Some Inuit children also attended, often because their parents or the missionaries wanted them to learn English. The school term extended from October to July.[14]

For the first time, the Mission hired teachers for the school, instead of relying on missionaries to teach the students. The Makkovik teachers were initially all young, single women from Europe. Most were the daughters of Labrador missionaries or members of the Moravian Church in England. Alice Perrett Perrault, for one, was the daughter of Rev. Walter Perrett in Hopedale. She came to Makkovik from England in 1926, replacing Edna Perrett, her sister, who had been teaching at Makkovik for five years.[15] Kate Hettasch, who taught in Makkovik in the late 1920s before she went to Nain, was the daughter of Rev. Paul Hettasch.[16] Others, like Emily Johnson and Evelyn Shaw, belonged to Moravian congregations in England.[17]

The Mission's policy in the 1930s was to hire teachers for three years, then give them a nine-month furlough with the option to renew their contract for another five years. They were expected to be on their best behaviour. Rev. Frederick William Peacock, superintendent of the Moravian Mission from 1942 to 1971, claimed it was necessary that the teachers "live in a manner as to uphold the prestige of the Mission and the White races."[18] He outlined his expectations in a letter to a teacher in

Makkovik missionaries, teachers, and students, 1929 (courtesy of Them Days Archive).

1948: "Our conduct must be exemplary. We must provide examples for the people we serve."[19]

The teachers were neither well trained nor well paid. In 1937, for example, Emily Johnson received £90 as her yearly salary, £60 of which she had to pay back to the Mission for her room and board.[20] In reflecting on the schools years later, Moravian Superintendent Peacock conceded that while the teachers "were fine young ladies, . . . many of them had not the ability or the training to teach."[21]

The teachers' minimal training and poor salaries were not unique to the Moravian schools. Most schools across Newfoundland and Labrador were in the same situation at the time. They were rarely staffed with well-qualified teachers and were not well funded. Like the Moravian schools, they offered a religious education organized and administered by the colony's various churches. Many closed during the difficult economic times of the early 1930s, owing to a lack of funding, teachers, and suitable buildings.[22]

The teachers at the English-language Makkovik school did not have to learn Inuktitut, unlike the Moravian missionaries who were expected to learn the Inuit language. Communicating with Inuktitut-speaking students could be a challenge, as Evelyn Shaw explained in a letter to the British Mission Board secretary in 1934:

> Some of the new scholars cannot speak English, and I do not know very much Eskimo. So we try very hard to understand each other sometimes, and yet how it draws us together. One of my pupils, Sophia Daniels, could not speak a word of English four months ago. Now she can read quite nicely from a simple primary book, her writing too is rather good.[23]

The teachers, volunteer helpers, and paid local staff cooked, cleaned, and collected wood for the school. On occasion, students were also expected to work. Alice Voisey Andersen, who attended the school in the 1930s, found herself employed in the kitchen during her two years at the school.

> When I was twelve, I came up to Makkovik for school on the old *Harmony* [the Moravian Mission ship]. When I was supposed to be going to school down here I used to have to help the kitchen woman, the cook, so some days I wouldn't get any — I never had much schooling, not me. There was someone, I don't know, I'll never know I suppose, when I was in the kitchen down here, someone wrote to Daddy a letter saying I was such a bad girl, I used to get out through the windows in the night and run out after the boys. And that wasn't a bit of true. So he said when he heard, he wasn't going to leave me here. He took me home. They didn't want to let me go, the minister that was here. He took me out of it and carried me home. I went down here to the kitchen in November, he took me out of it the 19th of May, I can remember that. [I got paid] $19. I was doing the clearing up, washing and scrubbing and things like that. The drudgery work.[24]

Students' First Days

Most students at the Makkovik boarding school came from families who lived miles away. Mary Oliver Clarke from south of Makkovik had fond memories of the boarding school, which she started attending in the 1930s when she was seven years old:

> I thought one of the best times of my life was when I got to go to school. I started school at Makkovik. The teachers, that first year, were Miss Perrett (Mrs. Alice Perrault now), Miss Pascoe, and Miss Shaw (Mrs. Wilson Cave now). The next year, there was also Miss Glaser, who is now Mrs. Siegfried Hettasch. The first night I was at school, it was a boarding school, I thought it was the same as at home so as soon as I finished supper I thought I had to go to bed, so I undressed. Somebody came into the bedroom and told us we didn't have to go to bed yet. There were three of us, three little girls. Miss Shaw came and told us she wanted us to go to her room. I thought it was great to stay up late. I was seven years old. She took us, one on each arm and one on her back and carried us to her room. She gave me a dolly to play with and gave the other two girls a book each. When they finished looking at the books we traded. Miss Shaw played with us until it was time to go to bed. It was a strange place so it took us quite a while to get to sleep.[25]

Muriel Lucy Andersen, who turned 100 in 2017, recalled arriving at the school in 1924:

> We lived about 30 miles from the station and we had to go by a dog team, you know. . . . My grandfather took me there. . . . And I was the littlest girl. I don't know how many — I'm not very tall now. I was the littlest girl for a long time. And the big girls, the big girls there in the school, oh, they was lifting me up to put me

Miss Potter (teacher) and children on Makkovik pier, 1929 (courtesy of Them Days Archive).

> upon the bench, big long bench by the teacher's table. . . . My first teacher was Miss Rowe her name, Miriam Rowe from England. We had three teachers — Miss Perrett and Miss Rowe and Miss Allsopp. They were good to us.[26]

Muriel remembers her excitement at going to school from her home in Adlavik Bay:

> The day had come, 1924, I was six in September and old enough to go to school at Makkovik. I remember being very excited. My mother and grandmother were busy washing and sewing and getting ready my few garments. We were a poor people, but grandmother's house was always clean and tidy. . . . I couldn't stay still and I talked the whole time as I was a real little chatterbox. I kept telling my Aunt Cateleena about the big house I was going to. I wondered to myself how my grandmother could

> look so sad, and once or twice I saw tears in her eyes. I wanted everyone to be so happy. I was to learn about the sad looks 'cause there came a time when I had to put two little girls in a boarding school.[27]

Muriel's daughter, Ruth Andersen Flowers, had a different experience. Both she and her sister, Annie Andersen Evans, were sent to live at the Makkovik boarding school in the late 1940s and early 1950s. Ruth remembers how she felt when she first went to the school:

> I was born in Makkovik, but I grew up for the first seven years of my life in a bay called Adlavik Bay with my mom and dad. There was only two families there, so we were a very close-knit family. Going to boarding school was — we were very very sad. . . . It was thoughts between, do our mother and father really want us? Or . . . But we soon learned that, yes, we had to go there to get an education, and was told that if we didn't go, our Family Allowance would be taken away from us. . . . There was such a change from living with my family in Adlavik Bay. My sister Annie Evans and I both went at the same time.[28]

A few students at the Makkovik boarding school came from Inuktitut-speaking families. Sybilla Pamak Nitsman arrived at Makkovik from Hopedale, but her journey started in Okak. She had lived there until the Spanish flu devastated the community in 1918 and killed her mother. When Sybilla arrived in Hopedale with her two aunts at the age of seven, the missionary sent her on to Makkovik to attend the boarding school. "That was the first time I went to school. Two men and a Kamutik [a sled pulled by dogs] took me in February or January to Makkovik and I was in Makkovik only six months, 'til June."[29]

Manasse Pijogge was another student from Hopedale whose mother tongue was Inuktitut. He went to Makkovik to learn English:

> I was living in Hopedale before I went to the Makkovik school. Our people was wanting to learn English. That's where I learned my English from. The people in Makkovik couldn't speak Eskimo, not all of them, a few of the old ones. The first year I went up I couldn't talk English at all so we used to have an interpreter then, one of the children that could talk. I liked the teachers right good. I didn't find it too hard to learn. We were just taught in English.[30]

Another student, Silpa Sillitt Edmunds from Hopedale, went to the boarding school in 1939 on the recommendation of the missionary, Rev. Paul Hettasch:

> When I was seven years old, Mr. Hettasch came and said to my parents that I had to go to Makkovik to learn English because we did not speak English in Hopedale. We were all Inuttitut[31] speaking people. No settlers then.
>
> So I had to leave my parents on the [S.S.] *Kyle* [the government-run coastal boat] to go to Makkovik to learn English, which I never did pretty good, very good at it. There was some more children my age who went to Makkovik and then on the *Kyle*. . . . Our teachers came from England on the ship.
>
> So I couldn't speak English and I couldn't communicate with the teachers. They'd be talking to me and I didn't understand what they were saying, and I found it really hard. . . . We had English teachers and no Inuttitut speaking people there. Then again, there was an old lady, Aunt Bertha [Andersen] was the only one who spoke Inuttitut, she would say things to me.
>
> I think that's how I survived. She would say things like, old people like saying few things to me where I couldn't speak English at all. . . . And then when my dad picked me up in March, Easter time on dog team he said whether you learned English or not, you're not going back again so I didn't go back to school, but I finished my grade three![32]

School Curriculum

School subjects at the Makkovik boarding school ranged from academic topics to practical skills. "Reading, writing, arithmetic, grammar, dictation, songs, history, Scripture, general knowledge, singing, music, knitting, sewing and repairs, sealskin bootmaking and repairs, washing clothes, housework and cleaning, cleanliness, [and] sawing and splitting firewood" occupied both the students and the teachers in 1923.[33] Former teacher Alice Perrett Perrault later recalled a curriculum that covered the basics: "The curriculum then was just ABC's or 3 R's as it was referred to then. Wasn't much, but then we put in different subjects like geography, history, grammars, spellings. The textbooks came from England, some of them."[34] A former student, Jim Voisey, remembers the curriculum as being religious and Eurocentric:

> They were teaching you how to read, to write, and history and stuff like that. Bible stories, a lot of that, Bible, Old Testament. American history — how Columbus come across the ocean and the old English stories, old timers like Oliver Cromwell and what's his name that put his coat on the ground for Queen Elizabeth to walk across.[35]

The school divided students into a "top class" and a "lower class," depending on their abilities. Some, like Hilda Dicker, moved between the classes for different subjects: "For reading and writing and spelling, I was good, but when it came to the reckoning [math], long division and stuff like that, I'd always have to go down to the lower class."[36]

Teachers also taught music. Miriam Rowe, from Bedford, England, started teaching in Makkovik in 1922.[37] She was especially remembered for teaching children how to play the piano. One of those students was Inga Andersen, who played the organ in the Makkovik church until she was into her nineties.[38] Inga herself also taught at the school in the early 1940s as a teaching assistant, as did other former students.[39]

Students in Makkovik school, ca. 1925. Left to right, back: Rachel Daniels (Hopedale), Susie Mitsuk (Hopedale), Gladys Chard (Ailik), and Violet Andersen (Makkovik); middle: Edward Voisey (Voisey's Bay), Margaret Evans (Ben's Cove), ?, and Lavinia Edmunds (Ailik); front: Bill Andersen, Jim Andersen (Makkovik), Muriel Lucy, and Susie Lucy (Adlavik Bay) (courtesy of Them Days Archive).

By 1937–38, the curriculum had not changed much at all, as shown in the following timetable:[40]

Monday to Friday

9:00–9:45	Scripture
9:45–10:45	Arithmetic
11:00–11:45	Reading or Writing
2:00–2:45	Dictation, Reading, or Writing
3:00–4:00	Girls: Sewing / Boys: Drawing
4:00–5:00	Girls: Mend their clothes or boots / Boys: Carry wood, make shavings. Comb all children's heads.

Saturday

9:00–9:45	Prayers
9:45–2:45	Girls: Scrubbing, weekly mending / Boys: Carry wood, make shavings
3:00–4:00	Walk
4:00–5:00	Girls: Mend their clothes or boots / Boys: Carry wood, make shavings. Comb all children's heads.

Memories of School

For some students, the school routine felt confining. Jim Voisey recalls being made to follow a strict schedule:

> Up 7:00, breakfast by 8, lined up to go in the classroom by half past 8, be in there 9:00. Then, half past 11, we'd be out for dinner. After dinner, out in the yard for about 10 or 15 minutes playing, exercise I suppose that was supposed to be. Somewhere around half past 1, we had to line up again to go back in, and 4:00 that's when we had to do our homework — or 5:00, we'd be at our homework, homework was done in the classroom. Half past 5, back to the same old thing, line up to go to supper. We had to line up and march to the dinner, supper table. Boys in one line, girls in the other. After supper, wasn't much free time, play around there for about half an hour. Start getting ready [for bed] by 7 and be in bed by 8, washed up, cleaned the teeth, stowed away this and that, and was in bed by 8:00.[41]

Annie Andersen Evans describes a similar routine at the school:

> We went to bed at 7 o'clock and we got up at 7 o'clock, from like 7, 6 or 7 years to 11. When you were 11, you were a big girl, you stayed up 'til 8 o'clock and mended. And we helped to clean and we dried the dishes, the big girls, 11 up, washed the laundry, helped the housemother wash the — our housemother was good to us — washing laundry. The boys got in all the wood. . . . At 1 o'clock in the afternoon, we went for a walk for one hour and we started school again at 2. School started at 9 in the morning and then at 2 in the afternoon to 4 and then at 5 o'clock we had homework. They called it prep, preparation for the next day. It was some hard times in school.[42]

Students were expected to do chores on top of their school work. Sealskin boots needed constant attention, and the buildings always needed wood for the stoves. Boys and girls attended to both chores, as the *Periodical Accounts of the Moravian Missions* reported in 1927:

> The boys are then busy cutting wood or fetching water; the girls are washing up, or scrubbing, or sewing. Moreover, a lot of the mending of the children's clothes has to be done by the teachers, and some come to us so poorly attired that mending begins soon after their arrival.[43]

Sometimes, the students' work extended beyond these tasks, as Rev. Harp describes in a 1947 letter:

> On Sept 21st, the mail boat arrived for the fifth time, bringing us 25 children for the boarding school, also one of the teachers. . . . The first week after arrival was a time of freedom from lessons.

Students in Makkovik chopping wood (courtesy of Them Days Archive).

> The boys were given tasks of digging potatoes etc and stowing firewood in the sheds for the winter. The girls spent every moment picking berries and these were put in barrels in the school store room for use during the winter. As a reward for all this work the 25 children were taken on an all-day picnic on an island in the vicinity.[44]

School Discipline

Mission staff used discipline to ensure that children followed the boarding school rules. They often saw the tolerant parenting approach with which the students were raised as an impediment to their efforts. As Rev. George Harp, the missionary in charge of the school from 1946 to 1951, put it: "Our Labrador children are all very spoiled in their homes and are consequently very undisciplined when they come to school. School discipline is a problem for the teacher just beginning, and she needs to exercise with much tact and justice."[45]

In taking the children away from their homes, the boarding school allowed the missionaries and teachers to exert full control over the students. Rev. Siegfried Hettasch, the son of Rev. Paul Hettasch and the brother of Kate Hettasch, taught day school at Hopedale in 1944. In a letter to Rev. Peacock, he expressed his frustration with his inability to discipline his students. He wished that they could be sent to the boarding school, beyond the influence of their families: "They should all be forced by law to be in Makkovik where the parents cannot help them or else we need a boarding school here in Hopedale where the missionary in charge will have full control and power to say and do what may be of need."[46] As Siegfried had learned, total authority over students was only possible in the seclusion of a boarding school.

Children who attended the Makkovik school often were not in a position to question the disciplinary authority of the Mission staff. But they resented the power they wielded. Ruth Andersen Flowers told the 2011 Truth and Reconciliation Commission sharing panel in Hopedale that "If someone was speaking to you [at the school], it was almost always, 'Don't do this, don't do that. Do this, do this.' Every sentence with an adult was almost like a command."[47] Ruth's sister, Annie Andersen Evans, also talked about school discipline at a Healing and Commemoration session held in Makkovik in 2018:

> It was some hard times in school. Like, they did use a — not the leather strap, but it was the pointer that made a long thick stick for the teacher for pointing at the blackboard, and you'd get strapped with that. . . . I guess we were like — we were their responsibility and we couldn't tell anybody, we couldn't go home. And the way it was back then maybe like our parents knew the difference, but to us it seemed like the teacher was always right or the minister was always right.[48]

Institutional Food

For many children, the boarding school food and rigid mealtime schedule made the adjustment to living away from home difficult. Students had no control over what they ate, how much, or when. Institutional food was often different from the country food served at home. Many of the children grew up in homes where families did not enforce strict rules around eating or scheduled mealtimes. Memories of the food therefore stand out for many former students. As Jim Voisey recalls:

> Emily Gear was doing the cooking the last year I was there. Miss Perrett would supervise the cooking. Monday's dinner was leftovers from the whole week. Say if you had partridge or deer meat Sunday dinner, perhaps salt trout for Sunday's supper, well, leftovers were saved all through the week and then sometimes you'd have beans or perhaps peas, salt beef, rice soup, whatever they had, that was saved and come around Monday, eh, that was all mixed up together. That was Monday's dinner. I didn't like it, no one did. I suppose they were trying to save.[49]

Gladys Chard Burdett went to the boarding school in the late 1920s. She could still remember meals in vivid detail when interviewed in 1978:

> What we had for breakfast was porridge, boiled the night before with molasses in it, cold and warmed over, lumps in it. I can taste it now. If you didn't eat your breakfast, well, it was there for dinner, and if you didn't eat it for dinner 'twas there 'til supper 'til you did eat it. If we wanted anything we needed to hold our hand up.[50]

The staff could be cruel in forcing children to eat the food. Gladys remembers an incident in which a nurse, M.E. Tatterson, behaved in a brutal and callous manner with a sick child:[51]

> I saw Nurse Tatterson come in one morning, there was a little Flowers girl there, a pretty little girl, and she was sick. Since then I heard she had TB, and she couldn't eat this porridge and she cried. Now, I saw Nurse Tatterson take the spoon and spoon it up and put it in her mouth, and when she's get in her mouth she'd vomit it back in her plate. Then she'd make her eat it again. That would turn anyone's stomach.[52]

Staff also used food to discipline children. Gladys remembers being sent to bed without supper once as punishment for something she had not done.

> I started to cry when I got in the bedroom and I cried and I cried. By and by down comes Mrs. Lenz [the missionary's wife]. "Vat is the matter now?" "I'm hungry. I laughed when I was doing my homework and Miss Hettasch [the teacher and housemother] won't let me have no supper." She said, "Okay, dry your tears, get out of bed, put on your clothes." She helped me put on my clothes. She was a nice old soul. She washed me face and we went out and she told the girl in the kitchen to get me supper. So

> that was okay. I had me supper. I didn't care then and I went to bed again. After a while I heard her come downstairs. Miss Hettasch's room was next to our bedroom with only just a wall between, you could hear everything. She went in to her, I don't know what she said but she was going to her in German, right mad. By and by I heard Miss Hettasch crying. I said, "I wonder what she's crying for?" The two of them came out and I heard Mrs. Lenz come in the bedroom. "Gladys," she said, "She (Miss Hettasch) said she was sorry she blamed you for telling a lie." Oh, I was some glad she got some calling off. She thought she could run it sometimes.[53]

Some former students remember not having enough food at the boarding school. Muriel Lucy Andersen describes how hungry children tried to get more food:

> They was hard sometimes in the boarding school. And all we used to have for lunch was a piece of hard bread. And the poor ol' boys used to be so hungry they be jumping up at the — the teachers used to have an old wooden tray. The poor ol' boys used to be jumping trying to get it. They broke into the store one night, they was really hungry. The minister had to come down and he boxed their ears.[54]

In their official reports, missionaries claimed that they always fed the children well. But adequate funding for the school was a constant concern, and the missionaries managed the food budget carefully. In 1940, Makkovik missionary George Sach dismissed complaints about children going hungry. He wrote in the *Periodical Accounts*:

> One small plump Eskimo girl was sent to the missionary, because she told her teacher she was starving. When asked what she had had for breakfast, she replied: "I had three cups of tea,

> three slices of bread and butter, and two plates of porridge." When she sent her plate for the third portion of porridge, the teacher thought that she had had enough. Two young men standing by were asked what they had had for breakfast, and gave their answer: "Bread and tea." Dry bread and raw tea, the usual Labrador breakfast.[55]

In later years, students often did not recall being hungry. Muriel's daughter Annie describes how the cooks and the children did their best with a monotonous menu:

> I went to school when I was seven and because it was Confederation then, if you didn't go to school you didn't get your family allowance. . . . The first year I went to school, after we got there, we was all kind of like — like a family more or less. It was good in the beginning. . . . We had three meals a day. We had breakfast, we had porridge and a cup of — half a mug of molasses tea and a slice of brown bread buttered. And then at noon we had either beans or peas or rice soup, fish — usually we had the fish for supper — and at the noon meal we had another half a cup of molasses tea, but we didn't have any bread with that. And then for supper we had — usually it was fish, cod fish, salt salmon or salt trout. Sometimes we had . . . a wedge of raw turnip and a slice of brown bread and half a mug of molasses tea, but we — we must have got used to it, I suppose. We were fortunate that we had a good cook and the things she made was really good. I mean, if you didn't like the — what you had, you had it again for dinner, eh, the supper. So it was better to eat it.[56]

Bullying and Abuse

Bullying at the boarding school was common. Teachers were not always present to supervise the children, and students often picked on each other. Those with power — both students and authority figures — could abuse others without much fear of accountability. Both sisters Ruth Andersen Flowers and Annie Andersen Evans were bullied while at the school. As Ruth says:

> There was a lot of bullying going on in school when Annie and I went there. Bullying like you would not believe. There was this one girl who was the bully, and she had packs — so many days, girls would be on her side. On another day, she would have three or more. Everything was done to us. A lot of them people are gone now that would remember that. One night, the bullying was going on, and they were demanding [that I] go and pinch my sister Annie. She was sleeping at the foot, and I was sleeping at the head.[57]

Her sister Annie describes the same situation:

> And like there was the bullying in the bedroom after and all day, and we were so afraid to say because the bully was a relative of, you know, whatever. And that was hard, that was really hard because you couldn't — you was always living in fear.[58]

The fear of reprisal meant that children at the boarding school rarely had anyone they could turn to for help. Ruth also suffered a traumatic sexual assault that she kept secret for years before she felt ready to seek help. "I have dealt with it, and I have gone past it. No one should have to go through that. You shouldn't have to be thinking about things like that."[59]

In summarizing her reflections of the school, Ruth said:

> I was glad to get some education, but the way we had to get it was so horrible. I think that if we didn't have to live with that fear of what was happening to us with the bully, we would have gotten a better education.[60]

Voluntary Attendance before 1949

For years, Makkovik was the largest boarding school on the north coast. Although the missionaries wanted children in the region to attend, not all did, and school attendance was not compulsory until the 1940s. While the Commission of Government made school attendance mandatory in 1942, Rev. Peacock commented as late as 1950 that "compulsory attendance at school is more or less a farce."[61] Before that time, parents decided not to send their children for several reasons. Some found organizing a trip to and from Makkovik to be difficult; some did not require their children to attend school once they had learned how to read and write. For others, the school fees were too expensive or the time apart from their children was too long.

Transportation Not Easy

Children often travelled far to attend the school. In the early years, the Mission ship, the *Harmony*, transported students from their homes to Makkovik. But in 1926 the Mission sold the *Harmony* to the Hudson's

Kate Hettasch and schoolchildren on ship (courtesy of Them Days Archive).

Bay Company, along with its trading interests. It then had to rely on other boats to bring the children to the boarding school.[62] This presented a problem if the commercial boats could not or would not take the children. In 1928, for example, the mail boat could not get through to Nain, so only one teacher and a few students got to Makkovik for school. The other two teachers, Alice Perrett (coming from Davis Inlet) and Kate Hettasch (coming from Nain), only arrived in Makkovik after January, when they could travel by ice.[63]

The experience led the missionaries to consider opening another English-language school in Nain. As Makkovik missionary Rev. Lenz wrote:

> It may not be possible to realize this in the near future, but the desirability of such a plan strongly suggested itself to our minds by these late difficulties. We shall endeavour to have the children come to us earlier hereafter, to prevent the recurrence of a similar upset. Another difficulty in the way of the northern children is that the small northern mailboat is hardly fit for ladies and children to travel on. Some of the parents will not send their children on the same to us, except there is somebody trustworthy travelling with them.[64]

Lenz reported the same challenges the next year in his annual report:

> We were sorry that again some children, that were expected from Nain, could not come in the end on account of adverse travelling conditions. Only from Davis Inlet and Hopedale we had seven children. In all twenty-four children visited the school last winter, against twenty-five the previous year.[65]

A few years later, in 1934, only seven children arrived at Makkovik. The captain of the Hudson's Bay Company supply schooner, the M.S. *Fort Garry*, had refused to take children from Davis Inlet, where several

Handwritten caption underneath photo reads: "School Children Arriving at Makkovik, Nov. 26, 1927, S.S. Kyle" (courtesy of Them Days Archive).

Settler/*Kablunângajuit* families lived. "This was a shame, because their parents are eager to send them," wrote Rev. Paul Hettasch to Samuel Hutton, the secretary of the British Mission Board.[66] "After the *Bay Nain* [a Hudson's Bay Company boat] stopped, I didn't go anymore," Clara Voisey remembers. "Daddy wouldn't send us on the other, there were only freight boats then, like *Fort Garry*. . . . I don't think they took the children on the *Fort Garry*."[67]

Just Reading and Writing

While many parents valued literacy, most believed that children also should learn how to master the land-based skills needed to thrive in the Labrador environment. As a result, some families made use of the school only for as long as they thought their children needed it. They then withdrew them so that they could complete their education at home in skills such as sewing sealskins, fishing, hunting, and trapping.

An American visitor to Makkovik in 1932, Rhoda Dawson, described in a letter how the parents of children at the Makkovik school held specific expectations for their education: "The fathers are coming along now to take their children home from school. . . . Their parents can't do without them for long. . . . As long as the child can read and write that is all they want."[68] Rev. Lenz regretted that parents needed the labour of their teenaged children at home, saying, "some parents are still unable to realize the growing importance of some schooling. At ten or twelve years of age, and in some cases even earlier still, the children become very useful at home, and the parents think that they cannot spare them."[69]

The parents' decision to encourage their sons, especially, to develop the skills and knowledge needed for a hunting and trapping way of life is clear in the ratio of boys and girls at the school. In the late 1920s, many more girls than boys attended:

> We had the same number of pupils as last year, twelve boys and twenty-two girls. It is harder to get the boys to come to school than the girls. The former are wanted at home. At an early age they get introduced to the use of the gun and to handling dogs and commatic [*sic*], which they find much more interesting than the uneventful regular work of school.[70]

Lenz also reported that parents were reluctant to force children to attend school when the children did not want to go.

> In some cases also the parents are not willing to prevail upon a child if it does not want to come. There are very few children, though, of that kind; for the most part they are only too anxious to come, even if after a while they get tired of the regular school hours.[71]

Students often attended school for only part of the year. Parents would arrive in the spring to collect their children if it saved them a trip later. Alice Perrett Perrault, a teacher at Makkovik in the late 1920s and 1930s, describes how the school year tapered out when parents started taking their children home in the spring:

> Sometimes, if parents came around Easter time, they took the children back with them. So they wouldn't have to come again in boat, you know. Took them back up by Kamutik and dogs. [Their school year] was from October or November until March, some of them. But then, those who stayed, we had to wait until the first mail boat came, which was probably the end of June or the beginning of July, all depends on the ice. They weren't kept — we didn't have proper schooling, you know. I don't think [the difference between the education of those who left and those who remained] was that noticeable. You see, after when spring came, nobody felt like . . . you see, the boys looking out the window, watching the birds, the snowbirds and things like that.[72]

Poverty

An inability to pay the school fees also kept children out of school. Many families could not afford the weekly payment of $0.50 for a child's board and schooling. In some years, the markets for fur, fish, and sealskin failed to provide families with much income. As trade was often done by barter instead of cash, families sometimes did not have money on hand to pay for their children's boarding school.[73]

In 1922, for instance, difficult economic times meant that parents of the majority of students (17 of the 31) did not contribute anything towards the school. The missionaries discussed how to deal with the matter:

> Ought we to encourage children to attend with little or no prospect of payment, when the school already is a serious burden to Mission finances? (Oh, for some endowment!) On their own initiative several parents have solved this problem for themselves (and for us, too) by refraining from sending their children last term. One is sorry for the children.[74]

Seven years later, when Lenz was reporting from Makkovik, financial challenges remained an issue:

> Some parents again are reluctant to bring their children, because they may not be able to pay the small fee we ask. Surely, fifty cents a week is an insignificant amount, but when the child is here for twenty or forty weeks it adds up and they do not know then how to produce the money. Several people hardly handle any of the latter, but do most of their trading by barter. Nor does the Store pay out any money except for fur. But we are convinced that this work should be encouraged and carried on.[75]

Too Far Away

The deaths of two children at the Makkovik boarding school in 1927 and 1939 underlined the separation between the students and their families. The missionaries provided medical attention and periodically weighed the students to document any healthy weight gains throughout the year.[76] But they were not trained doctors, and outside medical help was not often available. Infectious disease caused many deaths in northern Labrador until the 1950s, and mortality rates were high.[77]

Losing two children so far from home would have been devastating. Alice Perrault remembers the death of the two students, Millicent Flowers (1929–39) and Amos Voisey (1913–27), as "[t]wo of the saddest incidents" that took place while she taught at Makkovik. As she recalled, "the children died while at the school. One little girl from Davis Inlet, she died of meningitis, and a boy from Nain, he was, I believe, 13 years old. He died, but I don't know exactly, I don't remember the cause."[78]

Rev. Paul Hettasch, the missionary in Nain at the time, told the Voisey family about their son's death. It was a "sad occurrence. . . . The only boy and only child of one of our Nain settlers had died quickly far away from his father and mother, though well cared for at Makkovik school. It was a hard task to break the news to the bereaved parents on my return."[79]

The health and medical care of the children was a constant concern. In 1949, flu spread through the boarding school, but this time medical assistance was available. "We were much troubled by 'Flu' during the winter, and at one time, all the school children were in bed," reported Rev. Harp. "Our cook made a wonderful nurse, staying up nights and doing her work during the day. . . . Penicillin and Sulfathiazole came to our aid."[80] Despite all efforts, illness and epidemics at the boarding school remained a concern for both parents and teachers.

The Government Steps In

Mission finances, long a source of anxiety, became dire in the 1930s and throughout World War II. The situation was so desperate that the British Mission Board applied to the Commission of Government in Newfoundland for financial help for the schools. According to Rev. F.E. Birtill, the secretary of the British Mission Board, Labrador parents paid or donated about $425 of cash or goods in 1939 to the Nain and Makkovik schools. But the Mission spent about $8,700 to operate them. "We therefore make application: That a per capita grant be made for children in the Moravian Mission Schools on the same scale as is made for children in denominational schools in Newfoundland and elsewhere."[81]

Makkovik schoolgirls, October 1929 (courtesy of Them Days Archive).

Other schools in Newfoundland received $6.50 per student from the government. Church education authorities were also eligible for "augmentation grants," depending on the teachers' qualifications.[82] The Moravian Church asked for the same. In response to Birtill's request, the Commission of Government agreed to contribute $1,000 to the Moravian Mission for the 1941–42 school year.[83] But before it would release any augmentation grants, the government wanted more information about the Moravian teachers' qualifications.

The new Moravian superintendent for Labrador, Rev. Peacock, was determined to address the government's administrative demands. He sent extensive descriptions of the Moravian teachers' education to the Department of Education, but only his wife, Doris Peacock, fulfilled the requirements for an augmentation grant. While Doris had a university degree and a Diploma of Teaching, the other Moravian teachers had only elementary or secondary school education, and no formal training in teaching.[84] In frustration, Peacock wrote a letter to the federal Minister of Mines and Resources in Ottawa for information about how the federally funded residential schools in northern Canada operated. Hoping to compare the Moravian schools with these other schools, he asked, "Are fully trained teachers required, if not what qualifications are desirable"?[85]

Despite the Newfoundland government's critical assessment, Moravian Mission officials believed that their choice in teachers was appropriate for Labrador. "The training given in these schools, though it is not given by professionally trained teachers, is not only adequate, but in fact well-suited to the children of the coast," argued Birtill from London.[86] The Moravian Church relied on young women who were willing to exert themselves for the Mission "at salaries of a vocational standard," as Birtill described it, "not according to 'market rates.'"[87] The Mission also hired former Inuit and *Kablunângajuit* students as teaching assistants. Inga Andersen, Susie Mitsuk, and others provided invaluable help to the Mission by offering their bilingual skills and cultural expertise in the boarding school.[88]

Young, single women could be hired for low wages, but their teaching careers would end if they decided to get married. Over the course of four years, between 1936 and 1940, five European teachers married, most to members of the non-Inuit elite: Nora Mowl married Newfoundland Ranger Bragg (and then tragically died in childbirth the next year),[89] Evelyn Shaw married HBC manager Wilson Cave, Emily Johnson married Rev. Grubb in Hopedale, Frieda Glaser married Rev. Siegfried Hettasch in Nain, and Alice Perrett married Thorwald Perrault of Makkovik.[90]

These weddings took a heavy toll on the number of Moravian teachers on the coast. The British Mission Board was already finding it hard to recruit teachers. "It is so difficult to find the right type of person," wrote a Mission Board official from London in 1938.[91] In 1940, faced with staffing issues at the Makkovik school, Rev. Sach decided to hire a man from Newfoundland, Malcolm Sparkes, as a teacher, and paid him significantly more than the Mission was paying the female teachers. Sach's decision caused much consternation among his colleagues. His superiors at the British Mission Board, who had made all hiring decisions up to this point, did not appreciate losing their control over staffing. "We have no knowledge of this man," Brother Birtill wrote, "nor of his teaching ability or his powers of maintaining discipline."[92] Superintendent Paul Hettasch in Nain had other concerns: "At $20 a month plus room and board, he is more expensive than a lady teacher and does not do any of the mending or cooking."[93]

Some missionaries felt that teachers needed qualities other than formal training to succeed at the boarding schools: "A lot has been said I understand about some of the teachers not having sufficient education," wrote Rev. Grubb in Hopedale to Rev. Peacock, who was stationed in Nain.

> It is not always the one with the certificate that is the best teacher, and any intelligent Christian young woman who has had even only elementary schooling at home will be able to teach the children here as far as they can hope to get in our schools. Certified teachers are no doubt desirable, but a good conscientious intelligent young woman is a lot better than none at all, and would be more likely to do the matron tasks better, as certified teachers have a habit of being teachers only.[94]

Makkovik school children and teachers, 1931 (courtesy of Them Days Archive).

Others, led by the Rev. Peacock, newly appointed as the Labrador Mission superintendent, and his wife, Doris Peacock, recognized the deficiencies in the teachers' education. They were determined to improve the quality of the schools. Rev. Peacock's frustration with the situation is evident in a letter he wrote to Rev. Harp in Makkovik in 1945:

> With regard to the ability of the teachers; for almost five years I have been urging M.B. [Mission Board] to send us only trained teachers, for I do realize that the teaching in our schools is inadequate and the teachers we have had in Makkovik have been hopelessly incompetent. Mission Board are at their wits end to obtain teachers and they have had to take what they could get.[95]

Two-Tier Education System

Rev. Peacock was not alone in his criticism of the teachers' qualifications. Many within the region were dissatisfied with the Moravian schools in the 1940s and 1950s. Their concerns illustrate the underlying class- and race-based segregation that divided people of the region into Inuit, Settler/*Kablunângajuit*, and white (*Kallunât*) populations.

Since the beginning of the twentieth century, several *Kablunângajuit* students from northern Labrador had attended non-Moravian schools in the south. Families of former HBC employees, such as the Fords from the Nain area, had occasionally sent some of their children to the International Grenfell Association's orphanage in St. Anthony. As early as 1910, retired HBC clerk George Ford brought his adopted son, Bertie Lane, to live at the IGA Children's Home in St. Anthony after George's wife had died.[96] In 1929, Elsie Ford and a younger George Ford spent the year at school in St. Anthony, as had other children from Ford's Harbour throughout the 1920s.[97] In 1941, families associated with the Hudson's Bay Company post at Davis Inlet chose to send their children to the IGA's Lockwood boarding school in Cartwright instead of Makkovik.[98] The Mission worried that the government might harshly judge the Moravian schools if the Department of Education learned of the families' decision to avoid its school.[99]

At the same time, the Moravian minister in Makkovik from 1933 to 1944, George Sach, did not want to send his own children to the Makkovik school, not least, perhaps, because it was common practice for the Labrador missionaries to send their school-aged children to European boarding schools for their education. He revealed his attitude towards Labradorians when he wrote to the British Mission Board in 1941:

> I am anxious to send my son Ernest to school in 1942, to Canada or St. John's, Newfoundland. . . . Owing to the war I suppose he had better stay on this side [of the Atlantic]. . . . Our time is too full to teach him here, and the morals of the children are so appalling that we cannot think of sending him downstairs. We tried it last fall.[100]

Just as telling, white (*Kallunât*) officials at the wireless communications Marconi Company in Hopedale refused to send their children to the school in Makkovik or to the Inuit school in Hopedale. Instead, they explored the possibility of starting an independent school for their children in the mid-1940s. Concerned about the competition such a school would create, Rev. Peacock approached the Newfoundland Department of Education to dissuade it from supporting the idea.[101]

The Newfoundland Secretary for Education, George Alain Frecker, visited the north coast communities in 1948. He, too, noted the dissatisfaction among white families about the education provided by the local Moravian schools. He characterized the education as being two-tiered: adequate for the hunting and trapping lifestyle of the Inuit and *Kablunângajuit* children, but inappropriate for the white children of the commercial and religious elite:

> The type of education suited to either of these groups [Inuit and *Kablunângajuit*] is not suited to the needs of the straight white population. The Missionaries themselves recognize this and send their children to England to be educated. The people most seriously handicapped educationally are the Post Managers. They too will have to send their children away to school, probably to Newfoundland. But this is expensive and involves the separation of children from parents when still very young.[102]

Frecker portrayed the idea of separating *Kallunât* children from their parents "when still very young" as a shocking option, yet accepted the practice among the Inuit and *Kablunângajuit* without comment.

Walter Rockwood, the director of the Department of Northern Labrador Affairs, also commented on the situation in 1953. He saw the white elites' refusal to send their children to the Moravian schools as a double standard and an indictment of the quality of education provided at the schools:

> Much has been said concerning the education work being done by or through the Moravians. Many and varied have been the opinions regarding the adequacy or otherwise of the services being

> rendered. . . . [Yet] the Missionaries send their own children to England (or some other part of Europe) as soon as they are of school age. This would seem to indicate that the educational services being provided on the coast are not considered adequate by the Missionaries themselves for their own children. The Depot Manager at Nain sends his oldest child to St. John's to attend school, and plans, it is understood, to send the others here in the near future. The Wireless Operator at Hopedale has engaged a private teacher for his children. Some settler parents, possibly with the cooperation of the Moravians, have sent their children to North West River, three hundred miles or more away, to attend school.[103]

Fire!

Worries about finances and the quality of boarding school education caused the missionaries considerable concern. So, too, did the possibility of fire in the wooden, stove-heated buildings at the Mission stations. These worries were realized when, on 28 January 1948, flames swept through the Mission complex in Makkovik, destroying the church and the other Mission buildings.[104]

When the fire first started, chapel servant Sam Jacque urged the station missionary to tear down the wall where the chimney fire had started. But his advice was not taken in time, and the buildings burned.[105] Former student Millie Mitsuk Martin remembers the day:

> We were in school one afternoon and I don't know what happened but everybody, we all had to run out in the winter, that was in the winter. And we had nothing, only what we had on. So we lost everything, all our clothes and everything. Anyway, we had to go in with the people in the community 'cause it all burned down the old dorm. But I had a cousin married to [an] Andersen I think, they took me in. Eric, my brother Eric from Hopedale, Eric Webb, he came up and took us home. Myself and Chesley, I

> s'pose Harry too I s'pose. And took us by dog team from Makkovik to Hopedale, took us back.[106]

Except for parts of the dormitory, the fire destroyed all the buildings. At first, the missionaries discussed the possibility of closing down the Makkovik station.[107] But concerns about the future of the Moravian Church in Labrador soon prompted the missionaries to change their minds. Pentecostalists had recently established themselves in nearby Kippokok Bay, and the Moravians saw them as a threat:

> The Pentecostalists have commenced a school and some of our children attend. There are a lot of places in Labrador where these people could help men, women, and children living miles away from anywhere, but they have to come where others [missionaries] are working already. It is a great pity.[108]

The Mission did not want to give the "competition" a chance to advance further onto "Moravian territory" by abandoning Makkovik. So they worked to rebuild the station. Members of the Makkovik congregation dismantled the church at nearby Ailik and rebuilt it in the community. They also renovated an unused store building and used it as a temporary school.[109]

School started again in September 1948. "We have done wonders," Rev. Harp declared in his annual report. "To produce as modern a school as possible from an already erected building is by no means easy."[110] He was also pleased to announce that all 40 students were able to use the newly built fire escapes (which doubled as school toilets) in seven seconds flat.[111]

Hopedale Parents Demand a Day School

Despite the renewed energy invested in rebuilding Makkovik, misgivings about the Makkovik school grew louder. In a March 1948 letter, the missionary in Hopedale, Rev. Grubb, conveyed his community's feelings about the school to Superintendent Peacock: "There have been some complaints about the way the children have been looked after this winter [at the Makkovik boarding school]."[112] Families in Hopedale wanted to build their own community day school:

> Natan [Frieda, the chief Elder] informed me about the views of the people here, their idea is, that the house you have here on the shore, dismantled, could easily be re-erected and used as a school, and as the main portion of the boarders in Makkovik are Hopedale children, it would save them the journey to Makkovik and back, especially on ice in the cold weather. I pointed out to him the lack of fuel, but he said that the men would see to that.[113]

The next year, the conflict between Hopedale parents and the Makkovik school came to a head. A 1949 Newfoundland Ranger report describes what happened:

> During the first part of March this year a number of children, about 13, from Hopedale and the area north of Hopedale to Davis Inlet were evacuated from the Makkovik School. The parents of most of these children were contacted and such reasons as: the children were hungry, Eskimo children were not treated on a line with the White children, and work other than ordinary school work was put upon the school children to do, were given.
>
> Rev. Harp, missionary at Makkovik, was interviewed in connection with the above excuses and he informed me that none of them were true. He further stated that the whole trouble arose out of the termination of a Hopedale employee of the school and her dislike for the school cook. He informed me also that he has requested a thorough investigation into the matter by some Official of the Department of Education during the coming Summer.
>
> As to the validity of the excuse given above re the children being hungry, this in my opinion is untrue. Rev. Harp informed

> me that each child gained in weight from four to thirteen pounds since the beginning of school last Autumn. As to the racial problem, it is something to be expected from the Eskimo.
>
> The ordinary work around the school, such as, wood work, bringing water, shovelling snow, etc., is another dislike of many of the parents. When queried further as to this, Rev. Harp stated that it is a practice and will continue to be so, he gave details as to the amount of [illegible] to be incurred if men had to be hired to do the work.
>
> One parent kept her children from the Makkovik school this year because one of them had his foot frozen last year while working at wood. It would appear that the Hopedale people dislike all rules and regulations governing the Makkovik school. This dislike for the school is believed to have arisen when the school in Hopedale was closed a number of years ago.[114]

The Moravian and Ranger authorities may have dismissed their concerns, but families in Hopedale stood firm in their refusal to send children to Makkovik. Their determination forced the missionaries to accommodate their demands. As Hopedale missionary Rev. Grubb described it:

> Several years ago there was some sort of a day school at Hopedale, open between Christmas and Easter. But so many children went to the boarding school at Makkovik that hardly any were left on the station and the school was closed. This year a number of parents took their children away from Makkovik and refused to send them back again. There was little time to prepare for a school in the coming Fall. The superintendent decided that a school should be started and Miss Margaret Fountain, who was with us on her way to Makkovik, was asked to stay and take charge. . . .
>
> I should like to mention how well both children and parents responded when I issued a call for help in preparing the school house for school to be started. Women and girls washed and

> scrubbed the walls and ceiling, the men repaired doors and windows and fixed the stove as well as getting firewood. I did not need to pay out any wages. We started school on September 27th.[115]

Frustrated with the Makkovik boarding school, Hopedale families combined efforts to ensure that their children could stay home for school. They also likely wished to avail of the new Family Allowance program that became available after Newfoundland joined Canada on 1 April 1949. The Family Allowance gave families monthly payments for each child under the age of 16. But to be eligible for the program, children had to attend school. If children attended boarding school, families were required to pay at least $5 per month for the room and board of each child to qualify for the program. Because the Family Allowance payments could not be sent directly to the boarding school by the government, parents had to forward the money to the school.[116]

Since families in Hopedale were already unhappy about sending their children to Makkovik, Moravian Superintendent Peacock was concerned about the impacts of the Family Allowance eligibility policy. He claimed that families would either decide to stay in the villages so that their children could attend day school, or that they would take their children with them to their fishing, trapping, and hunting places. Those children would then receive no education at all.[117] Peacock argued that giving parents the choice of paying their Family Allowance to the boarding schools or going without the allowance "will mean the end of Boarding Schools."[118] Pressure on the government eventually led the Department of Public Welfare to issue grants of $5 per month to parents of boarding school students.[119] When parents forwarded these payments on to the school, they qualified for the Family Allowance. However, this practice only started in 1953, well after the Hopedale community had re-established a day school for their children.

Members of the British Mission Board also partly attributed the Hopedale families' motives to the Family Allowance. In a letter to the Newfoundland Department of Education in 1950, Brother Birtill argued that the cost of starting a day school in Hopedale constituted a new expense for the Mission:

> The insistent demand of the Eskimos last Autumn for a school in Hopedale — partly due to the fact that family allowances were not payable if the children were away at the boarding school in Makkovik, led to a day school being started in Hopedale and an additional teacher being engaged with the resultant increase in costs.[120]

However, Margaret Fountain, the teacher hired to teach at the Makkovik school before being rerouted to Hopedale, saw the new school as a positive move. She outlined its financial and social benefits in a letter to the British Mission Board, the contents of which were reported in the minutes of a board meeting on 23 November 1949:

> Miss Fountain (22 Nov) reports on the beginning of the day school in Hopedale. She compares the cost of running the school with the cost to the Mission of transporting and boarding Hopedale children at Makkovik School, and finds it to the benefit of the Mission to hold school in Hopedale. There is much voluntary labour given, and eagerness on the part of the children to learn, and on the part of the parents to get their children to school.[121]

As Margaret Fountain suggests, enthusiasm and involvement in the local school thrived when the community united to achieve its goals. Years afterwards, government officials used the story of local initiative in establishing the Hopedale school as an example of what could be achieved when a community stands together.[122]

Closing the Makkovik Boarding School

With the opening of the Hopedale day school, enrolment dropped at the Makkovik boarding school. From 41 boarders and one day pupil in

December 1948, the numbers fell to 24 boarders and 12 day pupils in 1950, and to 14 boarders and 19 day pupils in 1953.[123]

When construction of an American radar base in Hopedale started in the early 1950s, more families moved into the community. The increasing numbers of families translated into more students attending the Hopedale day school.[124] Rev. Harp of Makkovik struggled with how to encourage more families to send their children to the boarding school at Makkovik. In July 1949, his letter to the Newfoundland Department of Education illustrates his frustration with the situation. He wrote asking whether the government could force students to attend the school:

> For a great many years there has been a Boarding School in Makkovik run by the above Mission. . . . Some parents have availed themselves of this service whilst others have not. Now we would like to know whether children can be compelled to go to a Boarding School miles away from home. If not, it will be well nigh impossible to educate the children in this part of the world as the people live in widely scattered places.[125]

The increase in government administration in Labrador after 1949 offered a possible solution. With the Family Allowance payments tied to school attendance, government officials became very interested in tracking the movements of Labrador students and their families. They established accounting systems for Moravian missionaries and teachers to report on the attendance records of their students, in an effort to enforce compliance with the new regulations. In addition to sending in monthly school attendance records, Rev. Harp corresponded frequently with J.G. Parsons of the federally funded Division of Family Allowances in 1950 and 1951. Harp sent Parsons the details of various students' school attendance. This included the reasons given for their absence and the contributions their parents had made to the boarding school as school fees or in-kind donations.

It was an arrangement that benefited both the government and the Mission. Parsons used the information to address his office's concern with calculating how much Family Allowance to give each family, based on school attendance and contributions. Rev. Harp, on the other hand, was intent on steering the government's authority towards enforcing more school attendance. "I wish to make the following report," he wrote to Parsons in 1951.

> [Name] living in [place] with Mrs. [name] is not in school. He is eleven years old. This child did not come to school till January last year, and the only excuse I get is "He is not ready yet." It is true he lives about 15 miles away from Makkovik, but other children come greater distances than that, and we pay their fares on the steamer. [He] could get on the ship at the same time.[126]

A letter to Harp from another child's mother states that the family was going to take the child home from the boarding school in April. Handwriting under the note reads, "Removed by parents after discipline of child. Excuse unsatisfactory as we take children home first open water."[127] Harp then sent Parsons a telegram reporting the student's name, Family Allowance number, and the comment: "Taken from school on April 11th. Excuse unsatisfactory." In handwriting, the word "Collect" is written underneath, presumably indicating that Parsons should recover Family Allowance payments from the family.[128]

The Family Allowance payments were not insignificant. In fact, in 1950, Rev. Harp described the program as providing more money to families than many had seen in recent years:

> The outlook was somewhat brightened at the time and for the future by the family allowance cheques. In fact, some of our people receive more in family allowance cheques per month, than the wage earner has been able to make in a month for many years past. In our district alone there will be over five hundred dollars per month in family allowances to spend.[129]

The payments were not insignificant to the Makkovik boarding school, either. In 1951, Rev. Harp estimated that "ninety nine percent of school fees are paid in Family allowance cheques."[130]

By collaborating as Harp and Parsons did, the Moravian Mission and government officials expanded their control over local families after 1949. Many families felt compelled to send their children to the boarding school. Pressure from the missionaries, the recognized need for education, and the importance of the Family Allowance to their income obliged them to surrender their children to the Makkovik boarding school. Yet the government–Mission collaboration was not enough to save the school. Problems with the administration of the school endured. The Mission continued to struggle to recruit teachers, especially after the Department of Education exerted increasing pressure on the Moravians to hire qualified teachers. In 1951, the missionaries discussed handing over control of the schools to the government. Brother Birtill from the British Mission Board in London explained his position to Rev. Peacock:

> We naturally do not want to let the control of the schools pass from our hands if we can avoid it, but with the difficulties we have of obtaining teachers, it is becoming increasingly apparent that a change will have to be made before long. The demands of the Department of Education are getting stiffer each year and we are finding it increasingly hard to supply the staff with the requirements needed for our work in Labrador.[131]

In September 1953, with student enrolment down to an all-time low of five boarders and 13 day pupils, the future of the Makkovik boarding school seemed precarious.[132] The previous summer, a teacher had refused to return if the school continued to operate as a boarding school. She worried that they would not be able to manage if an epidemic spread among the children.[133] The minister for Makkovik had resigned, and the remaining two schoolteachers were running the station alone.[134]

In 1955, the Mission decided that the Makkovik boarding school had run its course. "After the summer, the Superintendent decided to close the Boarding school," wrote Rev. G.J. Vollprecht in the 1955 *Makkovik Annual Report.*

> This was only right, because we hardly had no children for it. We would have had no more than 7 or 8 children, only 4 from outside places, and this is not enough to keep the boarding school open. The boarding school in Nain became bigger and so our children would have had the chance to go over there, but nobody went. Aunt Gladys [Broomfield], our boarding school mother[,] was called to come to Nain, but she had to go down with her children to Happy Valley. She worked with the mission for more than 10 years and it is worth to say thank-you to her.[135]

Also in 1955, the Mission formally asked the Newfoundland government to take full financial responsibility of the Moravian schools.[136] This transfer of authority would eventually lead to widespread changes in education on the coast. Moravian Mission control — over the curriculum, the hiring of teachers and staff, and the approach to educating Inuit and *Kablunângajuit* children in Labrador — gradually diminished.

Although the boarding school shut its doors, the day school in Makkovik continued to serve the growing community. More families from the bays moved into the village when construction started on an American radar site at Cape Makkovik in 1955.[137] With more students, the community decided to build a new school building using volunteer labour, community contributions, and $600 worth of materials from the provincial Department of Education.[138]

In 1959, the Moravian Mission, the International Grenfell Association, and the provincial government directed an ill-advised and chaotic eviction of Inuit who lived at Hebron, north of Nain. About 30 families from Hebron, including many schoolchildren, were forced to relocate to Makkovik.[139] The provincial Department of Education built a new school in 1962 to accommodate the students from Hebron. The federal government provided partial funding for the four-room school through the Federal–Provincial Committee on Financial Assistance for Indians and Eskimos in Northern Labrador.[140] When it opened, the new school offered kindergarten to Grade 8. Students who wanted to continue on to high school were expected to go to North West River.

By 1975, the school had expanded to eight classrooms, with construction again partially funded by the federal government. Makkovik residents, including Ted Andersen and Fred Hall, pushed for high school classes. In 1976–77, the community successfully lobbied the school board to offer Grade 9, and Grades 10 and 11 over the next two years. In 1979, Tama Jararuse and Liz Evans, the daughter of former boarding school student Annie Evans, were the first Grade 11 graduates of the school in Makkovik.[141]

From its modest beginnings in 1896, Makkovik had gone from a tiny collection of houses to a community of over 300 people. Families moved in from the surrounding islands and bays, and they were joined in 1959 by Inuit evicted from Hebron. The largest boarding school on the coast was now one of the largest day schools. Its student population, once predominantly English-speaking, became a mix of English and Inuktitut speakers.

Control over children's education had also shifted from the Moravian Mission to the community as the school came under provincial authority. While Hopedale parents had played a major role in the closure of the Makkovik boarding school, Makkovik parents were equally assertive in the 1960s and 1970s, as Chapter Twelve describes. They were vocal in demanding the type of education they wanted for their children, from larger school buildings to high school classes in the community. In naming their new school after Johann Christian Erhardt, the first Moravian missionary in the area, the people of Makkovik acknowledged the role of the Moravian Church in education in their community. By the 1970s, however, they had assumed control of school affairs through the school board and the community council. The J.C. Erhardt Memorial School continues to provide education for the children of Makkovik, with the strong support of the community.

CHAPTER FIVE

The Nain Boarding School

"We do feel that if we can capture these boys and girls for Jesus Christ, the whole community here can be remoulded into a finer pattern."
— Reverends Paul Hettasch and F.W. Peacock, 1938

Once the boarding school at Makkovik fully opened in 1920, the Settler school in Nain closed. But missionaries continued to offer day schooling in Inuktitut into the 1920s. They held classes between Christmas and Easter, four days a week for a few hours a day. Both local Inuit teachers and missionaries taught the students reading and writing in Inuktitut, arithmetic, Scripture, church history, and geography. Girls received instruction in sewing and knitting as well.[i] After 1926, however, the schooling arrangement shifted. Economic changes forced Inuit families and their children to spend more time away from Nain. School attendance dropped, and so did the Moravian Mission's influence on the children's education and socialization. Anxious about their diminishing impact, the missionaries reconsidered their approach to Inuit schooling.

Ever since they arrived in Labrador in 1771, the Moravian missionaries had encouraged Inuit to live at the stations for as much of the year as possible. But to support themselves, Inuit families needed to hunt, trap, and fish over a large area. The Mission's involvement in Inuit trade, sealing, and cod fishing throughout the nineteenth century eventually convinced more Inuit to stay in the villages, if only between Christmas and Easter. In the 1920s, however, changing trade conditions made staying at the Mission stations during the winter virtually impossible for most families. After almost 150 years as the main trading company in the north, the Moravian Mission had decided to withdraw from trading. Prices for fur and fish had plummeted, and the Mission's practice of extending credit to its congregation had proven too costly. Its finances were in terrible shape. In 1926, the Mission gave up its monopoly and leased its trading authority to the Hudson's Bay Company (HBC).[2]

The HBC's trading policy differed greatly from that of the Moravian Mission. The Company offered very little on credit and wanted fur instead of seals.[3] To trap fox and other fur-bearing animals, however, Inuit families needed to spend much of their time in the winter on the land and away from the Mission stations. This, in turn, hampered their children's Moravian education, as Rev. Walter Perrett, the superintendent of the Labrador Mission from 1917 to 1929, explained in 1928:

> The problem of the education of our Labrador children is growing more and more acute as more and more families become non-resident at the station. For the advantages of the church services and of the school, people would prefer living here, but it is so difficult to obtain firewood in the vicinity and at the same time attend to the trapping on which they must depend for a living.
>
> A man needs so many miles of country over which to hunt and trap that they hinder one another when living too close together, so necessity compels them to scatter as much as possible in order to squeeze a bare living out of the country. Fur prices were very good last winter, and if fur-bearing animals were plentiful a good living might be made, but animals are not so plentiful.
>
> As it is men have to traverse many miles to keep their traps in order and to be constantly at it while the trapping season lasts, and yet they have so often to return home empty handed. The prices of

> goods in the stores are necessarily high, so at the best the Labrador men have a hard life and get very few comforts or luxuries.[4]

The missionary in Nain, Rev. Paul Hettasch, continued to hold classes for the Inuit children at the station. But their long absences from school discouraged him.[5] In his mind, the more time away from the Mission stations, the weaker the influence of the church. Hettasch feared that if Inuit did not receive a Moravian education, their attachment to the church would fade, since the ability to read influenced religious beliefs. So he suggested a new approach to Inuit schooling to ensure that more students would attend:

> When the people live away from the station they naturally take their children with them. But very few among them teach their children to read and write though there are hardly any among the grown-ups who are not fairly well versed in these arts. We shall always have to keep a school in Eskimo or else the people will in time become illiterate, and will return to superstitions of the worst kind.
>
> We, therefore, hope to make a trial with a sort of boarding-school after the style of former settler schools. Our people seem to understand the necessity of it. Yet when it comes to having to part with the children for a while, I fear there will be quite a few rocks ahead. However, try we shall, and may God guide us and bless the undertaking. This past winter we had out of twenty odd pupils seldom more than four or five actually attending [day] school. This must not continue.[6]

Rev. Hettasch believed they needed "not a day-school, but a boarding school with a teacher living with the children and able to exercise an influence for good on the children's morals. God grant that something of that nature will come about before too late."[7] However, in order to run such a school, the Mission needed a teacher who could also serve as a house parent. Although missionaries taught classes, they did not want to teach and look after the boarders full-time. The local Inuit teachers at Nain, Nathaniel and Frederike Illiniartitsijok, were aging, and no younger Inuit teachers had been apprenticed. Rev. Hettasch described their predicament to readers of the 1930 *Periodical Accounts of the Moravian Missions*:

> The beginners we had to leave in the hands of the old native teacher, Friedoricka. She has been teaching for about forty years, and her help has been most valuable in times past, but her age and the rapid failing of her eyesight makes us anxiously look out for a successor. To find one under the present circumstances is impossible, and our only hope is that it will become possible to have at some future time a devoted girl from the homeland, not only to teach but to exercise a wholesome influence on the moral development of the children.[8]

Frederike Illiniartitsijok and her students in Nain, pre-1929. Back row: Elizabeth Frey, Sarah Atsatata, Joshua Obed, Johannes Green, Judith Hunter, Boas Fox, Dina Frey, Kitora Hunter, Caroline Ikkusek. Front Row: Andrew Pardy, Leopold Saimat, Moses Andreas, Teresa Nathaniel, Agge Atsatata, Hermina Hunter (courtesy of Them Days Archive).

The MacMillan Moravian Mission School

The answer to Rev. Hettasch's prayers came in the form of an American friend. Commander Donald MacMillan was well known in northern Labrador in the late 1920s. Captain of the *Bowdoin* and leader of a scientific expedition to collect information on Arctic environments for explorers, MacMillan and his crew spent the winter at Anaktalak Bay, 25 miles southwest of Nain, in 1927–28.[9] He was familiar with the Moravian station and its people, and he supported the Mission's work.

In 1929, MacMillan donated materials and funding for a schoolhouse and teacher for Nain. He delivered the building supplies for a school and offered his crew for a few days to help with constructing the building.[10] His wife, Miriam MacMillan, explained his motivation for helping in her book, *Green Seas and White Ice*:

> With civilization working in on the coast, Mac had told me, he felt the children needed an education and clean and healthy living. And he admired the work of the Moravians and wanted to help them in their care of the young ones of northern Labrador. So he built this school. On the Bowdoin he carried all things needed to start it: lumber for the building, desks, small chairs, blackboards, chalk, erasers, an organ, a radio. There was an electric light plant, too, and a stove, sleeping bags, blankets, dishes for kitchen utensils and the table, towels, soap, food, and hundreds of books. All these he transported from this country. And every year since, he has landed provisions at their dock.[11]

When it opened in 1929, the Nain boarding school was the second large-scale attempt at a Moravian residential school, after the Makkovik boarding school. It was the first to offer schooling in the Inuktitut language. Unlike other Moravian schooling efforts, the Nain boarding school was also the first to integrate Inuit and Settler/*Kablunângajuit* children in a bilingual classroom. From the beginning, it was moderately well attended.

Rev. Paul Hettasch expressed his surprise at the support for his boarding school proposal: "We were trying a new experiment in the school: boarding children whose parents went away to the fall places. I was astonished to find that almost all parents were willing enough to leave their children here."[12]

Paul's daughter, Kate Hettasch, who had been teaching at the Makkovik boarding school since 1927, was called to Nain to teach at the new school. The first school year started on 16 December 1929 and continued until July. Kate recounts the experience in the Nain school diaries, now housed in the Moravian Archives in Bethlehem, Pennsylvania:

> I expected about fifteen or twenty scholars the first day, but to my surprise twenty came. Most of them were Eskimos and a few Settler children. Very soon the number went up to thirty-five pupils! The usual daily average was twenty-eight, or thirty children attending school. At first I found it awkward, teaching in two languages, especially as I did not understand Eskimo, and the Eskimo children did not understand any English; but with the help of the Settler children, who translated for me, we got on better, and now quite a number of the Eskimo children understand a little English and I am able to speak a few Eskimo words.
>
> I use the first hour of every morning in getting the children to do their hair and wash their faces and necks and hands; they clean their teeth and I find out how many of them have handkerchiefs and whether they have any holes in their clothes. At first several looked terribly dirty and almost in rags; but towards the end they really looked more respectable, and especially when the boys and girls all had on their school aprons and pinafores.
>
> From 9.45 till 10.45 we had a Bible lesson: I told the story in English, and then showed them the picture and asked questions and finished off by reading the story in Eskimo to them. How pleased I was when little Amos and Helena, one day in June, were able to repeat to me the Bible story in Eskimo: it gave me

courage to go on, and showed me that the work was not in vain, though many times I had almost lost heart.

The second hour I used for reading and writing, the Eskimos in their own language and the Settler children in English. They were nearly all beginners and knew nothing. I am glad to say that we have got so far that some of them are able to read those A.B.C. books with the beautiful red covers. Some of them kept their books very nice and tidy, but a few have got some terrible oil-marks on the covers, for which I had to scold them. The Settler children got on very well, too. A few are now able to write their first little letters and stories; and little Dolly, who has been to Makkovik school, writes quite nicely. In the afternoon we had arithmetic or drawing, singing exercises, and knitting and sewing — which boys as well as girls loved to do. I wanted to teach the boys how to carve a few little things out of wood, but have not got any carpenters' tools.[13]

MacMillan-Moravian Mission School, Nain, c.1930 (courtesy of Them Days Archive).

A Single Teacher

For the first two years, Kate Hettasch taught the students by herself and acted as housemother in the dormitory. She struggled with the Inuktitut language and the heavy teaching load. Fifty years later, she recalled her early despair at having to teach in Inuktitut. After spending 11 years in Europe at school, she had long forgotten any of the language:

> The little boarding school was opened and I was to be the teacher. And I was to talk Inuktitut. I had spoken it in my childhood days. I sang it as long as I could remember in school, Hosanna, sorrutsit kaititse, but as I grew older the language had vanished, and here I stood in this little class teaching Eskimo to the children and I didn't even know how to speak it.[14]

The number of students nearly overwhelmed their teacher in the first two years of the school. In January 1931, Kate Hettasch recorded in her school diary that school had started again after Christmas with 42 pupils: "With God's help got through morning lesson. . . . Those 4 rascal boys want each a teacher to them ownself."[15] But the number of students and the fact that the schoolhouse was too poorly insulated to house children during the coldest months made boarding school impractical during the winter. The missionaries decided that Kate should hold only day school from January until Easter. Her frustration with maintaining discipline among the children continued, and she resorted to desperate attempts at control:

> I assure you that not much was taught in those weeks, all I just managed was to keep them all busy and out of mischief and teach them how to behave and keep clean. . . . To keep those 45 mouths quiet was the hardest thing, and several times I had to make it pretty plain to them, that they had to learn to obey. And once when all warning and kind asking did not help, I told them that if they would dis-obey again I would plaster their mouth, they only laughed at this, till one day I really had to make use of

> it, as they refused to obey. I took a very narrow strip of adhesive plaster and put this square over the mouth of the worst ones. But already the next day the parents came to Dad to complain about the very cruel teacher and if it was not stopped at once, several parents would take their children away from school.[16]

In the end, some parents removed their children from the school after this incident. The community was vocal in their criticism of Kate Hettasch's approach to discipline. In her school diary, Kate describes how her father, Rev. Hettasch, handled the community's complaints about her behaviour: "Dad told me about men meeting: people disgusted with me and teaching, to cruel and so on [*sic*]. Father first told them what he thought of school and of them."[17] Protected by the authority of her missionary father, Kate continued on: "All the talking about the school, etc., did not stop [a family] to give us Bella [Winters Voisey],"[18] who cooked, cleaned, and helped with the children at the school in 1931.

The school was obviously understaffed. To help with the problem, Donald MacMillan offered in July 1930 to supply an extra teacher from the United States. But the Moravian missionaries resisted what they regarded as an encroachment on their authority. They complained that MacMillan had not consulted them, and that they did not know the female teacher whom he had suggested.[19] The British Mission Board thanked MacMillan for his gift, but told him firmly: "The selection and appointment of teachers will be our concern."[20] For the third year of the school, the British Mission Board transferred teacher Sylvia Potter to Nain. Originally from England, she had been teaching at the Makkovik boarding school for two years.[21] Once in Nain, she was assigned to teach the English-language students. Kate Hettasch was delighted: "Oct. 24th, 1931. Well, school life has started again. And this time we are two to look after kids, how happy this makes me. A proper God send."[22]

Segregated Classrooms

Starting in 1931, the school was divided into an Inuktitut class for the Inuit children and an English class for the Settler/*Kablunângajuit* children. Each class had its own teacher, but all the boarding students lived together in the schoolhouse. The dominant language in the dormitory was Inuktitut. Beatrice Ford Watts, a student in the English class in the 1940s, described the school's organization:

> Well, it was a different set-up, the Nain school was, we had the English school for English-speaking children and Inuktitut school for Inuktitut-speaking children. And I was in the English-speaking school but we all lived together in the boarding school part of it, but our classrooms were separated.
> [Interviewer]: Which language would you speak when you were with the other kids?
> Beatrice Watts: Everything. You know, Inuktitut a lot because that was the dominant language in the whole of Nain at that time and in order to survive you had to speak Inuktitut.
> [Interviewer]: What language did your parents use with you?
> Beatrice Watts: English.[23]

John Igloliorte, an Inuk student in the 1940s, described the same Inuit–Settler division in the school:

> The Settlers' children, from the families of white trappers and hunters, were in separate classes from us. They were taught in English, and we spoke Inuktitut. The teacher who taught Inuktitut was of German descent, and her parents were missionaries in Nain, along with some missionaries from England who ministered to us for a long time. It was our teacher's idea to have the separate classes; we were expected to live as our ancestors did, and learn our own language, but some of us, myself included,

> picked up some English when we were older, just by being in contact with white people.[24]

Both students and teachers learned some of both languages, despite linguistic separation in the classroom. Betty Ford Koch, who lived at the Nain boarding school in 1937, learned to speak Inuktitut during her time there: "I grew up in Nain, went there to boarding school when I was nine years old. I knew a lot of kids there, a lot of people and that's where I learned to speak Eskimo."[25] Rosie Voisey Ford Spurvey, another English-speaking child at the school, remembers her difficulties in learning how to speak Inuktitut:

> We used to go to school, used to be about 50 Inuit and only about 12 settlers and it used to be so hard. I don't think I learned anything really. . . . When I was in boarding school, we used to have to go to school in the morning and learn what you're supposed to learn in English, and then when you come out, you'd have to talk Inuttitut, learn how to speak Inuttitut, so it was really complicated, you know. It was hard, because you had to talk Inuttitut, that's the way the teachers told us to talk, Auntie Kate [Hettasch] and Mrs. [Ellen] Hettasch. . . . I don't think I really learned anything in boarding school, didn't have time. We went to school, you learned what you had to learn, come out and speak Inuttitut and then you had to do all your work.[26]

Sylvia Potter, the new teacher, describes how one little girl, Barbara, was "trying to tell me Eskimo names for things" on one of her first days at the school, and Sylvia came to learn and use Inuktitut words. Her entries in the school's diary from October 1931 to June 1932, which include words like "*ataata*" (father), "*anaana*" (mother), "*polacking*" (visiting), illustrate her growing understanding of the language.[27]

Moravian teachers were in fact expected and encouraged to learn Inuktitut. But it was often difficult to attract people from outside Labrador who would stay long enough to make real progress with the language. When Sylvia Potter was replaced by Lillian Matthews in 1932, Rev. Hettasch wrote of his hopes for the new teacher in the *Periodical Accounts of the Moravian Missions*: "We were very pleased to welcome Miss L. Matthews as a new teacher to help in the work, and hope that she will in time get a knowledge of the language so as to be enabled to be even more useful as a teacher and worker among the children."[28]

While English-speaking students and teachers were encouraged to learn Inuktitut at the boarding school, learning English was not similarly encouraged. Many former Inuit students remember Nain missionaries in the 1930s and early 1940s discouraging them from speaking or learning English. As Lucas Ittulak recalled, speaking through an interpreter:

> When he went to school, if he tried to speak the English language he would get a strap on the hand just for trying to speak in English, so the only way he grew up was using the Inuttitut language. When he tried to use the English language in school he got strapped for it by a great big belt, so that was one of the hardest things for Mr. Lucas to go through. . . . They used to get strapped just for saying English words.[29]

Moravian missionaries had consistently tried to keep Inuit and Settlers apart since establishing themselves in Labrador in the late 1700s. Maintaining linguistic separation in the early years of the twentieth century was in keeping with their policy of separating the Moravian Inuit from English-speaking outsiders. Paul Hettasch argued that these outsiders could be a bad influence and that Moravian education was the best protection:

> The enormous changes brought about by the trade passing into the hands of the Hudson's Bay Company are threatening to nullify the results of all earlier mission work. The ever increasing touch with Newfoundlanders, as well as the often very doubtful

> influence of the large staff of the HBC posts, are noticeably lowering the spiritual and moral standards of our people. There appears to be only one way of preventing greater harm viz. [namely] energetic educational work by which the children are protected from evil influences and made better capable to withstand them in later years.[30]

Although the missionaries of the 1930s and early 1940s supported Inuktitut literacy among Inuit, seeing it as a means to promote religious understanding and to preserve Inuit culture, they discouraged Inuit from learning English.

Educational Approach

The missionaries were optimistic that the Nain boarding school would allow them to influence the children on more than academic topics. Both Paul Hettasch and his daughter Kate believed that Inuit home life was a potential source of evil. They thought that children should be removed from homes to live at the school where missionaries could watch over them and train them to withstand immoral influences. "In their homes they hear and see things which by no means are fit for any child to know or hear or see," argued Kate Hettasch in 1931. "We are anxious to have a PROPER BOARDING SCHOOL, to have the children with us, away from the bad influence at home, only then can we have some HOPE for a following better generation."[31] When children did not attend boarding school, they were prone to fall under other influences, as she further explained: "Now last year one could try all ones best at day school, but out of sight the children were at once back to their old dirty ways, I saw very little progress."[32] Her father shared a similar view:

> Our hopes for the Eskimo are centred in our school. Our young people are so often led into temptation and fall so easily that we cannot stress too much the vital significance of the work that is

> done in the school-house. Unfortunately the influence we have upon the children is often heavily counteracted by appalling home conditions. It is very difficult for folk at home [in Europe] to realize how small, dark, dirty and overcrowded many of the Eskimo homes are; and consisting, as most of them do, of one room only, it is not surprising that many Eskimo have not high moral standards. In our clean and large school buildings the children are well housed and fed, and their spiritual needs are constantly before the teachers.[33]

The missionaries equated Inuit living conditions with low moral standards. In their eyes, Inuit failed to comply with European standards of cleanliness, both physical and moral. Through the boarding school, the missionaries hoped to train the children to adopt new attitudes and practices and thereby transform Inuit society into a more European-Christian version. "I am persuaded that the boarding schools are the only means of raising our people from their present low moral standard to a people cleaner in mind and body," wrote Rev. Hettasch in 1937.[34]

In the battle against evil influences, missionaries often portrayed sin and immorality as hidden in dark places. In removing the children to where they could be seen, the boarding school allowed the Mission to keep a constant and close watch over their future congregation:

> Our eyes have been opened to the depth of sin to be found in the very young already, sin so hard to fight because it is so hidden. All the more we see the urgent need of a place where children may be watched more carefully than in their own homes, and where they are debarred from the many evils which threaten to ingulf [*sic*] the little souls at a time, which we are accustomed to look upon as a time of innocency.[35]

Rev. Hettasch saw the boarding school as a means to train and transform the children:

Schoolchildren with Kate Hettasch and other staff, Nain, 31 March 1930 (courtesy of Them Days Archive).

> The children of to-day being the congregation of to-morrow, the schooling branch of our work is a very important one, even here in Labrador, so it behoves us to strive to train the children to fight the evils that surround them, and this can be done much more successfully, we think, if we have them continually under our care, as we should do in a boarding-school.[36]

Issues of cleanliness, control, and surveillance preoccupied the local missionaries in Labrador. Moravian officials in England expressed a more practical perspective on Inuit education. Still, the interest in reorienting Inuit ideas and allegiances remained. When Samuel Hutton, the secretary of the British Mission Board in London, wrote to the Newfoundland Commission of Government asking for financial aid in 1934, he appealed to their colonial interests. He described the Moravian approach to education as suited to the Inuit lifestyle but also as addressing the needs of the British Empire:

> Education is necessary, and this seems the only possible way. Nor does this education interfere with the learning of the crafts of hunting and housewifery, since the children are with their parents from Easter till October, and only are at school between the ages of six and twelve — for at twelve, they are so useful in the hunting and the home that their parents can no longer allow them to be away. We have five young lady teachers on the coast; three at Makkovik and two at Nain. They teach the children the three "Rs" with general and scripture knowledge, and such crafts as knitting, sewing, and woodwork: they endeavour to bring them up as good little Christian citizens of the British Empire.[37]

As he was making a case for financial support, Hutton was also eager to emphasize the positive impact the schools had on the children's health and moral character: "The boarding school system is improving the children in health and in morals as well as in education: they live on native foods as far as these are obtainable; and our effort is to make them useful citizens."[38] His stated goal — to transform Inuit children into citizens of the British Empire — differed slightly from the Labrador missionaries' goal of producing a congregation of the future. But both aimed to use the Nain boarding school as an agent of change in Inuit society.

A Suitable School Building

The Nain school quickly ran into financial difficulties. Captain MacMillan's support faltered in the early years of the Great Depression, as the stock market crash crippled the American economy. In 1933, with two years of unpaid bills and uncertainty about MacMillan's ability to further assist the school, the British Mission Board agreed to cover the outstanding expenses. But the Mission decided to cut costs by not running a boarding school that year or hiring any extra teachers.[39] Kate Hettasch was away on furlough for the year, and in her absence Lillian Matthews ran an English-language day school only.[40]

The schoolhouse MacMillan had donated in 1929 was also not ideal. The building turned out to be cold, cramped, and unsuitable as a home for children in the winter. Its condition had prompted the missionaries to cancel school during the coldest months of the year. "The trouble was," wrote Paul Hettasch in 1931, "that we had only very little room for the children to sleep in."

> Several considerations made us decide to discontinue boarding children until after Easter. Firstly there is not enough firewood in stock to carry us through the cold part of the winter. Then we found that during the cold "spells" the walls of the teacher's room and of the girls' dormitory got iced over and even the bedding got damp. So it seemed too great a risk to continue during the winter.[41]

As an alternative, MacMillan donated his building at Anaktalak Bay, 25 miles southwest of Nain, for the Mission to use as a school.[42] He had built the house for his scientific expedition when he spent a winter there in 1927–28, but it was no longer used. The missionaries discussed the possibility of operating the boarding school at Anaktalak Bay instead of Nain. Some thought the move might solve many of their current problems. The minutes for the 1933 Labrador Mission conference list the potential benefits of a move to Anaktalak Bay:

> The present schoolhouse in Nain is much too small for the number of children attending it, and is quite unsuitable for taking boarders during the winter months. Added to the lack of accommodation is the fact that the school house is right in the village, and the parents of the children interfere and complain far too much if things do not go as they think they should. This causes unpleasantnesses which are disturbing and trying for the teachers. Then there is the question of keeping the school supplied with firewood, a far from easy matter when parents are away at

Shifting the schoolhouse, Nain, 1936 (courtesy of Them Days Archive).

> their hunting and trapping grounds. The house in Anaktalak Bay is considerably larger than that in Nain, and it is away from all interference.[43]

But others at the British Mission Board felt anxious about leaving "two teachers, with their small charges, so far from the head station."[44] They questioned whether parents would allow their children to go there. In 1936, after two schoolchildren died while in their parents' care during an epidemic, the missionaries abandoned the idea of moving the school. They realized that the children would be too far removed from medical care if they lived at Anaktalak Bay.[45] The Mission eventually dismantled the Anaktalak building and moved it to Nain in 1946 for use as a school building.[46]

With the missionaries having abandoned their plan for moving the school to Anaktalak, the problem of properly housing the children remained. A solution presented itself in 1936 when the Hudson's Bay Company offered its cottage hospital building as a second school building.[47] The Mission decided to move the old schoolhouse away from the village and to a new spot next to the HBC building, which stood to the west of the church, near the water. Now, farther from the "interference" of parents, and with warmer and larger accommodations for more children, the school could operate through the winter. "The school work in the hospital building has been much more satisfactory than in the little school house," reported Rev. Hettasch in January 1937. "We were able to take 30 children as boarders, and all have been very happy and well during the first term."[48] As of 2019, the transformed HBC cottage hospital remained as the only Nain boarding school building still standing.[49]

Reliance on Local Labour

The Mission relied on local people to donate their labour, time, country food, and firewood to the school. Costs for the Nain boarding school were not as high as those at the Makkovik school because of the help locals provided and the periodic assistance from outside donors like Commander MacMillan. But the cash-strapped Mission still struggled to pay for food, teachers, and maintenance. The Nain missionaries used the Moravian Mission's publications to appeal for further donations from their supporters in Europe and America:

> All through autumn, winter and spring Miss K. Hettasch and Miss Glaser had their hands full with forty children boarding in the school. Again we had the valuable help of two former pupils, Miriam [Flowers Brown] and Rosie [Nukappiak Webb], the former excelling in doing all the rough work very willingly and the latter helping her and in between teaching the "babies." Minnie Voisey again acted as cook and supervisor. All went very smoothly from beginning to end, and we may say that the children show the benefit of the school in their behaviour when at home.
>
> But oh, my hair stood on end at times when I saw the quantities of food disappearing in the little mouths! Happy Commander MacMillan had again added considerably to our stock of food

> and clothing for the children, and so reduced very much the cost of the school. To him and the friends in America whom he and Mrs. MacMillan have interested in this work, as well as to all the faithful helpers in England, Holland and Switzerland, we would express our warmest thanks, and we would ask them to continue helping us and praying for this important part of our work.[50]

Unlike the Makkovik boarding school, where the Mission paid for much of the local labour, local women worked for free at the Nain school. The Nain school diaries for 1930–32, for example, describe various women at different times — Huldah [Green], Elsie [Ford?], and Bella [Winters Voisey] — who cooked, cleaned, went out with the children, helped them to learn Scripture verses, got water with the children, cut wood with them, and hunted and trapped.[51] These local workers often came from Inuit families who had a strong affiliation with the church. Many felt a responsibility to volunteer their time and efforts towards the Mission school. "The loyalty and devotion of the Sillitt family is a constant source of joy to us," wrote the Nain missionaries in 1943.

Minnie Voisey, cook in Nain boarding school, 1930s (courtesy of Them Days Archive).

> Two sisters, Sibilla and Katli [Katie Sillitt] assist in the work of the school, while the father and mother are always ready to help us when called upon. Then there is Juliana Merkuratsuk. . . . Juliana for a small remuneration keeps the school children's skin boots patched and in order. Each week twenty or thirty pairs of boots are given loving care; no matter how holey

> they are, or how hard, there is never a complaint or demand for increased wages.[52]

Besides the volunteer labour, the school also hired local people. One woman who worked in the boarding school in the 1940s describes her experience:

> We had a lot of work to do there. For my first year, I was paid $16, my second year $10 a month, and in my fourth year, $12 a month. School went from October 'til Christmas. We used to get a week off at Christmas until New Years. Then school went until May. After that we had to do the cleaning — the school, the sleeping bags, mattresses, everything. [During the school year], we used to help the younger ones memorize their hymns. That was mostly what was learned at school. We [helpers] stayed at the Boarding School too. We were allowed to go home two hours a week on Sunday afternoons.[53]

Children and Work

The missionaries expected the Nain boarders to help them run the dormitory and school by doing chores. They wanted the children to embrace the Protestant work ethic, but they also wanted to reduce costs for the Mission. Former student John Igloliorte remembers chopping wood and fetching water while he was at the boarding school:

> I had to go to school, starting every September. Our school was attended by students from all over Labrador, maybe about fifty children in four different classes. We all lived in the school, too, in two separate buildings, one for the girls, one for the boys. My bed was up in the attic of the main school building; the other kids and I slept on the floor, on long mattresses placed side by side.

> The school and the manse had lights from a small generator, which would be shut off at 11:00 pm, and we Inuit kids also used kerosene lamps.... In the winter, we kids were also outside to do the chores we had every day. The school didn't have a furnace, so after dinner we would go out to chop wood. Some of us weren't very experienced, so we weren't able to chop up very much wood. But we had a good time, and there was never a quiet moment, especially when we got to the point where we could chop a lot of wood and make shavings from dry wood to use as kindling in the morning. Somehow, the shavings always started flying around when it was just about time to go back inside!
>
> On very cold days, or during a fierce blizzard, we almost ran out of wood sometimes, and we children would have to bring in tree branches to burn. Then there was water to fetch. It took seven of us kids to haul the school's huge water tank on a sled, back and forth to the well, again and again, the runners of the sled always icing up and slowing us down. What a lot of work we did![54]

Chores were divided by gender. Boys chopped wood, made shavings, emptied honey buckets (chamber pots), and fetched water. Girls cleaned, scrubbed, and mended clothes. Kate Hettasch describes instructing the schoolchildren to do work in a letter to the British Mission Board secretary in 1938:

> First the teacher on duty gives out orders: "All hands, listen please. Miriam, you with these girlies go over into the other class and clean it beautifully, don't forget the corners and the doors. You, Rosie, with these three little ones, go upstairs and scrub the girls' bedroom thoroughly and shake the blankets. You three babes, help Minnie nicely in the kitchen, drying dishes. Malena and Emily, go over and scrub the passages, and you last two girls, scrub the storeroom properly. Now boys, listen, remember it is bathing day. So as soon as dinner is over, Willie, Elias, Albert,

> Eugen, James and Itok hurry up and fetch another barrel of water from the brook. Jerry and George, fetch the bathtub into the class here and put the 10 bundles of clean clothing tidily on this table.[55]

Julius Ikkusek also remembers the gender division in the work, and how the children were treated if they did not meet the teachers' expectations:

> 11 to 13 years old, they had to split wood, and they had to get wood from church to boarding school and they used to split wood . . . to start fire in the morning, 500. Each one of them, 200 splits to start the fire next morning, 500 doing this, and splits for starting fire, 500 each. If they didn't do 500, they had to stand up in a corner for one hour. . . . And they didn't used to like — they're not done good, they used say "not good enough" when they're starting fire. . . . The girls, they were little different — they used to

Bella Winters Voisey Leo with children at Nain boarding school, 1930s: Josasi Fox, Edward Sillitt, Marcus __, "Oma" Freitag, Amos Fox, and Marcus Hunter (courtesy of Them Days Archive).

> scrub floor, and mending socks, mitts, and clothes, and that's what the girls used to do, always mending clothes, mitts and everything that has to be mended. . . . Girls, they were taught how to clean the house and trying to keep the house clean, that's what the girls were taught, how to do like clean the house and things like women, women's work. But some girls like doing things that boys [do] and some of them were a lot smarter than some boys.[56]

Tabea Murphy, a pupil in the 1940s and 1950s, describes the school's reliance on student and local — and mostly female — labour:

> Some girls, because they were being used by the residential schools to clean up and all that. They didn't hire any people from the community, but they just used the school children when the older ones, when they become about thirteen years on, 'til fourteen, fifteen, they just used them to look after the boarding school, cleaning it, and mending clothes and stuff like that. In residential school the students worked really hard, like labour work, and this is the harder part of thinking about residential school, 'cause the children do a lot of labour work. The boys would — you see, at first, when we start going to school there was no oil stove, all wood stove. . . . The boys who are students, older boys would cut up, chop the wood, saw the wood and split the wood to make the starter and shavings, they call it shavings, you take a small piece of wood and take a sharp knife and make shavings to start the fire. These students really worked hard, and when winter time come, they would fetch water in a big ol' barrel and put it on Kamutik, big Kamutik and I don't know how many boys hauled it up and fetched water at the brook, there was a brook up there. They did a lot of labour.[57]

Rev. Hettasch described the cost savings that the free labour provided to the Mission in a letter to the British Mission Board in 1937. He pointed

Schoolgirls fetching water, ca. 1937. l-r: Silpa Sillitt, Katie Sillitt, Melena Barbour, Mary Sillitt (courtesy of Them Days Archive).

out that at the Makkovik boarding school, the Mission paid high wages for men to cut and split wood. But in Nain, the Mission saved money by relying on the boys for work:

> Here we are training the school boys to cut up all the wood, if at all possible, without the help of men. And if men must needs help, the work is to be done for free. By so saving a large expense I felt justified in letting the people off without charging for board, which is beyond their means of paying. . . . We save also in other ways. Water fetching, which is a big thing in winter, and is done at Makkovik by the servant and another man, is here carried out by the big boys or occasionally by big girls.[58]

As Hettasch explained, the money saved in wages at the Nain boarding school allowed the Mission to justify providing room and board for the children without charging their parents school fees.

Food

A large portion of the boarding school funding was spent on feeding the children. The "quantities of food disappearing in the little mouths," which so astonished Rev. Hettasch, consisted of store-bought Mission food and donations of country food. The Nain school diaries chronicle how parents periodically delivered seal meat, hares, and other local food for the children. Teacher Sylvia Potter described several such gifts from parents in November 1931:

> Sat 7th: Rosalie's *ataata* [father] came and brought a hare, also some material for a new *silapak* [Inuit-style coat] for her — I hardly knew how much to take, but fortunately Sybilla arrived at that moment so I got her to cut it out. Later someone else came and brought another hare and some berries for Lisetta — wasn't she pleased![59]

Potter also made note of what the children ate for supper and their reactions to the southern food: "Nov 11: For supper macaroni and black berries. The Inuks don't care for macaroni on the whole."[60] The Nain boarding school teachers kept track of every meal served at the school between 1936 and 1941. The notebooks, the "Macmillan Moravian Mission School, List of Dinners and Suppers," now reside in Kate Hettasch's collection at the Moravian Archives in Bethlehem, Pennsylvania. During one week at the school in 1937 (chosen at random), children were served the following:[61]

1937	Dinners	Suppers
Sunday, Oct 17	Pork & Beans	Buns & Cacao
Monday, Oct 18	Soup	Fish
Tuesday, Oct 19	Peas & Potatoes & Seal meat	Biscuits & Bl berries
Wednesday, Oct 20	Doughboys	Pipse
Thursday, Oct 21	Brewis	Carrots
Friday, Oct 22	Split Peas	Black Berries
Saturday, Oct 23	Soup	Buns

Some students disliked the food served at the school, especially if it was unfamiliar to them. Abe Flowers, for example, in describing his time at the Nain boarding school in the late 1940s to the Truth and Reconciliation Commission in Hopedale, talked about the food:

> I remember vaguely about going to Nain. I remember we got there in the night. We went from a place called Newfoundland Harbour, outside of Flowers Bay, where I was born. Me and my brother Garfield and sister Millie. It was almost dark when we got there. We went ashore, had a lunch,[62] I remember, and we had to go by the Moravian rules, which was, as some people know, very strict. First thing I had to do was put on a pair of pyjamas. I didn't know what that was. I cried and I cried. Finally got an older boy to convince me to put them on.
>
> After that, I went to school. The worst thing, I guess, was the grub. I wasn't used to that diet. I remember the worst thing — I mean, a lot of people could eat what they served, but I couldn't. I think the worst thing was seal fat and dried capelin. I could eat the capelin, but I could not stomach the seal fat.
>
> And after that, the school in the winter, everybody knows what a honey bucket is. Going to school in the morning, they'd be froze. They'd put them on the stove where we was to thaw them out. And imagine the smell. My brother was telling me, if you did anything bad, they were very strict. He said that he and his friend were having a little row, and they got in a little fight. In comes, I think it was one of the teachers. She thought they were having some kind of sex, so they got punished for that. I went to Makkovik the next year, things were a little better but still the same.[63]

Julius Ikkusek, speaking through his interpreter, recalled being hungry during his time at the Nain school: "When they were at home, they didn't use to be hungry but in boarding school they used to be hungry, and like nothing much to eat but when they go home they used to be alright, they had enough to eat at their home, but not in boarding school."[64] Julius also disliked having to abide by a schedule of eating meals only at set times. The practice was so different from his upbringing in an Inuit household: "When they're home, they were allowed to eat anytime — pitsik and nikku, but in boarding school they have . . . in the morning, 8:00, and noon, and supper time, that's all, they used to be quite hungry."[65]

Authority and Discipline

In the late 1930s and early 1940s, the Nain missionaries used their authority to pressure parents into leaving their children at the boarding school, even when the families stayed in the village. Children were allowed to visit their families only on Sundays for a few hours after church. The Mission could not force children to stay at the school, but it could support parents who obeyed its wishes and sanction those who did not. As one man told anthropologist Patrick Flanagan, in describing why families agreed to send their children to the boarding school, "In them days, you agreed with the missionary."[66] When times were harsh, many families also likely used the boarding school as a means to feed and clothe their children.

The new practice of boarding all students gave the Mission even more control over the children's development. Julius Ikkusek was one of the children who stayed at the boarding school while his family lived in Nain. Speaking through his interpreter, he described having to live at the school:

> Since he was 5–6 years old, he stayed over to boarding school, up to 13 years old he was in school. Even though his parents were in Nain, he had to stay in boarding school. From October to March, even though that his parents were here, he had to stay over to boarding school. . . . Sundays, after church service he used to visit his parents, but he had to be back at 12 to boarding school.[67]

Tabea Murphy likewise stayed in the boarding school although her parents lived in Nain:

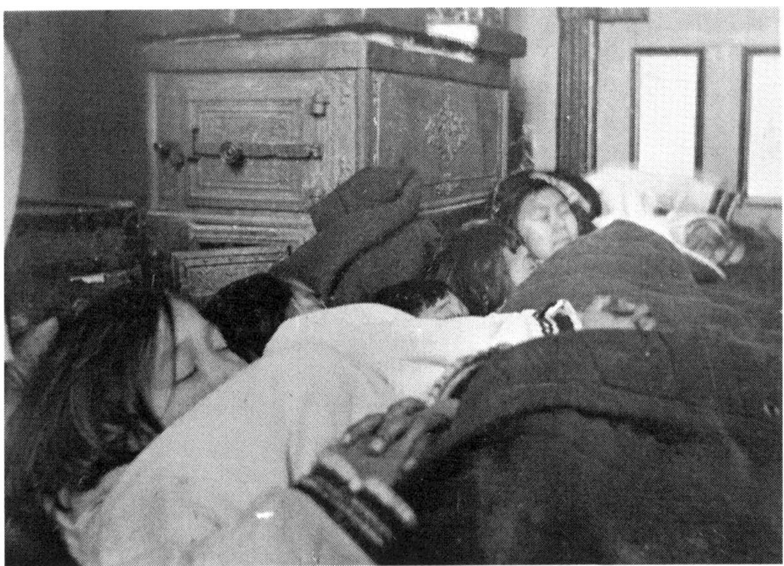

Nain schoolchildren sleeping in the boarding school (courtesy of Them Days Archive).

> We stayed in what we call boarding school, really was residential school and even though our families were here, in Nain, they took us! Anybody that was six years on, 'til I don't quite remember how old, possibly 'til about thirteen. . . . We only used to go and visit our family every Sunday, one week before we seen our family, 2:00–4:00 in the afternoon on Sunday, only time we see them.[68]

A woman who worked at the boarding school in the 1940s also recalls the rigid supervision with which the missionaries and teachers ruled the lives of both the children and the local workers:

> The place was a prison to me. I never worked so hard in my life. . . . Kate [Hettasch] used to eat her meals at the Minister's house and when she went, she'd lock us in. I don't know what we would have done if there had been a fire, try to get out a window I suppose. We got one hour a week free to go out. We could only visit

> with relatives and if there were any outside-the-family males that were in the house we couldn't go in, and if they came in while we were there, we had to leave. One day on the way to church, Jimmy Mobil [pseudonym], who wasn't married to my sister yet, said hello to me and I said hello back to him. I had to stay in for two weeks for that. I blamed it all on Kate. She treated me worse than Dad would treat a dog.[69]

Both Julius and Tabea still remember the suffering they endured while at the school in the 1940s. "Even to this day," Julius Ikkusek's interpreter translates:

> he thinks about the hardship that they had when they were growing up, and maybe just because there was war on and the Germans, they didn't treat them well, even out of other people — they were looking after kids, Inuit people, but they were kind of cruel and that's why even to this day he thinks about being compensated by what Germans did to them when they were growing up, even to this day he thinks about that.[70]

Tabea echoes similar feelings:

> [It] really was hard on me. I don't know why they had to do that to me. I suffered a lot because I was only five years old when the old man who run the residential school, and his daughter, old man Hettasch. Paul Hettasch and his daughter was running the boarding school, he was a supervisor. That used to get hard, only later years — only after Newfoundland and Labrador became a part of Canada, then everybody had to go to boarding school, and before that we was not allowed to speak English, that was what the old man and his daughter said, very strict about that, anybody who learned to speak English used to get punished. Punishing means that there's a strap, leather strap, I don't know how long, maybe a

> foot long, real thick, and they used that for punishing the children just for speaking in English, saying a word in English, learning it from the settler children. It was really, really hard.[71]

Tabea attributes most of her hardships at the school to the strictness of the Hettasch missionary family. But her stories also show that Inuit — in this case, her grandfather — could challenge the missionaries' control and assert their independence:

> The hardest time I had was in the first year at the residential school. We went home on the first Sunday of Advent. This day was chosen by the church committee called church elders — men only in those days used to be on the church committee. . . . I was so happy to see an Advent tree, and my Advent stocking with presents hanging on the nail that my mother had to hang it for me. We was not allowed to go home to hang our stocking on Advent Eve. On Advent, I was so happy when I went home and opened my presents from what was called in those days Father Christmas. My mom was cooking partridge for supper. I thought to myself, if only I could stay home for supper like I used to. I could have some Advent supper with my family. Before too long, the girls come in to pick me up. I said "No, I want to eat at home." They just tried to get me dressed, put my hat on and mitts on me. I cried and fought. My grandfather said, "Let her stay. She can go back to school tomorrow morning."
>
> So they left without me. Nothing Kate Hettasch could do, for my grandfather was on the church committee. I was five years old. In those days, especially Rev. Paul Hettasch and daughter Kate Hettasch had no respect on Inuit special celebration. They were like royalties. I remember when we go to church. We children were to stay in the porch until the missionaries come in to church. We children were together to say, "Good evening!" like they were royalties. We started to have teachers

> then come to Nain. One teacher, a man, come into the porch and went to church and sang with us. When he saw that, he quietly laughed about our royalties. Before you know it, it was over. No more "good afternoon," "good evening." I guess our royalties had to step down and become ordinary humans.[72]

In later years, after the Hettasches were no longer in charge, the school continued to emphasize disciplined behaviour. Brigitte Schloss, a Swiss Moravian teacher who worked at the Nain school in the 1950s, later reflected on her experiences in teaching Inuit children. For her, the differences between Inuit child-rearing practices and the teaching methods used in the school were striking:

> [M]any children being allowed to do just what they please, how they please and when they please, find it an interesting and amusing change to meet up with discipline. But whatever the reasons behind it, their eagerness to go to school was and is a great help to the teachers.[73]

Modernizing Moravian Education

In the late 1930s, Rev. Frederick William Peacock and his wife, Doris Peacock, came to Labrador. Their arrival marked the beginning of significant changes to the Mission's educational approach. Wartime politics no doubt played a role in the 1939 decision to appoint the young Englishman as the Mission's new superintendent. Despite his relative inexperience, Peacock replaced Rev. Paul Hettasch, a German national. Rev. Peacock had plans to modernize the Mission. His wife Doris was keen to modernize the Nain school. With a B.Sc. from the University of Cardiff and an education diploma, she also had the educational background to support her ideas. As Tabea Murphy recalls, until this point the Inuit classes had used the limited Inuktitut-language teaching materials that the missionaries had developed themselves:

Nain schoolchildren with teaching assistant Rose Nukappiak Webb, ca. 1940s (courtesy of Them Days Archive).

> When I start going to school at first, when it was all Inuit children, the only material we have written in Inuttitut was the bible, no other material. . . . The reason why they just used the bible, because they didn't want us to learn the English language. . . . This is why we know more of the bible things, my age people anyway, because of what we had to use — just the Inuttitut bible, that was our only resource, written in Inuttitut. Later on they come out with what we call Alpe-pat [A-B-PAT], ABC's, there's little stories in it, about children, what they do when they're learning in school, other things like that. That was a better resource than the Inuttitut bible, easier.[74]

Under the Peacocks' influence, the Mission schools extended the range of subjects they offered. "Formerly in our schools it was thought sufficient to teach the three Rs," wrote Rev. Peacock in 1943, "but within the last few years the curriculum has been greatly widened. History, Geography, Basic English, Nature Study, Art and Native boot making are all new subjects."[75] The broader range of subjects required the missionaries to develop new teaching resources in Inuktitut. These included a history and geography curriculum written by Doris Peacock and translated by Makkovik missionary George Harp. Kate Hettasch recorded her first attempt at teaching geography in Inuktitut in her 1941 school diary: "Thursday 13th: We had our first Geography lesson in Eskimo. It will do to mention the facts that pleasure from it conquered all dread and fears and aversion to have to try it in Eskimo. Results were a few wonderful-shaped maps of Labrador."[76]

Rev. Peacock also translated *The Story of Mankind, Part I* (from 4000 BC to 323 BC and Alexander the Great) by Henrik Van Loon into Inuktitut.[77] Although it is unclear whether the school ever used the translated work, Peacock's choice of textbook provides some insight into what he thought important for use in Inuit schools in Labrador. *The Story of Mankind* tells the classical history of the world, starting with the Egyptians and the Greeks, and climaxing with France, Britain, and the Industrial Revolution. Inuit and other Indigenous peoples are not included in its version of history. By translating the text into Inuktitut, Peacock aimed to expand the breadth of materials used in Inuit classrooms. His choice of text, however, maintained the conventional Eurocentric curriculum of the time.

While the Peacocks endeavoured to transform the curriculum, they also wanted to address financial challenges at the Moravian schools. Since the early 1930s, Moravian officials had been asking for financial assistance from the Commission of Government for teachers' salaries. Shortly after arriving in Labrador, Rev. Peacock could see the need for the government to assume a larger role in the region. "I know we are living through a Depression and times are hard," he wrote to the British Mission Board in 1936. ". . . But I say that the Commission of Government for Newfoundland should be made aware that it has a deep and lasting responsibility to make better provision for the Eskimos and Settlers of Northern Labrador."[78] Some Newfoundland officials also felt that the government needed to accept more responsibility for the Moravian schools. The government agent for northern Labrador, Walter Rockwood, penned a memo in 1945 about Moravian education for the Department of Education that outlined his position:

> However the Department may feel about the matter, it will not be easy to ignore the problem of education in Northern Labrador indefinitely. . . . The Newfoundland Government is no less responsible for the education of the Eskimo and settler children in Northern Labrador, than for the children in other parts of the Island.[79]

But the government was reluctant to fund education without having some control over it.[80] If Newfoundland was going to help pay for teachers' salaries, it wanted to assess the teachers' qualifications, and it expected them to be familiar with the Newfoundland curriculum.[81] Since the Nain school opened in 1929, Kate Hettasch and other young women from Moravian congregations in Europe had taught the classes. They had little formal training in teaching and were poorly paid. The Mission believed that this was the only possible way to run its schools, which cost it over £1,000 per year:

> The Mission Board does not contemplate the possibility of sending out teachers with full professional qualifications. It would be impossible to get an adequate supply of such teachers and still more impossible to pay the salaries which would be required for such a qualified staff. . . . The Board believes that a more modest scheme of education [that] is at present carried out meets the present needs of the Coast, and can best be carried out under the responsibility of the mission itself.[82]

In response to the Mission's request, the Commission of Government agreed to pay $1,000 towards Moravian educational efforts in Nain and Makkovik for the 1941–42 school year, but it asked for more information about the schools, including proof of teachers' qualifications and the number of students.[83] The new funding marked the beginning of increased government involvement in Moravian education. Annual government support grew to $2,000 in 1945 and to $4,000 in 1946.[84] The Newfoundland government also agreed to fund two students from Nain to attend high school at an International Grenfell Association school in St. Anthony or North West River.[85]

Further Education

Until the Peacocks modified the Moravian approach to education in the 1940s, missionaries had been reluctant to send Moravian Inuit to other schools for further education.[86] A few children of Settler/*Kablunângajuit* families, such as Edgar "Ted" McNeill of the Makkovik congregation, pursued further schooling elsewhere, but few Inuit children were encouraged to seek higher education.[87]

Moreover, Moravian Inuit education did not position children well for attending a school elsewhere. The missionary teachers in Nain had been unwilling to teach English to their Inuit pupils and had punished those who spoke the language. The Moravian schools also did not have grades, which made it difficult for students to transfer to other schools. "In the old days of school," recalls one former student, "we used to have the same thing over and over again — every year the same things. There were no grades — we never knew if we passed or failed."[88]

Rev. and Doris Peacock brought a new attitude towards the idea of higher education for Moravian students. With financial support from the Newfoundland government, they encouraged bright students to continue their schooling at the International Grenfell Association schools in St. Anthony and North West River. Students could then complete grades higher than what was available in their home communities.[89] The Peacocks also sent students to vocational schools in other regions.

Several students were sent to St. Anthony, including Silpa Sillitt Barbour of Nain in 1946:

> My friend Hilda Hunter and I went away to school when we were thirteen years old. At that time, we did not know what grades were. The minister arranged our passage, and we left in September. The very next day after our arrival in St. Anthony, Newfoundland, we started school. We were asked what grade we were in. It is no wonder we didn't know what grades were; our teacher in Nain had never explained the grading system to us, had not used it, and had not told us anything about it. At that time, in 1946, they tried to put us into Grade Nine, but later, we ended up in Grade Six. It is no wonder we were put down, because we knew nothing about history, geography, or literature. It was very difficult for us. We were told to return the next year. Although we had been told to return and had agreed to it, I decided not to go back, because we had been starving in the orphanage. I can say, though, that I did pass my Sixth Grade.[90]

Despite doing well in school, Silpa was determined not to go back. She stayed in Nain, worked at the Nain boarding school, and taught at the Nain school. Both Moravian and Grenfell officials were disappointed that she had decided against returning to St. Anthony. Rev. Peacock reported on her resolve in a 1949 letter:

> She said that she was not happy there and, as is the way with Eskimo parents, her folks acceded her request to stay home this winter. I am awfully sorry about this but when I spoke to the parents they said that they would not force the child to go back. It is a pity in many ways as Miss Bean told me that she was the most clever child they had in school in St. Anthony and it seems to me to be such a waste of good material.[91]

Gradually, more students from Moravian schools attended high school at St. Anthony or North West River, vocational school, or nurse's training in Newfoundland. Rev. Peacock later reflected with pleasure on the opportunities the training provided to the young people:

> The progress in our schools and the progress of our Eskimo children who come south to schools is a source of joy to us all. In a few short years the educational standard has been raised tremendously and we can hope that within a few years we may have a steady trickle of Eskimo children who will want to continue their education by going on to University and Vocational school.[92]

With the arrival of the Peacocks, Moravian attitudes and policies became more open and supportive of higher education. As Sam Andersen in Nain noted, Confederation further opened the doors to increased choice in education:

> We were no longer under the tight control, that we had these pressures . . . where we had to go to boarding school. Then you were under direct control of the Moravian Mission and you had to do everything they said. . . . But after Confederation, all that changed. Suddenly freed up. The parents had a choice of where they were going to send their kids. They could go to North West River or to some other school if they wished one. Well, prior to that it was the Mission who said where you could go to school. So they more or less dictated to you what you could do.[93]

The Shift to English

The Moravian schools gradually adopted the Newfoundland curriculum. Doris and Rev. Peacock developed a course of study based on the Newfoundland curriculum in 1941, but they soon found that the material did not suit the realities of northern Labrador. When the Secretary for Education in St. John's heard about their troubles in following the material, he encouraged them to develop a more culturally relevant curriculum:

> [A visitor] mentioned to me that you were a little concerned as to the difficulty in following the Curriculum in use in the schools of Newfoundland and Labrador generally. Please do not feel that you must do this. Wherever the Curriculum can serve as a guide by all mean use it. Otherwise arrange the course that you and Mrs. Peacock, with your knowledge of the situation, can do much better than anyone not on the ground.[94]

Educational authorities in Newfoundland, however, did not generally share the Secretary of Education's opinion. Over the next 10 years, Moravian teachers found themselves under increasing pressure to align their work with the Newfoundland curriculum and educational approach. In a letter dated 27 February 1950, Rev. Peacock outlined his frustrations to George Alain Frecker, the Deputy Minister of Education:

> One thing worries me very much and that is the insistence that we should conform to the Newfoundland curriculum. If we do this our children will get a very low grading; whereas we feel that it is our duty not so much to give an academic education but an education which will enable our children to fit into life in the Eskimo community. Mr. Carter [of the provincial Department of Natural Resources] has publicly stated that it is his avowed intent to make the Eskimos into White Men.
>
> In the first place, I would argue that this is a presumption, the Eskimos as Eskimos have a contribution to make to the world, by their specialized culture. . . . Surely our aim in educating Native peoples should be to fit them for the business of living not to turn them into a poor imitation of another race. For example, the art of building snow houses is dying out in Labrador, I therefore decided that snow house building should be introduced into the school curriculum. . . . To my mind, the ability to build a snow house is more essential to the Eskimo than the ability to do fractions.[95]

Despite Peacock's concerns, pressure from the government to revise their curriculum resulted in the Moravian schools making changes in the 1947–48 school year. By 1951–52, almost all teaching, except for Scripture, was provided in English and was based on the Newfoundland grading system.[96]

The demand for change came not only from the government. Rev. Peacock noted in 1943 that Inuit parents also wanted to see changes in their children's education:

> Our Eskimos are realizing that they need more education and the parents are taking far more interest in the school work than they had done formerly. The parents are clamouring for the children to learn English but I am thankful that they have no wish that the children should neglect their mother tongue. During the past year, I have conducted English classes.[97]

Years later, Abel Leo of Nain reflected on the transition to English in the Inuit school and the Elders' regret in advocating for the change:

> If you spoke English in school, you would probably get a slap for it. The Elders tried for years to get English taught in the schools without any success and finally after Confederation, they did have the opportunity to see English being taught in the schools. ... They found then that this went a little bit too far. After a number of years they realized they had made a mistake.... It was the community Elders themselves who wished to have English taught in the schools in the first place because they hadn't had the opportunity to learn English when they were going to school.[98]

Julius Ikkusek of Nain remembers this time of transition as being imperfect and arbitrary:

> While they were staying over to boarding school, they were not allowed to speak in English. Only in Inuttitut, that's how they

> were taught in boarding school, only Inuttitut. . . . They didn't even have to try to speak English, if they find out, if they been doing that, same thing used to happen, stand up in a corner. . . . After two weeks when they turn 13, Reverend Peacock used to teach them how to — like simple words in Kalungatitut [English] every two weeks, only when they turn 13.[99]

Former student Tabea Murphy recalls the transition to an English curriculum and a non-segregated school as difficult, at least at first:

> When Newfoundland and Labrador became part of Canada, our whole school was turned upside down. Mrs. Doris Peacock, the wife of Reverend Peacock, was our English teacher in the smaller schoolhouse. Before, we never entered that building, only the Settler people's children were allowed — the English-speaking kids. For some reason, Mrs. Peacock took me to her classroom from the Inuktitut classroom. I was very shy. I hardly know English language — only very few words. She put my desk right by her desk, and when she teached, she pointed to my workbook and showed me where we are. I cried, finding it hard, not being able to read English. She just carried on.
>
> In about one week, I used to catch up reading. She used to teach Sam Andersen, one of her students, stand and talk to others, learning to be at a meeting, to become a speaker at a meeting when he grew up. I used to wish I could be like Sam, getting to be like a speaker. Within a few weeks, my Inuktitut classmates moved to our smaller English classroom. I was very happy to see my first classmates.[100]

Not all classes were taught in English. Scripture, Rev. Peacock argued, should be taught in Inuktitut because Moravian church life in Labrador takes place in Inuktitut. He felt that people should "associat[e] their mother tongue with their religion. . . . Each individual speaks to God

Nain schoolhouse (left) and dormitory (former HBC cottage hospital) (right) (courtesy of Them Days Archive).

more from the heart if he is using his own mother tongue, and he does so simply because he has more command over language in his mother tongue." Rev. Paul Hettasch's son, Siegfried, who was a missionary in Hopedale, insisted that the Mission should adopt English entirely. Rev. Peacock disagreed. In a 1944 letter to Siegfried, Peacock outlined his thoughts on the importance of Inuktitut:

> With reference to your suggestion that we abandon the Eskimo language in Hopedale and start everything in English because of the increasing influence of "the Outside World." My personal opinion is that this increasing influence is a very good reason why we should retain Eskimo language. We Europeans have destroyed so much of the Eskimo culture that to abandon the Eskimo language would be, in my opinion, the final insult.[101]

Despite differing opinions within the Moravian Mission, the pressure to teach subjects in English persuaded the Mission teachers to adopt an English curriculum. Rev. Peacock believed the changes in the school were beneficial:

> In our schools too there has been marked and very evident progress. We have now changed entirely over to English for all teaching except religion. We have also adopted the Newfoundland Education Departmental curriculum with a few modifications which seemed necessary because of geographical position. We now have children in our school doing Grade 7 work which is far above what children in the Eskimo Schools in other parts of the Arctic attain, for the highest grade recorded in the Canadian Government statistics for Eskimos is Grade 3.
>
> But not only are the children making progress academically, there is a marked improvement in cleanliness. This fall, for the first time, there has been a Government inspection of our schools; Mr. Raymond Ivimey, the Government school inspector reported that our school in Nain was far above the average in Newfoundland outports not only as far as learning and teaching were concerned but the children were better behaved and cleaner than the Newfoundland outport children.[102]

To Peacock, the students' educational achievements and standard of cleanliness indicated that the changes were a success. However, Kate Hettasch, whom anthropologist Shmuel Ben-Dor describes as "a Moravian with the zeal of the olden days," did not see the new curriculum as progress. For her, "the changes mean that the 'soul' was taken out of the educational work."[103] Others, including student Tabea Murphy, thought that the changes to the Moravian school curriculum and approach were valuable:

> I'm very thankful when Newfoundland and Labrador became part of Canada that we changed into English, and we had a

> chance to learn English without being told off. I'm very thankful that we learned to speak English that we can talk wherever we go, or if we go to conferences like this. I'm thankful for that.[104]

Staffing

The Mission struggled to staff the schools and dormitory with both local domestic workers and qualified teachers. Local women who did the cooking and cleaning were now finding other wage opportunities elsewhere in Labrador. They also received social security payments that had become available after Newfoundland joined Canada on 1 April 1949. With the new sources of income, Nain women and girls no longer seemed interested in working at the boarding school. Doris Peacock explained the challenges in a report on the Nain school:

> At the opening of the past school session, 1950–51, we were faced with the difficulty of obtaining satisfactory domestic staff for our boarding school here. The younger girls from among whom we have been in the habit of recruiting domestic help are in receipt of children's allowances until they reach the age of 16 years and this precludes them from working for wages. Widows are now independent, and as there was only one unemployed girl, aged 17 years, here we were very worried and only managed to keep boarding school open by getting domestic help from Nutak.[105]

Rev. Peacock pointed out another reason for the lack of interest among Nain women in working at the boarding school. In a letter to the British Mission Board in London, he wrote, "It is becoming increasingly difficult to obtain labour for school (domestic)."[106] He then compared wages at the Nain school with wages at the International Grenfell Association boarding school in North West River. In Nain, the cook and laundress were each paid $6 per month, while the maids and assistant teachers were each paid $3.75 per month. The IGA, on the other hand, paid domestic staff about $42 per month.

The Mission's financial struggles continued even when, in 1951, the province increased its grant to the Moravian schools by $2,500. As Rev. Peacock made clear, other provincial government policies also increased the Mission's school expenses:

> The newly formed Division of Northern Labrador Affairs raised the rate paid for labour in Northern Labrador from 25 cents to 50 cents an hour, without consulting or informing Moravian Missions. This raised costs of labour for schools by nearly two thousand dollars p.a. [per annum] and thus almost nullified the value of the new grant.[107]

In 1954, the Nain boarding school closed for the 1954–55 school year because the Mission could not find a cook. The school ran as a day school only.[108]

Teachers were also difficult to recruit. A 1946 telegram Rev. Peacock sent to a congregation in Alberta shows how desperate the Moravian Mission had become in trying to find the right kind of staff: "Urgently require one lady teacher, over twenty one years of age for Boarding school. . . . She needs courage and determination matriculation if possible."[109] Given the scarcity of teachers, the Mission decided it should support local students who might train to become teachers themselves. In 1946, two students from Nain — Beatrice Ford Watts and Robert Lyall — signed contracts in which they agreed to return to Labrador at the end of their training and teach for two years.[110] They were given $150 each and sent to finish high school at the International Grenfell Association boarding school in North West River. Although Robert eventually decided not to pursue teaching, Beatrice studied at North West River and then Memorial University of Newfoundland in St. John's. In 1951, she wrote to Brother Birtill in London to express her appreciation and hopes for her future career:

Dear Sir:

Thank you for your letter. It was indeed a pleasant surprise. On behalf of the people in Northern Labrador, I would like to express my sincere thanks to the Moravian Mission for their unselfish and sacrificial service they have done. Ever since childhood, my aim was to become a teacher, with the hope that someday, I too would be able to help our people. With the aid of Rev. and Mrs.

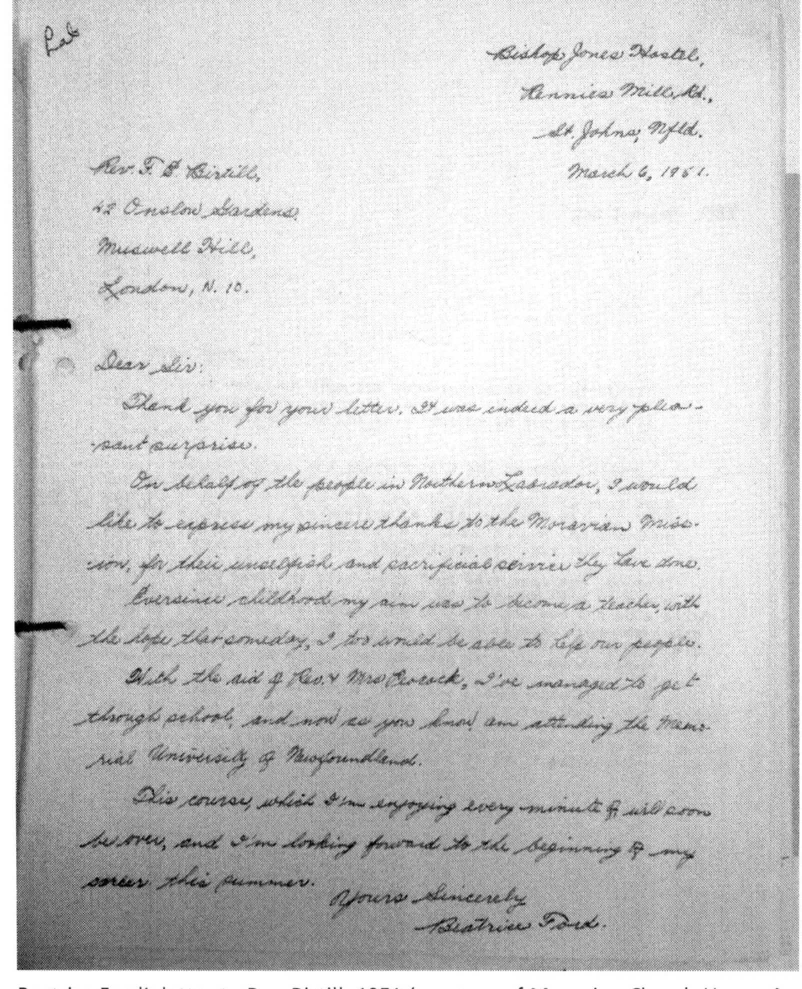

Lab

Bishop Jones Hostel,
Pennies Mill Rd.,
St. John's, Nfld.
March 6, 1951.

Rev. F. P. Birtill,
42 Onslow Gardens,
Muswell Hill,
London, N. 10.

Dear Sir:

Thank you for your letter. It was indeed a very pleasant surprise.

On behalf of the people in Northern Labrador, I would like to express my sincere thanks to the Moravian Mission, for their unselfish and sacrificial service they have done.

Ever since childhood my aim was to become a teacher, with the hope that someday, I too would be able to help our people.

With the aid of Rev. & Mrs Peacock, I've managed to get through school, and now as you know am attending the Memorial University of Newfoundland.

This course, which I'm enjoying every minute of, will soon be over, and I'm looking forward to the beginning of my career this summer.

Yours Sincerely
Beatrice Ford.

Beatrice Ford's letter to Rev. Birtill, 1951 (courtesy of Moravian Church House Archives, Muswell Hill, London).

> Peacock, I've managed to get through school, and now as you know am attending the Memorial University of Newfoundland. This course, which I'm enjoying every minute of, will soon be over, and I'm looking forward to the beginning of my career this summer.
>
> Yours sincerely,
>
> Beatrice Ford[111]

Beatrice Ford Watts returned to Nain that year as the first trained bilingual teacher. She taught at the school for years before becoming principal of Yale School in North West River. She later worked as an Inuit curriculum and Inuktitut language specialist for the provincial Department of Education.[112] Beatrice went on to become a well-known leader in Inuit education in Labrador, and, in 1992, received an honorary doctorate from Memorial University of Newfoundland.[113]

From Mission Control to Government Authority

The Newfoundland government's role in education and other aspects of life in northern Labrador increased significantly in the mid-twentieth century. Once almost entirely absent from the region, government officials became more active in Labrador in the 1940s. In 1942, the Commission of Government assumed responsibility for the trading posts in northern Labrador. The move came after the Hudson's Bay Company announced that it was leaving the region because it was unprofitable. The government's new division, the Northern Labrador Trading Operations, brought new state involvement to the Moravian district.

Also in 1942, Newfoundland passed the School Attendance Act.[114] The new law required all children aged 7–14 to attend a local school if they lived within two miles of the school.[115] However, the government did not immediately enforce the law in northern Labrador, much to the frustration of Rev. Peacock. In a 1943 letter to Newfoundland Ranger Tilley, Peacock lists a number of students who were not attending school.

"Should you wish to make it known that school attendance is now compulsory I shall be glad to co-operate with you in this matter," he writes.[116] He seems to have secured the Rangers' co-operation by 1950. In a memo about the Labrador Mission, he describes the arrangement:

> Finally in Nain, it is possible to enforce the compulsory school attendance act — a thing that has been impossible on the other stations. This has partly been due to the fact that Newfoundland Rangers have extended cooperation by maintaining that the 2-mile limit for compulsory [attendance] was non-operative in an area where there was a residential school. Although the action of the Newfoundland Rangers in this matter has been illegal it has helped us a great deal in our school work.[117]

Despite the unlawful practice of forcing children who lived beyond the two-mile limit to attend school, the Mission and the Rangers felt justified in asserting their power. A few months later in 1950 the Newfoundland Ranger Force, established in 1935 to provide a range of policing and community services to northern and remote communities, was disbanded and folded into the Royal Canadian Mounted Police.[118]

In the ensuing years, the Moravian Mission turned more and more to the Newfoundland government for help in overseeing and financing its schools. In 1951, the British Mission Board and the Labrador missionaries began to consider handing complete authority over the schools to the province.[119] Financial troubles that had plagued the Moravian schools through World War II and its aftermath had forced their hand. After much deliberation, the British Mission Board instructed Rev. Peacock to negotiate with the Department of Education about transferring control.[120] In 1955, the Mission requested that the government assume full responsibility for the schools in Nain, Makkovik, Hopedale, and Hebron. The missionaries asked only that they be allowed to continue teaching religious classes. "The Moravians would request access to the schools to give religious instruction," wrote Rev. Peacock to the Deputy Minister of

Education, George Alain Frecker.[121] He also asked that the Mission be allowed to maintain its authority as guardian of the Inuit: "I would like to point out that in my opinion the Eskimos themselves are not yet capable of taking part in school management. If it is possible we would, naturally, like a Moravian to be the chairman of the school board which would be established in N. Labrador."[122]

The Newfoundland government consented. In taking over control of the schools, the government assumed responsibility for hiring and paying teachers. But only candidates with provincial credentials would now be considered for the job. The government also refused to hire Inuit teaching assistants who spoke Inuktitut and taught Inuit skills, although the Moravian Mission had done so for years. Rev. Peacock described his frustration with the change in policy:

> When the schools came under Government control, the mission retained the boarding part, but the native aides were no longer employed in the school because they were "untrained." There was a typical failure to understand that these "untrained" natives were craftsmen and women of rare and incomparable skill.[123]

Without Inuit teaching assistants, Inuktitut-speaking children at the school were left to struggle with the English curriculum. The students also lost the opportunity to learn traditional skills from Inuit teachers like Kristianna Sillitt, who had taught sealskin boot-making at the school for years.[124]

The new hiring policy also impacted the boarding school. At the Nain school, teaching positions had always involved much more than simply teaching. In the 1940s and 1950s, teachers took turns living at the boarding school and looking after the children in the evenings. Former teacher Brigitte Schloss described the arrangement in a *Them Days* interview in 2000:

> In the winter, the teachers took turns sleeping in the boarding school, a week at a time. For a while we were housed in the very

> poorly insulated Anaktalak building, next to the school. The oil heater refused to work properly — always. Every other day or so, Doris [Peacock] would come and clear out the fine, oily soot. It needed to be done, so she did it. There was not much she would not tackle.[125]

After 1955, however, many teachers hired by the provincial government did not want to assume this additional work. Rev. and Doris Peacock moved to Happy Valley–Goose Bay in 1957 and could no longer attend to dormitory duties, so local Inuit took over the role of house parents at the Nain boarding school. Organized through the Moravian Church, these supervisors were often couples who lived at the dormitory with the children.[126]

The Newfoundland government now covered the cost of hiring teachers and operating the school, but the Moravian Church still had to cover the costs of the boarding school. Facing grave budget concerns, Rev. Peacock requested that the provincial government also pay for the dormitory expenses.[127] In 1956, the provincial government agreed to pay a grant of $5,000 "to the Moravian Mission authorities at Nain in return for operating a student hostel (dormitory)."[128] The government paid this grant each year until the Nain boarding school finally closed.

As more families moved to live permanently in Nain, attendance at the boarding school continued to fall. From a high of about 55 boarders in 1942–43, when the Mission encouraged families living in the village to send their children to the boarding school, the numbers dropped to 36 boarders in 1948–49.[129] In 1951–52, the boarding school temporarily closed when Kate Hettasch left Nain for personal reasons.[130] In the mid-1950s, an average of 25 children stayed at the boarding school, except for the 1954–55 school year when, as noted above, the dormitory closed again because the Mission could not find a cook.[131]

Through the 1960s, the number of children who stayed at the boarding school in Nain declined as more families moved into the community. At some point, the informal agreement between the police force and the missionaries to ignore the two-mile rule in the compulsory education regulations evaporated. Instead, children who travelled with their families to their *aullasimavet* — their fishing and hunting places — were sometimes given binders of school work to complete while away from the community.[132] Other children were forced to stay at the boarding school. Paul Jararuse was seven or eight when he went to live at the school for two years. His family went off in the spring and the fall to their *aullasimavet*, but left Paul and his siblings in Nain: "My parents found out that we had to go to school because the government said, if we didn't go to school, they were going to stop my mother's family allowance."[133]

Several families continued to live at their homes in the bays around Nain if they could manage it. But many decided that their economic and social situation would be better if they lived in the town. Parents of the few families still living outside of Nain, such as the Webb family, were pressured to send their children to the boarding school. Sarah Webb recalls the power the missionaries held over parents:

> The minister, church ministers had all the say. The parents had no say; just the ministers. Whatever the minister said, the parents had to listen. And, when I turned five October 12th, and on the few days after mom and dad left me in boarding school and went up the bay, because they said I had to stay here. So, I was five-years-old . . . . And, you couldn't even complain about them because your parents couldn't do anything, even if you complained about how you were treated by the ministers and stuff. They couldn't do any — they couldn't say anything.[134]

Sarah and her brothers decided one day in December to run away from the boarding school and return to Webb's Bay, about 35 kilometres from Nain. Their story has become a well-known episode in Nain's oral history:

> It started on a Saturday afternoon. We went down sliding down on the point. We never had no plans to go up to the bay. Nothing.

Nain boarding school children, 1963. Back: Sarah Webb, Jim Webb, Regina Maggo, Bill Webb, Joan Martin Dicker (daughter of housemother Susan Martin); front: Bertha Kairtok, Eliza Webb, Chesley Webb, Herman Webb, Joe Webb (courtesy of Them Days Archive).

But, we were down there sliding, and we was looking up and they said, "Oh Webb's Bay is just over there. Why don't we walk up?" There was Jim, he was 12; I was 11; Herman, he was 10; Joe was 9 or 8 or something. I can't remember. Eight or nine, and Ches was the youngest — he was six. So, Joe must have been 7. And, Bertha Barbour, she was the same age as me. She was Bertha Kairtok then. . . .

We got lost. One place we got lost. I suppose we got lost. There was a place where the brook never freezes over, and we went in and around, because when the dog team came looking for us, they kind of lost our tracks there. But, that's where the brook never froze. So, we had guardian angels, because just after we got there [Webb's Bay], the biggest blizzard hit. We made it. Yes. We left here 1:00. Jim and Herman got there 10:00. . . . Jim and Herman went ahead of us. So, they said they would go get the help for

> us. And, when we went over Sandy Point, you could see this light. There was the lamplight, I guess. So, this little light you could see. And, when it went out, I panicked, and I said — yelled, "Somebody come and get us! Somebody come and get us!" So, we had a guardian angel. . . . We got told off bad. And, when we came back, Auntie said — she had a rope with big old knots. "If you run away like that again, you're gonna get hit with this." And, we got, like, told off by everybody because, I mean, they were in church praying for us and everything, figuring we was all dead.[135]

Other children ran away from the boarding school because they were abused. Paul Jararuse lived at the Nain school in the early 1970s. At a Healing and Commemoration session in Rigolet, he describes having no escape from nighttime assaults.

> They used to tell me, "Don't go over there [to the boarding school]. They will do something." And I couldn't do nothing. . . . We used to run away to grandfather's because we didn't like the boarding school, but they still had to pick us up. And, after we ran away, they used to lock us up in our rooms only allowed to get out, just for something to eat, dinnertime, suppertime. . . . We had to listen to them anyway. We had no other choice. . . . We'd be more in trouble if we tell someone. . . . I was some glad when this stuff [about abuse at residential schools] came out, later on years, instead of keeping to myself.[136]

Final Days

The boarding school in Nain continued to take children until 1972, when it closed its doors for good. In March 1973, Rev. Peacock's replacement as superintendent, David J. Dickinson, returned the $5,000 annual grant for 1972–73 from the provincial Department of Education. The new Moravian superintendent informed the department that the boarding school was no longer in operation. Dickinson also reported that the provincial economic development branch, the Northern Labrador Services Division, was using the building as a store, since fire had destroyed its own building that winter. "I am therefore returning the cheque to you," he wrote, "as it does not appear that we shall be boarding any students in the near future. Last year was similar. From what I can gather, there have only been one or two students there."[137] Dickinson also offered to return a $6,000 surplus that had not been used over the last few years because so few children had stayed at the boarding school, but the department agreed that the money could be used instead for a school project.[138] The boarding school closed, but the Nain school continued as one of the largest day schools on the coast.

Since the creation of the Nain boarding school in 1929, the Mission's efforts to transform Inuit society through its influence and control of children had widespread but mixed results. While the missionaries

Nain boarding school children, 1963. From left: Sarah Webb, Eva Okkuatsiak Nochasak, Chesley Webb, Joe Webb, Juliana Merkuratsuk (assistant housemother), Jim Webb, Maggie Ittulak Jararuse, and Bertha Kairtok Holeiter (courtesy of Them Days Archive).

maintained Inuktitut education until the 1950s, their focus on removing children from the "harmful influences" of Inuit home life and their close surveillance of the students created much resentment and pain in the community. Kate Hettasch, the first teacher at the school in 1929 and a dominant figure in Inuit education until she retired in 1973, offered a poignant and possibly telling message to her former students before she died in 1987: "To all my boys and girls I was permitted to teach, I say forgive where unknowingly I may have hurt you. Do find Jesus, the friend of all. This little light of mine, let it shine, let it shine."[139]

CHAPTER SIX

A New Boarding School Considered

"Hebron had a school but we'd always be off at camps, Saglek and Ikkigasatsuk, so we didn't go to school at all, not until we moved down here."
— Lizzie Semigak, Nain

Once it opened in 1929, the Nain boarding school catered to families in the Nain area. Children who lived in more northerly regions had fewer opportunities for schooling. Okak had closed after the Spanish flu epidemic of 1918 devastated the community, and the Moravian stations at Ramah and Killinek had closed in 1907 and 1924, respectively. The missionary at Hebron served his dispersed congregation along a coastline of more than 100 kilometres, from north of Hebron to the Hudson's Bay Company post at Nutak in Okak Bay.[1] Children of families who lived at Hebron for the winter could go to the small day school there between Christmas and Easter, but most children in the Hebron and Okak Bay area did not attend school at all.

The Hebron missionary from 1934 to 1940, Rev. George Harp, described the situation in 1937:

> There are over two hundred and eighty men, women and children connected with Hebron and Okak, and to visit them one has to travel many miles. . . . It is unfortunate that we get so little chance to mould the lives of the young, but this can be done only

> in school. We hold day school in winter, but only twelve attended this year, and it is seldom there are more than this number. Some of the children live miles and miles away, and therefore cannot attend a day school. This year an Eskimo woman took morning school, and my wife afternoon school, and I took over from my wife when not travelling. Each child here and those living away also have an Eskimo ABC book but much more than this is needed if our children are not to grow up in ignorance, and the darkness which surrounds them.[2]

Harp felt that "the only solution lies in the amalgamation of Hebron and Okak in a new station in a well-wooded district near Okak, with a boarding school."[3] The potential cost of building a new station was too much for the cash-strapped Moravian Mission, but the idea of a boarding school in Okak Bay endured.

By the early 1940s, over 60 children in the Hebron and Nutak region were not getting formal schooling. Rev. Peacock, the new Labrador Mission superintendent, suggested to the Commission of Government that it contribute towards building a new Moravian boarding school at Pussekartok, on Martin Island inside Okak Bay.[4] The government agreed and proposed a 50:50 split of the construction costs. But World War II created financial difficulties for the British Mission Board, and it postponed all plans until after the war.[5]

The idea was revived again in 1950. This time, the provincial Department of Education budgeted $5,000 for the new Okak Bay boarding school.[6] When asked about the idea, however, Inuit living in Okak Bay argued that Pussekartok was too far from the trading post at Nutak.[7] The Mission stalled on the scheme.

In the meantime, about a dozen students travelled from the Nutak area to attend the Nain boarding school.[8] One such student was Nellie Andersen Winters, who lived with her parents and her brothers' families in Okak Bay. Nellie went to the boarding school in Nain in 1949, when she was 11:

> I used to go to school here in Nain, boarding school, from down there. We used to come up on the last boat in the fall, the [provincial government's Northern Labrador Trading Operations supply schooner S.S.] Winifred Lee, and stay in the boarding school until the spring, go back on dog team. That's the only time I've stayed in igloo. Children, some of the younger ones, younger than we were, were really pitiful when they were being sent to school. The first time we went, the younger ones were crying all the way to the Kilapaits [mountains]. And the captain on the boat, the Winifred Lee, said, now, I'm having my dinner, and if you don't stop crying by the time I'm finished my dinner, you'll be thrown overboard. Well, they were pitiful, I tell you. Just trying to stop them from crying, you know? We had to do a lot of work in school, you know. We didn't only have to learn, we had to do a lot of work besides. We had to eat things we didn't like. But I think in one way, it made us work harder, and do things.[9]

Boarding school students could connect with far-away parents when the missionaries organized radio communication in Nain in the late 1940s. The radio station broadcast Sunday services, educational material, and nightly prayers in Inuktitut and English. The missionaries also invited the boarding school students to send a message to their parents over the air.[10] Nellie Winters still remembers the opportunity:

> But, one good thing, like they had something set up — there were two men down there, Peacock and Mr. Grubb. We had some kind of a radio set up that we could talk home once a month. Yes, and we used to go down and [call] back home . . . somebody saying, "Send me another pair of skin boots. Mine is holey." And then Sid Dicker [a musician and songwriter from Nain] used to sing a song in between.[11]

While a few children from the Hebron and Nutak areas attended either the boarding school in Nain or the seasonal day school in Hebron, many more did not receive any schooling. Their families lived outside Hebron or in Okak Bay at places better situated for hunting and fishing but too distant to easily attend school. Provincial officials such as Walter Rockwood, director of the Division of Northern Labrador Affairs (DNLA), insisted that the formal education of these children should not continue to be overlooked:

> The most neglected area in Northern Labrador, and in fact the whole Province, is the Okkak and Hebron sections. . . . It is a fact that there are about eighty children of school age in the Okkak Bay section today, and no school. Nor has there been a school there for many, many years. True some children from there attend the boarding school at Nain. On October 19th, 1952, for example, four or five children from Nutak and Hebron came south to Nain on the M/V Winifred Lee. It is unlikely that more than this number are attending school from Nutak and Hebron this year.[12]

In the summer of 1953, Moravian and provincial officials toured Okak Bay to examine Pussekartok and several other potential sites for a new DNLA trading depot.[13] But plans for a boarding school in the Okak Bay area again evaporated in the 1950s. The International Grenfell Association (IGA) had become the main medical service provider in northern Labrador, and its staff's views on the "Eskimo problem" were influential. Representatives of the three non-Inuit agencies working in northern Labrador — Rev. Peacock of the Moravian Mission, Doctors Anthony Paddon and Charles Curtis of the IGA, and Director Rockwood of DNLA — debated the viability of an Inuit way of life based on the land. Their discussion cast doubt on the future of Inuit society in northern Labrador.

The officials argued that a fishing and hunting economy was outdated and that the Inuit north of Nain should relocate to southern communities. Once there, Inuit could access better education, housing, health care, and wage-paying jobs in new or proposed industrial and military developments. "The old Eskimo way of living off the land by hunting is irretrievably lost," contended Dr. Paddon, who was the IGA director of Northern Medical Services at the North West River hospital. "The only future for the Eskimo lies in community life, better education, and gradual adaptation to Canadian life."[14] He suggested moving "all the people north of the Kiglipaits . . . into one modern planned community in an approved site" at Pussekartok or Tessiujuk.[15] The new community would be "planned from the ground up" and "subject to rigid guidance by . . . an appointed committee representing the various agencies in the town, such as school, church, trading post, medical personnel etc."[16]

Rev. Peacock also believed that centralization was the best option for northern Labrador in the 1950s. He saw how difficult it was for Inuit fishermen to make a living when fish prices were low, and was convinced that people would eventually have to move south for better-paying jobs. "If the Eskimos are to have a chance to live as decent citizens of this Province with a fair living standard we must do all we can at once to equip them to meet the challenge of civilization," he wrote to the provincial Minister of Mines and Resources, Frederick Rowe.[17] This would involve education and medical treatment, so "they will be fit to leave the north and go where there is a decent living for them."[18] Peacock also identified another benefit of moving Inuit to southern communities. "Centralization of the Eskimo communities is desirable," he argued. "At the moment owing to the scattered nature of the population overhead expenses to both Government and the Mission are much too high."[19] The money spent on governmental and missionary services could be saved if the northern communities of Hebron and Nutak were to be closed.

Dr. Charles Curtis, the superintendent of the IGA in St. Anthony, found yet other reasons for centralization after he made his first visit to Nain in 1955. He was shocked at the poorly built Inuit houses, and believed that living conditions contributed to the high rate of tuberculosis. When Dr. Paddon told him that the housing was worse farther north, Curtis advocated for moving Inuit to southern communities. "Surely," he wrote in a letter to government officials, "along with any attempt to treat any disease among these people . . . money should be spent in moving them to better surroundings and in building better houses as soon as possible."[20] Curtis saw no value in keeping northern Inuit settlements or even in building a new northern community. He recommended the agencies "bring the Eskimo at Hebron and Nutak south."[21]

Walter Rockwood of the provincial government was more reluctant to dismiss the value of life in the north. Having lived for years in Labrador, he understood Inuit life better than visitors like Dr. Curtis. Instead of advocating for relocation, Rockwood argued for providing better services north of Nain:

> Ultimately migration to other areas may be necessary, but for the present it is neither practical nor politic to attempt this, and for the majority the next two or three decades will probably be spent in the familiar environment of the North. A vigorous Health programme is already underway and this must be matched by equally vigorous programmes in the fields of Education and Welfare.[22]

Inuit were not invited to join the authorities' discussions about closing the northern communities. But on hearing vague reports about plans for their future, the Inuit Elders at Hebron wrote to the Newfoundland government in 1956 to express their views:

> We Hebron People have heard that Hebron is to be closed, but we have not been told enough about it. . . . We do not want to be moved from our land and customs with all our doings and game hunting as this seems the best for us. The seal-hunt and trouting and deer-hunt and others which all are good for our livelihood, and it would seem that we would suffer hardships (in moving south).[23]

The Hebron area had long been at the heart of the northern Labrador Inuit homeland. It was a prime location for hunting and fishing, hosting the most lucrative char fishery on the coast. The Hebron people had close ties with other Inuit farther north and in Quebec, and their Inuktitut dialect and way of living differentiated them from Inuit in the Nain area and farther south. Their ties to the Moravian Church were also more recent and less established than at Nain and Hopedale, and they spent less time at the Mission station and more of the year on the land.[24] The prospect of moving away from their rich and distinct homeland was altogether uninviting.

The debate about life in northern Labrador had direct relevance to boarding schools in the region. If the new plan involved helping Inuit "get used to community life" and abandoning their land-based way of life, then boarding schools would no longer be needed. As the debate swung towards this conclusion, plans for a new boarding school in Okak Bay faltered. In September 1955, Peacock commented that, with poor prices for cod and Inuit moving south, the government might consider closing Hebron and Nutak. If that were the case, he argued, the Mission should not continue with the plan for a boarding school in Pussekartok until the situation became more definite.[25] The missionaries scrapped the idea for the last time.

As an alternative, the Mission and the provincial government drew up plans for a bigger boarding school in Nain. They intended the school and dormitory to accommodate children from the Hebron, Nutak, and Okak Bay regions, as well as from the Makkovik boarding school, which had closed in the summer of 1955.[26] The Department of Education would administer federal funds through the 1954 Federal–Provincial Agreement to build a larger school building in Nain. Officials at both levels of government stressed the need for adequate schooling facilities for the young cohort in northern Labrador, whose numbers had been increasing since Confederation as birth rates rose and infant mortality rates fell.[27]

The Department of Education therefore asked the IGA to share blueprints for a newly built dormitory in North West River with the Nain missionaries. Dr. Paddon sent the requested blueprints to the Deputy Minister of Education, George Alain Frecker. In his accompanying letter, Paddon also offered his perspective on the need to teach the Inuktitut-speaking Inuit in English:

> I think much of the future success of any programme to integrate the Labrador Eskimo into the Canadian State will depend on a good educational system. . . . I should think from an outsider's point of view that instruction in the language of Canada will be essential for these little Canadians.[28]

Paddon then stressed the significant expense and challenge of running a dormitory. Always an advocate for the North West River school, he questioned whether an expanded dormitory in Nain would not duplicate the efforts of the Grenfell dormitories:

> I am curious to know whether there are to be any duplication of facilities provided by this building, and the three Grenfell Mission dormitories. We ourselves suspect that the need for boarding school accommodation in Labrador will probably decrease as more centralization of population is achieved and more and more of the Labrador communities grow by absorption of the outlying hamlets to a size where they can maintain their own public schools. It would be my impression . . . that the solution to the problem of northern Labrador will be a southward drift of the population and the successive abandonment of the Hebron and Nutak communities. . . . I am therefore curious to know exactly what population will attend this boarding school. At the moment it could be filled up with the children of families who live in remote areas outside Nutak and Hebron. Most of the Nain people have moved into Nain proper and generally speaking nearly all of north Labrador is already living, or will very shortly be living in major communities.[29]

Dr. Paddon's letter planted doubt about the long-term need for boarding schools in northern Labrador in Dr. Frecker's mind. Once again, uncertainty about the future of Inuit land-based life and a growing consensus among the non-Inuit authorities that the people of northern

Labrador should live in towns weakened support for a northern boarding school. A few days after receiving Dr. Paddon's letter, Dr. Frecker wrote to Rev. Peacock about his indecision about expanding the boarding school at Nain:

> Our original plan was considered altogether too costly, especially in view of the fluctuating situation up north. This southward trend that everybody is talking about, and the visions of a more concentrated population in more southerly sections of Labrador, have made it extremely difficult to come to grips in a satisfactory way with the Nain project. . . . The more I think about the problems involved, the more difficult I find it to come to a positive decision in my own mind as to whether we should go all out for the project or abandon it for the time being to see how things will develop. Would a dormitory built to accommodate one hundred children become a white elephant in the space of a few years? . . . Would it be practicable and desirable to abandon the idea of a boarding school at Nain in favour of transporting children from the ages of ten and on to North West River by special boat each season?[30]

The provincial, Moravian, and IGA authorities gathered to further discuss the "Eskimo problem" at a 1956 Labrador Conference in St. John's.[31] Without consulting the people of Nutak or Hebron, the three agencies decided to move the northern Inuit to southern communities. They envisioned a future in which Inuit lived in large communities, worked at wage jobs, and had easy access to health care, housing, and education. While the Moravian schools had focused on educating children "to live as far as possible in the traditional manner of the Eskimos," as the chairperson of the conference, Frederick Rowe, described, a new and modern approach was needed: "Today the aim is to equip them to take their place as citizens and to absorb them into our society without violence to the native culture."[32]

Accordingly, the authorities moved northern Inuit into southern communities and championed the role of education in assimilating Indigenous peoples into the dominant society. Nutak was closed in 1956, and the people of the surrounding area were forced to move south to Nain, Makkovik, and North West River. As Paddon anticipated, the eviction of the people of Hebron followed in 1959 when the authorities closed the store and withdrew health services. With the closure of Nutak and Hebron, the northern Inuit were ousted from their homeland and expected to build new lives in the south.

The evictions caused upheaval and heartbreak. They displaced 158 people from Okak Bay and 233 people from Hebron to new and foreign environments, forcing them to adopt a village-based life.[33] Their Inuktitut-speaking children found themselves in English-only day schools in Nain, Hopedale, Makkovik, and North West River. They received little support in learning the new language, and some experienced discrimination because they were different from their classmates.[34] The number of schoolchildren living in Nain, Hopedale, and Makkovik swelled. As a result, the Moravian missionaries and the provincial government abandoned plans for an expanded Nain boarding school. Day schools became the sole focus of educational administrators in coastal Labrador.

Years later, upon reflecting on the chaotic and controversial decision to relocate Nutak and Hebron, Moravian missionary Siegfried Hettasch highlighted education as a crucial factor:

> Of course there are two sides to the story. Again, whereas the Eskimos would love to go north with their young people, go fishing and hunting like in the old days, we must not overlook that white people and governments are very concerned about building up an education at the same time to help the Eskimos. But how can you do both? Whereas the parents are in need of their children for the work they are doing, the sawing-up work, the hunting and fishing, to continue to exist like they would like to, like they have enjoyed to. And yet at the same time we would like

> to put them back at the school bench. So what is it that we want? What is it that is best? Are we trying to make their future or are we going to let them form their own future?[35]

The Moravian Mission, the IGA, and the provincial government decided unilaterally in the 1950s to "try to make their future" by forcing Inuit "back at the school bench." They did not invite Inuit to "form their own future." Instead, they used education as a justification for moving Inuit to southern communities, causing widespread social disruption in the process. A boarding school at Pussekartok might have presented an alternative to the process of forcing Inuit into community life, but its potential impact will never be known. Like the relocations, the Okak Bay scheme involved little Inuit involvement or support. The plans also relied on the assumption that education was a requirement of modern Canadian life and was therefore a rationale for the extensive social engineering of Inuit life in Labrador.

PART THREE

The International Grenfell Association Boarding Schools

CHAPTER SEVEN

Wilfred Grenfell and the Grenfell Mission

"In Labrador there is no poor-law system as in this country, and so when parents die the unhappy orphans might starve, were it not for the kindly, prompt sympathy of other families well-nigh as poor and hard-pressed as the bereaved. It is just here that the Mission has been able to exert a most beneficent influence. Families have been found in more favoured parts of the world willing to adopt the poor little orphans."
— *Among the Deep Sea Fishers*, July 1903

While the Moravian Mission was establishing stations and schools in northern Labrador, Inuit life in central and southern Labrador was following a different trajectory. Outside Moravian control, families in the region were free to maintain Inuit cultural practices that the missionaries farther north were trying to erase, such as spiritual beliefs, burial practices, and "shifting" between seasonal homes.[1] Inuit families were also free to associate with the growing tide of fishers and merchants from Newfoundland, Europe, and America who exploited the rich coastal resources of fish, whales, and seals each summer.

The fishing grounds attracted many to the coast. American whalers and fishers from New England travelled to southern Labrador in the 1700s and 1800s, bringing with them cheap goods to trade.[2] In the mid-1800s, a smaller French fishery brought over 1,200 fishers each year to the coast between the Strait of Belle Isle and Hamilton Inlet.[3] But the Newfoundland fishing fleet brought the largest wave of visitors to the region. Thousands of Newfoundlanders travelled each summer to fish "down on the Labrador," especially after the end of the Napoleonic Wars in 1815 when Newfoundland fishers were forbidden to fish along the French Shore in central and northern Newfoundland. In 1825, for example, over 260 ships carrying about 5,000 fishers sailed to Labrador to fish for the summer.[4] Most of the fishermen remained on their schooners for the fishing season. Others, known as stationers, claimed plots of land on the coast where they lived, dried fish, and stored equipment. Many stationers returned to these "rooms" year after year. Newfoundland and British merchants also established trading posts in the region, and they often hired servants or local people to guard their premises over the winter.[5]

The seasonal flood of fishermen to southern Labrador had a profound impact on the local population. Innu families spent much of their year inland, so they had little contact with the newcomers. But Inuit families lived on the coast during the summer and fished the same waters as

Fishing vessels, Indian Harbour, Labrador, before 1937 (courtesy of The Rooms).

the southern visitors. Although Inuit gained access to trade goods and trading partners, they faced intense competition for their resources. They also contracted infectious diseases and watched as these visitors depleted the environment. Some Inuit welcomed the European men as members of their family when stationers and trading post servants decided to start a new life in Labrador. A new mix of Inuit–European kinship developed that melded with the Inuit society of the region.[6] By the 1870s, about 1,000 to 1,300 permanent residents lived on the coast between Chateau Bay and Sandwich Bay.[7]

As elsewhere in Labrador, the Inuit and Inuit–European families (hereafter referred to as NunatuKavut Inuit) lived in dispersed homesteads. They fished for salmon, cod, and herring on the coast in the summer, and hunted migratory birds and seals in the fall. In the late fall, they moved to homes in sheltered and wooded bays for the winter, where they trapped for fur. Families lived in wooden houses during the summer and in sod houses or wooden structures during the winter.[8] European men relied on their Inuit partners for their knowledge of how to survive in the unforgiving territory. They relied on a network of Inuit family support that shared food and labour in times of need, and learned the skills needed to sustain themselves.[9]

By trapping, fishing, and hunting, the NunatuKavut Inuit families enjoyed a more diverse livelihood than the Newfoundlanders who relied solely on the summer fishing season, but both were entangled in the system of trade on the coast. In some years, the fishing was lucrative. More often, fishermen found themselves in debt to the Newfoundland merchants who controlled the market. The truck system, as it was called, was a cashless economy. Merchants equipped the fishermen with provisions and fishing gear at the beginning of the season on credit. At the end of the fishing season, they set the prices for both the fish and the goods taken on credit.[10] Fishermen found themselves dependent on the merchants and in constant debt. As a result, both Newfoundland and NunatuKavut Inuit families faced poverty and difficult working conditions. When combined with the resulting poor health and the almost complete absence of

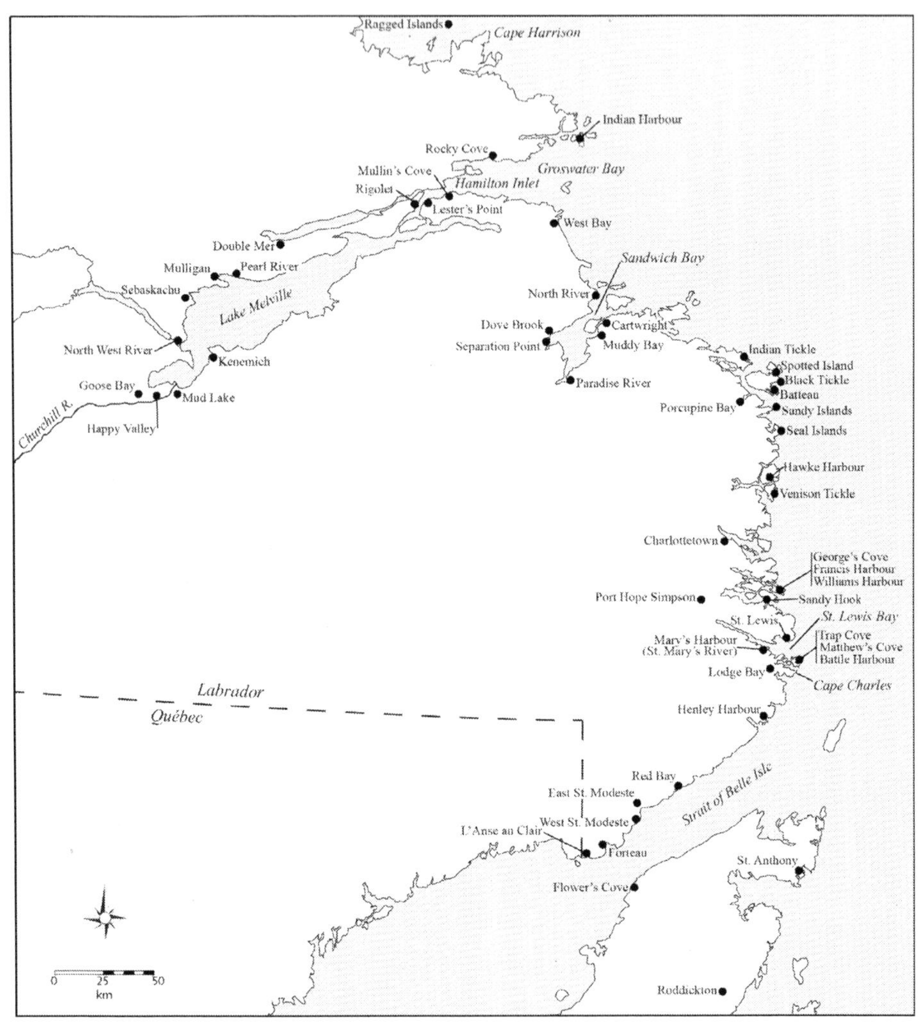

Map 3: Central and south coast of Labrador, and Northern Peninsula of Newfoundland (map by Peter Ramsden).

Pardy family, Huntington Island, Sandwich Bay, 1893 (back, l-r: Levi Pardy, Martha Davis Campbell, Lydia Campbell, and Tom; front, l-r: William, Alvina, Sarah Davis Pardy holding Harriet, Edward, Jim, and Manuel) (courtesy of The Rooms).

Newfoundland fisherman Joseph Goss and his wife, Inner Sandy Islands,1893 (courtesy of The Rooms).

government provision of justice, governance, and medicine, many endured hardship.[11]

News of the conditions in the isolated region reached the wider world in 1891. At the request of the Newfoundland government, Francis Hopwood, a member of the British Board of Trade and the Royal National Mission to Deep Sea Fishermen, travelled to Newfoundland to investigate the medical care given to coastal fishers in Labrador.[12] Outraged at what he discovered, Hopwood published an account of the fishermen's precarious life. He described their poverty and their perpetual dependence on merchants. His shocking account galvanized the public in Britain, Canada, and the United States to demand action.[13] The next summer, the Royal National Mission to Deep Sea Fishermen, a charitable organization dedicated to meeting the medical and spiritual needs of the British North Sea fishing fleet, sent a hospital ship to the Labrador coast. On board was a doctor named Wilfred Grenfell, who was sent to provide medical assistance to the fishermen.[14] The experience inspired the young Englishman to dedicate himself to activism in the region. As biographer Ronald Rompkey writes, "From the time [Grenfell] set foot in Labrador, he was seized with the desire to reform it."[15]

Charlotte Webber Paulo, Fox Harbour [St. Lewis], 1893 (courtesy of The Rooms).

Wilfred Grenfell convinced St. John's-based merchants to fund the Mission to Deep Sea Fishermen's medical work in the Labrador fishery. He returned in the following years to build small hospitals at Battle Harbour and Indian Harbour, central locations for the thousands of Newfoundland fishermen who descended on Labrador each summer.

When needed, the Mission also treated the local resident population of NunatuKavut Inuit, but the Mission's initial focus was on supporting the Newfoundland fishers.[16]

Grenfell worked tirelessly to extend medical services. He raised funds, convinced staff and volunteers to join him, and collected equipment for the work. He spent his summers travelling the coast in a hospital ship, tending to the migratory fishery and surveying their living and working conditions. In the winter, he toured across Canada, the United States, and Great Britain to raise more money for the new branch of the Mission to Deep Sea Fishermen that he called the Grenfell Mission.

In 1904, the Grenfell Mission opened its medical headquarters in St. Anthony on the Northern Peninsula of Newfoundland. The choice was strategic, as St. Anthony was located halfway between the Labrador fishing grounds and the home communities of the Newfoundland fishermen.[17] Over the next 75 years, the Grenfell Mission was to play a major role in the medical and social development of northern Newfoundland and Labrador.

The scope of the Mission soon extended far beyond the medical. Under Grenfell's influence, it expanded to encompass the social, economic,

Oliver family, Pottles Bay, Hamilton Inlet, 1893 (courtesy of The Rooms).

and educational affairs of the region. Grenfell believed that providing medical care was not enough to improve people's lives. Many of the health problems he encountered, including rickets, beri-beri, and tuberculosis, were the result of malnutrition, poor housing conditions, and poverty.[18] The Newfoundland fishermen's diet of white bread, tea, and salt cod was insufficient, and the truck system kept them in such debt that they struggled to improve their situation. What the region needed, Grenfell maintained, was social and economic development. Accordingly, the Mission organized local co-operative stores to break the merchants' monopoly on trade. It initiated nutritional education and agricultural projects, and a "no spitting" campaign to fight the spread of tuberculosis. It also established schools, a handicraft production program, and even an ill-fated experiment to introduce reindeer with their Sami herders to the Northern Peninsula.[19]

Wilfred Grenfell has been described as a social reformer, a "spiritual adventurer," and a "manly Christian."[20] Born in 1865, he was driven by Victorian notions of heroism, imperialism, and self-sacrifice for a higher purpose. From his earliest days in Newfoundland and Labrador, he spun a narrative about his role in the region that echoes these ideals. Enthusiastic supporters in 1903, for instance, boasted that Grenfell's arrival "was the most fortunate thing that ever happened to Labrador. For the misery that Dr. Grenfell encountered, the hopeless suffering he found, so cried out to him that he decided then and there to devote his life to bringing what alleviation he could to the unhappy souls that were imprisoned in ice for half the year, and cursed with privation and sickness always."[21]

Grenfell's initiatives were idealistic, but they often failed to engage local advice or participation. The Mission invited outside experts to the region to develop and organize programs. Equipped with British and American education, wealth, and confident know-how, Mission staff aimed to usher local people into the twentieth century. They saw Labradorians and northern Newfoundlanders as quaint and hard-working, but perhaps not capable of managing their own affairs. The control of the Mission's work, from its administration to the design of rug-hooking patterns, was therefore most often left to the Grenfell staff.[22] As anthropologist John Kennedy notes, Labrador and northern Newfoundland residents viewed these well-intentioned but often patronizing Grenfell workers with a mix of appreciation and resentment.[23]

According to his biographers, Grenfell was a mediocre doctor.[24] But his energy, charisma, and determination to effect social reform in northern Newfoundland and Labrador attracted many Americans, Britons, and Canadians to his cause. The Grenfell Mission relied almost completely on philanthropic support. After several disputes with the Mission to Deep Sea Fishermen about the cost and direction of its efforts, the International Grenfell Association (IGA) was incorporated in 1914.[25] The IGA included the branch committees that Grenfell had established in Canada, the United States, and Great Britain. These branches were crucial to the IGA's fund-raising efforts. Often driven by "lively and resourceful women," they collected money and donations of clothing, toys, and hospital equipment for the Mission.[26] The IGA's Board of Directors, based in New York City, was responsible for the financial and administrative management of the organization. It represented the Grenfell Association of America, the Grenfell Association of Great Britain and Ireland, the New England Grenfell Association, the Grenfell-Labrador Medical Mission, and the Grenfell Association of Newfoundland.[27]

From the hospital headquarters in St. Anthony, Grenfell and his staff ran summer hospitals at Indian Harbour and Battle Harbour. They relied on the Mission hospital ship to transport patients, staff, and goods throughout the region. When the English doctor Harry Paddon joined the Mission in 1912, he identified the need for a winter hospital in central Labrador as well. Paddon established himself first at Mud Lake and then at North West River.[28] As the organization grew, the Battle Harbour hospital became a year-round institution. The complex at St. Anthony expanded to include a school, orphanage, and Industrial Department. The IGA later built other nursing stations in Labrador and northern Newfoundland, including at Cartwright, Spotted Island, St. Mary's River (Mary's Harbour), Forteau, Flower's Cove, and Roddickton.[29] It also built

Grenfell Mission wops (workers without pay), St. Anthony, 1912. (l-r: William Logan Fox from Harvard University, S. Frederick Cushman from Amherst College, William Moore Carson Jr. from Harvard University, and Mr. Raley from Oxford University) (courtesy of The Rooms).

schools, co-operatives, and handicraft centres in various communities, and established itself as a leader in community development.

As Grenfell's fame grew, doctors, nurses, and volunteer workers flocked to the IGA. Most came from wealthy families in Britain and the United States, drawn to the opportunity for meaningful work. Many highly trained professionals offered years of dedicated service in communities throughout the region. Until the start of World War II, it was fashionable for students from elite American colleges to travel north each summer to volunteer as wops (workers without pay) at the Grenfell stations.[30] Harvard University students worked at St. Anthony; Yale University students went to North West River; Columbia University medical students worked at Spotted Island; and Johns Hopkins students went to Battle Harbour.[31] They volunteered as teachers, medical assistants, or manual labourers, acquiring valuable life experience and satisfaction from helping others. They also gained membership into the Grenfell social network of prominent and wealthy Americans. IGA staff and volunteers formed many fond memories and relationships with each other, and their solidarity ensured that support for the IGA continued long after they returned home, in the form of financial donations and well-attended reunions. Within communities in Labrador and northern Newfoundland, however, the Grenfell staff's education, privilege, and habit of maintaining an elite social clique often alienated local residents.[32] IGA staff made it clear that they were socially distinct from the people they had come to help.

A great publicist, Grenfell wrote many books and pamphlets, and went on lecture tours promoting his work. He relied on stories of extreme poverty and suffering to invoke sympathy among potential supporters, exaggerating and embellishing as needed. His fundraising efforts targeted the wealthy classes of New England, Canada, and Britain, who were willing audiences for stories of hardship. Those closer to home often felt more ambivalent about his fundraising approach. Grenfell's tales of misery riled the Newfoundland establishment, who complained that his stories harmed their business interests and created a poor image of the colony. In 1917, their complaints even launched an inquiry into the IGA's use of its charitable status in its economic efforts, but the organization was cleared of any wrongdoing.[33]

In his public lectures and promotional writing, Grenfell often capitalized on tales of suffering children, many of whom were Inuit. Aiming for greatest impact, he knew that stories about innocent children garnered more sympathy than stories about grown fishermen. In one of his most publicized stories, Grenfell describes his rescue of "Prince Pomiuk." Pomiuk was a young Inuk boy who had been on display at the Eskimo Village at Chicago's 1893 World Fair. The American promoters of the exhibit had given him the title of "Prince" because his father was an Inuit leader in Nachvak. Pomiuk suffered physical abuse at the hands of his stepfather in Chicago, and by the time he returned to Labrador his injuries had become badly infected.[34] Grenfell's story begins with finding Pomiuk "naked and haggard, suffering from an insidious hip disease, lying on the rocks beside a tiny tubik [tent]" at Nachvak.[35] The doctor took him aboard the Mission ship and brought him to the Battle Harbour

Pomiuk on deck of the *Sir Donald*, ca. 1896 (courtesy of The Rooms).

hospital. Through his fundraising efforts, Grenfell garnered financial sponsorship from a congregation in New England for the "Corner Cot" that Pomiuk occupied.[36] Hospital staff cared for the boy until his final days. "In a sheltered corner of a little graveyard on the Labrador," Grenfell wrote, "rests the body of this 'happy Prince.'"[37] The Mission used Pomiuk's story for years afterwards to encourage support for its work. "There are others still as desolate as was Pomiuk," noted an article in the 1904 issue of the Grenfell magazine, *Among the Deep Sea Fishers*: "many little sufferers to fill the cots as fast as they can be provided in the hospitals."[38]

Elizabeth Kirkina Jeffreys Mucko was another Inuk child who features in Grenfell's stories. Born in 1893, she also benefited from the charity of the same "Cornerers" congregation in New England a few years after Pomiuk's death. At four years old, Elizabeth had frozen both legs at her home in Groswater Bay. To prevent gangrene from spreading, her father had chopped off her lower legs with an axe. As some versions of the story go, Grenfell staff brought her to the Indian Harbour hospital where she learned English.[39] Wilfred Grenfell renamed her "Kirkina," and the name stuck. A nurse took her to school in Halifax, and on returning to Labrador she stayed at the Battle Harbour hospital for two more years. The resident doctor, John McPherson, made her a temporary set of artificial legs, which the "Cornerers" congregation later replaced with cork legs. When Dr. McPherson and his wife returned to their home in New England, they decided to take Kirkina with them and, "with true Christ-like love and pity, to provide for the child."[40] Grenfell conveyed the story to show the Christian charity and generosity of the Mission's work:

> Does not the record of this little girl's life, as it is, and as it might have been, bring home to us all the grand work the Mission is doing, and which would be left undone but for it. This is only one of many cases where a life of constant suffering has been changed into one of health and usefulness — and you and I may have the gladness and honor of sharing in this Christ-like work if we will.[41]

Benjamin Cumby (on crutches) and Kirkina Jeffreys, Battle Harbour, 1909 (courtesy of The Rooms).

Kirkina lived with the McPhersons until she returned to Labrador as a young adult, at which point she learned that her father had died in 1897, shortly after she had first been taken to the hospital as a child. While her Grenfell caregivers had known of his death, they had not shared the news with her. In anger and grief, she threw her artificial legs over the side of the ship. She spent the rest of her life in Labrador. After losing her husband in 1920, she trained and served as a nurse in Rigolet and Happy Valley. Four decades after her death in 1970, a women's shelter opened in Rigolet and was named in her honour.[42]

Labrador Inuit were not the Grenfell Mission's initial focus, but they played a disproportionately large role in the IGA's fundraising efforts. Pomiuk, Kirkina, and other Inuit children featured prominently in Grenfell publications and funding campaigns. The IGA's Industrial Department sold hooked mats and embroidered handicrafts with Inuit figures and motifs in New England, Canada, and Britain. The "Innuits, children of the Northland," as Wilfred Grenfell patronizingly called them, provided the IGA with a marketable image that served the organization well over its years of fundraising.[43]

In its early days, the Grenfell Mission approached the challenge of poverty in Labrador and northern Newfoundland by finding a solution elsewhere. Grenfell and his staff sought to help children from poor or struggling families by sending them away to live with other families. "In my boyhood," Grenfell wrote, "I used to collect postage stamps, butterflies, and birds' eggs. When we sailed to Labrador, however . . . I started to collect children."[44] Among the first were a little girl and her brother whose parents had died and left them destitute. Grenfell took them to a family in England, "and today, forty years later, they can look back on a happy and useful life."[45] Others included an abandoned five- or six-year-old who was adopted by the British skipper of the Mission hospital ship. In a 1903 letter to Grenfell, the skipper described how happy he was with the little girl:

> She is all that one could wish. My wife was very pleased with her, and she is a little lump of love. If I had a pick of ten thousand children — and that is a lot to say — I would not pick a better child. . . . There have been two or three people asking if Dr. Grenfell had got any more like her, and if so, ask him to send them along. . . . I will endeavor to do as far as lies in my power for her. I want her trained for the Lord, because I believe she was sent from Him for a purpose. Please send me her age, if you can tell

> it, because we should like her to have a birthday. Praying that God may make you a power for good, I remain, yours sincerely, S. Farman.[46]

Grenfell sent other girls to Canada, the United States, and England for work and training as ward maids and domestic workers. "I have taken away to be trained quite a number this year," he wrote in 1902, "and some good friends in Canada are acting as a sort of registry and home on a small scale to look after them, when they have found them places, and try to see that they are happy and well trained."[47] The following year, the Mission reported that "Dr. Grenfell has this year taken seven girls from poor homes on the coast and found them good situations."[48] The parents of one such girl wrote a letter to show their support for Grenfell's proposal to take her away:

> Hunt's River, Sept. 13, 1903.
> Dear Dockter Granvil.
> I received your kind letter about E___, and she is willing to go, and both me and my wife have consented. We know that you will look after her and see that she is in a good place. . . . Dear Dockter we know who you are, and what you is. We know that you are doing your best for God's people wherever you go. . . . We all pray for you dear Dockter.[49]

The Grenfell Mission also instituted the practice of sending students away to the United States, Britain, and Canada for education early in the twentieth century. Exceptional students from across Labrador and the Northern Peninsula pursued higher education at institutes elsewhere, funded by Mission supporters. Edgar ("Ted") McNeill from Island Harbour, Labrador, was Grenfell's "first scholar."[50] He was educated by Moravian missionaries in Makkovik, and then asked to work for Grenfell in return for more education. After attending school in St. Anthony, he went to the Pratt Institute in New York in 1908. He returned to work for the

Mission in St. Anthony as a construction foreman and superintendent of Mission buildings.[51] In 1927, he built the hospital in St. Anthony, and another Pratt graduate from Labrador, Wilfred Mesher, installed the heating and lighting system in the hospital.[52]

When Wilfred Grenfell in 1909 married Anne MacClanahan, a wealthy and well-connected woman from Chicago, the scholarship project became her focus. Under her leadership, the program expanded in size. In 1921, the Carnegie Corporation of New York agreed to provide grants of up to $5,000 per year for seven years for the scholarships.[53] Students attended the Pratt Institute in New York, the Wentworth Institute in Boston, Berea College in Kentucky, nurses' training schools, business schools, and other institutions in the United States.[54] Other students later went to Ryerson Institute of Technology in Toronto and to other Canadian schools. Between 1921 and 1928, over 89 young people from Labrador and northern Newfoundland obtained training through the scholarship program.[55] On their return home, most applied their skills in the schools, dormitories, orphanage, hospitals, and offices of the IGA stations. As

Students educated abroad by the IGA, 1920s. Front left: Violet Stone Moores from Battle Harbour; back right: Horace McNeill from St. Anthony. Also in photo: Edmund Pike from Port Saunders; Alice Simms from St. Anthony; Michael Walsh from Flower's Cove; and Winnifred Pye from Cape Charles (courtesy of The Rooms).

Anne Grenfell commented in 1927, the students received an education that promised to transform both them and their communities:

> They have brought home very different standards and ideals of living than they could have acquired otherwise, and their own people would naturally be more influenced by their report and their teaching than they could be by that of the staff of the Grenfell Association.[56]

The Mission offered transformative higher education opportunities for exceptional children, but for others it aimed simply to remove them from their home situations. Mission personnel saw poverty and cultural difference when they looked on families in the region, and their solution was often to take children away. Some children went willingly with the Mission, with their family's approval, but others were taken by force from their homes by Grenfell staff. Grenfell had been appointed as magistrate for the region, and he often exercised his authority to make unilateral decisions about other people's lives. In his autobiography, for example, Grenfell describes how he decided to "rescue" two young boys from their family in Eskimo Bay (Hamilton Inlet):

> We soon found the two small boys. They were practically stark naked, but fat as curlews, being full of wild berries with which their bodies were stained bright blues and reds. They were a jolly little couple, as unconcerned about their environment as Robinson Crusoe after five years on his island.
>
> Soon the father came home. I can see him still — the vacant brown face of a very feeble-minded half-breed, ragged and tattered and almost bootless. He was carrying an aged single-barrelled boy's gun in one hand and a belated sea-gull in the other, which bird was destined for the entire evening meal of the family. A half-wild-looking hobbledehoy boy of fifteen years also joined the group. It was just beginning to snow, a wet sleet.

> Eight months of winter lay ahead. Yet not one of the family seemed to think a whit about that which was vivid enough to the minds of the mate and myself.
>
> We sat down for a regular pow-wow beside the fire sputtering in the open room, from which thick smoke crept up the face of the rock, and hung over us in a material but symbolic cloud. It was naturally cold. The man began with a plea for some "clodin." We began with a plea for some children. How many would he swap for a start in clothing and "tings for his winter"? He picked out and gave us Jimmie. The soft-hearted mate, on whose cheeks the tears were literally standing, grabbed Jimmie — as the latter did his share of the gull.
>
> But we were not satisfied. We had to have Willie. It was only when a breaking of diplomatic relations altogether was threatened that Willie was sacrificed on the altar of "tings." I forget the price, but I think that we threw in an axe, which was one of the trifles which the father lacked — and in this of all countries! The word was no sooner spoken than our shellback again excelled himself. He pounced on Willie like a hawk on its prey, and before the treaty was really concluded he was off to our dory with a naked boy kicking violently in the vice of each of his powerful arms.[57]

Grenfell's depiction of taking the boys — James and William Shuglo[58] — illustrates his certainty that he is doing the right thing. He is equally confident that his audience will also approve of his actions. The story positions the doctor as benevolent and wise — vastly superior to the "feeble-minded half-breed" father, who is portrayed as socially deficient and incapable of supporting his family. In this story and in others told throughout the early years of the Grenfell Mission, the heroes are clearly Grenfell and his staff, who describe themselves as saving the poor children from the wretched hand-to-mouth existence of Indigenous life. The British, American, and Canadian public embraced this story and rewarded the Grenfell Mission with generous donations. Grenfell was knighted in

1927 by King George V for his medical, educational, and social work, and "Sir Wilfred" was celebrated as one of the greatest medical missionaries of his time.[59] Although failing health forced him to cut back his activities by the end of the 1920s (he would die in 1940) and he formally resigned his management of the Mission's work in early 1936, the work Grenfell began would carry on.[60]

The Grenfell Mission's attempts to improve the lives of orphaned or poor children changed over time. Its practice of removing children from Labrador and northern Newfoundland to the United States or Britain peaked in the early 1900s. The organization then adopted other approaches to child welfare. One of the new approaches involved establishing an orphanage for what Grenfell called his "increasing family" of destitute children.[61] As the next chapter will show, the "Children's Home" in St. Anthony played a prominent role over the next 60 years in the lives of many children from Labrador and northern Newfoundland. "Even though Gabriel, Prince Pomiuk, never lived within its walls," Grenfell wrote, "the real beginning of the idea of our Children's Home was due to him; and one feels sure that his spirit loves to visit the other little ones who claim this lonely coast as their homeland also."[62]

CHAPTER EIGHT

The Children's Home at St. Anthony

"A little helpless child was presented to us to care for, and later, five more whose father . . . had died. It wasn't a question of wanting to take them. By all the laws of humanity we had to take care of them, so we did."
— Wilfred Grenfell, January 1920

In the early years of the Grenfell Mission, Wilfred Grenfell and his staff arranged for the adoption of children they felt needed to be removed from a difficult home life. Grenfell relates how he "rescued" children from poverty, neglect, or ill-health by sending them to live with families in the United States, Canada, or Britain, to hospitals, or to the care of Grenfell Mission staff members.[1] As doctor and magistrate, Grenfell believed he had the authority to apprehend children and make decisions about their future. But finding homes for the children could be difficult. Grenfell staff started to reconsider the wisdom of sending children to live in other countries. An orphanage that kept the children in the region appeared to be a better option. But where to put them?

In 1904, the Indian Harbour hospital doctor and his wife took in a few children, including "Emmie, Prissie [Priscie], and Tommy [Roberts from Seal Islands], orphan children of an excellent man . . . who died last winter."[2] When Indian Harbour closed for the winter, Dr. George Simpson and his wife May moved with their new wards to the Grenfell hospital at St. Anthony. May Simpson took the lead on organizing supplies for an orphanage. An English nurse, she had worked at Indian Harbour before marrying the doctor. "I am sure you will be very much interested in our orphanage and more so in the three children we had with us last winter as its first instalment," she wrote to supporters. "The training of children is most delicate work, touching as it does the Unformed characters of our men and women of the future, but it is very interesting and enjoyable. Dr. and I found our winter very happy with them around."[3] On closing the letter, she provided a detailed list of the types and quantities of clothing that Mission donors could send to the new orphanage.

Emma White and children at St. Anthony orphanage, ca.1910 (courtesy of The Rooms).

In 1904, St. Anthony was a small but growing village. The Methodist church and the Grenfell Mission hospital, co-operative store, and guest house sat on one side of the harbour, facing the Church of England and houses on the other.[4] The hospital had opened in March 1904, but it was not a suitable place for the orphanage; the children needed a building of their own. In the fall of 1904, the Grenfell Mission started building "a small house in which we might accommodate a dozen orphan children."[5]

Construction of the orphanage continued over the next year, with local people hauling logs and Mission carpenters working to erect the building. "We hope," Grenfell wrote in 1905, "that we shall be able to place our children in the new building before the winter is too far advanced to do any more work at it."[6]

An "Orphanage for Helpless Children"

The Children's Home, as it was called, officially opened in 1906 with seven children. Four came from Labrador: the two older Roberts children, Emmie (age 12) and Tommy (10) (while their younger sister, Priscie [2], went to live with a Captain Ash in St. Anthony),[7] their cousin, Davy Gill (10), also from Seal Islands, and John Newell (14) from Winter's Cove in Hamilton Inlet.[8] The other three children came from Newfoundland's Northern Peninsula: Lizzie Hedderson (7) and her brother James (5) from Noddy Bay, and Hayward Patey (12) from HaHa Bay.

All of the children except for Hayward had lost one parent, and the Grenfell staff felt they needed care. At the 1906 Grenfell Mission annual meeting, Dr. Simpson described how the Roberts children were "living on scraps which the neighbours could ill afford to let them have."[9]

> I shall never forget going to get these children. The father had died, and the mother, poor soul, did not know what she was going to do in the winter — absolute starvation faced her. We pleaded with her to let us have the children. What was she to do?[10]

Along with the Roberts children, the Simpsons had also taken John Newell and Davy Gill into their care at the Indian Harbour hospital a few years before the orphanage was established. John's father had died, and his older brother had been looking after the other four children. According to the IGA records, John had a weak constitution, "having been starved most of his life," but was "a quiet lad and a good worker" with the "straight black hair and the olive complexion of the Eskimo."[11] He had spent time recovering in the St. Anthony hospital before moving into the Children's Home in 1906. Dr. Simpson described Davy Gill as "one of the flotsam and jetsam of this wild coast, having no home" after his mother had died.[12] The Hedderson children's father had also died the previous winter, and Grenfell staff found their mother and her five children living in a neighbour's home.[13] Hayward Patey lived with an uncle because his parents could not support him. He came to the orphanage for 10 months while he underwent treatment for his eyes, and although the Grenfell staff wanted him to stay longer, they reported that "his uncle insisted on having him back."[14]

After settling these children in St. Anthony, Dr. and Mrs. Simpson returned to England. The Children's Home needed a house parent to look after the group, so Grenfell searched for someone "who understood the problem of running the Home. She — how often it is 'she' — was found in England, a volunteer by the name of Eleanor Storr."[15] Miss Storr, a "lady of social rank" with a midwife's certificate, came to St. Anthony "at her own expense . . . because," according to Grenfell, "she thought she could work better miracles in a Labrador orphanage than she could in her London house."[16]

On the front of the orphanage a large wooden sign proclaimed, "SUFFER LITTLE CHILDREN TO COME UNTO ME." The biblical text (Matthew 19:14) quotes Jesus, who told his disciples, "Suffer little children and forbid them not to come unto me, for of such is the kingdom of heaven." The passage suggests that even the small and weak deserve care and that heaven will be open to those who, like children, are humble and meek. A Baptist church in Roxbury, Massachusetts, had made the sign and had sent it to the orphanage as a gift for its opening.[17]

Jessie Luther, a crafts teacher from New England who helped create the Grenfell hooked mat industry, arrived in St. Anthony in 1906. She witnessed the first years of the Children's Home: "The orphanage, not fully completed but livable, is a frame house without cellar, the walls bare boards, the outside clapboarded. The seven orphans, varying in age from five to fifteen years, assist in the housework. Miss Storr and Miss Bayley have done the cooking."[18] Jessie introduced the art of weaving to residents in the community and patients at the hospital as both an economic skill and occupational therapy. She also encouraged children at the orphanage to learn the technique.

> One of the orphanage children, twelve-year-old Emmie [Roberts] from Labrador, is bright and so capable I have taught her to make warps and wind bobbins. There are two looms ready, one for pattern weaving, one for homespun. Emmie is now making a heavy warp for rugs. She seems interested and is willing to work for a while without interruption, which I was told might be doubtful.[19]

Mary "Mae" Bird Burton was another of the early wards of the new Children's Home. She arrived when she was four and stayed there until she was 17 before returning home:[20]

> I went to the orphanage in St. Anthony, Newfoundland in 1908 when I was only four years old. There wasn't very many children there then, I was the youngest of them all.
>
> My mother, Emeline Martin (Mrs. Thomas Martin) was left a widow at Cartwright. She had been born somewhere down around Mulligan, near North West River. When my father died, she was left with six of us to rear up, three older than myself. . . .
>
> In the spring or summer, when I was four years old, Doctor Grenfell came in the *Strathcona* [the Grenfell Mission hospital ship] and took me to the orphanage at St. Anthony. There was a doctor's wife on board, Mrs. Stewart, and when we came to

> Spotted Islands, they brought a boy aboard by the name of Albert Elson. I got used to Mrs. Stewart and Albert. Albert would look after me when we were out on the deck.
>
> When we got to St. Anthony, they had to tie me on with a little horse's rein to keep me from running away as I wanted to go to Mrs. Stewart. The next day, they started calling me Mae (at that time there were two other Marys and another Lydia). As I was the new one, they took the R out of Mary and called me Mae. I would yell and tell them my name wasn't Mae. . . .
>
> We had good times at the Orphanage. Of course we had all kinds of rules to go by, and also the bell. The bell would ring before every meal so you would have to wash and stand in your place at the table and wait for Grace. You could not speak one word while at the table or you would have to leave the room. I guess, since it was all English matrons, it was English rules. They were very strict. We went to bed early every night, the oldest of us at 7:30 pm. We had work to do after supper, so we would hurry through that and try to get out for a few minutes to play Cat, baseball as it is called now. Now I have the Matrons and the Orphanage to thank for my good health. . . . I often wondered, after I grew up and went back to Cartwright, why I was the only one sent to the Orphanage as there were three older than me and two younger. Mother didn't really know.[21]

The original orphanage building was built to accommodate 25 children. In 1909, renovations doubled its capacity, thanks to a donation from Francis Sayre, a volunteer at the orphanage in the summer of 1908.[22] Sayre was the type of wealthy American volunteer that Grenfell tried to recruit for the Mission — as the son of the vice-president of Bethlehem Steel, and the future son-in-law of American President Woodrow Wilson, Sayre proved to be a valuable connection.[23] The orphanage housed 18 children in 1910; in 1911, 12 girls, aged five to 17, and 12 boys, aged six to 15, lived there.[24] The number of children kept growing. In 1917, the

The St. Anthony orphanage, partially financed by Francis Sayre, ca.1909 (courtesy of The Rooms).

orphanage housed 37 children.[25] Mission staff began to think about replacing the wooden building with a larger, more durable brick structure.

The orphanage numbers increased in part because of Wilfred Grenfell's impulsiveness and high-handedness. According to his biographer, J. Lennox Kerr, his enthusiasm for collecting children for the orphanage seemed endless:

> [Grenfell] picked up children and brought them to St. Anthony, with no thought for the fact that the orphanage there was already overcrowded and that, no matter how eager the staff were to save more children, there were physical limits. He just dumped the children on the wharf and left some one to "finish the job."[26]

Like many initiatives that Grenfell started, other members of the Mission had to tackle the work and manage the everyday realities. His methods exasperated many of the IGA staff. The surgeon at the St. Anthony hospital in the early 1900s, John Little, disagreed with Grenfell's focus. "Grenfell built an orphanage, which Dr. Little didn't approve of at that time because he thought the hospital was much more important," wrote an IGA doctor years afterwards.[27] Frustrated with the situation, Dr. Little resigned in 1917. But Grenfell continued to concentrate on the orphanage work.

Determined to take in as many children as he could, Grenfell sometimes resorted to coercion in convincing parents to allow their children to live at the orphanage. In 1905, for example, he asked a father for permission to "take care of and educate a small derelict boy of 10 years of age" from Seal Islands — a cousin of the Roberts children, David "Davy" Gill.[28] The father refused. "It so happened," Grenfell related, "that police constable Dawe . . . was with me at the time."[29] The constable, taking Grenfell's side, "skillfully portrayed the terrors of the law that were sure to overtake any who neglect their children." The intimidation worked. "He finally succeeded in persuading the man to let the child go. His uniform

Wilfred Grenfell with St. Anthony orphanage children, 1930 (courtesy of The Rooms).

the first ever seen here, was his most persuasive argument."[30] The IGA's records for the Children's Home contain other examples of similar coercion, as well as cases of parents refusing to give up their children.[31] Most records state that IGA staff brought the child to the orphanage, without details of the transaction, but a few describe parents asking the IGA to take their children.[32]

In 1918, the Spanish flu swept through the orphanage, infecting nearly everyone and killing Elizabeth "Bessie" Blake from the Rigolet area on 23 November.[33] Earlier in the year, Noah Karle from Davis Inlet had died from tuberculosis.[34] Katie Spalding, who had taken over administration of the orphanage from Eleanor Storr in 1916, reported the sad news:

> For the first time in the history of the Orphanage we have to record the loss from death of two of our children. In March our eldest boy, who had developed tuberculosis more than a year ago, died in the hospital where he had been a patient since the previous summer. In the fall of this year the Orphanage suffered from an epidemic of Spanish influenza from which only three of the children escaped. Several were very sick and one girl of sixteen unhappily developed pneumonia and died after a few days' illness. This was the only case of pneumonia we had, and, considering the serious nature of the epidemic, it is a cause for great gratitude that all the others recovered without complication.[35]

The epidemic devastated Labrador, killing many in Sandwich Bay and almost the entire populations of Okak and Hebron.[36] The victims of the Spanish flu were often adults, so many children in the region lost one or both parents in the epidemic. In Sandwich Bay, where over 70 people had died in a district of 320, almost 40 children lost one or both parents.[37] Family members took in most of these children until Rev. Henry Gordon built a boarding school at Muddy Bay in 1920 (see Chapter Nine), but several were sent to the St. Anthony orphanage. In a 1976 interview, Edward Pardy described how two of his siblings were taken to the orphanage after

Children's Page

HAVE YOU A PLACE IN YOUR HEART FOR US?

By Etta V. Leighton

THAT is the message the cold north wind is bringing us from down North and even if by the time it reaches our far South or our golden California, the wind itself has grown warm and pleasant, the message is still as penetrating, still as searching as when the north wind took it up from the sighs of little orphans in Newfoundland and the Labrador.

We understand it the minute the breeze brings it to our ears, for it comes from little children speaking our language and even thinking our thoughts. For the blood that flows in the veins of these little orphans is the same as that which flowed in the veins of Abraham Lincoln and Garfield and Jackson and Grant. Back of these children stretches the splendid line of heroes we all love, and in their little hearts is the same courage that Daniel Boone and the other heroes we read of in history showed when they lived under the hard conditions of the frontier.

THE WORLD NEEDS COURAGE.

Today the world needs courage more than ever, and the little children of the lands served by the Grenfell Mission are born to courage. Their fathers and mothers are full of courage and keep on hoping even when the fishing is bad or the hunting fails, and it is only when poverty and disease and death are too strong for them that their little ones come finally to the shelter of the orphanage.

You remember how in the war time we would do anything to help the soldier in the front line trenches? Well Labrador and Newfoundland are front line trenches, the frontiers of civilization. We must help the people who live there to fill that country with prosperous happy homes, just as Daniel Boone and Abraham Lincoln's father and the thousands of other pioneers changed our wilderness into a rich country.

Newfoundland and the Labrador are very beautiful and the children there love the high cliffs, the rushing waves, the majestic icebergs, the great forests with a deep love. But it takes a strong, healthy people to live in such a country, and little ones who lose one or both parents can not grow strong and courageous when they haven't enough food, no warm clothes, no comfortable homes. We are cheating the world of the courage it needs, if through carelessness, we leave one little orphan uncared for.

WELL BEGUN IS HALF DONE.

The new orphanage *is* well begun. Think of the hard work done in digging out the cellar! All those big boulders that you saw in the pictures in the October magazine had to be hauled out by men and dogs. Oh, it was hard! Have you worked as hard to earn and buy bricks as you would have to work to dig out even *one* of those great rocks?

CHILDREN BRINGING BRICKS TO THE ORPHANS

EACH BRICK IN PLACE COSTS 25 CENTS
WILL YOU HELP BY SENDING 20 BRICKS?

Keep the Picture but send this slip with the money and your name and address to

The Grenfell Association of America, Inc.
156 Fifth Avenue, New York City

Fundraising for St. Anthony orphanage in the January 1921 issue of *Among the Deep Sea Fishers.*

their parents died of the flu near Cartwright: "Jim and [Henry] went to St. Anthony. Dr Grenfell took 'em. And I stayed with Uncle John Learning."[38] The IGA records lists four children from Sandwich Bay who were admitted into the Children's Home in September 1919: Katie Lethbridge (10) and her brother, William Lethbridge (8), from Grady, and Levi James Pardy (13) and Silas Henry Pardy (6) from Packs Harbour/Mountaineer Cove.[39] The Lethbridges' father was dead, and both parents of the two Pardy children had died of the flu, leaving six children.[40]

Wilfred Grenfell informed the Newfoundland colonial secretary that the Mission was doing its best to care for children affected by the Spanish flu, despite the almost complete lack of assistance from the Newfoundland government:[41] "I have assumed the care of just as many destitute children as I can provide for at St. Anthony, as well as one widow, and together with the Reverend Mr. Gordon [at Muddy Bay] we are making preparations to see that as few more as possible die from neglect."[42]

With the growing number of children at the orphanage, the IGA decided it needed a larger building. It launched a Brick Orphanage Fund campaign to raise funds for the construction of a new Children's Home. The IGA's magazine, *Among the Deep Sea Fishers*, featured various appeals for donations: donors could pay 25 cents per brick, $2,500 to endow a room, $450 to pay for a schoolteacher's salary, or $125 to care for a child in the Children's Home for a year.[43]

To build support for the cause, orphanage superintendent Katie Spalding wrote a book in 1920 with Dr. Grenfell's wife, Anne. The book consisted of fictional letters from an orphanage superintendent that offered witty depictions of conditions in the old building:

> Feb 28: This building rocks like a ship at sea; the roof continually leaks, the windows are always "coming abroad," and the panes drop out at "scattered times," while even when shut, the wind whistles through as if to show his utter disdain of our inhospitable and paltry efforts to keep him outside. On stormy nights, in spite of closed windows, the rooms resemble huge snowdrifts.[44]

A Boston church magazine also ran an advertisement in 1918 for "the Children's Brick Home Fund, Dr. Grenfell's Home for Labrador Orphans."[45] The ad reminded the public of the children that Grenfell had famously "rescued:" "Let us honor the memory of Pomiuk, Tommy, Kirkina and their companions by providing room for these homeless children."[46] "Have You a Place in your Heart for Us?" asks another advertisement in the January 1921 issue of *Among the Deep Sea Fishers*, with an illustration of "children bringing bricks to the orphans."[47]

The campaign motivated many to donate to the project, including charitable foundations, Sunday school groups, and hundreds of individuals from the United States, Canada, and Britain. Most of the individual donors were women, the names of whom are listed in the back of the IGA's publications.[48] By 1920, the campaign had raised almost $30,000 from the multitude of people who donated $2 or $25 towards the cause.[49] Many American college students volunteered to help dig the foundations of the new building in St. Anthony. "The[se volunteers] certainly did credit to Yale, Harvard, Princeton, and their various schools and colleges," Grenfell wrote. "They christened themselves as usual by the honourable title of 'The Wops' [workers without pay]."[50]

The brick orphanage was completed in 1922. The new three-storey building looked "simply magnificent in its solidity and its design for economy and convenience."[51] It provided beds for 50 children and featured a modern kitchen, running water, and electricity. The new orphanage superintendent, Frances Baier of Troy, New York, took over from Harriot Houghteling, a childhood friend of Anne Grenfell.[52] The children moved from the old building to the new one on 13 December 1922, and the orphanage hosted an open house on New Year's Day. About 160 people from St. Anthony and the surrounding area joined the children and staff to inspect and celebrate the new building.[53]

Millicent Blake Loder from Rigolet was one of the children to live in the new orphanage. She represented a new type of boarder — a student from Labrador who came to St. Anthony to continue her education. Millicent had completed Grade 6 at the Labrador Public School in Muddy Bay

The new brick St. Anthony orphanage, 1945 (courtesy of The Rooms).

and travelled to St. Anthony in 1928 to get her final three grades. The orphanage became her home while she attended school. In her memoir, *Daughter of Labrador*, she describes her memories of the place:

> I can recall quite clearly my first sight of St. Anthony. . . . Up from the wharf were several large buildings that belonged to the IGA. There was a large shed and farther up, enclosed by fences, was a large yellow box-like building. This was the orphanage, where we were to live.
>
> Five Labrador girls and a number of boys had come to attend school that year. We were met and warmly welcomed by a jolly, smiling, motherly sort of lady. This was Miss Karpik, the Head Mistress. Her greeting convinced me from the first that this school would be more to my liking than Muddy Bay. Miss Karpik took us around to our room. This was called the Labrador Girls' Room. Other children are everywhere in the halls and

> in the dining room. Some had been there for years, while others were newcomers as we were. The dining room had lots of tables and when we all filed in they were all full. It was like a big family.
>
> Miss Karpik and her helpers sat at the table with us, quite a change from Muddy Bay. Miss Karpik told us all about the rules and regulations. She told us that she would be glad to help us out with anything at any time. I loved her from the first. . . . I told Eva [Shiwak] I was going to like it here. After we got in bed we chatted about the place, the Head Mistress and expectations for the future. We fell asleep happy.[54]

With the larger building, the number of children grew. Sixty children lived in the orphanage each year in the early 1930s, and between 65 and 75 lived there in the mid-1940s.[55] For the first time, the IGA hired co-superintendents for the Children's Home. Linwood Brown and his wife Rachel took over administration of the orphanage from 1936 to 1945. The couple had worked at a children's home in New York State, and both "have had training in the management of children along modern lines."[56] Linwood tried to enforce the use of the name, "The Children's Home"

The interior of the new St. Anthony orphanage, after 1923 (courtesy of The Rooms).

instead of "The Orphanage," but the original name stuck. Unofficially, the new building was also known as the "cracker box" or the "old biscuit box."[57] Rachel Brown, a trained nurse, described the layout of the building during their time there:

> A corner light area kitchen, with a monstrous wood-burning iron stove, whose ovens would bake-off a dozen loaves of bread at a time. . . . The laundry room was next with huge set of tubs, and yes, hand scrub boards! . . . There was also a huge food storage room, which was well secured by locks! Many staple foods came in barrels: flour, sugar, molasses. There were bins for root vegetables, shelves for canned goods, and more perishable foods. In addition, there was a large shower room, washroom and toilets for boys use. Across the hall was a work shop. . . .
>
> First floor dining rooms were for the children, and there was a serving kitchen where the food was sent up from the kitchen by "dum-waiter" [*sic*]. Sinks for washing and sterilizing dishes were used at mealtimes. Two rooms off this serving kitchen provided the domestic help with dining and sitting rooms. The staff dining room, living room, and dish pantry, were on the back of the building on the first floor. Also, was the Director's office, coat rooms, clinic facilities, and washroom-toilets for the girls, and an activity room or games room. There were boys and girls stairwells leading to the second floor. Dormitories for small and large boys, with bathroom facilities between, and adequate storage for clothing. There were dormitories for little girls, and a nursery with cribs and youth beds, bathrooms, and clothing storage. On the third floor, were dormitories for the larger girls, staff rooms, and bathrooms. Here was the ever popular "Sewing Room" . . . .
>
> Daily routines included: One hour knitting, sewing or mending for the girls. Under the supervision of Francisca Mayer, who was skilled in these techniques. The smaller boys filled wood boxes, split wood, working on the fish stage curing salt

cod in season, mending fish nets, repairing shoes or skin boots. Older boys worked at the Mission barns, dog kennels, and hen house. The wood working shop was open only when supervision was available as the machines required supervision. Many fine pieces of furniture were produced in this shop.[58]

The School Curriculum and Orphanage Activities

School-age children at the orphanage and in the community attended a Grenfell Mission school in St. Anthony. The number of orphanage children at the school varied over the years. In 1945, about a third of the 180 students came from the Children's Home.[59] The proportion declined in the 1950s and 1960s as the number of children at the orphanage decreased. By 1958–59, the school had grown to 238 pupils, of whom only 38, or 16 per cent, lived in the orphanage.[60]

Wilfred Grenfell had established the St. Anthony school in the early 1900s. Although the town already had Anglican and Methodist schools, he wanted to build a school that was open to everyone. Grenfell disagreed with the religious segregation and the inefficient duplication of Newfoundland's denominational education system. Church control of the schools made it feel like people in the colony were "still living in the Middle Ages," he argued.[61] When he could not convince the other schools in St. Anthony to combine their efforts, he opened a non-denominational Mission school in 1907. For the first few years, until a new schoolhouse had been built, the Grenfell school used both the Methodist schoolhouse and the Church of England schoolhouse across the harbour.[62]

A non-denominational school was an anomaly, and teachers at the Wilfred T. Grenfell School initially endured local criticism and low enrolment.[63] To counter the public's skepticism, the Mission tried to attract well-qualified teachers, the earliest of whom were well-educated American and Canadian volunteers.[64] Ruth Keese of Chelsea, Massachusetts, was the first to teach at the school. The daughter of a Congregational minister and a graduate of Vermont State College, she travelled to St. Anthony for the position in 1907.[65] "Little Miss Keese," as she was known among Mission staff, taught at the school for a few years until she returned to the States after marrying John Mason Little, a Grenfell doctor stationed at St. Anthony.[66] Olive Lesley joined Ruth Keese in 1910 to teach kindergarten at the Grenfell school. Olive had co-founded the Lesley School for teachers in Cambridge, Massachusetts, with her sister, Edith, and specialized in training teachers in kindergarten methods.[67]

In 1910, students at the Grenfell school no longer had to use the Methodist or Church of England schoolhouses. The new two-room Grenfell schoolhouse stood about 750 metres from the orphanage. When it opened, Ruth Keese was ecstatic:

> It really is perfectly gorgeous in the new school. We had the Christmas tree there and introduced it to the general public and the general public was enthusiastic. It is just a joy. When we get furniture for this school it will be hard to beat. It is one of the pleasantest rooms I have ever seen.[68]

The Grenfell schoolhouse in St. Anthony, 1913. The inscription above the door reads: "All thy children shall be taught of the Lord and great shall be the peace of thy children" (courtesy of The Rooms).

Student numbers increased as the school's reputation improved. According to Magistrate Squarey, who investigated the Grenfell Association's activities in 1917 as a result of complaints filed by the Newfoundland business community, children from neighbouring towns stayed at the local inn in St. Anthony while attending the Grenfell school. He was impressed with what he saw: "The Association has established a splendid school at St. Anthony. Nearly one hundred children attend. People come to St. Anthony every winter and board at the inn solely for the purpose of attending the school — a fact illustrative of their appreciation of its existence."[69]

Grenfell teachers and orphanage staff aimed to provide an education that set a high standard of academic achievement and extended well beyond academic subjects. They expressed their hopes that both the school and the orphanage would profoundly change the children who attended them. As Wilfred Grenfell wrote in 1911: "It is our great desire that the schools should stand for more than mere teaching school-book learning. They can be centres of real civilization."[70] Grenfell staff also felt their work at the orphanage existed on "the frontiers of civilization."[71] Accordingly, the orphanage would serve as a "factory to raise boys and girls [in] Christian ideals of life and service."[72]

Grenfell's philosophy of "work, service, worship and play" influenced the school curriculum and orphanage activities.[73] Teachers and orphanage staff organized programs designed to teach the children practical skills, sportsmanship, creativity, and play. They also socialized the children in the norms, values, and behaviours that the IGA staff felt were essential for their future lives. "Education as we see it," Grenfell wrote, "means the training that enables one most completely to correspond to one's environment, together with the development of a healthy body, and primarily of a spirit which makes living to serve the world the first objective."[74] To adapt the teaching to the needs of the students, as the teacher Alice MacNair explained, the school curriculum focused on "Arithmetic — adding and subtracting was most needed of all, for the making and understanding of a simple bill; the composition of a letter; some spelling, some local geography leading out to the larger world."[75]

Snowshoe race in the annual St. Anthony Sports Day (with the orphanage in the background) (courtesy of The Rooms).

For Grenfell, play was important for children because it fostered "the ineradicable love of athletics and sport" that was a distinguishing feature of "Anglo-Saxon" superiority.[76] As Grenfell saw it, the love of sports gave the English an "advantage over competitors" in addition to their "racial attributes."[77] But when Grenfell and the volunteer teachers first came to the coast, they did not see any recognizable toys or games among the children — at least not the kind one would see in the homes of children in Britain and America. They aimed to fill this void, in the name of British imperialism. Ethel Gordon Muir, a summer teacher with a PhD who co-ordinated the Mission's volunteer teachers in the early 1900s, shared Grenfell's belief in the need to encourage games and imagination among the children. Muir likewise saw the lack of play as a sign of a flawed childhood: "Where life is so serious and hard, as it is on this coast," she wrote in 1911, "it is surely no wonder that the children are sadly lacking in imagination."[78] Accordingly, "organized play was carefully introduced on the coast," and sports days and annual competitions became a tradition in St. Anthony.[79]

Staff also tried to instill a spirit of service by encouraging students to use their knowledge and new skills to help others upon their return home. Phyllis Blake, a child at the orphanage from Mud Lake, Labrador, wrote an article for *Among the Deep Sea Fishers* magazine in October 1922 that illustrates her ambition to serve Labradorians. She describes the poverty, starvation, and poor health of many in Labrador, yet affirms her wish to improve conditions: "But in spite of all the privations of the far north land, I still love it and when my nurse's course is finished (it hasn't begun yet), I will return to my native land and try to help the people in every way possible."[80]

The orphanage also provided training in practical skills. In 1922, the first boys' worker, Paul Claggett, reported his plans for the boys at the orphanage. These included organizing a Boy Scout troop and adding training in gardening, arts and crafts, construction, and woodworking to the school curriculum. "The boys who leave the orphanage to make their own living must have a good knowledge of the use of tools," he maintained.[81] For group instruction, he envisioned "[s]ports and games, physical fitness, tools and handicraft, woodcraft, mechanics, popular science, camping, reading and public speaking, wild animals, birds, gardening, citizenship, and vocational training."[82] The children seem to have enjoyed the activities. Teacher Alice MacNair reported that "The favorite subjects were manual training, sewing, music and the worship service."[83]

Orphanage staff also introduced the children to current American social values through their training and activities. One such example involved a visit from a representative of the American Humane Association and Animal Rescue League of Boston, who arrived in St. Anthony in the early 1930s. Maude Phillips tried to promote the organization's values among the orphanage children by launching a humane society called "Sir Wilfred's Crusaders." To become a Crusader, children had to make the pledge, "I promise to be kind to every living thing, people, animals, birds, trees, and flowers."[84] The children were encouraged to shelter their dogs, to make kennels, to feed bread to the birds and to be kind to each other. When asked to perform a kind deed, the children laid flowers on the

Domestic science class at the St. Anthony school, 1930 (courtesy of The Rooms).

grave of a child who had recently died — an act that impressed their reality on Maude Phillips.[85] Like other missionaries, she used gardening metaphors to describe her work. In an article published in the IGA magazine, Phillips wrote that she was sowing seeds of humane values in the "soil" of the children's hearts and minds.[86]

In the late 1930s, under the supervision of Linwood and Rachel Brown, the orphanage children were given more manual training to supplement their schooling. Linwood felt it "imperative that our children be given every possible opportunity to become self-sufficient."[87] A local fisherman taught the boys how to fish, and Dr. Curtis, the IGA superintendent, taught the older boys "how to raise and care for cattle and pigs at the Mission barn. During the summer the younger boys and girls are busy in their vegetable garden. Next year I hope to be training the boys in poultry raising."[88] Linwood Brown also taught the boys furniture-making, while his wife ensured the girls learned "cooking, sewing, and every phase of housekeeping."[89] Rachel Brown offered the girls training in other practical homemaking skills as well:

> They are also taught to can the local products, make jam and jellies from the locally grown berries. Our canning and preserving figures for the past year are quite impressive: twelve hundred tins of salmon, hundreds of pounds of jams and jellies and many jars of vegetables and greens. Besides the valuable training this affords the girls, these things go a long way in augmenting our winter's food supply.[90]

After the Browns left St. Anthony in 1945, a similar carpentry program ran for a few years in the late 1950s.[91] Aimed at Inuit boys from northern Labrador, it was funded by the provincial Department of Natural Resources. Stanley Hodge and Albert Styles, two Grenfell school graduates who had gone to the Ryerson Institute in Toronto for technical training, ran the program.[92] As the January 1957 issue of *Among the Deep Sea Fishers* notes:

> A new venture has been started this year by bringing to St. Anthony five Eskimo boys from Labrador to a small manual-training school that we have established under the charge of

Orphanage boys splitting fish on wharf, St. Anthony, 1931 (Bill Burden, Israel Rumbolt, Jimmy Turnbull) (courtesy of The Rooms).

> Stanley Hodge. These boys are receiving instruction in plumbing, carpentry and diesel engineering so that they will be able to take their place in the many new activities that are opening up in Labrador.[93]

The Moravian missionary in Hebron, Siegfried Hettasch, describes the experience of two of the Inuit students for the *Periodical Accounts of the Moravian Missions*:

> We have one 17-year-old man, who is an orphan, and in his days here in Hebron has been pushed around from one home to another and for a while he was labelled as a bad boy. But there is a great deal of good in him. The Government is paying for additional education for him at the Grenfell Mission Trade School in St. Anthony where he is getting much valuable training. He is now in St. Anthony for his second winter. This summer he came home for several weeks, when he showed us quite a lot of the blue-prints for house-building, which he had learned to design. He is very happy about it all and seems to be getting on well. We feel quite proud of him.
>
> Another boy with an artificial leg was taken to that same school this year. The reason of his leaving Hebron was that he wanted to get away from his relatives who were drunk too often for his liking. He has only little knowledge of the English language as yet, and had also very little schooling, nevertheless, we hope that he too will be able to learn something to help him in the future.[94]

The trade school program came to an end in 1960, when the provincial funding ceased.[95]

The Children at the Orphanage

Children at the St. Anthony orphanage came from families throughout Labrador and northern Newfoundland. In his early publicity, Wilfred Grenfell often claimed that most were Labradorians, perhaps in an effort to convince skeptical American donors of the need to support such a cause. In 1919, for instance, he wrote:

> One of our boys is from Cape Chidley itself; others come from as far south and west as Bay of Islands in South Newfoundland. So many erroneous opinions seem to persist regarding the difference between Newfoundland and Labrador that I am constantly asked: "But why do you have a Children's Home in Newfoundland? Can't the Newfoundlanders look out for themselves and their dependent children?" As I have tried to make clear . . . North and South Newfoundland should be sharply differentiated as to wealth, education, climate, and opportunity. Though for purposes of efficiency and economy the actual building of the Home is situated in the north end of the northern peninsula of Newfoundland, the children who make up the family are drawn almost entirely from the Labrador side of the Straits; unless, as is often the case, the poverty and destitution of a so-called Newfoundland family on the south side of Belle Isle makes it impossible to leave children under such conditions.[96]

The existing IGA records from the Children's Home are incomplete, but they provide a more detailed picture.[97] From when it opened in 1906 until 1919, the orphanage took in more children from Labrador (53) than children from Newfoundland (34).[98] However, the ratio switched in the 1920s and the number of children increased, especially after the larger brick orphanage opened in 1922. Between 1920 and 1929, more Newfoundlanders (81) than Labradorians (54) were admitted.[99] This trend continues in the 1930s, when the orphanage took in 80 children from Newfoundland and 26

Children at the St. Anthony orphanage, ca. 1929. Back, l-r: Mary Spurrell, Priscilla Burden, Margaret Fequet, Jessie May Bownes; front: Alice Parsons (courtesy of The Rooms).

children from Labrador.[100] In the 1940s, the number of children continued to decrease, with 48 children from Newfoundland and only eight children from Labrador.[101] The IGA records list a total of 141 Labradorians and 243 Newfoundlanders admitted into the Children's Home between 1906 and 1948.[102]

While a few came from northern Labrador (including Ford's Harbour, Davis Inlet, Makkovik, and Aillik), most came from central Labrador (including Mud Lake, North West River, Rigolet, and Sandwich Bay), southeastern Labrador (including Batteau, Spotted Island, Seal Islands, Grady, Ragged Islands, Tilt Cove, George's Cove, Fox Harbour, Venison Tickle, Boulter's Rock, Battle Harbour, and Cape Charles), southern Labrador (including Red Bay, West St. Modeste, Forteau, L'Anse au Loup, and L'Anse au Claire), the Northern Peninsula of Newfoundland (including St. Anthony, Griquet, Back Cove, Flower's Cove, Hare Bay, Daniel's Harbour, Englee, and Conche), and other communities in Newfoundland (including Bonne Bay, Lewisporte, Hampden, Springdale, and King's Point).[103] The names of children in archival records less than 100 years old cannot be published, due to privacy restrictions,[104] but the April 1930 issue of *Among the Deep Sea Fishers* lists 63 children who lived at the orphanage on 31 December 1929 (see Appendix 1).[105] Based on their family names, it can be deduced that about half of the children came from Labrador. The majority of those from Labrador were of Inuit ancestry.[106]

Until the 1930s, Grenfell staff kept detailed records of the orphanage children's appearance and behaviour. Using racial terms from colonial and American slavery contexts, they made judgements based on their assumptions of the children's ethnicity and ancestry. Comments such as "she is dark and has Eskimo blood in her," "looks like a pure Eskimo," "a quadred," and "a dark child but seems remarkably bright and intelligent" contrast with "blue eyes and sallow complexion with light hair . . . he has a rather sainted expression" and "fair — bright looking and seems very intelligent."[107] One boy from Francis Harbour — a "redheaded little Eskimo!" — caused the staff some confusion about their categories: "never saw the dark skin and red haired combination before . . . ."[108]

Children stayed in the orphanage for shorter periods of time as the years went on. In the first 15 years (1906–20), the children stayed for an average of six years in the orphanage.[109] In the 1920s and 1930s, the average stay was about four and a half years, while in the 1940s, as more children were staying at the Children's Home for a year or less, the average

Children at the St. Anthony orphanage, before 1949 (courtesy of The Rooms).

length of stay was two years.[110] These changing trends were the result of changing reasons for children to be at the orphanage. When it opened, the institution acted as a home for children who had lost a parent and who were often facing destitution. As the years went on, children came to the orphanage for other reasons as well. In 1960, a report on the IGA's educational efforts surveyed the children in the three IGA dormitories in St. Anthony, Cartwright, and North West River.[111] The report, written by Senator William Wall at the request of the IGA Board of Directors, found that the largest group of the children (37 per cent) stayed in a dormitory because their community had no school or they lived far from a school.[112] The second largest group, at 22 per cent, involved foster children and children with one or both parents in the hospital.[113] Another 15 per cent of the children had one parent deceased, and 10 per cent of the children came from "poor home conditions — broken homes, immorality, etc."[114] Ten per cent of the students lived in the dormitories in order to attend high school.[115] The smallest groups, each with 3 per cent, were children who needed medical attention and those with special circumstances.[116]

Children with One or No Parents

In its first four decades, the St. Anthony orphanage often housed children who had lost both or — more commonly — one parent. In 1929, for instance, most of the 17 children admitted to the Children's Home that year fell into this category:

> Of the children admitted eleven are from Newfoundland and six are from Labrador. Three new girls have come from Muddy Bay [Grenfell boarding school] and one from Cook's Harbor [Newfoundland] for schooling. Frank Cove, a little boy of six, was sent to us in the summer from Labrador by Sir Wilfred. His parents were both drowned at Ragged Islands the winter before while out trapping, and left three children. Frank is a cute little fellow and a favorite with the older boys who sometimes lend him one of their ties to wear on a Sunday — a great honor. By special

Children at the St. Anthony orphanage, ca.1932: (l-r) Frank Cove, Joey Ward, and Jim Turnbull (courtesy of The Rooms).

> request he always sits at table with the older boys for meals. A little boy of three came from Jackson's Arm, Newfoundland, with his two sisters aged eight and six. They had recently lost their mother. All the others admitted have one parent only.[117]

When their surviving parent remarried, the children often returned home. Those who had lost both parents often stayed at the orphanage until they reached the age of 16, at which point they left St. Anthony to work, to undertake more schooling, or to live with other family members. The Grenfell Mission helped some of the earliest residents at the Children's Home to find employment in the early 1900s at the logging mills on the Northern Peninsula, on fishing crews, or as domestic help.[118] A few children were adopted into other families in the 1930s and 1940s. New parents signed an adoption agreement promising to be responsible for the child "physically, morally, and spiritually until he is eighteen years of age."[119] If they failed to do so, the Children's Home superintendent had the authority to withdraw the child from their care.[120] In 1949, when the federal Family Allowance program began in Newfoundland and Labrador, the new income allowed families to keep their children at home. IGA staff saw a significant decrease in the number of impoverished children admitted into the orphanage.[121]

Boarding at St. Anthony for School

Not long after it opened, the orphanage housed other children who came to St. Anthony to attend school. Wilfred Grenfell described the new approach to recruiting more students to the school with enthusiasm: "Being an unrecognized school, and so far off, some years went by before the innovation of bringing up scholars from our northern districts entered our heads."[122] Frank Davis of Mullins Cove, near Cartwright, was sent to St. Anthony in the early years of the orphanage by his mother, who wanted him to take advantage of the education that the IGA provided. His future wife, Blanche Davis, also lived in the orphanage and later trained as a teacher in the States before returning to teach at the boarding school in Muddy Bay, but Frank decided not to pursue further education abroad:[123]

> I come to go to St. Anthony school just by accident. Sir Wilfred Grenfell used to come on the coast and he used to get women to make moccasins and things out of deerskin, boots and all that see. Now when he come to Mullins Cove, poor Mother asked if he'd be calling in on the way back. He told her that he wouldn't be calling again — he had a visit there so he was satisfied with that. Poor Mother told him that if he called back that he could have me for two years. And that's how I come to go to St. Anthony for school, only by accident. Poor Father didn't want me to go, but poor Mother told Sir Wilfred I could, so that was that.
>
> I had the chance to go to England, too. Sir Wilfred was interested in what he called the smartest of the people, interested in taking them away and putting them through school and all that. It was a Miss Muir was interested in me and, as far as I know, that was the one that took away Blanche.... She took Blanche and two or three more. I come back from St. Anthony for a cruise with my

> family before I went away to England and then they wouldn't let me go back. I would like to have gone, but just the same when you take it all-in-all, 'tis only a living, whatever you do.
>
> I don't think I was too smart altogether, but they called me one of the smart ones. I got to the fourth grade and that was as far as I ever got. That was a good grade for them days, because there was lots that wasn't able to read. I was thirteen when I went to St. Anthony and fifteen when I came back. . . . It was lonely at first when I got to St. Anthony, but I fought that off and got over it all right.
>
> Poor Father said I could go to England if I wished but I knowed he was against it so I stayed home to satisfy him. I was sorry in my own mind. I would have liked to get out and get an education.[124]

A number of children at the orphanage, like Redgeway Snook from Trap Cove in southern Labrador, came to St. Anthony in the late 1930s to finish high school:

> I went to St. Anthony to take my grade eleven. . . . I was homesick as could be. I really missed my friends and family. It was especially hard because we were a close family. I was a very lonely person. I was a bit lucky when Charles Stone from Henley Harbour came over and I got to visit him. Cornelia Stevens and Lillian Rumbolt came over to work in the orphanage. That helped a bit to get to see someone from home. I made a few friends but it was still hard.[125]

Florence Goudie Michelin from North West River also finished high school in St. Anthony. An orphan at nine, she had lived at Gibbons Cottage, the IGA dormitory in North West River, before moving to St. Anthony. Once she graduated from Grade 11, the IGA sent Florence to study nursing in St. Catharines, Ontario.

Children at the St. Anthony orphanage, 1926 ("The beginners' sewing class") (courtesy of The Rooms).

> I stayed in school in North West River until I was 13 and had my Grade Six. Old Dr. Harry Paddon wanted me to go on, and in order to get further education I had to go to St. Anthony, Newfoundland. It was strange there at first because I didn't know anybody but I got into it. I liked it at the Orphanage and I did pretty good in school.[126]

In the 1940s, the Moravian Mission in northern Labrador sent other children to live at the orphanage while they attended school in St. Anthony. Hulda "Hilda" Hunter was one of four students who came from Moravian schools in Nain and Hopedale. Being immersed in a new school system was a challenge, as she describes:

> Before Newfoundland was under Confederation in 1949, when I was twelve or thirteen years old, they were recruiting some students to go to school in St. Anthony, Newfoundland. There was four of us, two girls and two boys: myself and Silpa Barbour from Nain, and two boys — John or Jack Edmunds (we called

him "Jack" all the time), and David Mitsuk. There was four of us went in a little schooner-type boat called *Winifred Lee.* We got aboard of that, and we were sent off to go to school in St. Anthony, Newfoundland, and we stayed in the orphanage. And from then on, I went back and forth for five years, back and forth going to school. . . .

When we got to St. Anthony, they tested us to see what we knew 'cause we didn't have no records or anything to take with us. We had to go to the principal and go through what we learned while we was in Nain or Hopedale. When he tested us on the blackboard to see what we knew, how much we knew, we didn't know English very good. We could hardly speak because of shyness — we didn't know all them students that were there. They put us in the classroom upstairs in grade nine, ten, and eleven. And he start asking us and looking at some math and English and whatever, and asking us.

But the grade nine, ten students watching us and laugh[ing] at us and everything else. They wasn't very nice, and I don't think anybody, any teacher, should ever do that to kids who got another language and hardly know the language of Newfoundland English. Anyway, come to find out they put us into grade six. I got to laugh, I often wonders — I must have been in grade five when I left home! I was thinking after, too, I must have been in grade five for five years, because that's all I knew when I was five and first when I went to school, we was doing the same thing we was doing when I left home and went to school in Grenfell School in St. Anthony!

That's how funny to me it was after a while. And then we were in the orphanage and we had to walk over a mile, it must have been, over to the school every day, every schooling day. Rain or shine or whatever, but cold. We could only wear little old things like dresses all the time, no pants. It was cruel in a way, I found it. I guess you get used to it after a while, when you go back and forth so much.[127]

When Silpa Barbour decided to remain in Nain upon her return home after a year at St. Anthony's, Audrey Frieda from Hopedale took her spot. The four students — Hulda, Audrey, John, and David — stayed at the orphanage and attended the school for four or five years. Hulda's last year was 1953. She and Audrey trained to become nurses, and Hulda transferred to North West River to work in the hospital there.[128]

Beth Green Solis from Nain also lived in the orphanage at the same time as Hulda Hunter and Audrey Frieda. Her parents had died when she was seven years old.[129] At first, she lived with her grandmother and her aunt. But then the Ogletrees, an American couple who taught at the Moravian school in Nain, adopted her. Years later, she described her early memories of Nain and of going to the St. Anthony orphanage before she joined the Ogletrees in the States:

> We were very poor but happy. I remember having to trap snowbirds and going to the island to fish. My favourites were dried capelin, ovelooks (mussels), pipsi with siva (dried cod liver), and nikku. I missed all these when I left for St. John's in the summer of 1950, little did I know that I would end up in St. Anthony orphanage at the end of that summer. . . . I was 16 years old and very scared, knowing just enough English to get by but in less than a year, I was able to write letters to the Ogletrees in the USA. We were very obedient in the Orphanage to Margie Byrne and Miss Parker our house parents. Drs. Thomas, Curtis, and Paddon were there then. We learned so much in that year, 1950 to 1951. We sewed, mended, made homemade bread, cooked, knitted, cleaned, took care of younger ones. We sang and danced. The boys milked cows and made ice cream. We went to movies and we served in the kitchen and dining room. We ate a lot of oatmeal with molasses or brown sugar. We had to take ugly old cod liver oil every morning. And we learned to be very responsible.[130]

Them Days magazine published a letter that Beth wrote to the Ogletrees on 4 October 1950, from St. Anthony. The letter illustrates her efforts to learn English:

> Only me and Hulda and Audrey are in the house all the other girls are town to the movies and I didn't want to go because Hulda and Audrey didn't go and because I'm stateying (studying) tonight. I loves learning English only some of them are hard for me. Our teacher's name is George Fields his right nice teacher. He [teaches] grade 8, 7, and 6. He told me and Audrey that his going to help us and try to teach us hard so we can go to grade 7 after Christmas and his going to try to led (let) Grade 7 go to Grade 8. His nice teacher. When I go stutying in the evening Hulda always helps me, she's right nice. She's Grade 7 now. Me and Audrey and Hulda go stutying together in the evenings. We are having some fun now.[131]

Eva Elson Luther leaves St. Anthony to fly home to Spotted Island, ca.1965 (courtesy of Them Days Archive).

In 1959, the Newfoundland government launched the Confederation Bursary program to celebrate 10 years as a province in Canada. The new program enabled high school students to attend school in larger communities if their own schools did not offer higher grades. Lloyd Stone from Henley Harbour in southern Labrador described the program in a *Them Days* interview:

> Many kids quit around Grade Nine or Ten. For those who wished to continue beyond Grade Ten, there was a $500 bursary available to attend a Regional High School in a larger centre. Some of the students went to the St. Anthony Grenfell Mission boarding school, while Lloyd and his brother Paul went to Bishop's College in St. John's to study grade eleven.[132]

Many of the high school students who stayed at the orphanage relied on this bursary program to fund their room, board, books, and other expenses.

Boarding at St. Anthony for Medical Services

Other children who lived at the orphanage came to St. Anthony for medical reasons and attended school while they were there. The IGA took Bella Butt Brown to St. Anthony from her home in East St. Modeste, southern Labrador, because of illness in 1923. She describes how she later went to an American school:

> In March, I was rushed off to Forteau hospital with an infected lung. In August, I was sent to St. Anthony to the Children's Home. There I would be near a doctor and could attend school. My father was quite upset over the move because he hadn't been told about it. He always said that I was kidnapped.
>
> Four years went by, and I was still at St. Anthony. He became anxious and sent a telegram to the matron, stating that if I wasn't sent back home, he was coming to get me. A message was sent back to my father telling him that I was going to be sent out to

> the United States to school. In those days, the Grenfell Mission had a fund to send students away to the United States or Canada to further their studies, and this year, I was one of those chosen to go.
>
> Within a few days, I was on my way with Mrs. Grenfell as my guardian. I wrote and told my father about it, saying that it was only for two years. It turned out to be five years. In 1932, I went home to what I thought would be a surprise arrival. . . . It was a happy reunion.[133]

Alice Rumbolt from the Mary's Harbour region was another child who was sent to the St. Anthony hospital and lived in the orphanage while she attended school: "I had to go to the hospital and the orphanage. I supposed I was eight or nine years in the hospital and then I was reared in the orphanage and that's where I got my education, Grade Eleven."[134]

After Confederation, even more children came to St. Anthony for medical reasons. Funding from the federal government for Inuit and Innu medical care starting in 1954 prompted the IGA to embark on an ambitious campaign to treat tuberculosis among people in Labrador. It built a 50-bed sanatorium in St. Anthony, and the expanded tuberculosis program brought many patients to live in St. Anthony.[135] As Dr. Curtis reported in 1955: "The Children's Home now houses about thirty children, many of them from Labrador, who are living there and attending school while their parents are undergoing treatment at the Hospital."[136]

Fran Frieda Williams from Hopedale, who had tuberculosis twice as a child, recalls being sent to the North West River hospital in 1949, and then to the new facility in St. Anthony for a few years after 1955. She lived in an annex for female patients when she first got there, then in the sanatorium for a year before moving to the orphanage for her final year: "My dad died of TB, so did my uncle, and I've had TB twice as a child; when I was 5, in hospital for a year, and when I was 11 in St. Anthony for two years."[137] Laura Millie, who was relocated from Hebron in 1959, moved to the St. Anthony hospital for three years in 1962 at the age of 11.[138]

William Palliser, who was born in 1947 in Rigolet, arrived in St. Anthony when he was five. He came to receive medical treatment after being hit on the head with a rock, but he contracted tuberculosis while there and stayed almost seven years.[139]

The Heavy Hand of Social Services

The orphanage also served as a home for children who had been apprehended by social services. As in Wilfred Grenfell's day, the IGA continued to act in its unofficial capacity as child welfare and social services provider until the Newfoundland government took over the role. In 1931, Newfoundland passed child welfare legislation. But with only two staff members assigned to child protection for the entire province, the government relied on the IGA to provide child welfare services in the region. More than a decade later, in 1944, the government passed the Welfare of Children Act and expanded the Division of Child Welfare under the Department of Public Welfare.[140] Still, government staff and resources remained limited. The Department of Public Welfare depended on the IGA, the Newfoundland Rangers, and the Division of Northern Labrador Affairs to co-operate in dealing with children taken as wards of the state.[141]

In fact, until it closed its doors, the St. Anthony orphanage maintained its original purpose of providing housing for children whom authorities deemed at risk. Rosina Kalleo Holwell of Nain was one child placed at the St. Anthony orphanage as a ward of the state. In an interview during a 2018 Healing and Commemoration session, she describes the pain she felt at being separated from her family:

> I was really hurt, because I was taken away from my home, from my family, and my sisters, because I always took care of them. When my parents were drinking and drunk, I always had to be there for them. My two brothers were older. My brother, John, I believe, was on his own somewhere on the island. And, my other brother, William, was in the St. Anthony orphanage already.[142]

Rosina recalls her sadness and loneliness at being taken so far from home:

> Selma and I used to be very close, and we were homesick, and we started counting the days. She was in grade 3, and I was in grade 4. And we made our own calendars, and we used to say, "Gee, we can't wait. Too bad we can't run away. We can't run away and go home. I wish we could run away. I'm sick of this place." And, we used to hug each other and cry. And, Selma said, "We can't. We're in Newfoundland. We can't go. We can't go back home. And we used to cry ourselves to sleep. . . . I don't know why, but I can never remember ever going back home from North West to Nain either. I don't know why. It was just so overwhelming, I guess.[143]

Rosina suffered sexual abuse by another student. She also experienced hunger while in St. Anthony:

> Another time, we were so hungry in the orphanage. . . . [The dumb waiter] I used to call it the tilt for some reason. It used to go down and bring up our food, eh, from the basement. We were so hungry, there was four of us. We went down in that. And, I can't remember the boys. They had to be strong, because they had to use the rope, a strong rope, to bring us up and down. We went down and we stole some vegetables, potatoes, cabbage, turnip and carrots in one of our aprons. Whoever had the biggest apron had to carry it. So, we stole some, and we let them know that we were ready to be brought back up. So, sure enough, then we got caught.[144]

Yet not all of her memories are bad:

> I mean, we had good days. . . . I remember clearly we were in grade four. We were allowed to go and visit the farm they had

> there at St. Anthony. . . . We used to count the days on the calendar when we were almost getting ready to go home. That was good. At the end of May, we would make our own little calendars in our classrooms, in the back, at the orphanage. And, we just used to cross the X's off. "Oh, so many days. Yay, we're going back home soon!"[145]

Enoch Obed was another child placed in the orphanage by social services. In a 1999 article, he describes being relocated from Nutak to Hopedale in 1956. The eviction caused relentless upheaval for him and his family:

> In the relocation, I lost touch with who belonged in my family. I was 9 years old when I got separated from my family due to a respiratory disease. I lost my mother to food poisoning. My family wasn't used to new materials to store our food in. I wasn't allowed to attend her funeral at North West River. I was taken to the St. Anthony orphanage without my father's consent. When my father died, it was three months later I was told, although the caregivers knew of his death.
>
> In my early year at the Orphanage, I went through physical, emotional, mental, and even sexual abuse. I recall the beatings, going to bed with no meal because I'd spoken in Inuktitut. When I went there I was fluent in my language. Somehow, through the brainwashing, assimilation and punishment, my language was lost. It's like a burn in my brain. Anyway, I got kicked out of the Orphanage. I was too full of rage, bitterness, hatred and shame.
>
> Today I realize those that worked there thought they were doing God's will and simply followed orders and policies set by the government. When I returned to Hopedale, I had lost my identity, my culture, my language and my dignity. I could not communicate with my family anymore. The age and cultural gap seemed unbridgeable. I didn't know how to tell my story. It

Enoch Obed at the St. Anthony orphanage, ca. 1965 (courtesy of Them Days Archive).

> was too shameful. All my emotions were bottled up and frozen. I did manage to get an education and a number of trades.
>
> But I became an alcoholic and drug addict. My heart was so full of despair and grief. Many times I thought of suicide as a way out, and did try a number of times. Most people don't know how many times I agonized and wished that things would have turned out differently. In my own hurting, I hurt those who were closest to me. I loved each one of my family members, yet I could not show that love.[146]

Authorities also took K. Naeme Merkuratsuk of Nain to the orphanage after first placing her in North West River:

> My sister and I were not permitted to come back to Nain to spend summer here with my mom and we were asked where would we like to go. I think we were asked if we'd like to go to St. Anthony. And I asked my sister what she would like to do. She and I decided to go to St. Anthony for the summer. But we enjoyed St. Anthony so much — it was so much like home; there were hills and motor boats and everything, berry picking, so much like home — that we decided to be there instead of going to what they call flat North West.[147]

Eventually, K. Naeme was allowed to return temporarily to Nain. Dr. Gordon Thomas, the IGA superintendent from 1959 to 1979, agreed to let her stay at home longer:

> I wrote to Dr. Thomas and asked him if I would be permitted to stay in Nain and look after my father because he had artificial legs and all that. . . . And I was given permission to stay. And then two years after that, I wrote to Dr. Thomas, again, asking permission for Joanna to be sent home to help me look after my father.[148]

While in state care, children experienced the authorities' absolute control over their lives. Government and IGA officials determined where the children lived, what they ate, what language they spoke, whether they could attend family funerals, and even when they were to be told of family deaths. As a result, many felt frustration, anger, and resentment towards the institutions and the political structure that exerted such authority.

Fundraising to Stay Afloat

In the early years, the Newfoundland government paid the IGA to care for many of the children at the Children's Home, as it did for other orphanages in the colony.[149] However, government grants only covered a fraction of the costs. And the orphanage was not the IGA's only expense. Its hospitals, schools, and social programs were increasingly costly. By 1918, the IGA's budget was already more than $90,000, and it ballooned over the next 50 years.[150] The organization depended on financial support and donations of used clothing, equipment, books, and volunteer time from its wealthy supporters in the United States, Canada, and Britain. Wilfred Grenfell, a phenomenal fundraiser, enthusiastically accepted the challenge. He collected almost $1 million for the IGA's Endowment Fund in the 1920s — an enormous sum for the time.[151]

Much of the fundraising focused on children. Stories written in the early 1900s to elicit donations from sympathetic readers chronicled how the orphanage transformed its wards from physically and morally deficient children into strong citizens of the Empire:

> Some of our boys have done splendidly. Instead of growing up weak, rickedy, dwarfed, ignorant, and all that means morally as well, they are now doing splendidly for the world. Several fought in the war. Freddie Blake, the oldest boy of the original family presented to me, fought with the New England troops. Archie Ash brought in 40 wounded with his stretcher patrol one day. He was mentioned by the General in France the day before he was killed, actually carrying men in. He sleeps in France. Our girls are also giving good service to others as nurses, cooks, seamstresses, etc. The Home . . . badly needs hurrying along.[152]

The IGA also recruited the children themselves to help raise funds. In the 1930s, it circulated descriptions and photographs of orphanage children whom generous donors could sponsor. Women from Britain, such as the students at the Ladies College in Harrogate, England, and other individuals each sent the IGA $125 a year to support a child.[153] The children at the orphanage also performed operettas for visiting tourists on the Clark Steamship Line. The steamship offered cruises to "the far-famed Grenfell Missions in outposts of civilization on the fringe of the Arctic," as an advertisement in the April 1938 issue of *Among the Deep Sea Fishers* proclaimed.[154] Lizzie Lucy, who lived in the orphanage in the 1930s, was photographed dressed in traditional Inuit clothing as she collected donations from the passengers.[155] These operetta performances were successful fundraisers, collecting enough money to purchase laundry equipment and chairs for the children's dining rooms.[156]

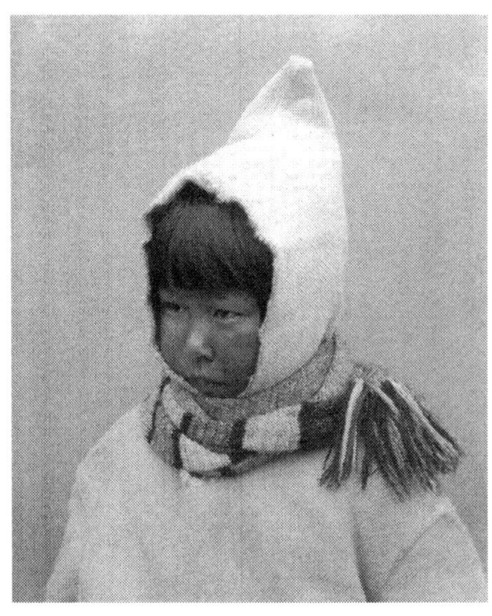

Lizzie Lucy at the St. Anthony orphanage, ca.1932 (courtesy of The Rooms).

Hard Times

Despite the constant fundraising, the orphanage remained an expensive endeavour for the IGA. Dr. Charles Curtis, the IGA superintendent from 1936 to 1959, felt that the high cost of the orphanage was unwarranted. Since at least 1910, the Newfoundland government had provided funding for the children in the orphanage.[157] In the 1930s, the grant "for the support of children whose father is dead" was $65 per child per year and in 1942 this support increased to $80.[158] But the cost of running the orphanage extended well beyond these payments. Curtis argued for limiting the admissions criteria for children:

> The whole question of taking care of children at St. Anthony should be reconsidered. I do not feel that such a large building is justified by the results we are obtaining from the children. . . . I suggest that the [IGA] Directors consider a smaller building for a Children's Home. I suggest that in the future no children should be taken unless they are full orphans.[159]

In order to track the institution's impact, the IGA staff had kept records about the children's lives after they left the orphanage. They noted how and where their former wards lived, whom they married, and any "improvements" in moral principles or standard of living. For example, they commented that one young man was "supporting himself comfortably and is planning to study for the ministry . . . he is turning out very well" and that another now had "one of the leading families" in his community.[160] A young woman was "now married [but showed] no improvement in standards over those of her family."[161] Another record laments, "he is living in the same miserable condition as [when he first came to the orphanage]. Evidently the only good accomplished here was that he acquired a love of reading. He is as dirty as ever."[162]

The mixed outcomes and the expense involved made some IGA staff members feel uneasy about running the Children's Home. In 1942, for example, Dr. Curtis felt the institution was having a positive influence on the children of the region. "For many years," he wrote, "the Orphanage was mostly a rescue home and dubious results were obtained in many cases. Now, I think we are making some progress."[163] However, a few years later, Curtis again argued that the cost of the Children's Home was too great. "The orphanage expense has gradually increased during the past several years so that it now costs us $400 per year per child. This I consider excessive for this country."[164] With 66 boarders in the orphanage for the 1944–45 year, the gross cost of running the institution was $28,715.08. After deducting all sources of income, the IGA still needed to pay $20,100.60.[165] "The cost of operating the orphanage at St. Anthony causes me considerable concern," Curtis wrote again in 1946 in his report to the IGA Board of Directors.[166]

It was at this financially difficult time for the IGA that Linwood ("Brownie") and Rachel Brown left St. Anthony to return to the United States. The couple had worked together supervising the orphanage for almost 10 years. At least one person saw their departure as the start of the orphanage's long, slow decline into irrelevance. Long-time IGA staff member and Assistant Superintendent Horace McNeill (son of Ted McNeill from Island Harbour, Labrador, and Grenfell's "first scholar") later wrote:

> Rachel and Brownie made the place tick and when they left there seemed to be a vacuum and with the uncertain economic outlook the orphanage was phased out. The Browns gave those in their care, the best of home life atmosphere, gave the children a sense of well-being and self worth. Never before had this been entirely fostered.[167]

While the Browns' departure affected the orphanage, the changes that occurred after Newfoundland and Labrador joined Canada in 1949 were even more influential. Social and economic conditions improved with federal social welfare programs such as the Family Allowance and Old Age Pension. The new money given to families directly contributed to the decline of the St. Anthony orphanage. In 1950, Dr. Curtis reported to the Board of Directors that the number of children at the orphanage was decreasing: "An average of 25 children were in residence during the year. . . . Owing to the family allowances and increased social benefits there are fewer applicants for this institution."[168] The October 1951 issue of *Among the Deep Sea Fishers* reported the same trend: "The Children's Home at St. Anthony has fewer children than in years past because widows now receive generous pensions and family allowances thus enabling them to bring up their families at home which is far better than placing them in an institution."[169]

Plans for a Regional High School and Dormitory

In 1960, the orphanage housed 31 children, six of whom came from Labrador.[170] Half of the children had been placed there by Newfoundland's Division of Child Welfare, and none were full orphans.[171] It cost about $1,000 to house each child annually. The provincial government provided grants of $234 to $360 per year for each child in state care, while the IGA paid the rest.[172] The low numbers of children combined with the high cost of their care led the IGA to consider using the orphanage building for other purposes. One option was to build a regional high school in St. Anthony and to house out-of-town students in the orphanage building. The Newfoundland government offered grants for the construction of regional high schools, so Dr. Gordon Thomas, who would succeed Dr. Curtis as the IGA superintendent, suggested in 1952 that the government convert the orphanage into a dormitory and then manage it. He anticipated that high school students from southern Labrador and northern Newfoundland could then attend a regional institution:[173]

> We also have on the Grenfell Mission here, a large building which is presently used for an Orphanage. The need for a boarding school is becoming more apparent and we would be interested in having the Department of Education establish here a regional

> high school, and take over our Orphanage for the housing and maintenance of the children who would come to school here.[174]

The provincial government replied that it would not involve itself in managing student accommodations, but the IGA still pursued the idea of turning the orphanage into a student dormitory for a regional high school.[175] Dr. Thomas reiterated his plans for the orphanage in a letter to the Department of Education in 1961:

> We are hoping next year to make it more of a dormitory for High School children than a residence for Foster Children of a younger age group, as we feel that the building is better suited and would be better used for this purpose. Therefore, if we can obtain sufficient children to come to school here in St. Anthony, we will be happy to make our dormitory facilities available to them. I would appreciate you letting the various Superintendents and responsible officials such as school supervisors aware of this. Where possible we would be glad to bring children into here under the indenture scheme so that they can be resident in the dormitory and go to the Grenfell School here in St. Anthony until a proper Regional High School is built. This dormitory could be particularly useful to children living in isolated areas of Southern Labrador.[176]

Despite the IGA's enthusiasm for the project, establishing a regional high school in St. Anthony proved challenging. Conflict among the local school board, the IGA, the Anglican authorities, and the community led to much frustration. It also slowed construction of the building, the plans for which had been approved in 1960.[177] Although a partially completed school was in use by 1962, disagreements between the parties continued.[178] A year later, Dr. Thomas recognized "the local rising feeling of a large element to run their own affairs with no interference from outsiders."[179] He suggested that the IGA withdraw from the educational sphere in St. Anthony. Accordingly, the IGA Board of Directors decided to step away from its participation in the local school board: "We have reached the conclusion that the time has now arrived when the people themselves are ready and willing to administer and control their educational facilities without the advice and assistance of the Grenfell Mission."[180]

The days of the St. Anthony orphanage were numbered. In North West River, IGA administrators were urging authorities in northern Labrador to send their students to live and attend school there instead of St. Anthony. The IGA staff also discussed changing their policy for housing children in care so that fewer children would be sent to St. Anthony. In 1964, Dr. Thomas wrote to Dr. Anthony Paddon at North West River with a proposal: "I suggest . . . we now decide that St. Anthony dormitory will no longer take children from middle and northern Labrador through the Welfare Department, but in the future we will refer all these children to you and consider that you will be able to take care of them."[181] The shift of the IGA's educational and child welfare work in Labrador from St. Anthony to North West River was almost complete.

Olive Matthews, who worked in St. Anthony in the early 1960s, describes the final years of the orphanage in a letter published in *Them Days*. She had come to St. Anthony after having been in charge of the dormitory at North West River for four years:

> St. Anthony was very different. The orphanage was running down, and apart from a few children sent by [IGA nurse] Louise Greenfield from Spotted Islands, etc., young people from Newfoundland preferred to "board" in the Village, and a small amount of money was then being given to would-be high school students. We had 35–40 children, one helper and myself. It was never the challenge or the quality of North West, much more occasion for social life, better food, etc. . . . And again we got excellent results from the few high school students we had. Gladys Elson from Spotted Islands got her 11th grade and every prize going, then went to St. John's to train for her teaching, later

> going back for her degree. . . . In spite of a large social life, it never compared with North West dorm. St. Anthony closed down about two years after I left, and the building was used for staff quarters. I remember it with mixed feelings.[182]

The new regional high school, Harriot Curtis Collegiate, officially opened on 3 September 1964. While the orphanage continued to house a few students, financial difficulties led the IGA board to look for ways to reduce spending. On 7 February 1969 they decided "To close down St. Anthony Children's Dormitory as of June 30th, 1969, for an estimated saving of $20,000 this year and $40,000 in subsequent years."[183] The IGA converted the dormitory into a residence for medical staff. It later transferred the building to the province when it handed responsibility for health care and the ownership of much of its property to the Newfoundland government in 1981.

A former IGA worker, who visited St. Anthony in 1978 after a 48-year absence, recalls:

> When we arrived in St. Anthony I was escorted to an apartment put at my disposal for a couple of days while its owner was in Nain. Where was I? In the orphanage, of course! But orphanage no more — it was now an apartment house for the staff. The orphanage had been abandoned some years ago. The infant mortality rate had decreased, the longevity rate had increased, and the government has stepped in between. Result — not enough orphans to fill the building![184]

The St. Anthony orphanage had undergone a pronounced transformation over the years. From its idealistic but imperious beginnings to its decline in the 1960s, the orphanage had played a significant role in the care and education of children in Labrador and northern Newfoundland. The International Grenfell Association had arrived in the region when the Newfoundland government was uninterested and uninvolved in

Labrador. In the government's absence, Grenfell and his organization assumed jurisdiction over educational, social, and medical affairs, and established the orphanage, schools, and hospitals. The IGA staff operated these institutions and took control of child welfare concerns, based on their own cultural ideals and assumptions about what was best. As Newfoundlanders and Labradorians increasingly resisted outside interference in their lives, the IGA bowed out and the orphanage closed.

In the IGA's final year, the superintendent, Dr. Thomas, reflected on the nearly 90-year evolution of the organization. He recognized the need to step aside and allow the local communities to make their own decisions:

> This organization started in 1892 under the colonial system of Great Britain, during the heyday of Queen Victoria's reign. This was a time when the affairs of such an organization as the Grenfell Mission were conducted in an extremely paternalistic although well-motivated manner, by outside persons and with no local opportunity for involvement in the running of its affairs. These philanthropic-minded individuals felt themselves to be very much "bearing the white man's burden." That the Grenfell Organization was to survive, especially following Newfoundland's joining the Canadian Confederation, was due to its ability to change with changing times.[185]

CHAPTER NINE

The Cartwright Area Boarding Schools

"'M' is for Mothers: they are far, far away"
— Peggy Bird, "Dormitory," 1943

The first efforts to establish a school in southeastern Labrador occurred at Battle Harbour in the mid-1800s. The Anglican Bishop of Newfoundland, Rt. Rev. Edward Feild, travelled to Labrador in 1848 and noted the complete lack of educational facilities in the region. "There is no teacher, of any character or denomination, till you come to the Moravian establishments at Nain and Hopedale," he wrote to the British Secretary for the Colonies.[1] He suggested establishing a school at Battle Harbour, "the most populous and most important place on the whole shore."[2] By 1864, his suggestion had taken shape, and the Anglican minister at Battle Harbour was holding school at his house for 20 or so children.[3] Over the next few decades, the Anglican Church also operated summer schools at Cape Charles, Venison Tickle, and Matthews Cove. The schools accommodated the children of both NunatuKavut Inuit families and seasonal Newfoundland fishing families.[4]

All schooling in the colony was administered through the churches and funded by the government in St. John's. In addition to organizing day schools, the Anglican Church and the Methodist Church hired itinerant teachers periodically in the late 1800s and early 1900s for the Sandwich Bay and Lake Melville areas.[5] Itinerant teachers would stay with a family for a week or a month at a time, teaching the local children, before moving on to another homestead. Neither the summer schools nor the itinerant teaching was an efficient method of education. "Labrador is not a favourable country for the establishment of schools," noted a visiting official in 1869.

> The people there are so scattered that, with very few exceptions, it is impracticable to get a sufficient number of them together for that purpose. The general and most effective mode of instruction is by supplying books to the isolated inhabitants, and thus enabling them to learn at home by their own firesides, where they teach one another.[6]

In the early 1900s, the Grenfell Mission also organized summer schools in fishing communities in Sandwich Bay and further south. The teachers were summer volunteers, usually college students who were untrained in teaching but keen for adventure. So, while they taught reading and writing, they also addressed other issues that they or the community

Rev. Henry Gordon with dog team, Sandwich Bay, ca.1920 (courtesy of The Rooms).

identified as important, such as nutrition or first aid.[7] Grenfell recruited two well-educated volunteers, Ethel Gordon Muir and Elizabeth Criswell, to co-ordinate the summer schools. Both women soon recognized the limited impact of the brief schooling sessions on children's education and recommended establishing longer-term schools.[8]

When Anglican priest Henry Gordon arrived in Cartwright from England in 1915 to take over the Sandwich Bay Mission, he also recognized the challenges involved in educating the children. The families of his parish lived in over 40 scattered homesteads along a 200-mile coastline between Batteau, Lake Melville, and Cape Harrison.[9] Most moved seasonally between winter homes in sheltered bays to summer fishing villages on the ocean. While Cartwright's population could support a day school, most of the other sparsely populated settlements were only visited by itinerant teachers. On his way to his new post in Labrador, Rev. Gordon started organizing. He stopped in St. John's to hire three teachers: one to travel around the Hamilton Inlet area, one to visit the communities in Sandwich Bay, and one for the day school in Cartwright.[10]

But Rev. Gordon knew the itinerant schooling system was not ideal. Students spent only a few weeks with a teacher before the teacher moved to the next settlement, and the children of poor families did not get any access to an education if they could not afford to house the teacher. Gordon was keen to discuss how to improve schooling with the local people. He soon became friends with Charlie Bird, a Labradorian who "was a man of very real vision as regards the future of Labrador and shared my own great hope for some improved system of education."[11] Gordon also discussed the issue with Dr. Harry Paddon, an English doctor who had come to Labrador in 1912 to work with the Grenfell Mission and who was building an IGA medical station at North West River. The two had met in 1915 aboard the *Carthaginian*, the ship bound for St. John's from Liverpool, and their shared Oxford education and interest in Labrador cemented a firm friendship.[12]

The Boarding School Solution

Henry Gordon, Charlie Bird, and Harry Paddon discussed various options for improving education in the region. One alternative to the itinerant system was to build a central boarding school on the coast that students could attend for extended periods of time. The Grenfell Mission had been encouraging promising pupils and impoverished children to go to the orphanage in St. Anthony and elsewhere for further education, but Gordon felt that a local institution was needed. He regarded the practice of sending children away for their education as a colonial way of superseding local independence:

> I had for some time realized the danger of arresting a people's own development by, if I express it correctly, over-colonisation. There was much that Labrador could gain from the outside world, but one didn't want it to be at the expense of its own "personality." That was why I completely disagreed with people who maintained that our children should be sent out of the country to receive a training as teachers and mechanics, so that they could return to instruct the others. Dr. Paddon was of the same opinion, and Charlie [Bird] was like-minded. It was on this view that the project of the Labrador Public Boarding School was conceived.[13]

Rev. Gordon envisioned constructing at least two boarding schools: the first for the Cartwright area and a second for Groswater Bay. The schools would house and teach children for periods of up to six weeks. Gordon hoped that they would serve "to educate the people enough to give them an independent voice and a choice of their own welfare."[14]

Plans for constructing the school were developed with the support of Rev. Dr. Edgar Jones and his parish of St. Thomas' Anglican Church in St. John's. To raise funds, Rev. Jones formed a committee at St. Thomas' that included representatives of the governor of Newfoundland, the Anglican and Methodist churches, the International Grenfell Association, the HBC, and prominent members of the St. John's business community.[15] Gordon also formed a local committee of leading authorities in Labrador to raise funds. Members included the IGA's Dr. Paddon and Hudson's Bay Company (HBC) staff at Cartwright.[16]

By the summer of 1918, the committees had collected over $2,000.[17] Rev. Gordon wrote to Clara Ashall, a teacher in his former parish in England and his soon-to-be wife, to ask her to teach in the new school. He emphasized the need to "get the children away from their homes" in providing them with schooling:

> Very little at present is done in the way of education down here: the efforts of such teachers as we can get, can do no more than touch the fringe of the work. To get the children away from their homes, and place them in a building where they can be given a good Christian education, is the only solution that I can see. . . . You are the very person if you would only consent to undertake the work.[18]

Clara agreed. When delayed in coming to Labrador in 1918 because of passport issues, she spent the next few months studying the Montessori method[19] of teaching, as, she later wrote, "I felt that it was going to be of inestimable value in the kind of educational work that lay before me."[20]

The community raised funds for the school as well. At an Easter Fair in Cartwright, which "overflowed with people and dogs," residents raised over $100 for the School Fund. As Gordon reported, the contribution "has done much to increase peoples' sense of independence."[21] Enthusiasm about the project was building.

Then disaster struck. Over the course of eight weeks in November and December 1918, more than 69 of the 320 residents of the Sandwich Bay district died of Spanish flu. By the end of the year, about 40 children had lost one or both parents.[22] Rev. Gordon and the few other healthy adults struggled to feed and nurse the living and bury the dead. The government in St. John's ignored all calls for help.[23] Families in Cartwright, Dove Brook, Paradise River, and throughout the district readily took in the children who had lost their parents, but Gordon and others believed that the boarding school would now need to double as an orphanage:

> [Dr. Paddon and I] talked long and earnestly about the future, and especially the care of the orphaned children. He was heart and soul in favour of the immediate erection of the School, and its use as a Home for the children, and offered to do all he could towards the cost of the venture. . . . I knew his co-operation was all the more sincere and valuable because he was going counter to the declared policy of his [IGA] directors, who, at this time, advocated the removal of children to [the St. Anthony orphanage in] Newfoundland.[24]

As Chapter Eight describes, the International Grenfell Association continued to gather orphans in St. Anthony, and some children from Sandwich Bay were temporarily sent to the Children's Home there. The IGA pressed its supporters for more donations to build a larger orphanage building in St. Anthony so it could accommodate more children. As for a boarding school in the Cartwright area, Henry Gordon knew that Wilfred Grenfell did not initially support the idea: "I felt that he was not in favour of our project of a local School, but he was too large-hearted a man to do anything to damp our enthusiasm, and he wished us all success."[25]

Dr. Harry Paddon pressed the IGA to reconsider its focus on relocating needy children. He had always disagreed with Grenfell's habit of adopting children out to families in the United States or Britain. He felt that even St. Anthony was too far away to send Labrador children. In 1919, Dr. Paddon described how he and others worked to change Grenfell's approach to child welfare:

> We have won over my beloved chief [Dr. Grenfell] from treating Labradorians as an interesting group of tragic individuals who

> can only be saved by bringing them out of their country. He now realizes that they are worth giving a chance to, in their own country; which is well able to support them, if only they are given fair play.[26]

Henry Gordon, Harry Paddon, Charlie Bird, and others remained resolved to build a local institution and keep children "in their own country." When Rev. Walter Perrett of the Moravian Mission passed through Cartwright on his way to St. John's in April 1919, the two ministers shared their heartbreak over the Spanish flu epidemic and discussed future plans. Rev. Gordon was "particularly interested in [Perrett's] scheme for a Moravian boarding-school, which it is intended to start at Makkovic [*sic*]."[27]

Harry Paddon took up the cause with IGA supporters through the organization's fundraising magazine, urging them to recognize the efforts of other groups working in Labrador in the aftermath of the epidemic, especially Rev. Gordon and the Moravian Mission. He asked them to "realize that our people are not all paupers, though life presents a stern struggle to the majority."[28] He encouraged IGA donors to support the local efforts of Labradorians and Rev. Gordon in caring for the orphans through a boarding school near Cartwright. He reported that the people of Sandwich Bay and Lake Melville had donated $1,400 towards the boarding school.[29] In the summer of 1919, families of Sandwich Bay continued to show their support for the project by further contributing towards the new school. Henry Gordon described their support as "a thank-offering for their recovery from the 'flu, and (to me) conclusive evidence of their whole-hearted backing of the project."[30] Their donation of over $600 was "an extraordinary amount for such a small community."[31]

When the Newfoundland government finally responded to the Spanish flu epidemic by sending help to Sandwich Bay, it was June 1919. Six months after people had died from the disease, the government sent 1,500 board feet of lumber for coffins.[32] The general neglect displayed by the Newfoundland government towards Labrador had always angered

Henry Gordon, but this thoughtless shipment of materials for the already buried dead infuriated him.

> The attitude of the Newfoundland government towards Labrador has always been a scandal but this is adding insult to an already long list of injuries. Labrador pays at the very least $10,000 a year in taxes to the Newfoundland government, she has not one single representative in the House of Assembly, she has no resident magistrates, police, relieving officers, no roads, no winter wire or wireless communications, no railways, nothing that any people need for the advantages of life. And to think that governing body, which takes all and gives nothing, should deliberately condemn a magnificent race to starvation and death. One's heart has been almost broken with the sufferings of these poor people. Does no one care?[33]

The insensitive shipment showed that, like most other aspects of life in Labrador, responsibility for the orphans of the Spanish flu fell to the local people and their local minister. The government obviously would provide little help. The coffin-building materials, labelled "Labrador Relief," were nonetheless put to good use: "We were given a present of the fine pile of lumber," Gordon wrote, "which I at once appropriated for the use of the coming School."[34]

Fundraising efforts increased as news of the devastating epidemic spread. By the spring of 1920, the combined efforts of the St. Thomas' committee in St. John's, a lecture tour undertaken by Henry Gordon in the winter of 1919–20 in England, appeals in English newspapers, and Harry Paddon's fundraising efforts in the United States attracted widespread support. Together, they gathered over $25,000 in donations for the Labrador Public School — more than enough to build and run the school.[35] The committee officially registered "Labrador Public Schools, Inc." as a legal entity under Newfoundland law, and construction started that summer.[36]

On Charlie Bird's recommendation, Rev. Gordon chose a site for the

Labrador Public School at Muddy Bay, mid-1920s (courtesy of The Rooms).

new school at Muddy Bay, four miles from Cartwright.[37] Charlie had built a now abandoned commercial fox farm at Muddy Bay in 1915 for a former Grenfell volunteer, the American entrepreneur Clarence Birdseye.[38] Although Birdseye had left Labrador, his bungalow remained at Muddy Bay, where Charlie Bird and his family also had a house. The site was isolated from Cartwright, a community of about 70 people with a Hudson's Bay Company post and an Anglican church, school, and parsonage, but Muddy Bay was accessible by sea and by an overland trail to Cartwright. Gordon and Bird both felt that it was the perfect location for the boarding school.

The St. Thomas' Church committee shipped building materials and expert carpenters to work with local men on construction.[39] The building was erected quickly in the short summer season. Clara Ashall describes visiting Muddy Bay in July 1920: "Work was already going on there on the site — foundations being dug, and part of the outer frame going up. The work, so far, had been in the hands of local labour, but a foreman and three carpenters were to come down from St. John's on the next steamer."[40] A subsequent visit in August impressed her with how far the construction had progressed:

> I could scarcely believe my eyes when I saw how the building had gone up. The concrete basement was finished, most of the framework was up, and the ground floor in place. At the present rate, there seemed to be every chance of the school being ready for the children to take up residence well before the winter.[41]

Exceeding all expectations, the school was finished in late fall. The governor of Newfoundland, Sir Charles Harris, arrived in early September to lay the school's foundation stone.[42] On 25 October, on one of the last freight runs of the year, the *Sagona* supply ship delivered beds, bedding, and food supplies for nine months.[43] The school opened at the beginning of November 1920.[44] "November 1st was a day long to be remembered," Henry Gordon wrote. "It was settling-in day; the first day's life in our great venture of the Labrador Public School."[45]

The Labrador Public School

At the time of its opening in 1920, the Labrador Public School building was one of the largest in the area. It stood at 100 feet by 35 feet, and 30 feet high, with over 70 windows.[46] Twenty-eight children enrolled in the school's first year, "most of them at least part orphans."[47] Ten staff members lived at Muddy Bay with the students. In 1921–22, the number of students rose to 40, and the staff had to refuse admission to others.[48]

In its first year of operation, school staff consisted of Clara Ashall as principal and teachers Miss McKenny of St. Thomas' Anglican Church in St. John's and Sidney Lawton of England. They were supported by a nurse from Liverpool named Amy Astbury, who acted as matron. Charlie Bird served as the general manager with help from Wilfred Shiwak of Rigolet. Hetty Dawe from Newfoundland worked as cook, Mrs. Brown was in charge of the laundry, and Aunt Liz Williams of North River was responsible for the sewing and mending.[49]

The school welcomed visitors and family members, many of whom brought country food for the children. As Clara Ashall notes with pleasure:

Some of the first children at Labrador Public School, ca.1920 (courtesy of The Rooms).

"There was seldom a day when we did not have visitors calling in. . . . Instead of these being a drain on our resources, they were a considerable help, as they very often brought us fresh meat or fish — of which we seemed to consume an enormous quantity."[50] In return, school staff gave out clothing that had been donated by supporters in the United States and England.[51]

Teachers and staff alike intended the Labrador Public School to provide an education appropriate to the Sandwich Bay area. They hoped that the pupils would share what they learned with their families at home.

> The aim of our school is a very definite one. Fully convinced that Labrador's development can only be effected from within, we are giving our children what might be called an "intensive" education. It is not our desire that any of the children should have to leave their country, but rather that they should return to their own homes and infuse their own people with the new ideals and hopes which the school has given them.[52]

Clara Ashall described the approach as a "belief that our children should be identified with the life and occupation of their native land as much as possible."[53] Having trained in the Montessori method of teaching, she encouraged child-driven learning, outside activities, and ample time to play. She scheduled lessons from 9:30 a.m. to noon, and from 4:00 p.m. to 6:00 p.m., "so that they could have the afternoon for play and fresh air when possible."[54] Henry Gordon reported that the approach was proving "a huge success. Rewards and punishments are practically in the hands of the children themselves, who have learned to regard as the worst offences those which injure the well-being of the community."[55]

After the school's first year, Clara Ashall and Henry Gordon married, and Clara resigned her post as principal of the school. While the Gordons remained closely involved in the school and Clara continued to do some teaching, they withdrew from daily oversight of the institution.[56] Agnes Hamilton of Nova Scotia was hired as a replacement principal for the next three years.[57]

While Clara's Montessori teaching methods may have influenced the other teachers, the school assumed a more traditional approach to education after she resigned. However, the teachers maintained their goal that the school should prepare the children for life on the coast. The school's curriculum concentrated "on a useful and industrial training":

> Certain hours are devoted to elementary training and the rest occupied with "utility" instruction. The boys are taught to use their hands and learn the importance of being able to do their own work. Under a splendid local handy man, Mr. Charles Bird, manager of our outside department, they are quickly learning just those things which will make them more prosperous in later years. . . . In similar manner, the girls are taught the ideals of housewifery — cooking, sewing, laundry and above all cleanliness. We are most careful to avoid any extremes in their training, for one realizes the great value of preserving the joyfulness of their childhood.[58]

The school founders aimed to provide an education that complemented local life. But staff also recognized that the school's teaching marked the students as different from the rest of the population. A temporary summer schoolteacher, arriving in 1921, noted the difference with approval. She credited the change to the practice of removing the children from their families:

> I am thoroughly convinced that Mr. Gordon's idea of educating these children in a boarding school is the proper way of reaching them. They are thus taken out from under the immediate influence of their homes, which is not a refining influence. It seems like a most worthwhile effort.[59]

Labrador Public School boys, Sandwich Bay vs. Groswater Bay football game, between 1920 and 1925 (front, l-r: Finley Lemare, Warren Goudie, Henry Goudie, Holman Mesher; middle, l-r: Henry Voisey, Jack Williams, Harry Heard, Harvey Bird; back, l-r: John Heard, Charlie Williams, Tom Bird, Jack Mugford) (courtesy of The Rooms).

Indeed, after just a year in operation, Rev. Gordon already noticed the school's effect on the children: "It is an honest fact that some of the children have altered so much that their relatives did not know them."[60] Other staff noticed the impact of schooling on the children as well. Greta Bidlake took over as matron of the school when Amy Astbury married Charlie Bird in 1922.[61] On visiting families around Sandwich Bay, she was pleased to see the difference that the school had made in the lives of its pupils: "I was able to visit a few houses while there and compare our children with others I saw. Without a doubt the Cartwright School has done much. The children in the school show plainly that they have had greater advantages than others."[62]

School routines and regimented chores structured the lives of the children. In describing a typical winter's day to IGA readers in 1922, Rev. Gordon revealed a strict schedule:

> We (at least the adult portion of us) rise about 6 a.m. and begin stoking up the stoves. Breakfast is at 8 o'clock and consists of porridge or brewis (a very satisfying mixture of bread, pork-fat, and salt fish, far more palatable than it sounds). From 8.30 to 9.30 the girls are busy upstairs, while the boys split up wood, and fill all the wood boxes by the various stoves (there are about fourteen). From 9.30 to 11.30 school. At 11.30 dinner, consisting of either partridges, rabbits, hash, or pea soup followed by a boiled pudding. From 12 o'clock to 1.30 the wood boxes are replenished, the water barrels filled, and the refuse carried down to the land wash, or poured through a hole in the ice. From 1.30 to 4 o'clock school again. At 4 o'clock comes tea of bread and jam or sometimes beans. Immediately after tea, wood and water are attended to once again, then comes recreation with football, sleighing, walking, etc. With dark indoor games are available. At 6.45 comes cocoa, 7.30 prayers and bed. So it will seem that we have not much idle time during a winter's day.[63]

The teachers incorporated British cultural practices into the schedule and routine, from the afternoon tea to the Empire Day celebration and the crowning of the May Queen.[64] In 1922, Clara Ashall (now Clara Gordon) described how they organized the pupils in a performance of that singularly British custom — a Christmas pantomime — while the staff staged a production of Charles Dickens's *A Christmas Carol.*[65]

The International Grenfell Association Takes Charge

The school and dormitory required an enormous amount of work to run and maintain. Henry and Clara Gordon found it exhausting. Constant money worries, problems with a lack of clothes for the children, and the wider responsibilities of the parish soon wore them out. Clara described her situation to an American donor:

> At present we have thirty-two children resident here and the problem of clothes is ever before us. It is fearfully difficult to keep such a large family looking neat and presentable, and it is a great relief and help to us to have your boxes of clothing to turn to as necessity arises. I do not know what we should have done without those gifts and we are more than grateful for all your help. . . . We are looking forward to the spring when we hope we shall receive the help which we so sorely need. We are very short-handed, and consequently get very tired and despondent occasionally, though we quickly climb the mount again. . . . Besides all this, the money problem — funds for the upkeep of the school — is a great and ever-present worry.[66]

The Labrador Public School worked to raise funds in a number of ways. Henry Gordon asked the Newfoundland government to provide the school with the same annual grant ($52 per child per year) it provided to orphanages in the colony. The Deputy Colonial Secretary agreed, and on 1 November 1920, the day the school opened, he recommended the government issue the grant.[67]

The International Grenfell Association also organized a Big Brother and Big Sister campaign to help pay for the boarding school. Donors were asked for $125 per year to sponsor individual children at the school. The IGA advertised the program in its quarterly publication, *Among the Deep Sea Fishers*: "The first donation of $125 is going to care for a little girl at the Labrador Public School by a woman who wants to pay her board and clothe her and hopes to eventually give her the advantage of higher education in the States."[68]

Despite all efforts, however, financial concerns persisted. In the summer of 1922, Henry Gordon received a letter from Wilfred Grenfell offering a solution to his problems. "With his usual frankness and delightful inconsistency [Grenfell] informed me that he had now become completely converted to our belief in a localized system of education and (with the full approval of his very powerful Board of Directors) offered to take over full responsibility for the Boarding School."[69] Gordon felt that it was the only viable option to the financial challenges of running the school. "I knew, in my heart, that this was the only thing to do, but before reaching any decision, I had a long talk with Charlie Bird, Hayward Parsons and one or two more of our local Committee. They all agreed that we should accept the offer."[70]

Henry and Clara Gordon moved to Cartwright from Muddy Bay in 1923, and he resumed his ecclesiastical work throughout the parish. Clara stopped teaching full-time, but she organized women's groups in Cartwright and taught Sunday school. They left Labrador in 1925 to return to England, bringing with them Violet Holwell, a graduate of the Labrador Public School from Spotted Island who had worked as their maid for years:

> After some considerable thought, we had decided to bring [Violet] back with us to England, where we hoped she could train as a nurse, and come back to help at her old school at Muddy Bay.

> Needless to say she was thrilled, and the envy of all her friends. We were very glad that her mother was so pleased about it.[71]

Violet later returned to Labrador to work as housemother for the IGA boarding schools at Cartwright and Mary's Harbour.[72] She married Ewart Young, the head teacher at the Lockwood School, in 1937.[73]

Although the early success of the Labrador Public School was largely attributed to the Gordons, Henry and Clara always paid tribute to the contributions of local people. "Mr. [Charlie] Bird has been one of our many blessings," wrote Rev. Gordon in 1921. "What we should have done without him is beyond the imagination to express."[74] Gordon credited Charlie Bird with many of the school's accomplishments:

> Our greatest mutual interest was in the educational welfare of the Labrador children. He shared my own belief that only a central Boarding School could adequately deal with the problem, and much of the future success that attended the achievement of this project was due to his enthusiasm and practical help.[75]

In recognition of the minister's efforts, the IGA tried to rename the bay "Gordon Cove" instead of Muddy Bay, but the name never caught on.[76] Nonetheless, Henry and Clara Gordon's legacy lives on through the Cartwright school that was renamed Henry Gordon Academy in 1968.[77]

When the IGA took over responsibility in 1922, it gave the school a more secure financial footing, but the Labrador Public School remained an expensive endeavour. Even with pupils expected to do their own chores, school administrators still needed several young women to help with the cleaning, cooking, laundry, and mending. Ida Lemare Lethbridge Sheppard (age 16), Lizzie Oliver (age 16), and Mary Jane Williams (age 13 or 14) were a few of the local people the IGA hired in the 1920s. When Miriam Hamel started working at age 13, she was paid $2 a month: "We started on $2, and it went up to $4. . . . Then we used to get $6 a month when we worked down there. We thought then you had a fortune."[78] It was hard work and, for Ida Sheppard, who worked at the school in 1922 or 1923, it was also thankless toil:

> I was working there like a slave. That's what we used to all call it, all we girls. . . . All young people working. We had to do all the work, like scrubbing and washing and cooking and everything like that. The big girls and big boys [the older students] had to do all their own dormitories and empty their own pails in the winter. And the big boys had to get water for the laundry and water for the kitchen, water for all the people. They'd be out in the storms hauling two barrels of water on a big old long *Kamutik*. Had to work hard there, maid, especially in the winter. . . . [We got] nine and ten dollars. That's as good as you could pay them times.[79]

Students also contributed to the costs by catching wild food, cutting wood, and carrying out general chores. An IGA staff member reported on their efforts in 1926:

> [The boys] caught four hundred rabbits. If these were bought it would amount to $100. Two thousand turn of firewood cut would be $50. Path making and helping haul has been also part of their work. They saw all firewood, cleave and carry it around to the rooms where it is required, and the fetching of water and other chores would cost at least $20 per month if it were hired help.[80]

The IGA continued to recruit teaching staff from England, the United States, Canada, and Newfoundland. It also hired graduates of Grenfell education programs who returned to Labrador after going to school elsewhere. Blanche Davis of Cartwright, whom the Grenfell Mission had sent to Boston for teacher training, came home to teach kindergarten and younger students.[81] Ethel Pye from Cape Charles worked as a teacher and a housemother at the school before moving to the same position at the new IGA boarding school in North West River.[82]

Labrador Public School children, ca. 1921 (courtesy of Them Days Archive).

Dr. Harry Paddon, long a supporter of the Labrador Public School and now permanently stationed at North West River, felt encouraged by the success of the school. After a visit to Muddy Bay he was impressed by what he saw. "They were certainly a jolly, healthy looking group, and I felt my conviction strengthened that herein lay the solution of some at least of Labrador's problems."[83] He started to plan for a similar boarding school in central Labrador. "I could not rest content till a second of the Labrador Public Schools should be built, and that at North West River."[84] In 1926, with funding from Yale University, he organized the building of a second Labrador Public School at North West River (see Chapter Eleven).

The End of the Labrador Public School

On 19 February 1928 the Labrador Public School at Muddy Bay came to a sudden and fiery end. Two disgruntled students being punished for a misdemeanour set the building on fire and it burned to the ground. Millicent Loder was in Grade 6 at the time:

> One cold Sunday evening in February, we were all in the dining room eating our supper . . . when one of the working girls came in and said something to the mistress. She always stood by the food table, watching us while we ate, and she said to us, "Children, get up immediately and file quietly out into the hall and go straight out the front door." We did as we were told. . . . As we passed the stairway, there was smoke coming down and we could hear the crackling of fire.[85]

Miriam Hamel describes her memories of the fire from neighbouring Goose Cove:

> You could hear the cans pop, pop, pop, with the heat. . . . They used to have sweet potatoes in tins. . . . I tell you that was some time. Oh my, the poor little children. Everyone was broken hearted, they lost everything. . . . That was done by Buck Michelin and Tom Toomashie. They said when the doctor was beating

Labrador Public School, 1920s (courtesy of Them Days Archive).

> them, I often heard that when the doctor was beating them they had their pants and everything stuffed out with grass. It never hurt them a'tall, my dear.[86]

Upon seeing the smoke, people drove their dog teams and *Kamutet* from Cartwright to Muddy Bay to pick up the children. "It wasn't long before the kind people of Cartwright came and took us into their homes and fed and comforted us, and gave us what clothing they could spare," recalled Millicent Loder.

> Next morning we learned that our school had burned to the ground and that one little girl [Lizzie Learning], who had been sick in her bed upstairs, had just escaped when one of the teachers had managed to get her out by handing her to people standing below the roof of the porch. Then he was forced to jump himself, and broke his ankle or knee.[87]

Buck Edgar Michelin, who was 14 or 15 at the time, was charged with arson and spent time in jail for setting the building on fire.[88]

Out of the Ashes: The Lockwood School and Dormitory

The loss of the Labrador Public School was devastating to the community and the International Grenfell Association. Undeterred, the IGA rallied its supporters to fund the construction of a new school. The school at Muddy Bay had been insured for two-thirds of its value, but more money was needed to construct a new building.[89] The largest contribution came from J.S. Lockwood[90] of Torresdale, Pennsylvania, who had been a long-time supporter of the International Grenfell Association.[91] In recognition of her generous donation of $25,000, the IGA named the new institution Lockwood School.[92]

Harry Paddon wanted the new school built closer to Cartwright and made fire-resistant: "In the reconstruction, when it came, at least one great fault was to be corrected by the shifting of the school to the shores of Cartwright harbour, to a magnificent location by a brook."[93] Chosen on Charlie Bird's advice, the new location was within sight of Cartwright, across the harbour from the larger community.[94]

IGA volunteers (wops) mixing cement during construction of the dormitory at Cartwright, 1930 (courtesy of The Rooms).

Construction of the Lockwood School at Cartwright, 1930 (courtesy of The Rooms).

The IGA also used the opportunity to transfer its medical station at Indian Harbour to Cartwright. The Newfoundland fishery, which had brought so many schooners and fishermen to the Indian Harbour and Battle Harbour Mission stations, was changing. The fishing fleet had shrunk by about 60 per cent, and far fewer fishers were working on shore.[95] "We have decided that the time has arrived when the beloved little old hospital on the island at Indian Harbor must sink to the level of a nursing station," Wilfred Grenfell wrote in 1929, "and Cartwright become the seat of all the northern activities."[96] Plans were drawn for a hospital, a school building, and a dormitory near Cartwright.

Led by former Grenfell student Ted McNeill of Island Harbour, Labrador, IGA staff organized construction of the buildings. Crews of IGA summer volunteers, the workers without pay (or wops) from eastern US colleges, constructed a dam for the new school and hospital building, and dug a half-mile of ditch for water pipes.[97] The building was designed to be modern and comfortable, with running water, a furnace, and electricity — unknown luxuries in the region at the time.[98] The Newfoundland government also agreed to build a road around the harbour, connecting the IGA station to the community of Cartwright.[99]

While the new school was under construction, most students either attended the Anglican-run day school at Cartwright or stayed at home. Three girls went to stay in the Grenfell orphanage while they attended school in St. Anthony in 1929, and six students in Grade 6 finished their year at Muddy Bay by living and taking classes in the laundry building.[100] The Hudson's Bay Company donated ledgers for the students to use as paper and wooden crates for desks.[101]

When the Lockwood School opened in the fall of 1930, the IGA congratulated itself on the achievement. The IGA's executive officer in New York, Alfred A. Whitman, announced that it represented "the realization . . . of Sir Wilfred's dream of a really adequate school on the Labrador."[102] In celebrating the new school, Whitman neglected to mention the Labrador Public School at Muddy Bay or the efforts of Labradorians and Henry Gordon. Instead, he claimed that the new Lockwood School "will take the place of the very inadequate schools conducted by itinerant summer teachers, which have been the only possible means to education in the little isolated settlement along the Labrador coast."[103]

With the opening of the Lockwood School, Elizabeth Criswell of Columbus, Ohio, acted as principal for the first two years, having been the principal of Yale School in North West River for the previous four years. She was assisted by women from Labrador who had been educated through IGA institutions. Eva Shiwak of Rigolet, who had lived in the St. Anthony orphanage while attending school there, assumed the post of assistant teacher at Lockwood for the 1930–31 school term and Violet Stone of Henley Harbour taught at the school in 1932–33.[104] Wilfred Grenfell was especially pleased with the new buildings at Cartwright:

> The new school house and boarding school, given by Mrs. Lockwood, are perfectly splendid. As one approaches, one notices the solid white wharf that has been built. . . . The wide road is well made and drained; it leads over a hill that was once a tangle of bog and tuckamore. The colors of the two buildings, showing over the trees, are very attractive.[105]

Plans for a new hospital were also in the works, and a site near the Lockwood School and the separate dormitory was chosen in the summer of 1931. But just four years after the new school opened, on 19 June 1934, the dormitory housekeeper, Janet Stewart, was heating floor wax on the stove when it caught fire. Lewis Brown, a pupil at the time, describes what he remembers:

> It was started by a can of wax on the oil stove. When [Miss Stewart] went to take it off she burned her fingers and dropped the can, then the wax went down in the oil stove and exploded. My sister Sevilla was there and instead of goin' downstairs and get out, she went upstairs, right to the last floor, five storeys up. She jumped out the window and hit the ladder, hit the second last

Dormitory at Cartwright, built in 1930, burned down in 1934 (courtesy of The Rooms).

> step from the ground, across her head. She survived but she wasn't the same after. She was up in her seventies when she died.
>
> Me and Solomon Elson was in bed with the chicken pox. We was asleep when the fire started. We just woke up and heard something like a rush out in the hallway. I went out and opened the door and looked out. The fire was right out in front of our door then. It was goin' up and spreading around. We ran for the door but, when we got down the steps to open the door to go out, the fire was blazin' under the steps. It wasn't long before the fire was out of control. Of course, it was out of control from the start, because they had nothing them times to put out fires with anyway.[106]

Elizabeth "Lizzie" Learning, who had been saved in the 1928 fire at the Labrador Public School in Muddy Bay, was "in isolation for a mild case of scarlet fever in a room on the top floor."[107] "She was just a young girl," describes student Chesley Lethbridge. "Apparently the top floor of that first dormitory was used as a kind of a nursing station and a little hospital, and I think she was there sick at the time."[108] This time, rescuers were unable to reach her, and Lizzie Learning, just 17 years old, died in the fire.

Lockwood School and Dormitory Start Over

The dormitory burned to the ground. But the school building, hospital, and most other IGA buildings remained undamaged. Once again, the IGA raised funds to build a new dormitory on the foundation of the first one, this time with asbestos and rock wool lining to ensure it would be fire-resistant. School continued for the 1934–35 school year with only 14 boarders, due to a lack of space. Violet Holwell from Spotted Island acted as housemother.[109] Other students likely attended St. Peter's, an Anglican day school at Cartwright, or stayed home. The next year, 1935–36, Principal Ewart Young reported that the school could take in five day pupils and 27 boarding students by housing the boys in the cooking shack and the girls in the school building (see Appendix 2 for the list of students).[110]

Construction of the new dormitory was completed in 1936. The bungalow in Muddy Bay, originally built for Clarence Birdseye, was moved to

Lockwood dormitory at Cartwright, opened in 1936 (courtesy of The Rooms).

Cartwright for Kittie Keddie of the Grenfell Industrial Department. On top of organizing Grenfell craft production, she taught students "deerskin sewing" and other handicrafts.[111] Dr. Hogarth Forsyth from London, England, moved from St. Mary's River to live at the Lockwood dormitory in 1938, when the St. Mary's River boarding school closed (see Chapter Ten). His wife, Clayre Forsyth, took on the role of superintendent at the Lockwood dormitory. A new era of institutional life at Lockwood had begun.

Life at Lockwood

The second Lockwood dormitory was a four-storey building with four large bedrooms for the older and younger boys and girls. It included kitchens, bathrooms, dining rooms, study rooms, staff living quarters, equipment rooms, a laundry, a carpentry shop, and a furnace room.[112] Former student Gary Elson lived there in the 1960s:

> There were approximately sixty kids, give or take, evenly divided between boys and girls, and we all lived in the Dorm. The upstairs was sub-divided, a boys' room and the girls, separated by a hallway. There were bunk beds, and we were responsible for making sure our beds were clean and our little locker area was cleaned up every day. I remember the place being very clean, very tidy and a lot of rushing around. It was a very structured facility.[113]

Initially, most of the students at Lockwood either came from small settlements and single-family homesteads around Sandwich Bay or from larger communities on the southeast coast of Labrador that did not have schools.[114] Between the 1930s and the 1960s, more families from Sandwich Bay moved into Cartwright, where their children attended St. Peter's day school.[115] Over time, a higher proportion of the students at Lockwood came from the communities of Seal Islands, Spotted Island, and Batteau. In 1960, for instance, 56 of the 62 children registered at the dormitory came from Seal Islands (14), Spotted Island (21), and Batteau

(21).[116] Other students at Lockwood came from schools in Rigolet, Paradise River, Separation Point, and other communities. Having attended the first few years of classes in these communities, they wanted to continue their education at the larger Lockwood School.[117]

As elsewhere in Labrador, schooling was not compulsory until 1942.[118] School officials did not usually enforce attendance until after Confederation, when they could threaten to take away Family Allowance payments if parents did not send their children to class. But even when attendance was officially mandatory, the boarding school at Lockwood often could not accommodate every school-aged child whose community did not have a school. In 1952, for example, the Lockwood dormitory could take only two of the 12 children from Hawke's Harbour, which did not have a school. The remaining 10 children did not go to school.[119] Children in the Roman Catholic community of Black Tickle, which lies across the bay from Batteau, did not attend Lockwood because of religious segregation. As one resident commented, children in Black Tickle had very limited educational opportunities:

> I used to go to Batteau and Spotted in the fall. I had friends there. They'd be gone. They'd be gone to Lockwood or St. Anthony, the old Grenfell schools. But we never went. And why we never went was we was part of that Catholic school thing, and that was in West St. Modeste and they had no boarding place. We had no schooling hardly growing up.[120]

Arriving at Lockwood

Every student at Lockwood had a different experience of living at the dormitory and attending the school, but the shock of being immersed in a foreign and institutional environment was universal. Mission staff picked up students from their home communities in the fall with the IGA boat and returned them home in June. Children from beyond Sandwich Bay rarely saw their families during this time and would spend Christmas and Easter at the school.

Millicent Blake Loder, who later became a nurse and worked for the IGA at St. Anthony, Mary's Harbour, and North West River, remembers arriving at the school at the age of 10 from her home in Double Mer, near Rigolet:

> When we arrived at Muddy Bay, the school looked monstrous to me. The staff and children of the school came down on the wharf to greet us. I was taken to the school and was handed over to the Head Mistress. She looked at me, then called one of the working girls over and said, "Take her upstairs and show her where she is going to sleep. Check her head, give her a bath and put some decent clothes on her." I was heartbroken. I was being treated like I imagined poor children were, and I knew that my mother had given me the best she could.[121]

Thirty years later, six-year-old Ethel Campbell felt the same humiliation upon entering the institution. Now living in Rigolet, she describes her initial enthusiasm when she and her cousin, Jane Shiwak, were picked up from their home at West Bay:

> I was 6 when I went to the dorm. I was kind of happy going; I didn't know where I was going. I was going on this boat, all the way up, eating apples, being happy. So we got to the dock, got out. People come and got us. We had our suitcase in our hands, going up to the dorm. All of a sudden, we were all going in this room, getting our heads checked, putting all this old stuff on our heads, burning my neck. Getting our hair cut, just like we were coming out of a cave or something.[122]

Betti Mesher Broomfield recalls a similar experience on her first day at the school:

> I remember when I got there, our orientation was to have a bath. You got your hair chopped off, your earlobes showing and a bang across your forehead. You were deloused if you had lice or not, swamped with some kind of solution to kill head lice. They really had to do that because if there was people and kids with lice the whole place would be infested. You were issued your clothes, which was cotton shirts with peter pan collars with rick rack and a pair of bibbed overalls with rick rack around the bib as well.[123]

Many remembered a strict routine that was signalled by a bell.

> The bell rang at 7 in the morning and you were out of bed. School time, the bell rang at 9 o'clock sharp and you better be in that door, and it rang again 12 o'clock sharp, rang again 1 o'clock sharp and again 3:30 in the afternoon, you know, and it rang for the meals and so on. When you heard that thing ring, you better get goin'.[124]

Loneliness

The impersonal and regimented life at the large institution was humiliating and hurtful for many children, some of whom were as young as four or five. They missed their tight-knit families at home. One man in Cartwright describes what it felt like to leave his family on Spotted Island for Lockwood, 100 kilometres away:

> You're taken away when you're seven years old and you are put in this strange place with what they call the housemother and the housefather. You're looking at two strangers, you don't know who they are and then right from day one, they take you away to your room and to your individual bed where you got to look after. It's very scary. It was very scary for a seven-year-old to have to go through that. . . . Especially taken out of a little fishing community, you know, you're only looking at probably 40 or 50 people in the whole community where everybody knew one

> [another], and you take us and put us aboard a [boat to] Cartwright and then, you know, another 80 or 90 kids or something that are from all sides and different places, it's very frightening. So every night you cry yourself to sleep.[125]

The prolonged separation from family heightened children's fear and loneliness.

> Every year since I started school I'd remember when they take us away in the latter part of August, first [of] September, and then in the Spring, the IGA, they'd take a lot of the school kids and started dropping them off to their Summer places like Indian Tickle, Spotted Island, Black Tickle, and Seal Island. We'd get dropped off by those little boats. And that would be in June month, so you'd get home then for a couple of months and then you'd go back again. But you didn't see your parents not from [when] they took you away September on to June. They had no way to get to see you. They had no way to get out there only by dog team. If you were lucky enough, probably sometime in the Easter time to get down and perhaps say hello or something like that, but that was it. But you never saw your parents from September to June.[126]

Life at Lockwood was vastly different from life in the tiny coastal communities. In the village, life was centred around the family; children were surrounded by a network of relatives who played various roles in their lives, from nurturer or mentor to caregiver or younger sibling.

> Every family was close. Every family, didn't matter if you had 10 or if you had 20 or you had 2, it was all the same thing. . . . When I was growing up as a kid, you didn't back-answer your parents, but they treated you with whatever respect they could. They treated you as a human kid. We knew we never had enough to eat

Elson children in Rocky Bay (winter place). The family's summer place was Spotted Island. (l-r: Eva Elson, Vadney Elson, Doreen Elson) (courtesy of Eva Elson Luther).

> . . . but you was always close [with your] family. . . . You [would] never go hungry. But what I got in that boarding school, now whatever they cooked for all of us kids, well, you had to eat.[127]

Jane Dyson Light, who went to Lockwood in 1960, came from the small fishing village of Batteau. In comparing life at Lockwood with life in Batteau, she contrasts the freedom she found at home with the restrictions she felt at the boarding school. In Batteau, she remembers feeling "at home, no matter what house you went in because you had so many aunts and uncles and then all the kids played together."[128] Her experience at Lockwood, she says, taught her to appreciate her family more. "Because I remember just before I left [Batteau], I couldn't stand the kids. But after you're away from them, you can't wait to get home to see them, so you — it taught me to appreciate my sisters and brothers."[129]

Hazel Williams Beaulac also felt that she became aware of the importance of others because of her experiences at Lockwood. Her mother had died when she was two. From a small village north of Cartwright, she was sent to the St. Anthony hospital at the age of three for back surgery, and then to the Cartwright hospital to recover. She started school at Lockwood at age five in 1948 and stayed until she was eight. When she was allowed to return home, she did not really know her father or her family.

> I was always called the farmer's child. Because they were fishermen and I didn't know what to do, like my sister did. I didn't know how to row. I didn't know what kind of rocks to pick up for the nets. . . . [But] I learned, I think, a lot of things probably I wouldn't have learned if I had been at home. I know what loneliness is like, isolation is like, and I think you learn to care for other people more — not to judge them. So that I am thankful for.[130]

Blanche Williams Coombs worked at the school at Muddy Bay in the 1920s, where she witnessed the separation of children from their families. Years later, with five young children of her own, she wanted to prevent

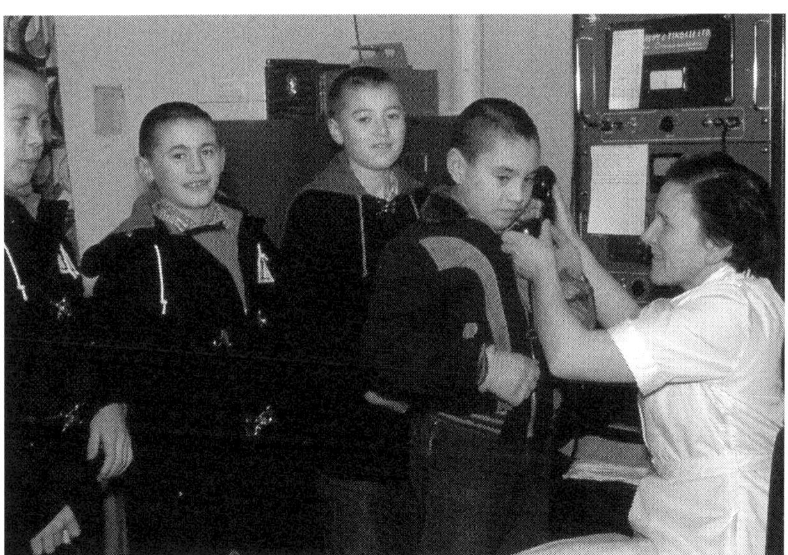

Children at Lockwood call home, 1960s (photo captioned, "Merry Christmas") (courtesy of Them Days Archive).

the same split happening to her family. When she developed a fatal case of pneumonia, her daughter Bertha Chaulk describes how this concern was foremost in her mind: "Her last wishes were for her husband to keep the family together, and for them to get a good education and not to send them to a boarding school."[131]

John Webber went to Lockwood in the 1930s at four years old, after his mother died and he had no one to look after him. He remembers missing his home on Spotted Island:

> When I was there I didn't like it, [and], you know, I think back at it now, I don't think I'd be able to go over on the Lockwood side if I was in Cartwright. I don't think I'd be able to stand it, to look at it. When I was there I always wanted to be home, I didn't like it then. We never had all that [much], [but] home was a real home. . . . [But] you wasn't hungry and you wasn't dirty [at the school]. I give them credit for that, even right from the first year. A lot of people says it was bad old food and all this, but I think I got to say it was better than we had at home.[132]

John spent five years at Lockwood, and the experience still upsets him: "Lockwood School, I don't think I'd feel very good now to go over there, when I'm in Cartwright, God, I almost gets panicky or something or other, to think about it."[133]

Chores and Discipline

Students at Lockwood were expected to do chores throughout the day. According to IGA staff, children needed "the discipline of regular hours and the stimulus of responsibility for a job which depends on their care."[134] Jobs were divided by gender: boys brought in wood, lit fires, shovelled snow, cleaned and took care of the hens, while girls cleaned, baked bread, and sewed. "Everyone took their turn doing chores," remembered Victor Mesher. "'Twas on a list that you had to do. We had to clean up after meals, wash dishes, wipe them and put them away. . . . We used to have to scrub all the floors, the hallway downstairs, the washrooms and everything."[135]

Bella Learning Gear described how the staff grouped the children into big girls and boys and little girls and boys to organize responsibility for doing the chores.

> The big girls used to have to take turns in twos, like they'd put two big girls together to go down and mix breads and stuff like that. We used to have to have a turn, doing dishes, help peel potatoes, clean carrots and stuff like that. Mostly helped out in the kitchen and we had to make our own beds.[136]

Two girls at Lockwood drying dishes, 1930s (courtesy of The Rooms).

Sometimes the work had its perks, as Bill Pardy describes:

> We were kept pretty busy all the time. In the mornings, before school, we had chores to do around the Dorm. Some of the boys would have to chop wood and bring it in. We'd have to do the same thing in the evening when we'd get out of school. We'd be assigned to different places, like Mrs. Keddie's place, that was the Industrial worker. She lived down in the Cottage and we used to have to get wood, water, and stuff like that for her. . . . Mrs. Keddie used to always give us a lunch when we finished our chores. Soon as our chores were done we had to go in and sit down for a little bit. We'd be looking forward to that because sometimes we'd be pretty hungry. At the Dorm, you wouldn't get anything between meals, no lunches or nothing like that, just the regular meals and sometimes you wouldn't like it. So we used to look

> forward to going to Mrs. Keddie's, getting her water and her wood in for her, cleaving it and storing up the wood in a shed.[137]

IGA staff and teachers enforced strict rules at the dormitories and at the school and disciplined disobedient children. Teachers sometimes punished students physically, while discipline at the dorm usually took the form of food deprivation. "They very often caned you if you deserved it," remembers John Webber. "My God, old Mr. Cook used an old twelve inch leather boot bottom. When he come down on your hand, you wouldn't do tomorrow what you done today."[138] Chesley Lethbridge went to Lockwood in the 1940s. He recalls his hunger from being punished at the dormitory:

> You were sent to your room and maybe you had to miss a meal. I'll guarantee you, to miss a meal then really hurt because you only got three meals a day and no snacks in between. If you missed a meal you were a hungry person before the next meal would come up.[139]

Bill Pardy remembers students being punished for small transgressions:

> The children were very good, they didn't do anything, as I can recall, that was really bad. Sometimes they wouldn't do their homework or forget to do their chores, then they'd get punished for that, probably have to write a hundred lines or five hundred lines or something, the older ones. They were very strict.[140]

As strict as the staff was, Chesley Lethbridge felt that it "prepared us for later in life":

> The discipline was really remarkable because we had, we were on just as rigid discipline as what you would have in the armed forces, you know, in that respect, eh. And I don't think that hurts

> anyone. No, I think that builds character and helps you out in later life, you know. I certainly never regretted any treatment that I ever received there.[141]

Others have negative memories of the harsh treatment they endured. One man in Cartwright describes a housefather who "carried a yardstick, a big long wooden stick":

> If you made a peep, buddy, I tell you . . . [he'd] take you by the hand and lift you out of bed, bend your arm and stick you in a dark corner with your hands over your head like this for so long . . . then he started [putting] books on your head . . . you know, those old arithmetic books, hard-covered books, until your arms started to fall. And the books would fall off your head and then you start to cry and then they leave you there 'til you stop crying and they lead you back, put you into bed.[142]

Jane Shiwak of Rigolet was only four years old when she went to Lockwood from her home in West Bay in 1959. From the start, she was abused by the housemothers when she could not bring herself to eat the food.

> I couldn't adjust to the food. I'd throw it up and had to eat it back again. All the kids watching me . . . I was only 5 years old. Stripped off and beaten in front of all the school children, with a leather belt. Every day they did that. Till it got reported, that was about March, I suppose, when it got reported. February or March. They had it in the records in Cartwright from Social Services, where I was abused, beaten. . . . And then my mom, so far away from me, couldn't get to me. I had to suffer from September till March before she knew what was happening to me.[143]

When the staff changed at the dormitory, Jane's life improved. The new house parents were kind, and she enjoyed the rest of her time at Lockwood.

Years later, when Jane was 12, the abusive housemothers visited her at West Bay to apologize. Her mother counselled her to be patient, but Jane never forgave them for the way they treated her.[144]

Many parents disagreed with the Lockwood staff's disciplinary measures. As Chapter One discussed, Inuit families use an approach to child-rearing and discipline that emphasizes patience over harsh penalties. According to accounts from both former students and the IGA, many NunatuKavut Inuit families found the Grenfell staff's method of controlling students much too authoritarian. In 1939, the doctor newly stationed at Cartwright, Dr. Forsyth, noted that "If the teachers at the Lockwood school discipline a child, the parents will often take him away from school or not send him back the next year."[145] Four years later, comments by IGA staff suggest they still had not learned to adjust their behaviour to accommodate cultural differences in parenting styles:

> Labrador parents will not send their children to any boarding school if the children do not want to go, and if the children were disciplined, they would not return a second year. This makes dealings with difficult children very hard and a few such had a demoralizing effect on the school as a whole.[146]

Meals and Class Distinctions

Mealtime at the dormitory served to remind the children that they were far from home. Many students found the food strange and new or institutional and unappetizing. At home, they ate wild food such as salmon, cod, caribou, rabbit, partridge, eggs, and berries, as well as staples of bread and tea. At Lockwood, they ate canned and dried foods that could be easily stored and cooked for large numbers of people.

> We lived on beans, a lot of different kinds of beans, and peas, lentils, and macaroni and cheese and various things like that was the most things that we got. Once in a while we'd get a meal of salt fish, yes, but that was maybe once a month or something like that,

> we would have what they called a Jigg's dinner, you know. And we would get desserts, but mostly for their desserts it would be a sweet pudding or something with a bit of sauce of some kind to go on our rice pudding. You'd get quite a bit of stews, you know, different vegetables all cooked up together and so on. But it seemed to be, like I say, we'd only get three meals a day, but it was good meals. It was rough food but it was good food and there was plenty of it, plenty of it. We would get enough to eat, you know.[147]

As part of the IGA's emphasis on agriculture and nutrition, the Cartwright station also kept gardens, pigs, and chickens as a source of food for the boarding school.

Mealtimes gave IGA staff members the opportunity to teach the children table manners and other cultural behaviours appropriate for American and British middle-class society. Gary Elson describes the rules:

> The meals were very organized and very English. Every Monday you'd be eating the same thing, certain type of soup or something like that. Manners were a must at the table, we weren't allowed to have two hands at the table at one time and you definitely weren't allowed to put your elbows on the table. You had to sit up straight and you had to wait 'til grace was said before you were allowed to be dismissed.[148]

Enforcing table manners and other social rules highlighted the distinctions between the staff and the children. With a few notable exceptions, IGA administrators and teachers tended to see themselves as a social class above the children, community, and domestic staff. This was clearly felt by both students and staff, as Millicent Loder explains:

> The staff was good to us, but always let us know that we were not their equals. The staff came from abroad and felt themselves to be missionaries, trying to bring a bit of England to the Labrador

> wild. In the same building, they ate apart from us, had different food and better living quarters.[149]

Dr. Forsyth and his wife, Clayre, replicated the class distinctions of an earlier era in Britain by assigning female students to serve as their maids. One such maid, Avis Lethbridge Kremer, a student at Lockwood from 1942 to 1946, recalls how the Forsyths created their own exclusive upper-class milieu:

> In my third year at Lockwood I was one of the ones selected to be "maid" for the Forsyths. I wore a black uniform with a white apron and I used to set their dining room table, help fix their supper meal, serve it and clean up afterwards.
>
> They had their own kitchen but cooked on the big stove in the large kitchen. Their dining room and table settings were very formal, using either sterling silver or silver plated flatware and serving dishes, etc., little individual salt and pepper shakers with silver tops at each place setting, crystal glasses and lighted candles. They would get dressed in semi-formal wear (we would call it today). They would have a little homemade wine, homemade cheese crackers (both made by Mrs. Forsyth) before their dinner. They would ring the little silver bell when they were ready for dinner to be served, at which time whoever was the Maid (we took turns) would proceed to serve the dinner. Throughout the dinner if they needed anything, such as dessert, coffee, etc., they would ring the bell.
>
> I was always so afraid that I wouldn't hear the bell. Everything was so formal, and I thought it was such an honour to be a maid, for a 12 year old I guess it would be. I remember I used to have to make little butter balls with two slatted, wooden paddle-type things that made a pattern in these little balls, which were served on a little silver butter dish.[150]

Not all IGA staff maintained the class-based divisions practiced by the Forsyths. Emily Thomas Bird was a teacher who came from Newfoundland to teach at Lockwood in the mid-1950s and early 1960s. She married Albert Bird of the Muddy Bay-Cartwright family, and was uncomfortable with having staff privileges such as a servant girl and a separate dining room:

> We didn't eat with the children, we ate in the staff room. Lots of times I went up and ate with the girls because I much preferred the food they had. We didn't eat the same things as the kids, normally. Edna McDonald was the staff girl, she would serve us. To me that was foreign at the time because I was used to sitting down with family and serving myself.[151]

Other IGA doctors refused to abide by the established hierarchy altogether. In 1943, the Forsyths took a year off and were replaced by Dr. Richard Spicer and his wife, Anne. Victor Mesher, who went to Lockwood at the age of seven in 1938, recalls how the Spicers rejected social distinctions within the dormitory:

> That's one thing I remember about Dr. and Mrs. Spicer, they eat the same as us. When they was there, whatever we had they had. Yeah, they seemed like more up on the level with us, like. But Dr. and Mrs. Forsyth, they was almost like the king there, you know eh, him especially. He was like higher you know. They always had their own food and everything, we'd probably have a bowl of soup and they'd probably have meat or something, vegetables. And Dr. and Mrs. Spicer, they was the same as we. What we had they eat. We had burned bread or burned toast, they had it too.[152]

Even into the 1950s and 1960s, staff still maintained British cultural rules and practices. Josie Curl Penny, a Lockwood student in the 1950s, wrote about her experience in *So Few on Earth: A Labrador Métis Woman*

Remembers. In her memoir, she tells of returning to the school to work as a cook 10 years later.

> As I look back, I realize that not much had changed at Lockwood. The policies and procedures and the way the children were treated were much the same. All the rules and regulations governing the school were carefully prescribed. Even though some of the house mothers tried to be compassionate, it was hard for them to break through Dr. Grenfell's rigid vision of how children were to be treated. What we referred to as "old English rule" persisted until Lockwood closed its doors forever in the mid-1960s.[153]

Recreation

School staff also taught students British and American cultural values and practices through special events, recreation, and sports. The staff devised elaborate celebrations for Christmas, Empire Day, and Halloween, introducing customs that were often foreign to the children. Jane Dyson Light's first exposure to Halloween, for instance, illustrates the cultural divide between staff and students. As she says:

> The only thing that scared me the most that I remember as a child that took me a long time to get over was I didn't ever know about Halloween. As a 7 year old and seeing all these cats and witches and ghosts and everything, I was petrified for weeks. I was scared to death because I didn't know there was such a thing existed and nobody explained it to me because we didn't have Halloween growing up. I didn't know what in the devil was going on.[154]

In the 1940s, under Clayre Forsyth's direction, Saturday nights were reserved for special celebrations, biannual general birthday parties, games, and English folk dancing.[155] Teachers also organized student concerts and plays throughout the year, as Chesley Lethbridge describes:

> Christmas time we would usually put off a concert. They were not just skits, like you see in schools today, but long plays that would last 2.5 to 3 hours. Usually we'd put off one at Christmas, one at Easter, and maybe one in between. I enjoyed acting in the plays and looked forward to it.[156]

Outdoor recreation, such as soccer, ice-skating, and the annual sports days against St. Peter's School in Cartwright were a highlight for many. "The 24th of May would be a holiday," remembers Raymond Mesher, "and that would be Sport's Day. They had races like running races, three-legged races, sack race, potato race."[157] For Jane Dyson Light, the recreation facilities at Lockwood were a source of fun:

> We had a really nice playground, a merry-go-round and a slide and some swing sets. So we did have that and then we had a ball field over there where we'd play kickball and everything. And then in the wintertime, the housefather would make us all a skating rink every winter, and he'd be up at nights making the skating rink so the boys played hockey and we figure-skated and things like that.[158]

A student skiing, Lockwood School, 1963 (courtesy of Them Days Archive).

Between 1953 and 1968, the United States Air Force operated a radar base on the hills above Cartwright. As former student William Max Clarke recalls, the Americans were generous with providing entertainment and recreation for the children at Lockwood.

> The Americans were very good to us. They had a base in Cartwright, a military base, a radar base. And come Saturday, they'd come down and they

> tried to teach us American football, which we didn't like. But anyway, they'd bring a movie. And, of course, Christmastime Santa Claus came from the American base. Thanksgiving they came and all of the special events which would take place during the year, the Americans always showed up with a movie and to play soccer with us. They couldn't teach us American football so they had to play soccer.[159]

Chesley Lethbridge also has good memories of Lockwood:

> I enjoyed . . . the companionship of the other children in the school, because there was fifty of us there and we were all the same as one family, really you know, we got along very well, because everybody more or less worked together and lived together as a family. But I enjoyed it very much there. We had good people taking care of us, good teachers and we had, what we called, a housemother that ran the dormitory, looked after everything there and

Birthday celebration, Lockwood School, 1960s (back l-r: ?, Dot Morris, Maggie Dyson, Phil Holwell, ?, Oswald Dyson, ?; front l-r: Roy Dyson, Emily Dyson, Charlotte Roberts) (courtesy of Them Days Archive).

> her husband was the doctor in the hospital there, so they worked very well together and made life, you know, pretty decent for us.[160]

Social Improvement

The goal of transforming the children's habits, manners, and morals into those of the British and American middle class remained an important aspect of education at Lockwood, just as it had been during the school's first incarnation as the Labrador Public School in Muddy Bay. Removing children from the influence of their own homes was a key step in achieving this goal. In a letter to the school's funder, J.S. Lockwood, housemother Janet Stewart described a visit she made to homes between Cartwright and St. Mary's River in the early 1930s. She reported finding conditions "so distressing" that she brought 12 children to Lockwood:

> The progress of four of them has been of great interest to me; they came to us from such hovels that it is a marvel to me they have turned out such bright, active young things. These four, along with others, of course, have returned to us for this winter. I was anxious to keep them away from their home environment as much as possible for a few years. I am sure they will then be able to improve conditions in their own homes without much urging from us. They will be so used to living a clean, healthy life that our training is bound to tell in the long run.[161]

Schooling aimed to teach children social values and practices such as notions of cleanliness and "proper" housekeeping, in addition to the standard educational aims of reading, writing, and arithmetic. By separating the children from the influence of their communities, the teachers and house parents could better instill their own values in the children. Betty Fyfe, who taught at Lockwood for the 1938–39 school year, described the social training provided by the school as a fundamental rationale for its existence. In an article in *Among the Deep Sea Fishers*, she asked:

> What is the use of this education? Why bring them up in a house with bathrooms and running water, when they are going back to some tiny wooden shack to spend the rest of their lives in fishing and trapping? Surely habits of cleanliness and methodical work acquired when they are young will persist even under less favourable conditions, and help them to make their own homes better and still better with each generation.[162]

Many IGA staff saw education as a way to spread their ideas and values to local families, and they focused on how their students fell short of those values. But not all staff felt this way. Betty Lloyd Chatham, who taught at Lockwood between 1956 and 1958, could see the children's independence and competence. She describes the students in loving terms:

> As for the children, they were a joy to know, very affectionate and very independent. They were able to do many things, from making bread, sewing and knitting from a very young age and capable of taking care of the younger children. The boys could handle a boat, fish and chop wood.[163]

Bullying and Abuse

Like children at other residential institutions, the students at the Lockwood School sometimes found themselves vulnerable to bullying and abuse. With little or no communication with the outside world, there was little public accountability for what transpired there. Children depended entirely on the benevolence of the staff and their fellow students for their well-being. As Martha Davis Compton, a former Lockwood student in the 1940s, described it, "You'd go down in September, just before school opened, and then we were there for the winter. You couldn't get home. There was no transportation only dog teams, them days. We had to stay there all that winter. Nobody knew if we was hungry or goin' without. That was it, eh."[164] As a result, while some enjoyed the experiences and gained useful training, others endured hardship and abuse that in some cases had devastating long-terms effects on their lives.

Josie Curl Penny gives a personal and heartbreaking account of her experience at Lockwood in the 1950s in her memoir. Over the course of two years, from the ages of seven to nine, Josie's time at the school "transformed [her] from a happy, carefree child into a rebellious, angry girl."[165] Her initial excitement at going to Lockwood turned to humiliation, loneliness, and feelings of abandonment as she was subjected to bullying and sexual assaults by older students. Years later, she struggled to cope with the experience. As others who have faced traumatic situations have also found, the experience affected her parenting and her ability to convey her feelings. "I raised four children and I wasn't able to be there emotionally for my children. That's the damage, that's really the crux of the damage — to not be able to share your emotions and express your emotions."[166]

When asked what she would tell younger generations about the boarding school experience, former student Jane Dyson Light had this to say: "I'd just tell them that they're lucky they didn't have to do that or go through that. They're lucky that they're home with their parents and home with their sisters and brothers."[167] Similarly, Raymond Dyson of Cartwright was adamant that the same situation would not be repeated today. "We've got a [young] fellow now who's 15," he said. "If he had to go somewhere to go to school, we'd have to go too."[168]

Financial Challenges

The Lockwood School and dormitory faced perennial staffing and funding challenges. Teachers were difficult to find, and the large buildings were expensive to heat and maintain. The IGA's magazine, *Among the Deep Sea Fishers*, served as a fundraising vehicle by publishing stories and anecdotes about the school and its pupils, letters of appreciation to its supporters, and appeals for help. One strategy championed in the 1930s was the "Grenfell Junior" clubs. These clubs consisted of enthusiastic children in the United States and Canada who raised money for the Lockwood

School. "Why not form your own Grenfell Junior Crew," an advertisement in the January 1934 issue of *Among the Deep Sea Fishers* magazine read, "and go to the rescue of Labrador children? Write your Grenfell Junior Headquarters of I.C. Gale for suggestions. They will chart your course."[169]

In 1935, the Commission of Government agreed to give a school grant to the IGA for teacher salaries and school maintenance, but this funding did not cover boarding costs.[170] The Mission was paying almost all costs for its three institutions — which in 1943, for example, was $43,000 to run Lockwood, the Yale boarding school at North West River, and the St. Anthony orphanage — and the vast majority of this money came from American and British donors.[171]

On the local front, the IGA asked parents of Lockwood students to donate fish, berries, and skin boots for their children, but during difficult economic times, staff reported that most did not. According to the IGA publication, this was due to extreme poverty in the region, which the organization used to further justify the existence of the boarding schools.[172] In private correspondence, however, the IGA recognized that this refusal to contribute might also be understood as an act of resistance on the part of the parents. Dr. Forsyth expressed his frustration with the situation in 1939 in a letter to Charles Curtis, the superintendent of the IGA:

> The Association built this large dormitory with all modern conveniences before it was demonstrated that the coast needed such a building. Very few day pupils come to the school as there is a government school in Cartwright. The boarders are drawn from the poorest section of Labrador. Originally these children were supposed to bring with them a certain number of pairs of skin boots, some fish, or berries towards their support, but this they do not do.
>
> The parents do not appreciate the benefits of education. They feel that they are conveying a privilege upon the mission

> by sending their children to school and do not feel obligated to send the boots or the food to help towards their education. If this matter is brought up with the parents, they simply keep the children home.[173]

Dr. Curtis, who, as superintendent, was wrestling with financial issues at the children's home in St. Anthony as well, argued that if parents did not have the option of taking their children out of school, they would be forced to contribute to the school. Still, he wrote in 1939, "As long as compulsory education does not exist in this country, nothing can be done about this situation; it is useless to argue with parents."[174]

Yet when the Commission of Government for Newfoundland passed legislation in 1942 making education compulsory, it did not solve the schools' financial problems.[175] The government did not initially enforce the rule in southern Labrador, as the region did not have enough schools to accommodate all the children. Until Family Allowances were initiated with Confederation in 1949, parents did not have any financial or legal incentive to send their children to school if they did not wish to do so.

So instead of enforcing school enrolment in the 1940s, the IGA attempted to exact the payment of school fees. Martha Davis Compton, who attended Lockwood in the mid-1940s, remembers how she was not allowed to attend until her family came up with the $40 entrance fee:

> I was about 12 years old when I went to Lockwood. I was late gettin' to school, see. It was hard to get to school them days, hard to get enough money to go to school. Everything was hard. We had to go from Sandy Islands to Cartwright, about 70 miles, on the *Kyle*, and you had to have money to pay your way on that. When we got there you had to pay your $40.00.[176]

Chesley Lethbridge, who went to Lockwood from 1940 to 1943, starting at the age of 10, also remembers the $40 fee:

> We had to pay our board, but you didn't have to pay it in . . . now $40.00 doesn't sound like very much now, but then $40.00 was a lot of money, believe me. . . . So if our parents killed a lot of caribou, they could pay in material, we'll say if they didn't have the cash. So sometimes the people that got caribou they would bring in meat to help pay the board for their children that was there. So then we'd get the bones. They'd take off all the meat, they'd clean off all the meat they could, from the bones, and can it for the staff. Then they would cook up the bones and that for us. There would be quite a bit of meat, sometimes, on the bone. Now that's the only time that we would see any fresh meat.[177]

In an interview with *Them Days*, teacher Emily Thomas Bird also describes how parents contributed as much as they could manage to the school: "Parents did a lot of things like that for their kids, as much as they could. They'd catch wild meat and send [it] down and things like that." She explained that they did so because they were grateful for what the school and staff were doing for the children.[178]

IGA staff had always selected which children could attend Lockwood. In her memoir, Josie Curl Penny from Spotted Island describes how, at seven years old, she had begged her mother to write to Mrs. Forsyth to ask if she could attend Lockwood. When she found out she was accepted, Josie was overjoyed.

> I never knew what transpired beyond the letter to Dr. and Mrs. Forsyth asking permission, but I think there was a fee or a cost. . . . Maybe Mommy paid the fees using the barter system, or perhaps she took care of the charges in cash, though I'd never seen money at that point. Maybe the fee was waived for a large family. In any case, I was soon on my way to Lockwood School.[179]

Parents sometimes complained when the school limited the number of students it would admit, but it was often done for financial reasons. In

Lockwood School students, 1960s. Front, l-r: Denis Bird,?, Lincoln Elson, Fred Holwell, Alex Elson, Lloyd Elson, Gordon Elson, Brenda Elson. Middle, l-r: Garland Mesher, Richard Morris, Viola Williams, Llewyn Holwell, Cylar Dyson, Don Elson, Judson Holwell, Kirby Elson, Ross Roberts, Bella Williams, Shirley Elson, Lillian Holwell. Back, l-r: Dot Morris, Doreen Elson, Minnie Morris, Jane Dyson, James Holwell, Oswald Dyson?, Ann Holwell, Lorelie Roberts, Violet Elson, Daphne Dyson, Rose Morris, Solomon Elson, Phyllis Dyson. (courtesy of Them Days Archive).

1942–43, for instance, Lockwood staff decided to admit only 26 to 30 pupils because the school had only a single teacher. "There has been some criticism locally that we do not admit more pupils and fill the school to capacity," IGA Superintendent Charles Curtis wrote.

> But our answer to this is that, firstly, it serves to bring home to the people the fact that admission to the school is a privilege that they must seek, rather than a benefit which is thrust upon them. In the past, they have tended to feel that they were doing the Mission a favour by letting their children come and felt under no obligation to contribute towards their support.
>
> Secondly, this plan allows the Doctor to exercise a certain amount of choice in the selection of pupils. This is important. . . .

> There are many difficult problems to be met with in the Labrador Boarding Schools not commonly found in other places. The hardest is the attitude of a large number of parents who are not ashamed to admit that they see no value in education for their children. By choosing the best children, those most anxious for an education, something may be done for the future. It will be much more constructive than filling the school up to capacity when half of those admitted would just come for food and clothing.[180]

Although it does not seem to have been official policy, some former students said that each child was given a limited period at the school so that others would also be able to attend: "There was such a backlog of children waiting to get into Lockwood School that each child was given not more than four years, having then to move out to let another take advantage of those few years which was, for some of us, a gold mine of knowledge," remembers Sarah Elson Holwell.[181] Other students remember doing two years of schooling in one, in order to make the best use of their time there.[182]

Lockwood School Closes

Lockwood School remained an expensive and challenging enterprise throughout its existence. The IGA continued to struggle with financial concerns, and finding teachers was often difficult. In 1941–42, with only 26 boarders, the school cost the IGA about $4,000 to operate. In 1947–48, with the dormitory "filled to capacity," the cost had risen to about $7,500.[183] School administrators found it difficult to convince qualified teachers to come to isolated northern communities, teach in mixed-grade classrooms, and live in sometimes spartan conditions, all for relatively little pay.[184]

As difficult as it was to find funding and teachers for Lockwood, however, it was even more challenging for schools in other communities of southeastern Labrador. Without the benefit of the IGA's financial backing, the acute shortage of teachers forced many schools to close temporarily.[185] The government examined the situation in 1952 by sending a Department of Education official, Gerald Day, to visit the region. He prepared a report detailing the widespread difficulties in finding teachers and in running community schools. Of the 28 classrooms between Rigolet and L'Anse au Clair, he reported, only 16 had teachers.[186] The remaining schools were closed. Rigolet had no teacher, nor did Fox Harbour (now called St. Lewis), with its 40 children and newly built school. Residents in Hawke's Harbour were determined to build a school in their community, but Day was pessimistic about the likelihood of finding a teacher to work there. He was sympathetic to people's efforts to build and operate schools in their own communities so that their children would not have to move to Lockwood to attend school. "It is of course quite natural that parents should want their children at home as much as possible," he wrote. "This sentiment is most prevalent in Sandwich Bay and in other areas where few children have been attending the school at Cartwright. Parents do not object so strongly when they know that their children are happy and want to return [to Lockwood] the following year."[187] Nonetheless, the Lockwood School impressed Day:

> The boys and girls are receiving at the boarding school an education equalled nowhere else on the coast. Not only are they instructed well in the academic subjects; they are taught how to live together. They have supervised games, a fair amount of sports equipment and a good playing field outside. Each student has some little responsibility. They look well dressed and are scrupulously clean.[188]

In 1952, the provincial government gave a $2,000 grant to the IGA for its Lockwood and Yale boarding schools in Cartwright and North West River.[189] Even with the additional funding, the Board of Directors found the institutions unduly expensive. In 1956, partly as an attempt to lower its costs, the IGA transferred control and administration of Lockwood to the Amalgamated School Board, but difficulties in finding trained teachers persisted. "Unless we can secure better teachers and make an impression on the education of these children," IGA Superintendent Charles Curtis wrote, "it has occurred to me that it might be necessary to close this institution."[190]

In 1957, having found only one teacher for the 60 or so students, Grenfell staff again raised the possibility of closing the school. Tony Paddon, the son of Harry Paddon and his successor as IGA doctor in North West River, sent a desperate telegraph message to George Alain Frecker, the Deputy Minister of Education in St. John's:

> Lockwood School still has only one teacher for nearly sixty prospective students. This dormitory will cost 30 thousand dollars to run this winter and with one teacher can accomplish practically nothing with type of youngsters in school. Alarmed Directors may order it closed depriving many children any hope [of] education. Can you possibly find teacher.[191]

Even after the provincial government increased the annual grant for the IGA dormitories to $4,000 in 1957, the financial situation at Lockwood seemed precarious.[192]

The parents also found themselves in a difficult position. With the introduction of Family Allowances in 1949, they were under significant pressure to send their children to school as the payments were conditional upon children attending school.

> What they told the parents, if your child don't go to Lockwood School to go to school, you would lose your family allowance. And family allowance was the only thing that kept them going after their husbands stopped fishing, besides going on welfare. And that was just enough to get you through, and barely enough if you had seven or eight youngsters in the family, right?[193]

Parents' options were limited, especially as teachers were scarce, and it was difficult to find a teacher to establish a school in the children's home communities. "We could have all pulled together and not go [to Lockwood], but then what if that did happen? I don't think we would have got teachers [for a school at home], you know? The teachers were very few and far between at this time."[194]

But local families possessed more clout in how and where schools were run than they realized. In 1959, after two Lockwood housemothers quit and Grenfell administrators were again struggling with the problem of finding teachers and school staff, they discussed the possibility of hiring school staff through the Mennonite Committee. "It would have to be done carefully as regards the Church of England," cautioned IGA staff.[195] The current Grenfell personnel seem to have been disliked by many in Cartwright at the time, and the IGA was obviously feeling the pressure to be mindful of local views. "The people feel we are reactionary and dictatorial, and the Labrador crowd never did take much from even the most enlightened women."[196]

At the same time, hiring Mennonites would risk alienating the Anglican Church, which was influential among the local residents. The Church could potentially open its own community schools, a move the IGA saw as competition for local students: "The Anglicans are talking of putting teachers in all the small communities," wrote Tony Paddon in 1959. "If this is done, it will seriously affect the number of children coming to the dormitory."[197] After launching an expensive but fruitless advertising campaign for other teachers, the IGA decided to hire three Mennonite teachers and a housemother for the 1960–61 school year, despite the risk.[198]

The move caused an outcry among members of the Anglican Church and the students' families. The new teachers held Bible study and asked the children to write home to their parents about religious matters. Parents believed that the Mennonites were attempting to influence their children's religious beliefs. The Anglican minister at Cartwright, Rev. Gordon Pevie, described the situation in a 1961 letter to his Church superior:

> The children are confused, the parents upset. I have had to be very outspoken. I have a letter here (from one of the children, to her mother) with me now and it hurts, "The girls down here are becoming Christians. Mommy, what is a Christian?" It's a nasty thing, and the dear little children are exposed to practically the same thing year after year.[199]

People from Spotted Island "seemed to have formed further unfavourable impressions of religious activities at Cartwright," Tony Paddon wrote.

> I tried to soothe things down a bit and tried to present our staff difficulties, [and the] fact that the majority of Mennonites had proved quiet and decent people who did good work and made no trouble, [but] the reaction of the people in the district was absolutely spontaneous. . . . They were upset by what their children were being told in the dormitory. I suppose the answer is to emphasize to our staff that they are welcome to hold any religious beliefs they wish . . . but should not attempt to influence or alter existing religious beliefs. We should hang on to our reputation as non-denominational, and if we get into religious arguments with the local people it seems to me that we are to blame.[200]

Local families decided to take action. In 1961, parents removed all their children from the Lockwood dormitory in protest.[201] As Anglican minister Francis Buckle at Cartwright later wrote, parents had long been unhappy with the lengthy period of time their children were away from home while they attended Lockwood. "The business of proselytizing was an additional reason for parents to keep their children at home and to take steps to provide schooling in their own communities."[202]

The next year, the IGA hired an Anglican couple from Newfoundland to take over as house parents, but the damage was done.[203] In 1964, the Anglican School Board decided to open schools in Batteau, Spotted Island, and Porcupine Bay.[204] As a result, the IGA expected very few

Children from Seal Islands waiting to go home from Lockwood (courtesy of the Maritime History Archive and heirs of Jean Smith).

children to attend Lockwood. Coupled with ongoing financial and staffing difficulties at the school and dormitory, the new IGA superintendent, Gordon Thomas, decided to close the boarding school.

> In discussions with the Anglican authorities, it was obvious that their policy and wish was that the children should remain in their own communities. The Cartwright dormitory has been undergoing many difficulties, as the Directors are aware, for many years and in fact as long back as . . . about 15 years ago. It became obvious to me that the only solution, at least for this year, was to close the dormitory at Cartwright, and as an emergency decision had to be made, I accordingly made that decision and closed the dormitory for this year. My own opinion is that we should keep this dormitory closed until there is change in the policy of the Anglican School Authorities in Central Labrador, and until this is done, the dormitory at Cartwright is quite superfluous.[205]

The decision was made internally within the organization, and the news of Lockwood's closure caught both the provincial government and some within the IGA community by surprise. The Department of Education sent its annual funding grant to the IGA in the fall of 1964, but was told that Lockwood had closed the previous summer.[206] Similarly, the Montreal branch of the IGA, which had just donated $1,000 for the creation of a library at the Lockwood dormitory, was surprised and upset to find that the school had closed by the time the books arrived.[207]

But the decision to close was final. St. Peter's School, the Anglican Church school in Cartwright, would later use the Lockwood school building for extra classroom space for its growing student population.[208] Lockwood itself never reopened, and the IGA withdrew from any involvement in education in Cartwright. The remaining Lockwood students attended other schools in their communities or transferred to other IGA boarding schools at North West River or St. Anthony. The dormitory remained standing until the 1990s, when it was demolished. The Lockwood school building, now condemned, still sits, as of 2019, next to the nursing station on the far side of the Cartwright harbour.

Lockwood School (left) and dormitory (right), after 1934 (courtesy of The Rooms).

CHAPTER TEN

The St. Mary's River Boarding School

The International Grenfell Association operated a small boarding school at St. Mary's River — today's Mary's Harbour — between 1931 and 1938. Because it closed before Confederation in 1949, the school was not officially included in the federal apology and commemoration activities, but it is an important part of the Labrador story. The boarding school opened when the IGA established a station at St. Mary's River, after closing its station at Battle Harbour.

The same changes to the fishing industry that prompted the Indian Harbour medical station to be moved to Cartwright in 1930 also impacted the IGA station at Battle Harbour. Once known as the "capital of Labrador," the island of Battle Harbour no longer served as a central hub for the seasonal fishery. As a result, IGA staff made plans to transfer their work to a new and more accessible station on the mainland.

Herman Moret, a Swiss doctor who joined the IGA in 1922, chose a location for the new station at St. Mary's River.[1] Dr. Moret and his wife Charlotte planned to build a boarding school as part of the new Mission complex. But just as the transfer from Battle Harbour to St. Mary's River started in 1930, fire broke out. On 4 November, fire destroyed the Grenfell hospital at Battle Harbour. Local people looted the building as it burned, carrying away towels, bedding, and other items.[2] As anthropologist John Kennedy comments, "this image of locals looting Grenfell's first hospital is at odds with the popular, even the academic Grenfell legend, one in which Grenfell and his mission are deified."[3] Instead, Kennedy argues, it was likely a "long awaited act of resistance" against the "often imperious" Grenfell Mission.[4]

Despite the loss, the IGA continued with its plans for the region. It requested that the Newfoundland government grant the organization ownership of 50 acres of land at St. Mary's River "for the purpose of erecting thereon a boarding school and hospital."[5] Princeton University students and faculty members volunteered during the summers of 1929 and 1930 to help build the new IGA station.[6] When funds ran low for the school's construction, university volunteers, including Larry Rockefeller (a third-generation member of the wealthy Rockefeller family), raised $1,500 towards what they called "the Princeton school" at St. Mary's River.[7]

Until the school building was finished in 1931, students attended a day school held in a warehouse on the wharf. Frances Conrow, an IGA teacher from Kansas who had taught for two years at Muddy Bay and at the Yale School in North West River, taught the children.[8] The class slowly grew over the winter of 1930–31:

> Thirteen pupils entered their names on the first day. Within three weeks we had enrolled twenty, and this was the average number for the winter. Our largest enrolment was twenty-three, but we did not hold to this very long for one family "shifted out" early and two boys had to leave the school because they were needed at home.[9]

The next year, with the schoolhouse almost completed, the new boarding school opened. Alice Toops, an IGA teacher from the United States, describes her first view of St. Mary's River, as she sailed up St. Lewis Bay:

> The school building, looking very minute, its white coat of paint making it conspicuous in the dark landscape, was visible almost from Battle Harbor. It was with the greatest pleasure that I looked

Boarding school at St. Mary's River [Mary's Harbour], ca. 1931 (courtesy of The Rooms).

> forward to seeing St. Mary's, for I had heard from other passengers about the new school and hospital and how pretty the surrounding country was.[10]

At 80 feet long and 20 feet wide, the schoolhouse was a large and imposing building.[11] It served as a classroom, a dormitory, a church, a concert hall, and a nursing station during the summer. Boarding students lived in one half, partitioned into a girls' room and a boys' room; the schoolroom, with a "new British flag, its big blackboard, [and] its numerous books," formed the other half.[12] The two teachers divided the classroom in half with a blue denim curtain. Alice Toops's beginner class sat on one side and Charlotte Moret's class of older students sat on the other.[13] "By October 15 [1931] we had thirty-four pupils including sixteen boarders. Another boarder came in February and another harbor girl started after Christmas, making our total enrollment thirty-six. Many of these boarding children were receiving their first systematic instruction."[14]

Millicent Bird of Cartwright, recently home from school in St. Anthony, was the first housemother for the boarding students in 1931.[15]

In an article in *Among the Deep Sea Fishers;* Alice Toops describes the children as assuming responsibilities for tasks that many seem to have already mastered:

> In the boarding school the children were just like a big family. Everyone had daily tasks for which he was held responsible. The girls made bread and kept the house tidy, and made and mended skin boots, which most could already do well. They made much of their own clothing, made the boys' overalls and helped with the mending and with serving the meals. They were given additional sewing in the school. The boys were responsible for the supply of wood and water to the boarding school and the schoolroom, carrying all supplies from the hospital, and for many other little jobs. We tried to get them to work together and assume joint responsibility for work. Overcoming individualism and substituting group work is one of the teacher's tasks. Warm shower-baths on Saturday in the hospital were a luxury looked forward to all the week. They loved them. The boys were urged to set traps. In every possible way we attempted to promote a normal Coast life which would carry over to the home when they returned.[16]

Eva Acreman Coish, a pupil at St. Mary's River during its early years, described how the IGA ran the school:

> They took in children from places where they didn't have a school, from north and so on. They'd go and collect them in the fall, before school would open, and bring them to Mary's Harbour. They had a housemother to take care of them. They had a great time, all those little children. In the spring, when school was over, they'd take them back home again, back to Seal Islands, George's Cove, and places like that.[17]

Boarding students came mainly from the St. Lewis Bay area, and from as far north as Seal Islands.[18] In 1931, the school also took in two children from Flower's Cove in Newfoundland, where the IGA had a nursing station. For many, living in a large institution was an unfamiliar experience. It was the first time that most children had seen a multi-storey building with running water. Charlotte Moret watched with amusement as one little boy figured out how to climb stairs when he arrived at the school in 1933. Another little girl "from Seal Islands had never seen water run out of the spigot, and when the stopper was pulled up, she squatted down under the basin to see what happened to the water."[19] The IGA requested nominal payment for the boarders and day pupils, but most families paid in country food, as Charlotte Moret reported: "Very few of our children can pay in cash for their schooling, but do try to help by bringing dry codfish, salt salmon, berries, seal skins and fresh meat; partridge, duck, seal or bear."[20]

Schoolchildren at St. Mary's River (Mary's Harbour), 1930s (courtesy of Them Days Archive).

The school curriculum was based on texts from Newfoundland. Students covered reading, writing, and math in the early years. "The upper grades had geography, geometry, literature, history and drawing in addition," wrote Alice Toops. "One period each week was given to handwork when the girls sewed, or both girls and boys drew, painted or did anything they wished. We hoped to have manual training for the boys another year."[21] The school also involved students in music, concerts, and plays: "The children love to sing and learned to sing together very well. We gave two short periods to singing each week in the school program. The children were taught favorite hymns and how to find them in the hymn book, old favorite songs and some of the Coast songs."[22] Most children at the boarding school were beginner students, but some, like Eva Acreman Coish, whose family had moved to St. Mary's River to work for the IGA, were more advanced students. Eva recalled taking Latin as her required foreign language in high school. "There was a choice — French or Latin. But [Dr. Forsyth] wanted us to do Latin and he taught it in school. I can still remember it."[23]

Over the next eight years, the school took an average of 16 to 20 boarding students and 20 day pupils each year.[24] The January 1936 issue of *Among the Deep Sea Fishers* lists the students registered for the 1935–36 school year. Their family names suggest that they lived between St. Lewis Bay and Seal Islands (see Appendix 3 for the children's names). Violet Holwell, who returned from England after training as a nurse, was hired as the housemother for the St. Mary's River school in 1933–34 before transferring to Lockwood in 1934–35.[25] Another local woman, Faith Stone, also worked as housemother, while teachers, including Boyd Hoddinott, Golden Killigrew, Seneth Rowe, and William Bradbury, came from Newfoundland.[26] For teacher Alice Toops, the boarding school provided children with a healthy environment of nutritious food, physical activity, and social development:

> For the boarding children we hope it meant increased physical resistance as well as an advance in knowledge. If just one thing

> which they learned at St. Mary's makes their lives better or more cheerful than they would have been otherwise, we can ask for no more.[27]

From an almost unpopulated cove in 1928, St. Mary's River — or Mary's Harbour, as it is now known — grew to an IGA post with a hospital, boarding school, wharf, storehouse, road, staff house, farm, and barn by 1936. Dr. Moret was instrumental in creating the new IGA station at St. Mary's River, despite the challenges, and his drive to establish the town irritated some. Many local people saw him as a tyrant, who "thought he owned Mary's Harbour," as one man told anthropologist John Kennedy.[28] Because the IGA officially owned the land, anyone who wanted to build near the community had to get permission from Dr. Moret. His exercise of this authority clashed with local people's ways of sharing land and further alienated the IGA from the NunatuKavut Inuit.[29]

But St. Mary's River never became the bustling centre that Dr. Moret had envisioned. In 1935, Moret and his wife returned to Switzerland. He was replaced by Dr. Hogarth Forsyth, who stayed in the community until Dr. Helen Hosmer from New York took over the St. Mary's River hospital in 1938.[30] The same year, the IGA closed the St. Mary's River boarding school, and many of its boarding students transferred to the Lockwood School.[31]

By 1941, only one family, the Acremans, lived at the IGA station. The hospital treated very few patients every year, but the station cost the IGA more than $7,000 a year to operate.[32] In 1942, IGA Superintendent Charles Curtis argued that St. Mary's River was an "ill-advised plan" that should be "written off as a bad mistake and abandoned."[33] However, the IGA decided to maintain a nursing station in the community.[34] In the 1960s, more families moved into town under the provincial resettlement program.[35] The school at Mary's Harbour, still called the Princeton School, operated under the administration of the Anglican Church, and its student population once again grew in size.[36]

CHAPTER ELEVEN

The Yale School and Dormitories of North West River

We returned to our families, but a new race
Aliens from a cold cruel place
Quiet. Neat as pins. Full of facts which make no sense.
We're now strangers in our own homeland.
— Rose Oliver, "Angels to Aliens"

At the beginning of the twentieth century, Inuit, Innu, and European families lived in the Hamilton Inlet and Lake Melville region. They educated their children to master the skills and knowledge needed to hunt, fish, trap, and survive on the land. Some also taught their children how to read and write.[1] The Methodist Church, which had established a mission at Lester's Point near Rigolet in 1883, provided a few itinerant teachers in the area.

The first teacher in the region was William Santaford of Bonavista, Newfoundland.[2] Santaford and the other itinerant teachers travelled widely. They would board with a family for a few weeks at a time in return for teaching the children. John Montague of North West River remembers:

> After so many years there was a teacher used to come here from some part of Newfoundland. She'd have a week here, a week to Mud Lake, a week to Mulligan, a week to Pearl River, a week to the head of Grand Lake, and a week to Butter and Snow and all

> these little places, and a week to Gillisport. By the time the week was up, it was time for her to go out, you know.[3]

The education was brief and had minimal impact, as Edna Campbell of Pearl River recalls:

> There used to be teachers just travelling around, you know, in the winter, and sometimes they'd get to our places for only a month, and perhaps not sometimes. But out of the crowd that was going around, sometimes it would be only ten days he would teach to our house, because they had to go from one place to another, so we'd get a little bit of learning, not much though.[4]

Some parents wanted a better education for their children. Bella McLean Shouse, who lived in Kenemish as a child in the 1920s, remembers how her father, Scottish immigrant Malcolm McLean, disliked the itinerant education system:

> My father was fighting all his life for a boarding school. The only means of education we had here was a traveling teacher from Newfoundland, usually a teenaged boy, just out of high school. . . .
>
> I remember, the minister came to our place once, and he had this young feller with him, and our father looked at him, and he said, "Who's this young man?"
>
> "Oh," he said, "that's going to be your teacher."
>
> "Oh no, he's not!" my father said. "He's younger than my sons who he's going to teach!" He said, "You can take him somewhere else for the fall."[5]

The End of the Itinerant Teacher

Not long after his arrival in Labrador in 1912, Dr. Harry Paddon began to tackle the challenges of schooling in the region. He worked first at the

North West River, 1920s, with IGA hospital ship, the Strathcona, in the foreground (courtesy Them Days Archive).

hospital in Indian Harbour and spent the winters at a temporary hospital at Mud Lake.[6] The Grenfell Mission staff had selected the Mud Lake location, which sat at the mouth of the Grand River (renamed the Churchill River in 1965 by Premier J.R. Smallwood), as the Mission's winter headquarters in Labrador.[7]

From the winter station, Paddon would travel by dogsled down the coast, treating patients in outlying settlements as far north as the Moravian Mission stations at Makkovik, Hopedale, and Nain.[8] It was on one such trip that Paddon first met the Moravian missionaries and witnessed their efforts at educating Inuit children. What he saw impressed him. While different religious denominations offered some schooling in southern and central Labrador, the Moravians had "outstripped everyone."[9] Instead of using itinerant teachers, they had started "admirable" boarding schools, which Paddon viewed as "the truly rational solution of the education problem in Labrador."[10] Soon enough, Paddon would have the chance to duplicate the Moravian boarding school model in central Labrador.

In the meantime, however, Paddon communicated with Wilfred

Grenfell about the problems with the Mud Lake location. Although a generous benefactor had loaned the use of three houses at Mud Lake for the Mission's hospital work,[11] it was difficult transporting supplies and equipment there each fall. So in 1915, Paddon moved the permanent winter hospital to North West River, where the Hudson's Bay Company had established a trading post in the 1830s.

From the outset, the efforts of Paddon and his staff of paid and volunteer workers at North West River extended well beyond medicine, encompassing industrial, social, and educational work.[12] In the new winter station's first year of operation, a volunteer nurse held classes for children one day a week; later, the Methodist Church ran a small and often understaffed school.[13] But Malcolm McLean and other parents wanted a more regular form of education for their children. As his daughter, Bella McLean Shouse, explained, her father was "quite keen" on education: "He was after the doctor, Dr. Paddon of the Grenfell Mission, to get a boarding school. Bring all the children into North West River, have a bigger school and more teachers."[14]

The success of the Labrador Public School at Muddy Bay, for which Dr. Paddon had been instrumental in planning and fundraising, encouraged him to build what he called a similar "child welfare institution" at North West River.[15] Urged on by parents like Malcolm McLean as well as itinerant Grenfell teachers, Paddon sought financial support for his vision. Donations flowed in from friends of the IGA. A former Grenfell volunteer pledged to pay $500 a year for five years for a boarding school. Varrick Frissell, an adventurous tourist from Yale University who had trekked up the Grand River in the summer of 1925, convinced the university's philanthropic organization, the Yale Board of Charities, to donate funding to the school. In return, the Yale board asked that the school be named after the university.[16] Young American and British students with the International Grenfell Association volunteered their labour in constructing the buildings,[17] and the Yale School opened on 3 October 1926 with 16 boarding students.[18] Years later, Bella McLean Shouse recalled the occasion: "and you know, in 1926 we finally got our boarding

Yale School at North West River, 1930 (courtesy of The Rooms).

school and the children came in from around the coast. And I was the first child to sleep in that dormitory in North West River."[19]

The school offered an education for boarders from outlying villages and day students from the local community. The first teacher was Alfreda Davis Blake, a Labrador graduate of the Methodist College of St. John's. She had fond memories of the early days:

> I first came to North West River in 1925. This was my first year of teaching, and I was the first permanent teacher for North West River. Prior to my coming to North West River, we had itinerant teachers. . . .
>
> I had a class of about sixteen and we were packed in this little room like sardines. I had students from beginning to grade six. . . . I suppose I punished some of the pupils, but I can't remember. They were precious children. We enjoyed our recesses as well as school hours. It was really a happy atmosphere.[20]

Boarders' cottage (Wood Cottage) at North West River, 1930 (courtesy of The Rooms).

The IGA also built a dormitory, called the Gibbons Cottage, in 1926, with funds donated by Martha Gibbons of Philadelphia, a long-time Grenfell supporter and summer volunteer at Indian Harbour. In its first year, Gibbons Cottage housed 14 children from small settlements around Lake Melville: "a few students came from Mulligan, two from Kenemich, some from Sebaskachu, and from a few other outlying places."[21] The following year, the Mission built another smaller dormitory, named after its American benefactor, George Wood.[22] The school and dormitory staff grew over the next decade, with a number of Labrador teachers and housemothers joining Alfreda Davis, including Ethel Pye from Cape Charles in southern Labrador, Annie Baikie from North West River, Bella Butt from East St. Modeste, and Blanche Davis from Sandwich Bay.[23]

A Different Approach

Yale School and its two cottage dormitories differed in many ways from the IGA's boarding schools in Muddy Bay and Cartwright. For one thing,

Gibbons Cottage and Wood Cottage were built to house fewer children — about 25 and 10 boarders, respectively — although they often held many more when student numbers rose in the 1940s and 1950s.[24] Unlike the larger Grenfell dormitories in Cartwright, neither cottage in North West River had indoor plumbing, nor did the IGA hire as many domestic staff members to help with the work. Yale School was also not physically separated from the community, as the Muddy Bay and Lockwood schools were. Boarding children from outlying settlements joined children from the North West River community in classes, with the boarders comprising about a third to a half of all the students at the school.[25]

Financial concerns likely drove the decision to build small cottage dormitories instead of a large institutional building, but Dr. Paddon also emphasized the educational philosophy that lay behind the practice. "I very much prefer the small group, the model home to the big institution, for child evolution and development," he wrote in his memoir.[26] "It is obviously far more likely to be an inspiration to the young homemaker of the future, besides allowing for far more individual observation and development." He describes how a book by "another pioneer in frontier education," Archdeacon Stuck of the United States Episcopal Mission to Alaska, influenced his educational philosophy. Stuck argued that the education offered by Mission schools in Alaska failed to provide sufficient training for life there. Upon graduation, a boy "could not grind his own axe, make his own sled, net his own twine, or do any of the hundred and one things that go to keep a frontiersman independent and successful."[27] As a consequence, Paddon "registered a vow that this reproach should never be made against Yale School if I could help it."[28]

However, Dr. Charles Curtis, medical officer in charge at the St. Anthony hospital and later the IGA superintendent, disagreed with Paddon's cottage philosophy. The two men often clashed over the IGA's educational and social development work. Curtis believed that safety regulations for the boarding school should have been prioritized over educational philosophy. In looking back on Paddon's efforts in 1942, Curtis argued that the cottages had posed a fire risk:

> In each cottage, the cooking and washing is done for that cottage under the most primitive conditions, the idea being to duplicate their home conditions. Dr. Harry Paddon and others had always thought that the plan at St. Anthony and Cartwright of housing students in modern fireproof buildings was wrong. I do not agree with their criticism. Surely in the past we have run a grave risk in Northwest River with children packed in these wooden buildings with only a woman in residence at night. With lamps and stoves, the danger of fire was ever present and on a stormy Labrador night, rescue of the children would be in the hands of a woman.[29]

Fortunately, the cottages in North West River did not burn throughout their existence as dormitories, although the IGA eventually replaced them with a larger, more institutional building in the early 1950s.

Despite skepticism from others, Paddon continued to defend his educational approach to the IGA Board of Directors. He had to advocate fervently in the early 1930s especially, when the Great Depression was eroding IGA finances and the expensive station at North West River was under scrutiny. Paddon argued that the Yale School and dormitories were providing a valuable service for the future of Labrador:

> [School] examinations are planned for professional life in Newfoundland rather than for effective citizenship in Labrador. Apart from the 3 Rs, and some History and Geography — taught in such a manner as not to leave the graduate either inarticulate or devoid of imagination — education in Labrador of today should be largely vocational. To be good wives and mothers, girls must get domestic science in all its branches; while boys must have the best manual training available, coupled with care of twine, tools, etc. Children of both sexes should be encouraged to take an interest in agriculture. All our teachers and housemothers are now natives of Newfoundland or Labrador — chiefly the latter — except the principal, Mrs. [Marjorie] Beard.[30]

Other debates occurring in the United States and Newfoundland about the role of education in the lives of the working class supported Dr. Paddon's position. Like him, educators emphasized the importance of teaching children skills that they would later need at home. In St. John's, the superintendents of education for both the Catholic and the Methodist churches had recently criticized school curriculum that was designed solely for the privileged few who would not have to earn a living by fishing. In the United States and elsewhere, vocational education had become increasingly popular, and educators created the field of home economics, designed to teach young women how to become better housekeepers.[31]

Paddon also believed that the boarding school children's diet should consist of local foods as much as possible. Instead of just wild foods, however, he envisioned a diet of locally produced and farmed foods. A barn, chicken house, garden, and cow provided Mission staff and the boarding school children with fresh vegetables, eggs, meat, and milk. Teacher Elizabeth Criswell described the cottage environment and healthy diet in the April 1927 issue of *Among the Deep Sea Fishers*:

> When we enter the building, we find an eager crowd just ready to sit down to supper around a plain deal table, where benches serve in lieu of chairs. The smoking hot cups of cocoa send a pleasant fragrance to the air, the hot dishes of potatoes and fish invite the healthy young appetites, and there are the dishes of bright red-berry jam which the children picked in the early fall.[32]

As part of their training for life in Labrador, the staff expected the children to work. "And how they do work!" exclaimed Principal Marjorie Beard in 1931.

> The girls keep the school and cottages clean and neat during the week, while the boys bring in wood and water and keep the fires and do the heavier work. They seem to make play out of it, too. . . .

> The boys made toys in the manual training class which were sent in Christmas boxes around the bay. Some of the girls made their own white dresses for the May 24th celebration. They do beautiful work — a tribute to the training of Miss Ethel Pye, who has been at Northwest River for five years as a housemother and domestic science teacher.[33]

Elizabeth Blake Osmond, a Yale School boarder in the 1930s, remembers the work:

> In the Wood Cottage, we had chores to do such as make our bed, set the table, wash clothes on the washboards and aluminum tubs, heat water on the wood stove and spread the clothes on the outdoor lines. We would iron the clothes using irons that were heated on the wood stove, and we would fold the clothes and put it away. One of our chores was to scrub the floor in the living room, wax it and then shine the wax with a cloth. As little children we worked really hard, we would clean the lamps and fill them. There were little chores that we would also have to do such as getting brown sugar from the barrel or get cream/milk in from the porch.[34]

Jean Blake Crane, born in 1929, also remembers the work. Although it was hard, she expresses appreciation for the skills that the experience gave her:

> My family moved from Naskaupi River on the trapline before I was born so we could be near the hospital and school. We lived on the south side of North West River and I was number twelve of thirteen children. We went across the river to Yale School at the Grenfell Mission. . . .
>
> I started school at age six in 1935. I had a few years at Gibbons Cottage, the big cottage had about thirty students, a cook

> and a housemother. I preferred the little cottage so I requested and spent most of my years there at Wood Cottage.
>
> We also had a cook and a housemother. . . . The cook made bread and cooked the meals on a wood burning stove, so everything had to be watched, not to get too hot. We learned cooking by helping, also we made our beds and helped do the laundry in the wash tubs with a washboard and hung it out on the clothes-lines to dry. In the winter, it froze like cardboard. We finished drying it inside and ironed it with a flat iron, heated on the stove. It was really good to have learned to keep house, by the time we grew up we could run our own.[35]

However much the educational approach and set-up of the Yale dormitories differed from the IGA's other residential institutions at Muddy Bay, Lockwood, and St. Anthony, they shared an underlying goal: to separate children from their home environments. As Dr. Harry Paddon wrote in his memoir, "The one hope for many of these children was to get them away from home, sad as such a conclusion was and great as were the responsibilities that it carried with it."[36] Like the IGA's other boarding schools, the Yale School and dormitories aimed to do more than provide the children with an academic education — they also set out to instill the social values and skills promoted by the school's staff.

Yale School and Dormitories Get an Upgrade

As the years passed, the Yale school building became increasingly worn down. In July 1943, almost 20 years after it was built, IGA Superintendent Curtis identified the need for a new building. Writing in *Among the Deep Sea Fishers*, he asked readers to consider supporting the construction of a new school as a memorial to Dr. Harry Paddon, who had died in December 1939 after more than 25 years of service in Labrador.[37] Curtis's appeal finally bore fruit in 1948 when the "long-dreamed-of new school building" became a reality.[38] By then, Paddon's son, Anthony

(Tony) Paddon, who had trained as a doctor in the United States, had returned to North West River to take charge of the work started by his father.[39] The new school building was constructed from materials from the closed Royal Canadian Air Force (RCAF) radio detachment on Spotted Island and was financed by the Department of Education and the IGA.[40] It boasted "lots of windows and central heating and electric lights" — a sign of modern times![41]

A few years later, Dr. Tony Paddon also pressed the IGA board for funding to build a new dormitory, as the overcrowded Gibbons Cottage was falling apart and was impossible to heat. Even worse, a child had recently fallen through the second-storey floor. "The building is ramshackle to the point of collapse," he wrote. "We, who seek to educate these children to a better way of life than the one they are familiar with, are putting them into greater squalor than they are used to at home."[42] In 1952, the IGA built a new dormitory, complete with indoor plumbing and central heating, and the children moved over in early December. Polly Taylor, an

New dormitory, built in 1952 (Wood Cottage in the background) (courtesy of Them Days Archive).

American who worked as an assistant housemother in North West River for the 1952–53 school year, described the transition:

> Now that we have no wood to chop and haul, no fires to light, no water to pump, and no pails to empty, we have mixed the boys and girls up indiscriminately on the jobs. We find that the boys do a much better job of mixing bread than the girls ever did and they also get the dishes cleaner, which may be partly because of the better sinks and running hot water. They aren't very good however, at sweeping and have no notion at all of cleaning basins and bathtubs.[43]

The new building could accommodate 52 students in four dormitory rooms that divided the children into older and younger girls and boys.[44]

Student Composition

Over the first few decades of the Yale School, boarding students came from small settlements in the surrounding region. By 1948, more students in the dormitory came from communities between West Bay and as far north as Nain. Their numbers grew as the IGA expanded its facilities in North West River, although the proportion of boarding students at the Yale School remained at about a third of the student population. The school grew from 98 pupils (of whom 35 were boarders) in 1940, to 176 (including 60 boarders) in 1952, to 167 (52 being boarders) in 1960.[45]

Although school attendance was voluntary until 1942,[46] Grenfell staff sometimes coerced reluctant parents to permit their children to attend. In his memoir, Harry Paddon described how he would occasionally rely on his authority as a magistrate to pressure parents to send children to the school:

> There was no difficulty about collecting the old scholars returning to the school, so far as the children were concerned, at least.

> In many cases, the new candidates were more than willing, having heard of the good times in store from older brothers and sisters. Occasionally, there was parental obstruction, but then, under the Children's Act, a justice had a strong lever.[47]

The 1921 Children's Act (An Act for the Protection of Neglected, Dependent and Delinquent Children) allowed Newfoundland magistrates to take children into custody when they thought it necessary. "Under the Children's Act," Dr. Paddon explained, "a justice could remove any child from a home where, on moral or economic grounds, the youngster's welfare was threatened, and this could be and has been a powerful lever with refractory parents."[48] Paddon describes using this "lever" and the threat of losing government relief payments to force a foster father to send one boy — or his brother — to the school:

> On one occasion, having determined to recover a bright young Eskimo whose foster-father was, I understood, opposed to his returning, I arrived at the encampment where a group of Eskimos were cod fishing, and finding the man in question away I kidnapped the wrong boy, who was more or less the double of the right one. However, when the irate parent protested and I challenged him to show that he could maintain the lad at home without government relief, he curled up [expressed shame]. So as Adam had been spirited away and could not be found, Allan had his berth.[49]

Parents found themselves increasingly pressured to send their children to school after legislation made attendance compulsory in 1942.[50] The pressure became even more forceful after Newfoundland joined Confederation in 1949. With the new and valuable Family Allowance tied to children's attendance at school, families could find themselves in a difficult situation. Nonetheless, some parents could decide whether and which of their children would attend school. A letter between Department

Children at Yale School, ca. 1930 (courtesy of The Rooms).

of Education officials in 1951 illustrates the relationship between IGA staff and parents about sending children to the dormitories at North West River: "Because it involves negotiating with parents in each case, it is impossible to determine in advance how many parents are willing to allow their children to go to North West River for the Winter."[51]

Despite the Newfoundland government's legislation and interest in ensuring that students attend school, not all children had educational opportunities. Other day schools in central Labrador communities often faced significant challenges in finding teachers, resources, and adequate buildings in which to operate. Church-run school boards organized the schools with grants received from the Department of Education, and church officials provided leadership on local school boards, overseeing school construction, staffing, fundraising campaigns, and building maintenance.[52] However, the effort and expense needed to run community day schools sometimes proved too great, especially as it was difficult to recruit teachers to teach in isolated one-room schools.

Dr. Tony Paddon estimated in 1953 that half of all schools in Labrador were closed because they could not find teachers to hire.[53] The school in Rigolet, for instance, was closed for years in the early 1950s because the Central Labrador Amalgamated School Board could not recruit a teacher.[54] In 1951, according to an Anglican Church report, about 15 children lived in the community, and about 20 children lived in the nearby settlements of Rattler's Bight, Bluff Head Cove, Ticoralak Island, Ticoralak Point, Double Mer, Kellick Point, Mullins Cove, and Cullingham's Cove.[55] With the Rigolet school closed, these children had little opportunity for schooling. Likewise, the school at Mulligan River had closed in 1953 because of the lack of a teacher, and the school at Mud Lake had "one school girl teacher with no training."[56] The children living in these areas therefore could either stay at the Yale or Lockwood School (if room could be found in the dormitories) or forfeit the opportunity to receive any formal schooling.

Still, the cottage dormitories at North West River could not accommodate all the children who applied to attend Yale School. In 1950, Tony Paddon described how the Gibbons Cottage, then almost 25 years old and falling apart, had been designed for 25 children but now housed 41 and "many more must be turned away."[57] Even after the IGA managed to raise money to build the new, larger dormitory in 1952, the problem of accommodating students continued.

The lack of resources in other communities created inadequate schooling situations, and some parents turned to the IGA for help. In 1965, for example, Pentecostal Church authorities in Postville were struggling to recruit and retain a teacher for their school. Students would often get only a few months of classes, or the school would shut entirely if the school could not find a teacher. If parents sent their children to North West River to attend Yale School, the Postville children were often placed in lower grades because of the limited schooling they had received.[58] In a letter to the Deputy Minister of Education, Paddon described how a Postville woman had asked that the IGA grant admission for her child to live in the already overcrowded dormitory. He quotes the mother as writing, "A lot of us worries about our children and there isn't any school for them to go to. It's hard on mothers and fathers. I guess there won't be any school this year."[59]

Children from settlements with inadequate schools were not the only ones to live in the dormitories. Changing social circumstances were also having an impact on who boarded at the school, as Tony Paddon remarked in 1955:

> Increasingly our dormitories are becoming either (a) homes for school children whose parents are sick in hospital or who still live outside of communities, (b) children who present special health problems, not sufficient for keeping them in hospital wards or (c) high school students whose own village schools are not able to carry them this far.[60]

The lack of adequate educational facilities in other communities allowed IGA staff in North West River to decide which children to accept as pupils. Tony Paddon enacted an admission criterion by making children request acceptance into the Yale School dormitories "in their own handwriting."[61] In fact, the school did not have an official admissions policy — a flaw noted in William Wall's 1960 review of the IGA's educational efforts — and Dr. Paddon seems to have made most of the decisions.[62] His role as the de facto admittance officer was confirmed by Polly Taylor, the assistant housemother in the early 1950s:

> Tony Paddon has been the entire admissions committee for some time now. He picks children whom he thinks will benefit, or whose homes are too bad to leave them in. As a result we have some kids who have had excellent home training . . . and some who are quite untrained. They all come from spots where there are no schools so they start first grade at any age — one of the boys just starting at 13.[63]

Financial Help over the Years

In 1935, the Commission of Government agreed to give the IGA schools an educational grant for teachers' salaries and school maintenance. In return, the schools agreed to teach the Newfoundland curriculum and to hire teachers who were trained in the Newfoundland system.[64] The IGA continued to operate and fund the dormitories. Parents of the students, as had been the case at the Lockwood School, contributed to the costs through school fees or donations of country foods for their children. The IGA's base of supporters, most of whom lived in the United States, contributed financially, with gifts of clothing, toys, and other items and with volunteer labour for the IGA stations.

While Wilfred Grenfell had been active in the organization, donations had poured in. But by the 1930s, with health issues keeping him from maintaining a leadership role and the Great Depression hitting financial markets and fish prices, the organization faced more difficult times. Fundraising relied on continued interest and communication, so the IGA encouraged students at Yale School to write letters to the Grenfell Juniors, an American youth organization it had started in the early 1930s. A section in *Among the Deep Sea Fishers* was dedicated to the Grenfell Juniors and features many of these letters.[65] When writing for the magazine, Grenfell staff also highlighted the accomplishments of the Yale School and its cottage dormitories, contrasting these with the "wretchedness and squalor" in the social situation around them, as if to underscore the need for the IGA's work:

> The dormitory has . . . made education possible for the outport children who would otherwise be condemned to do without. It has brought opportunity and hope to hundreds of children who would otherwise have known neither, and it has perhaps done more to alleviate human wretchedness in north and central Labrador than the hospital itself.[66]

Despite the enthusiasm expressed in the magazine about the social value of the IGA's educational work, not all within the organization believed that it should fund activities that normally would fall within the government's jurisdiction. The IGA Board of Directors in New York asked its staff to find ways to cut costs, especially in areas that did not directly pertain to the IGA's central medical mandate. As the government in Newfoundland and Labrador assumed more control over its northern regions, the IGA stepped back from educational affairs, including financing schools and paying for their teachers.[67]

By 1948, IGA staff had agreed to work more closely with the United Church at North West River to run the Yale School, although the IGA maintained sole jurisdiction over the dormitories. The two organizations formed the first Northwest River School Board, which later changed its name to the Central Labrador Amalgamated School Board when its jurisdiction grew to include Rigolet.[68] The school board assumed ownership of the school buildings and responsibility for the cost of their upkeep. Its formation enabled the Yale School to access government funding for teachers' salaries, materials, and building maintenance. It also allowed for more local involvement in the school's administration.[69]

With the establishment of the Central Labrador Amalgamated School Board, the IGA distanced itself from the day-to-day school operations, instead providing only administrative and political support. For years, however, Dr. Tony Paddon chaired the school board, alternating with Rev. Lester Burry of the United Church.[70] The IGA also stepped in when problems arose. In the early 1950s, a shortage of teachers caused a crisis at the school. The dormitories housed several school-aged children who could not be accommodated in the school because of a lack of teachers.[71] As a desperate measure, the IGA gave $2,500 to the school board in 1959–60 and $5,000 in 1960–61 to help pay for qualified teachers from England.[72]

The resources and efforts of the IGA gave North West River an advantage in facing the challenges of running a school and a dormitory in Labrador. Most smaller communities in the region did not have such a powerful backer. As a provincial Department of Education official commented in 1952, while many of the schools in southern Labrador were closed because they could not recruit teachers to staff them, the Yale School endured: "Rev. Burry and Dr. Paddon are giving a leadership in education which most of Labrador South lacks."[73]

Although the school board assumed responsibility for the school's expenditures, the dormitories at North West River remained a significant expense for the IGA. In 1952, the provincial Department of Education agreed to pay $2,000 annually to the IGA for costs of the Lockwood and North West River dormitories.[74] Although the grant helped somewhat, the IGA continued to bear the bulk of the expense, which grew to over $25,000 annually for the Yale dormitories in the 1950s.[75] More funding also became available after Confederation through per capita grants for each child at the dormitories from the provincial Department of Public Welfare, and provincial bursaries and scholarships for high school students paid for part of their room and board.[76] The IGA used some of these grants to pay for costs at the dormitories, while it funnelled others towards costs at the school.[77] In the late 1950s, for instance, the Central Labrador Amalgamated School Board received an additional $13 per month for each boarding student as a grant from the Department of Public Welfare. The board used the money to augment the principal's salary in order to attract high-quality candidates for the position, even though the boarders only made up one-third of the students in the school.[78]

By 1960, the IGA was paying about $100,000 for its educational activities, most of which it spent on its three dormitories in North West River, Cartwright, and St. Anthony.[79] With such a significant portion of its budget focused on the boarding schools, the IGA Board of Directors wanted to ensure that its investment was worthwhile. They approached William Wall, a senator from Manitoba with experience in education, to conduct a survey of the schools within central and southern Labrador and northern Newfoundland, and to make recommendations about how to improve education for the boarding students.[80] The approach allowed the IGA to highlight some serious inadequacies of the education system without being seen as meddling in provincial affairs.

Senator Wall's 1960 work, *The Wall Report: A Survey of Education Problems in Selected Study Areas in Northern Newfoundland and Labrador: A Report to the Board of Directors of the International Grenfell Association*, assessed the educational situation and the IGA's efforts to provide educational opportunities by operating dormitories at North West River, Cartwright, and St. Anthony.[81] He described the dormitories as "a tremendous effort by a non-governmental and service-minded organization to help equalize educational opportunities, since the net cost to the IGA is approximately $650 per dormitory child per year (for almost 150 children)."[82] He then outlined the deficiencies in the education provided to these boarders through the provincial system. Wall noted the challenges of recruiting and retaining teachers, the high dropout rate, and the lack of modern equipment, and he provided several recommendations for the IGA to maximize its impact on education.[83] His suggestions included reviving the IGA's scholarship and bursary program to help students pursue post-secondary education, and devising admission rules and practices for the dormitories.[84] He also recommended that the IGA stop paying supplementary subsidies for teachers' salaries at North West River, as salary grants and teacher–pupil ratio decisions were the responsibility of the Boards of Education and the Department of Education. The IGA had made significant contributions to the field of education, Wall argued, but it should be careful not to overstep its authority.[85]

IGA staff met the report with interest, although having an outsider appraise the organization's activities was a novel and slightly uncomfortable experience for an agency accustomed to autonomy. The IGA later implemented some of Wall's recommendations, including the scholarship program. It also agreed to stop supplementing teachers' salaries at North West River.[86] Dr. Tony Paddon, however, remained determined to continue with his hands-on approach to overseeing the school and dormitories.

The Paddon Family in North West River

Tony Paddon and his parents, Harry and Mina Paddon, dedicated most of their lives to their work in North West River. But the IGA did not always fully support the Paddons' efforts in the community. After Dr. Curtis in St. Anthony assumed the IGA superintendent's role in 1939, he was especially skeptical about the value of the North West River station, and he looked for ways to save the IGA money. "For years we have realized that North West River was a very expensive station to operate," he wrote to the IGA's executive director, three days after Harry Paddon had died suddenly of an infection.[87] Curtis suggested that the IGA close the boarding schools at Cartwright and North West River. He also recommended reducing the North West River hospital to a nursing station.[88] He was unsuccessful, however, and Mina Paddon, a nurse, took charge of the Mission station until the end of World War II, when Tony Paddon, now a doctor, returned home in 1947.[89]

Tony Paddon was equally as determined as his parents in his efforts to ensure that the North West River hospital, school, and other IGA

Dr. Harry Paddon (centre) with Inuit men, 1930s (courtesy of The Rooms).

efforts remain viable. But increasing competition, in both the medical and educational fields, threatened North West River's leadership position in central Labrador. During World War II, the Canadian and American militaries had built a large air base at Goose Bay, 40 kilometres from North West River, complete with modern medical facilities. Many Labradorians moved in from their homes along the coast to work at the base, earning cash wages for the first time. They founded the community of Happy Valley, downriver from Goose Bay, in the early 1940s. In 1944, Charles Curtis predicted that North West River would "never be important again medically" as it was too close to the medical services available on the base, and that North West River "will never be more than a nursing station."[90]

New schools built in Happy Valley provided education for children who might otherwise have gone to the Yale School in North West River. In 1943, for example, Alice Perrett Perrault, the former teacher at Makkovik, established the first school in Happy Valley for the children of the new community.[91] By the 1950s, Happy Valley had three schools, and by 1959, its school population was over three times that of North West River.[92] In his 1960 report, Senator Wall pointed out that the student numbers at North West River had grown rather slowly during the same time period.[93]

Happy Valley continued to increase in size after the war, from 257 residents in 1951 to 1,145 in 1956.[94] In 1961, construction began on a major hospital to serve the town, which the province recognized as the new administrative centre of the region. Although officially the supervisor of the new hospital from his headquarters in North West River, Tony Paddon acknowledged that the large facility would eventually eclipse his station.[95] In 1962, he wrote to IGA Superintendent Gordon Thomas in St. Anthony to express his anxiety about his jurisdiction and responsibilities diminishing in the future because of Happy Valley; "for me it would be miserable," he confessed.[96]

Dr. Paddon lobbied hard to ensure that his community and his IGA station would retain its purpose and prosperity. He proposed two measures to bolster the importance of North West River: first, to expand the IGA's medical jurisdiction to include Cartwright and Labrador's south coast, and second, to build a central high school in North West River and a larger dormitory to house students from coastal regions. In Paddon's opinion, North West River needed to expand in order to survive, as he revealed to Dr. Thomas: "The future value of my station and its future existence might well depend on it."[97]

Ambitions for a Central High School

The idea of establishing a central high school and larger dormitory at North West River consumed Dr. Paddon and local school officials for the next decade. In their new scheme, students from all communities between Batteau and Nain would attend the high school after Grade 6. The principal in North West River would act as superintendent of all the community "feeder schools."[98] Yale School staff described their vision of the benefits of attending a central high school for children from coastal communities in their submission to the 1967 Royal Commission on Education and Youth:

> Entering this school at Grade Seven, a child would have an adequate period in which to avail himself of the advantages of a larger school, and to adjust to, and prepare to find a place in, the larger and more advanced world outside his community.[99]

In his 1965 analysis of Labrador administration issues concerning Inuit, anthropologist Diamond Jenness describes Dr. Paddon's "rosy vision for his native community of North West River" and a new central high school as a means to enculturate Indigenous children in mainstream society:

> [The high school] would provide a dominantly white environment which teen-aged children from Eskimo and Indian homes in northern Labrador now lack, and would thus enable them to acquire the fluency in English and the invaluable background of

> general knowledge, as opposed to textbook learning, which they find so difficult to obtain in their present communities.[100]

Champions of the plan believed that five years at a central high school in a "dominantly white environment" would provide the needed socio-cultural and educational training to transform Indigenous children into well-adjusted members of the "advanced world."

North West River advocates garnered support for the central high school from other officials in Labrador. The Moravian superintendent, Rev. William Peacock, agreed with the idea, although he believed that children from north coast communities should only attend the North West River school after Grade 8.[101] Dr. Paddon also reported that principals at the schools at Nain and Makkovik found providing high school instruction to be "extraordinarily difficult and also wasteful of teacher resources, since relatively few of the students at these schools wish to go through high school."[102] A central high school at North West River would therefore serve the needs of many coastal communities, he argued, especially those in northern Labrador.

But a new school and dormitory would be expensive. Dr. Paddon hoped that he could access newly available funding for Indigenous education from the federal government. While preparing for an IGA board meeting in New York at which he planned to ask the board for funding for the dormitory, Paddon wired Premier Smallwood to confirm his support for a federal role in the project: "Respectfully submit federal government ought [to] contribute something to such a high school since nearly half enrolment will be Eskimo or perhaps Indian."[103]

After Confederation, the federal government had initially refused to accept responsibility for Indigenous peoples in Labrador. In negotiations with the province afterwards, it agreed to pay for two-thirds of Inuit expenses and all of Innu expenses related to capital expenditures for health, welfare, and education.[104] This money contributed to school construction and renovation projects in communities designated as "Eskimo" or "Indian."[105] Although North West River was not a designated community,

Students at Yale School, 1950s. Back, l-r: Irene Flowers (Rigolet), Ralph Lyall, Bernadette Blake, Cluney McNeil, Bernice Blake, Elaine Blake; middle, l-r: Herbert McLean, Jerry Michelin, Cora Best, Miriam Igloliorte (Hopedale), Katherine Baikie; front, l-r: Nanette Blake, Frances Frieda (Hopedale), Karen Montague, Marina Hopkins (Mud Lake), Lucretia Baikie (courtesy of Them Days Archive).

Dr. Paddon fought for the Indigenous funding. He and the Central Labrador Amalgamated School Board lobbied the Department of Education to petition for federal funds for their project.[106] The federal government eventually agreed to pay partial costs for the high school and dormitory, in proportion to the number of students who attended from communities included in the Federal–Provincial Agreement — Nain, Hopedale, Makkovik, Postville, Davis Inlet, and Sheshatshiu (then known as the Innu — or "Indian" — side of North West River).[107]

Dr. Paddon had succeeded in getting federal funding for the project. Lake Melville High School officially opened in 1971, with 20 per cent of construction costs paid for by the federal government.[108] Yale School (also known as North West River Amalgamated School) became Yale Elementary for kindergarten to Grade 6. In 1972, the Senior Dormitory also opened, with the federal government paying 60 per cent of the construction and operating costs.[109] The new dormitory provided accommodation for 72 high school students, the majority of whom came from the north coast (Nunatsiavut). The older dormitory became known as the Junior Dorm. It housed children between the ages of 6 and 12, most of whom were Inuit or Innu wards of the state. An IGA staff house, built in 1957 and known as Todd House, became the Infants' Home for preschool-aged children who had also been apprehended by social services.[110]

Education of Indigenous Students

The education provided at the school in North West River relied on the standardized English-language Newfoundland curriculum, taught by teachers from Newfoundland and elsewhere in Canada, as well as from Britain and the United States. The school's curriculum did not reflect its students' Indigenous cultural backgrounds, nor was it meant to. Instead, educators aimed to train Indigenous students in the dominant culture's values and understandings. In his 1967 submission to the Royal Commission on Education and Youth, Dr. Paddon used the example of the recent Hebron relocation to Makkovik to argue that education should train students to adapt to the "Canadian" way of life:

> Much time, money and ingenuity has been expended on assisting these natives in their transition from a very primitive and poverty-stricken life, to something more in keeping with Canadian standards. It is curious to me that virtually no concessions have been made in the school syllabus to the unique and special problems presented by the environment, the cultural background, and the language problem of northern Labrador.[111]

The concessions in the syllabus that Dr. Paddon envisioned did not involve incorporating Inuit values and language into the curriculum. Instead, he argued that Inuit needed to adapt to modern community living.

Using the Hebron relocation as illustration, Dr. Paddon asserted that schooling should teach Inuit students household and community living skills such as maintaining a house, managing a household budget, and cooking with imported foods.[112]

The need to address what Dr. Paddon termed the "special problems" of Indigenous students' "cultural background" and "language problem" reflected a belief in the benefits and inevitability of modernization. This view had crystallized at the 1956 Conference on Labrador Affairs, a meeting convened by the provincial government to discuss plans and goals for Labrador and its people. Although there were no Indigenous participants at the meeting, representatives from the IGA, the Moravian Mission, and the provincial government gathered to discuss the challenges of administering health and social services to such a large and dispersed Inuit and Innu population.[113] They critiqued the Indigenous fishing and trapping way of life, which most agreed should be replaced by wage-paying jobs. At the conclusion of the conference, representatives issued a formal statement clarifying their intentions:

> [The conference] served to confirm the view that the Eskimos and Indians cannot continue to exist as isolated minorities but must ultimately be integrated into the general body of our Society. A vigorous programme in Welfare and Education, particularly the latter, is required . . . to prepare these minorities for the Society of the future.[114]

The authorities at the conference saw the educational system as an integral part of modernization efforts to transform Inuit and Innu children from hunters, fishers, and trappers into assimilated and "productive" citizens. A few years later, IGA staff applauded the success of the North West River school and dormitories in achieving this social transformation among their students:

> Nearly every youngster in Northern Labrador who, in the past 43 years, has managed to attain high school education and subsequently to learn a skilled trade or vocation or to qualify in a profession such as teaching, nursing, laboratory worker, etc., has done so in the Grenfell Mission dormitory. We are naturally proud of this.[115]

Like Dr. Paddon and the other conference representatives, teachers at the Yale School believed that traditional Indigenous practices and ways of life had no role in the transition to modernization. They described that belief in a 1967 submission to the Royal Commission on Education and Youth:

> It is apparent that Labrador is expanding, and will continue to do so. It is also apparent that education is extremely important to this expansion. While it may be true that many of the coastal settlements will maintain the status quo . . . we are convinced that there is much good material on the coast, that there are many young people there who will be, or should be, dissatisfied with the old life and who can and should have a part in the development of their country, and enjoy the benefits of the twentieth century.[116]

The teachers and the local school board recognized that the program of study was foreign to some students, but they still thought it worth pursuing. They hoped that the education would encourage students to turn away from "the old life" and embrace a modern future. By providing housing for Indigenous students from coastal communities, both the school and dormitory system at North West River aimed to accelerate the modernization process. Once living in the dormitory setting, the students would be encouraged to learn the values and norms of the dominant white society as part of their formal education. As Dr. Paddon wrote:

> [The dormitory system is] intended to meet the problem of providing education for a group whose main problems arise from the fact that there is a strong Eskimo racial and cultural element in an isolated population. The Eskimo influence and attitude towards education, and the language problems in these bilingual groups is the factor we wish to mitigate.[117]

In short, Dr. Paddon and the school staff did not aim to support the bilingual knowledge or cultural identities of Indigenous students. Rather, they sought to overcome these racial and cultural "problems" by immersing the students in the North West River social setting and giving them an intensive English Newfoundland education.[118]

Their beliefs reflect widespread convictions of the time. Led by the tenacious Premier Joey Smallwood, post-Confederation Newfoundland was determined to usher its citizens into the modern world. The new government aimed to help people move from difficult lives in small coastal fishery outports across the province to the affluence of urban, industrial society.[119] And to make the leap, children needed to be educated according to the standards of dominant Canadian society.

As head of the IGA at North West River and superintendent of the local school board, Paddon clearly outlined the cultural outcomes he thought the educational system should teach Indigenous students. In the late 1960s, the school boards in North West River and in Sheshatshiu were planning to build large high schools on either side of the river. Federal government officials suggested that this duplication might be avoided if students on the North West River side were sent over to attend school on the Sheshatshiu side. However, Paddon argued against the idea "because we are trying to integrate them [the Innu children] into [the] Canadian way of life, and not vice versa."[120]

Dr. Paddon was not the only one to promote Indigenous "integration" in the late 1960s. In fact, he was simply following the latest thinking on policy towards Indigenous peoples in Canada. In 1967, the federal government's Hawthorn Report argued that Indigenous children should be taught in integrated schools instead of in segregated residential schools: "school integration represents the first step toward the dissolution of most reserves, because education makes it possible for the Indians to adapt themselves to the White Canadian's way of life."[121] Dr. Paddon believed that this "integration" of children at the school and the dormitory helped to dissolve cultural and social divisions between groups in Labrador. In 1968, he received a letter from Ed Schreyer, a member of Parliament in Ottawa (and later the NDP premier of Manitoba and then Canada's governor general), asking about the Grenfell boarding schools in light of changing federal policy towards Indian residential schools in other parts of Canada. Paddon replied that the dormitory in North West River was more progressive than boarding schools elsewhere:

> The dormitory is wholly integrated and the Eskimo and settler attend in full social and intellectual equality and live together contentedly. . . . I should like to stress that unlike some of the Church boarding schools in the Canadian Arctic, the North West River dormitory is wholly non-denominational and wholly voluntary.[122]

Student Experiences

To a great extent, students' experiences at the schools and dormitories in North West River reflected their teachers' attitudes towards Indigenous cultural difference and desire to integrate and modernize Indigenous ways of life. As with all the boarding schools, children had a wide range of experiences at North West River, and former students have shared a variety of recollections about their time there.

Homesick and Vulnerable

Many children suffered from homesickness when they first arrived at the dormitories in North West River. Bella McLean Shouse, one of the first students at Yale School, returned years later to work as a housemother in the dormitory. She described how, in 1943, Gilbert Saunders and his family moved from Davis Inlet to what would become the town of Happy Valley to work on construction of the Goose Bay airport:

> Because there were no school facilities for the children, [Frank and Andrea Saunders] were boarded at the Grenfell Boarding school at North West River for the school year. I was housemother at the Grenfell school. At that time we boarded thirty-two boys and girls ranging in age from six to eighteen years — one big happy family where the older children helped to take care of the younger ones.
>
> It was easy to feel, right from meeting Frank, that he had come from a large, loving and caring family. He made no problems but was very homesick, which caused me to lose some sleep. Nights I would hear sobs coming from the boys dormitory. . . . He just missed his family very much.[123]

Dormitory life also provided opportunities for abuse to occur, as children could find themselves in vulnerable situations. The effects can have a lifelong impact, as this anonymous student makes clear:

> I started living in the dorm when I was 5 years old. . . . I went there because my mother was a single mother and she figured it was a safe environment for me to be since Grandma, her mother, worked in the kitchen and could possibly look out for me. . . . The bad memories are few but took a toll on me later in life.
>
> I remember some of the boys would come in our room at night while we were asleep and I'd wake up with someone pulling off my panties. I don't remember who it was, one of the boys though. . . . So I couldn't imagine what was going on. I knew it was a private part and what he was doing was bad. I managed to kick him away and get my panties back on. I was afraid for a long time after that, thinking that if I went to sleep, something bad

> would happen. Maybe that's why to this day, I can never sleep through the night and sleep very lightly. . . .
>
> The worse part of the dorm was the lack of supervision by the house mothers and the lack of loving attention from them. It seemed the only attention anyone would get was to be disciplined in a physical manner and with an angry voice. There was no love or caring in those voices. I don't blame my mother or my grandmother or anyone for having me stay there. For all they knew, I was safe. It's all they know. I love my mother for doing what she thought right for me at the time. I'm sorry there were no other options for her.[124]

In some cases, children developed close friendships for mutual support and protection in the dormitory. Patricia Kemuksigak describes what happened when social services took her to live in the dormitory with her siblings:

> Some of the other people there, especially people that were from England, like they seemed to be really harsh and strict and stern. But I had some really good friends in the dorm. I was in a room with six — five other girls — six other girls and I'm always glad to see them, when I see them, because we only had each other and we had to try to protect each other. And sometimes the older boys would try to come after us and do things to us, but we all had to look out for one another because we knew what bad things could happen.[125]

Former students gave further accounts of sexual assault by school staff or other people in testimony to the Healing and Commemoration events in 2018 and to the Truth and Reconciliation Commission sharing panels in 2011.[126] These experiences traumatized them as children and have disrupted their lives ever since. Again, a lack of supervision and a blind respect for authority, as well as a societal acceptance of male sexual violence, often created the opportunities for their abuse. Most offenders were never held accountable for their actions, and many survivors continue to struggle with the pain of injustice.

Racism: The Failure of Cultural Integration

For many children from coastal communities, integration in North West River was a difficult experience. Some encountered racism for the first time — in the community, at the school, and in the dormitory.

Kitora Abel came to North West River from Hopedale for high school between 1969 and 1974. She recalls a sense of alienation upon her arrival to the community:

> As soon as we hit the dock when the plane landed and got off the plane, I could feel how out of place we were there. And it hit me right hard, I said, "Oh my God, I didn't think it would be like this." And that's when I, I think that's when I first experienced how hurtful people could be, and how much prejudice hurts.[127]

Rosie Mitsuk, also from Hopedale, remembers physical and verbal abuse:

> Verbal abuse all the time, and it was from the same group of people. I wonder why they were like that, I mean, what kind of upbringing did they have? To be like that, to treat people the way they treated us. The physical abuse was bad like being run after and I had my hair pulled on. . . . The verbal abuse was the worst. Being called "Skimos, Eskimos." And making fun of our language. Like talking funny, like [makes garble noises] — making fun of our language.[128]

Many residents of North West River did not see themselves as Inuit at the time. Abe Flowers, who came from a Settler/*Kablunângajuit* family near Hopedale, describes an invisible line that some drew between those who came from northern Labrador and those from North West River.

> If you were from north of North West River, you were called Inuit, even though we weren't Inuit. But they didn't call us Inuit, they called us "dirty skimos." Now today, some of those very same people are trying to get into the Nunatsiavut government. They're trying to be Inuit themselves now. I can't understand it.[129]

For students who experienced racism in the community, it is frustrating and hurtful that many of the people who called them names later claimed Indigenous status themselves. Many are now Inuit beneficiaries of the Nunatsiavut government or the NunatuKavut Community Council.

While some people in North West River treated him with respect, Jim Tuttauk remembers others making fun of him because of his skin colour and the language he spoke:

> I heard a little bit about racism living here in Hopedale. I used to hear the [American] black people talking to my grandparents and that, talking about racism and what was going on [at the US military] base here. When you hear the word racism, but you didn't know what the heck it meant. We didn't understand that, you know, at six and seven years old then, right? Went to North West River and, you know, there were really nice people there, but you know, being — being a different colour, talked differently, you know, people tend to make fun of you and — the first time I heard the terminology, called me Eskimo. I still can't fathom it today. . . . So a bit of that, and you know the sad thing about it, most of these were Inuit people and didn't know it.[130]

Ivy Andersen Strangemore of Makkovik also remembers a mixed reception from the people in North West River:

> Some of the people were really friendly, but a lot of the people were really not friendly and we were looked down at. And, we were always made to feel that we weren't as good as anybody else.

> We were always put down. That was the biggest thing that I found and the hardest thing that I had to overcome. When I finally got out on my own and went away to school and stuff, I really had to convince myself that I was just as good as the person next to me, and that I could do that as well.[131]

When the Truth and Reconciliation Commission hosted a statement-gathering event in Hopedale in 2011, Philip Abel came to share his story. He described his lonely and exhausting experience of having to deal with relentless racism in North West River:

> It was one of the hardest things I had to do. . . .The bullying that went on there was something that I was not used to. It was almost every day that we had to take care of ourselves — we had to fend for ourselves. We were called names, all kinds of names. We were called huskies, skimos, Eskimaw, whatever name they could come up with, that's what they would call you. And if you retaliated back, or tried to ask somebody for help, there was nobody there. You had to fend for your own self.
>
> There was always, always, forever the same people, every day for the 5–6 years that I was there. Same people. In class, outside the school, outside the dorm, anywhere at all. Same group. . . . I learned how to fight, whether I got beat up or not. Didn't even really matter anymore. That's what I kind of got used to. But I still remember those same people. I still, in my mind, to this day think, why were they like that? What did we do to deserve the treatment that we received? I tried my best, and I know a lot of people did, to get along with other people, to be nice to them, but I still got the same answer back — "shut up you old Skimo!"[132]

Hulda Nochasak, whose family was forced to move to North West River after being evicted from Hebron, describes the cruel treatment she endured as a child from the other children:

> I was born in North West. There were only five houses in the village which was relocated from Hebron. They would call us "The Village People." They'd be throwing rocks at us, calling us down to the dirt and all kinds of names. And then, me and my two sisters and my brother got took away from our parents. They put us in the dorm. . . . It never ever changed. They would still be calling us down to the dirt, calling us all kinds of names. It would be the same everyday. We'd go to school in the morning, and they'd be there behind you throwing rocks. They would be in the classroom pulling on your hair.[133]

Other children in the community and at school were not the only ones who made derogatory comments or looked at the Inuit students with disdain. In a 2010 documentary film about boarding schools in Labrador, Philip Abel describes his memories of disrespect from a teacher as well as from other students:

> When I was trying to talk to a couple of people from Nain, I tried talking Inuk, and the teacher told us to stop talking our language because they thought we were talking about them. "You talks funny. Stop talking you old husky, you old 'Skimo" . . . I got so used to it, it never even bothered me anymore. There was one day though that we were in the bathroom, and [a bully] happened to be there. He said, "Move away, you old Blacky." I said, "Look in the mirror. You're the same colour as I am." "Don't you get saucy with me, you old 'Skimo." No matter how hard you fight back, you lose and you lose. You are always losing.[134]

Evelyn Winters, who grew up in Kamarsuk and Nain, quit school in Grade 9 after an incident with a teacher at North West River:

> One of the teachers pointed at me. And you know they saw someone walking down the road who had quit school and was

> on welfare. And they said, you know, you're going to be just like those people out there. You're going to have kids year after year and you're never going to amount to anything. After when he said that, you know what? I took my books and I left and I never went back. I was just so hurt and sick.[135]

Laura Palliser Pardy arrived at the dormitory for Grade 9 at the age of 13. After growing up in Rigolet in a large family and spending a lot of time hunting with her father, she found the school at North West River foreign and bewildering. She felt unprepared, both academically and socially. The humiliation she endured in that one year affected the rest of her life.

> My father was very respectful to the people who said we had to leave. We had to. I was never so lonesome the whole year. I didn't know nothing about the school in North West. It was so different from Rigolet back then. I didn't know there were gym teachers, I didn't know things like that, little things, but to them, that's when the fun-making started. . . . I never felt so stupid in my life.
>
> One teacher was really negative, would bawl at me in class. I felt really belittled, and I didn't even want to go to his class. He would throw the books at me, throw the scribbler down. "What's this?" I didn't have a clue. It's hard to explain. I wasn't educated enough from Rigolet to know what he meant. I was so scared. I couldn't wait for weekend.
>
> The house parents were prejudiced, strict. My mom and dad were strict, but not strict like that. We had to go by rules [at the dorm], and I didn't ever go by rules [at home]. [We] just belonged, right?
>
> I even turned to alcohol. . . . I had to learn to be tough. I joined a gang and everything. I became like a very terrible person, a bully. I know if I was home, that wouldn't have happened. I was a bully, a real bully. I didn't understand why. I was angry at the world, didn't care.[136]

Irene Voisey grew up in Nain. She came to the dormitory in 1975 and stayed for two years. Her house parents looked at her as a stereotype and pegged her as a failure:

> It was hard trying to deal with the house parents because they were — they had their own mind made up about who you were going to be. . . . I always made sure that you know that you can do it just as good as anybody else. There's no such thing as that you can't do it. Just be kind and treat everybody with respect.[137]

Students reacted in different ways to the prejudice they encountered. Some learned to deny their Inuit roots. For example, in a letter sent to Premier Smallwood's executive assistant in 1966, Dr. Paddon notes that 16 of the 50 boarders show what he describes as "evidence of Eskimo inheritance in their physical appearance, [but they are] entirely English speaking and inclined to deny that they are Eskimo to any degree."[138] Others learned to hate themselves, to hate others, or simply to bury their emotions in order to survive.

Wanda Lucy remembers learning how to deal with the racism she encountered and the institutional life that left little room for individual attention and care:

> You had to take the abuse that we received. You had to be belittled. You had to accept it like that was the acceptable behaviour. You did nothing. You just said nothing, otherwise you would have comebacks at you, and vengeance, which you didn't want. You just really had to almost function like a robot. . . . We weren't human anymore. It was like a herd of cattle. Like animals, we were treated really like animals. You were fed certain foods. You were expected to behave this way. . . . We had no counsellors. We had nobody to turn to, really. We were out there on our own.[139]

For others, like Emma Ford Reelis, who was put in the dormitory in 1959 after her father died, the dormitory was a refuge from the abuse she suffered at home. But it was also an institution that failed her because she was Inuk:

> In the dorm, we were told that we weren't — you're not going to make anything of your life. You're going to be just, you know, an Eskimo and — because that's what we were called years ago by a lot of people, and we weren't going to amount to anything because, you know, you're this, you're that and whatever, you're stupid. . . . I was told I was stupid. I was told I wasn't going to amount to nothing. I think that just sticks onto you to this day. [I] ask, "Did I do it right today? Did I do this right?" I'm still asking the same question even though I'm 70 years old. So I'm still asking, am I doing the right thing?[140]

For other students, the dormitory provided a haven from the racism they experienced in the town and at the school. Kitora Abel, who did not feel at home in North West River, described in the 2010 film, *The Courage to Remember*, how she felt safe only at the dormitory:

> The only safe place I felt when I was in North West was the dorm because once you're outside that yard, you were, what do you call it, "bait" for them. You had to be careful when you went out, of who was around, who was outside of the yard. . . . You'd never go alone. That's how out of place we were, living in another world.[141]

Several years later she reiterated these feelings to the Truth and Reconciliation Commission:

> Me and my friends experienced a lot of shame, and we were made to think that being Inuit was dirty and that we should be ashamed to be Inuit. But we weren't called Inuit at that time, we

> were called skimos, huskies, eaters of raw flesh, all those names. It wasn't so bad in the dorm, we never heard those names — some of us were Inuit, some were settlers, some from Goose Bay area. . . . It wasn't [the] dorm that was so bad, it was the schools that deterred everyone from the education that they wanted.[142]

Not all school and dormitory staff treated the students with disdain. Jim Tuttauk describes how one dormitory worker's kindness and respect saved his life and helped him and many others retain their pride in being Inuit:

> Educators can be heroes, some of them are. And this one here, this lady, she came from the States, originally from Maine. . . . Her name was Ellen Bryan at the time, who is Natan Obed's mother.[143] She was a great support to me and a lot of us at the time. . . .
>
> Like, when they found out my [middle] name was Abia, I got tormented a lot and it made me ashamed to even mention the name anymore. But Ms. Bryan, God bless her heart, I still remember her words today. [They're] stuck to my head, will be for the rest of my life. "You have a beautiful name, you have a beautiful — your grandfather's name, your last name is a beautiful name. Never forget who you are."
>
> She truly was an angel sent from heaven, I believe. I know this in my heart right now today, my heart and mind, that if Ellen Bryan didn't come to North West River at that time I wouldn't be here today. I would have suicided, I know I would have. . . .
>
> She was very hurt when she found out that we went through all this residential school stuff, because in the letter she sent me she said, "How could they do this to my children?" And we were her children, that's who we looked up to there. It's the first white woman or any non-Inuit woman or person, for that fact, [who] had ever treated us with dignity, kindness. She was almost like a

> second mother, I guess. She was very young herself. And I know for a fact if it wasn't for her, I wouldn't be here today, and probably a lot of us.[144]

The Return Home: Disconnection

After spending time in North West River, many students found adjusting to the return home very difficult. Although they looked forward to seeing their families, the transition back to their communities could be painful and confusing. Everyone had changed to some degree, both those who had left and those who had remained at home, as Edna MacDonald McLean from Paradise River describes:

> When the school year ended, I went home for the summer . . . I felt rather "foreign," "changed," my parents and siblings didn't seem the same, and my old friends, while not exactly mean, neither were they totally welcoming. I was an outsider now and it seemed I no longer fit at home. In different situations, boarding school had set this pattern for my life for many many years to come. . . . It's so very emotionally draining sometimes but I let the good things in my life overrule these feelings most of the time. I have survived and learned to cope.[145]

The time away from family often created a disconnect that was difficult to rebuild. Philip Abel found that his once close relationship with his mother had changed when he went home to Hopedale:

> The hardest part I found about going to North West River was coming back, coming back home. It was like I didn't even know my parents anymore. I didn't even know my mother. Because we were away, away from home so long. We couldn't even talk to each other like we used to. We was always talking and laughing. She used to always tell me everything, tell us everything. I came back from my first year in North West River, she was like a stranger.

> She started talking to me in Inuk[titut], most times I answered back to her, but that first year back, I hardly understood what she said. The first year was a really bad year for me. It made me want to go back to North West River because I didn't know my parents anymore. We lost communication with each other.[146]

Back in North West River, Philip endured further heartbreak when he learned that his father had died in Hopedale.

Families at home also felt the disconnect when the students came back. Sybella Tuglavina remembers her brother returning to Hopedale from the dormitory in North West River and how different he seemed:

> He went to the dorms first, but we used to notice that when they used to come back from North West River the boys would come back with their long hair and headbands on, and they'd go strutting and people would be jealous. You know how they used to make remarks about them. That's how my brother was, he was part . . . hippie. He eventually quit though, I don't know why.[147]

People at home sometimes sensed that the students had adopted a new and disparaging attitude towards their Inuit heritage. They resented the students' new outlook, as Jim Tuttauk explains:

> Coming home — coming home was good and hard for some of us from residential schools after the school year. When we come back, some of us, we — we became home lost. We became white, the way we dressed, our slang, the way we combed our hair, the way we talked. . . . Some of us got shunned by our own family members when we come back home. We became too white, too proud was the word that got used, because I guess after being there for a while you kind of — kind of was embarrassed of your own people and it's so shameful to fucking say this, but it's the way they made you feel back when I was going there.

> And what hurt the most was coming back to our home communities and having this said to us by our own family members, some of our aunts, uncles, grandparents. "You're so damn fucking proud. You're so damn proud you're white." It still bothers me today that some of us had to go through that and it still hurts, stings, today. Because some of the people still in our community still have that same belief that we're still these proud people that are — that think that — think we're better than them, but that's bullshit. That's the farthest thing from my mind anyways. I don't think I'm any better than anybody.[148]

When students internalized the racism directed at them and felt ashamed of their Inuit heritage, their feelings often mixed with guilt in a confusing combination, especially for teenaged children. Marjorie Andersen Flowers describes the shame she experienced upon returning home to Makkovik from the dormitory, and how she has struggled against it since:

> I think the first thing that I remember coming home from high school was when I went in the porch and there was seal skins up in our porch and I went — it was the smell that hit me. I was so ashamed, I was ashamed of who I was, I was ashamed of my parents. I thought that I was a bit better than them. It took a lot of time to learn the difference and even in my head I'll hear it now. I still have to learn and grow and go back to where I come from.[149]

Hulda Pijogge found that no one acknowledged the confusion and pain that students experienced when they moved home, after they had been taught to despise their Inuit heritage:

> When I talk with my friends that I had from the dorm, all we talk about is the good times. We don't talk about losing our parenting

> skills, coming back home being called an "Inokutsi" [some Inuk you are]. 'Cause when we came back, I think a lot of us felt ashamed to try to go back to our traditions, to follow our ways. We wanted to be more like . . . 'cause we were made fun of so much in the dorm. We didn't want to be Inuks. We didn't want to follow our Inuk ways. We wanted to be more like them so that we could fit in, 'cause we spent more time there than we spent at home.[150]

Rose Oliver also describes how years at the dormitory in the 1960s instilled in her a sense of shame for her Inuit life. Then she became ashamed of herself for changing. She expresses regret and sadness about how her years in North West River affected her:

> My life was forever changed as I knew it. I had no guidance about the future. I left home a growing teenager learning my traditional ways and living with a big happy family. When I returned home after a few years of Dorm life, being ashamed of myself, the Inuit

Martin Sillitt from Nain, 1960s. Martin later became a ship's engineer; he died tragically on a hunting trip in 1979 (courtesy of Them Days Archive).

> girl, and being ashamed of my dear Mom and her ways, such as seal skin on the walls drying and the smelly house from having no bathrooms and the smell of fish cooking and seal cooking. I was confused. I loved my family but somehow it got ingrained in me that they were savages, dirty, and lazy. . . . When I returned I was a new race. I felt like an alien in my beloved home. I was a stranger now. Our values were different. I had an education and Mom didn't ever go to school. . . . I never did tell my family what happened to me in those four years at the Dorm. . . . I was too ashamed of myself for changing into someone I did not like or know.[151]

Students were not the only ones to experience the impacts of boarding school. Parents, siblings, and neighbours suffered the absence of the children when they left each September. When the students themselves became parents, their children also felt the repercussions. Kitora Abel describes how her time at the dormitory affected her parenting:

> We didn't learn to be good parents because our parents weren't there with us. We didn't learn how to respond to someone who was hurting, because we didn't know who to turn to. There were no adults telling us how we should react to someone who's hurting inside. This is how I act now, because I don't know how to respond, I don't know how to hug.[152]

Boarding school changed the lives of the students and their families for years. A comment from Marjorie Flowers summarizes the sense of loss that remains:

> I lost a lot. I lost a lot of my culture and parenting and role models. I did. I lost a lot. I gained my education but I lost a lot of me in the process. I almost didn't know who I was. I wanted to be someone else and it took a long time to come back and find my roots.[153]

Fighting Back: Friendships and Speaking Inuktitut

In the face of racism and institutional life, students developed ways of coping with their new life at the dormitory. Many built strong friendships and social networks that continued to provide support through adulthood. As Elaine Lane of Postville remarked, "We did make friends there. It actually filled in the void, being taken from your home and put into a place that you weren't aware of."[154]

At the age of five, Richard Rich was taken by the IGA plane from his home in Rocky Cove, a small settlement near Rigolet, to school in North West River. Although he found it lonely at first, he made strong friendships that helped him during his time at the dormitory.

> Within a month, I was alright, because I was took around, and people who [used to] live here [in Rigolet] lived in North West. [They] used to get me on the weekends, and showed me around, not be lonely. So I went like that for seven years, but now as you got older, you got better. 'Cause I had lot of friends from north, south, North West, even Goose Bay. And I still got them today. . . . We all helped one another, friends from north and south. We all shared what we had. Stole a lot of stuff out of the gardens! [*Laughs*][155]

Other students held on to their pride in their Inuit culture by speaking Inuktitut, even though its use was discouraged. As a child, Maria Brown Brazeau was sent to North West River hospital from Nain for eye treatment. School authorities pressured her parents to keep Maria in the school there, so she stayed at the dormitory for two years. She recounts her efforts to retain her language:

> On my way to the store I would meet some young children from North West River, and they would be calling me dirty Skeemo and all kinds of terrible things for a child to be called. And I thought the whole world is against me. But I had happy moments too. They had some kind of fairs or something and everyone was

> happy and enjoying that. So everybody was kind then, that was a good memory.
>
> But you never knew when it was going to crop up. So you grow up after a few times and as you grow older it builds in you, this feeling that you're inferior. They wanted you to feel that you are not like us, and I felt that way very strongly when I was a teenager, because things seem bigger in your — when you're a teenager. Like, it was like boiling inside of me, me and Bertha Ford.
>
> So we used to go in behind — there was big swings behind the dorm. We used to go on the swings and talk in Inuktitut to our hearts content, thinking of every Inuit word we could think of as long as we could, and that was like us getting back at them even though it wasn't — they couldn't do anything to them, but we knew that we would never forget our language and we never did, her and I. We never forgot our language. We fought to keep it. And so to be a strong — I'm Inuit and I know my language.[156]

For Sybella Tuglavina, preserving her language was less about defiance and more about staving off homesickness:

> It was quite a culture shock for me. One of the major things that I missed mostly was talking to my mum in Inuktitut everyday. And so, I was cut off from my mother, my mother and father, my brothers and sisters. I was left there alone and all around me were all people who didn't speak Inuktitut. So I tried to keep on communicating with my mum by writing letters to her and she would write back which was real good, and they were all in Inuktitut.[157]

North West River Perspectives

Residents who lived in North West River remember the "dorm kids" in their own ways. Katherine Baikie-Pottle recalls looking forward to playing with the dormitory children and credits Yale School with providing a

Children at the dormitory in North West River, 1952, l-r: ?, ?, ?, Nora Blake, ?, Elizabeth Pottle, Alma Blake, Jane Wolfrey, ? (courtesy of the Maritime History Archive and the heirs of Jean Smith).

good education. In 2008, when the Labrador boarding schools court case started and former Prime Minister Stephen Harper apologized to the survivors of residential schools in the rest of Canada, she wrote a letter to the editor of the *Labradorian* newspaper:

> We, children living in North West River, couldn't wait for September when our friends would be coming back to the dorm after being home for the summer. Of course, some were sad to leave home again for the school year, but we, as young children, could not have understood that, we were too excited that our friends were back! Maybe we were selfish in our delight to welcome the dorm children . . . we could not understand their grief of leaving home?
>
> If people in my town called dorm children names because of their race, I do not recall it during my days in school. I thought we all looked pretty much alike. Dorm children did have restrictions

on where they could go, how late they could be out playing, strict homework time, etc. BUT boy was I jealous! We had strict rules growing up, and before we could think about homework getting done under a kerosene lamp, we had to split, chop and carry wood in each evening, haul gas, kerosene and groceries, help with the house work. . . .

That type of thing was not mentioned in or outside the dorm. If the physical abuse came from teachers . . . many of us from the town or dorm received the same. No one was spared the book flying through the air, ruler smacks, hair pulling or the wide strap that hung under a principal's choir gown. Some of our friends from the dorm came to our house often, some to play, have an "outside" meal, to go hunting and fishing with my older brother and some helped us around the house with our chores. Those came from every community along the north coast and never did we feel better nor different than them . . . we were friends. . . .

Yale school was a model for education. It delivered students who are nurses, engineers, teachers, administrators, managers, many chose trades, and some of the very brightest came from the dorm. Many of those assisted in establishing the Nunatsiavut Government. Many of the people in my age group will always say, "Where would we be today?" "We might have starved only for the dorm." That is not to say everything was rosy and that they were not homesick. My generation appeared to have had a "decent" experience but for those who came after something appears to have gone wrong.[158]

Removed by Social Services

Newfoundland and Labrador's Division of Child Welfare (later renamed but commonly known as "social services") oversees the protection of children who are apprehended as wards of the state if social workers, police, or other authority figures deem them to be neglected or abused.[159]

Although the department expanded after World War II, it relied heavily on the IGA, the police, and welfare officers to enforce its child protection regulations and to take responsibility for the children in care.[160] The IGA orphanage at St. Anthony and the dormitories in North West River provided housing for these children, and the Division of Child Welfare paid the IGA for partial costs of their care.[161]

Children whom social services placed in the dormitories experienced the trauma associated with having their family connections ruptured. Dormitory life could not replace a family's love. Rosina Kalleo Holwell remembers the humiliation of seeing the authorities inspecting her family's living conditions in Nain before they took her and her siblings to North West River and St. Anthony:

> Social services used to always come to my parents' house and have a look in their cupboards. Without permission from my parents, they would — he would have an RCMP member with him, and just knock on the door, and come straight into the house, and go straight to our cupboards, and look to see if we had any food in our cupboards. . . .
>
> Maybe a day or two later, we were taken away from our parents and we were sent to the dorm. My younger sister, Harriet, was only a baby, so she was fostered. And, Justine was sent to North West River, up to the cottage, and I stayed in the dorm. I was really hurt, because I was taken away from my home, from my family, and my sisters, because I always took care of them. . . .
>
> . . . When we were taken away, we weren't allowed — I wasn't allowed to see my sisters. But I used to sneak over to the cottage and see Justine, even just to have a look at her. It was good knowing that she was okay and being taken care of.[162]

When Rosina was six, her mother came to North West River for medical reasons; Rosina was only allowed to talk briefly with her through a window:

> I said, "Good. I'm alone. I'm homesick." I was just kicking the sand. I didn't know what else to say, because I knew I wasn't allowed to go and see my mum. I wasn't allowed to hug her. And, she said, "*Panik* [Daughter], I have to go now. The nurses said we've got to go now."
>
> And, they had to close the window, and we had to leave again. Before I left, she threw down cookies for me. She had them tied in some kind of little rope or string, so they don't fall out. Those two cookies, I guess they were chocolate cookies, I brought them to the dorm, I had a small bite, and for two weeks I kept those two cookies under my pillow, because they had my mum's touch. Every time I touched those cookies before I had a bite, I knew there was my mum's touch on there, and I didn't want them to ever go away. But, every day for two weeks I just took a bite off of them knowing that my mum's touch was there.[163]

The children in care lived year-round in the dormitories; they often did not have a network of family and friends to look out for them. This made them especially vulnerable to abuse, as a woman in North West River told researcher Arie Molema: "Some people went through the dorm, and they . . . just didn't see the underbelly of life here. I guess you had to be a welfare kid or somebody that nobody cares about. [The worst abuses are] not going to happen to the ones that had family, and families that are vocal."[164]

Some children in care also faced additional ordeals in their lives that compounded their difficulties in the dormitory. Toby Obed, for example, has battled the intergenerational trauma of both relocation and the child welfare system his entire life, on top of boarding school. His parents were northern relocatees forced to settle in Hopedale in the late 1950s. When he was three, social services took Toby away from his family and placed him in the Infants' Home in North West River. He spent years in the dormitories and, later, in foster homes. He endured abuse and says he never felt loved. At a Healing and Commemoration sharing panel in Hopedale in 2018, Toby recalled the time his mother came to the hospital in North West River to give birth to his younger brother. It was the last time he was to see her; when she and his father later died in Hopedale, Toby was not allowed to go home to attend their funerals.

> When my mother was ready to have him [my brother] in North West River, the hospital right next door to the junior dorm, right next door. The day that my mother was ready to leave North West River and go home, we were told, "You got a half hour. Go to the hospital and see your mother. You got a half hour. Go see your mother." That's the only time I fucking seen my mum. The only time I seen my mum in my life. That's the only time I seen her, half hour. My mum . . .
>
> It's one thing to live through fucking hell and back, one thing. The shit that I went through I would never, never, never wish on my worst enemy, never. Things I've seen, things I've experienced. Nobody ever deserves shit like that, no one. . . .
>
> One thing I learned, keep my fucking guard up. Don't show weakness. Don't show weakness. That's one thing I learned. Always keep your guard up. Don't show your weakness to people. That's one of the first things I learned in North West River.[165]

Life in the North West River dormitories was a miserable experience for many children. Some, like Toby, endured untold suffering. Others faced their own difficulties. For most students, the months spent away from home resulted in splintered family relationships, a forgotten language, and a new-found shame of Indigenous culture. Students and their families decided this was not acceptable. As the next chapter describes, Inuit from the northern communities of Nain, Hopedale, Makkovik, Postville, and Rigolet challenged the boarding school system in the 1960s and 1970s. Like the families of children at Lockwood and the Makkovik boarding school before them, the families of students at the North West River dormitories demanded better. Together, they pushed for schooling opportunities in their own communities, so children did not have to leave home to get an education. The Yale dormitories' days were numbered.

CHAPTER TWELVE

Boycotts and Protests: *Inuit Demand More Control*

"What we don't understand is why some communities here on the coast have grade eight while other communities have to send their grade eight school children to North West River."
— Hopedale resident, in *kinatuinamot illengajuk* (1973)

Many students disliked living at the dormitory in North West River. But for children from the north coast communities of Nain, Hopedale, Makkovik, Postville, and Rigolet, there was no other option for getting a high school education. It was either attend the school in North West River or the one in St. Anthony, and both involved moving away from home. Students living in small communities on Labrador's south coast faced the same choice. Depending on the size of the community, schools there only went up to Grade 7 or 8, or they closed for the year if they could not find any teachers. But families wanted to see their children complete high school. In the 1950s and 1960s, most jobs in the expanding mining, hydroelectric, and military developments in Labrador required an education. So moving away for high school seemed to be the only option.

But why not have a high school at home? Young people asked the question and began to demand a better education system. In August 1962, students in Nain took a stand and refused to go back to North West River for the school year. After talking with their teachers in Nain, they announced that they would stay at home for Grades 10 and 11. Within the week, Moravian Superintendent Rev. F.W. Peacock and Dr. Tony Paddon of the IGA had arrived in Nain. The two men hoped to quell the protest and convince the students to change their minds. As a student later recalled:

> [They] came up here for a meeting with parents, students, and teachers, [and] said "You can't get the education here that you can get in North West River. The teachers won't be as good." Think of how the teachers here must have felt. We stayed, although the next year the kids went back to North West River.[1]

The two men promised to cover the fees of students who agreed to return to the dormitory. For Dr. Paddon, convincing the students to return to North West River was necessary to his plans. He wanted to convince the federal and provincial governments to support a regional high school and expanded dormitory in North West River. As a Moravian missionary noted in the Nain station diary, Dr. Paddon was "trying to procure enough high school students to establish regional high school for coastal area."[2] A Nain student also recognized Paddon's motive: "I think North West River was being built up as a centre at that time and that's why they wanted us to go out."[3]

Rev. Peacock also wanted students to attend high school in North West River. In a 1963 letter to the Minister of Education, he describes how people in Nain and Makkovik had refused to comply with these plans. In consequence, the schools in these two communities were forced to offer some high school classes that year:

> Although this arrangement [to send students to North West River] stands, we do not always get the co-operation from the parents and children and there is a reluctance among some to send their children as far away as N.W.R. especially since they cannot get home for Christmas, in consequence much against our will we

> are obliged to offer High School. This year Nain has 8 High School students in Grades 9 and 11 and Makkovik 3 in grade 9. I think therefore that we have to educate the parents to understand that it is far better if they will send their children to N.W.R.[4]

Students had been resisting the move to North West River for higher grades for years. For example, in his study of schooling in Nain, anthropologist Patrick Flanagan estimates that, between 1945 and 1965, only a third of the children from Nain stayed at the dormitory in North West River. Another third did not go, and the remaining third moved with their families to the Goose Bay area and received an education at schools there.[5] Between 1965 and 1978, attendance statistics told a similar story: as many as 205 children in Nain were old enough to go to North West River, but only 56 students (27 per cent) made the trip. Of those 56 students, only 10 received a high school diploma.[6]

Flanagan saw the issue in terms of social status. He wrote, "In terms of educational opportunity, class factors have emerged which seriously affect [northern coastal] people's ability to access the educational institutions."[7] Most of the students who stayed in North West River had close connections with the Moravian Church and its schools or were from families who could afford to go without the children's contribution to fishing or housekeeping. As a woman in Nain described it to Flanagan, "only the cream of the crop [went] to school" in North West River.[8] Of the children who did not go to the dormitory, more than half were from relocated families from Hebron or Nutak.[9]

For most of the Nain students who did not want to go to North West River, dropping out of school was their only option. Although she believed she had no choice but to continue, Sue Webb from Nain remembers how most of her classmates quit school rather than go to North West River:

> All the students that went to Grade 9, most quit because they had to go to North West River. There was no room in the big school [in Nain] for Grade 9 anymore. They managed to find a

> classroom, but there were only three of us, three girls in Grade 9. And, I managed to pass, so I had to go on to North West River. The experience I felt was, like, okay, I had no choice. I guess it was under government and if I didn't go, then my parents or whoever took care of me would stop getting family allowance or something.[10]

Parents in northern Labrador often had a negative view of the school. They recalled their own experience at the dormitory or heard stories from other families. As a result, some refused to send their children to North West River. In 1975, 16-year-old Maria Merkuratsuk wrote a letter describing her schooling experience to Tagak Curley, the leader of the national Inuit organization:

> I'm an Inuk from Nain and I have been to school but I quit in grade 8. My parents didn't want me to go away to North West River (where they go to school to the higher grades). They didn't like it, the way they heard about it, so I had no choice about quitting school. I wouldn't mind going back to school to learn more and my parents don't mind now because that's the only way I can get a job easily. They sure wish me to have a job instead of just sticking around doing nothing. There are not many jobs here in Nain — not for girls anyway.[11]

Angus Andersen came from another family in Nain that decided not to send him to school at North West River. Although his uncles and aunts had stayed at boarding schools, his grandparents chose to raise him instead. They wanted him to learn the skills needed to carry out a traditional way of life. While Angus sometimes wondered what he had missed, he appreciated the Inuit education he received with his family:

> I didn't go to residential school, not because I didn't want to, my grandparents were told not to send me there. Only instead of me

> going to residential school like my uncles and aunts, my Grandma Johanna kept me. So I lived with her, helped her, done chores for her instead of sending me to residential school because she's already heard, from her own kids, of issues and stories and hurt from North West River. And I guess being the first-born grandchild saved me from going to residential school. . . .
>
> I often wondered what did I miss education wise, what did I miss curriculum/athletic-wise because I was hearing all this great, positive stuff coming out from North West River; like, they got basketball, ice hockey teams, and floor hockey teams and we did not have that in Nain in the seventies. . . .
>
> But not going to that school, I got the opportunity to be raised by both grandparents, my father, my uncles out on the land. I got to learn about the land, the tradition passed on through generations, how to survive, how to use the stars, how to fish, learn the tides, how to survive off the land. . . . I thank my grandmother now for not . . . having me sent to North West River . . . I'm glad I did not go.[12]

Access to high school education posed a different challenge for Labrador's south coast residents. Year-round communities such as Cartwright, Port Hope Simpson, and Mary's Harbour were large enough to support high schools. So for the families that had resettled in these communities in the 1950s and 1960s, attending high school was not an issue. But many other families still shifted between winter and summer homes into the 1970s. In the winter, their children could go to school in Charlottetown, Port Hope Simpson, or Lodge Bay, for instance. But when they moved to their fishing places from May to October at George's Cove, Sandy Hook, or Francis Harbour, for example, they often did not receive any schooling.[13] The shortened school year limited their education and created challenges for students who wanted to graduate from high school.

By 1959, the provincial government had started a bursary program to support students who moved away for high school. Developed to commemorate the first 10 years of the province joining Canada, the Confederation bursaries provided up to $500 per year for students from small schools to complete Grades 9–11 in larger centres.[14] In Labrador, the program provided bursaries for students who had completed as far as Grade 6.[15] The funding allowed children across Labrador to travel to North West River, St. Anthony, or another community where they could live and attend high school.

The Confederation bursaries supported the IGA dormitories at North West River and St. Anthony by providing financial assistance for out-of-town students. The federal and provincial governments further contributed to this boarding school system by paying for the construction of the regional Lake Melville High School in 1971 and the new senior dormitory in North West River in 1972.[16] But support for a regional education system was fading, even as the opportunity for more coastal students to attend North West River grew.

Many Labradorians were unhappy that they were expected to leave home to attend high school. As the 1974 Royal Commission on Labrador reported:

> A significant number of parents, particularly from the north coast, send their children to North West River for the program offered in the new high school. Not all of them are happy with this arrangement or its results. There is dissatisfaction with the residence life which children experience. In addition, some parents remain unconvinced that a high school education is worth the toll in time away from home for children as young as 13 years, and regret the opportunities lost for the teaching of and exposure to culture and native skills.[17]

Despite recognizing that "many of those who endure it find it a very lonely experience," the Royal Commission felt that "the boarding school system exists as a necessary evil."[18] Students and their families disagreed. They decided to take a more proactive approach to changing the educational system.

The movement to provide high school classes on the north coast gathered strength through the 1970s as local people demanded more political control over their lives. In 1972, the Nain School Committee, a new organization of residents and school representatives, convinced the Labrador East Integrated School Board to hire a Grade 9 teacher for the 1972–73 school year.[19] Other communities, such as Hopedale, struggled to convince the school board to give them enough resources to offer Grade 8, but all communities strived for higher grades.[20]

The campaign to transform the schooling system in Labrador merged with the political aims of the Indigenous rights movement. The national Inuit organization, Inuit Tapirisat of Canada (now called Inuit Tapiriit Kanatami), was founded in 1971. Its leaders visited Nain in 1972 to encourage Labrador Inuit to create their own Inuit organization. They responded by establishing the Labrador Inuit Association in 1973.[21] The new organization aimed to promote the culture of Labrador Inuit and to assert their right to govern their own lives.[22]

Innu leaders were also outspoken in demanding recognition of Indigenous rights in Labrador. In 1972, Bart Jack from Sheshatshiu attended the fourteenth meeting of the Federal–Provincial Committee on Financial Assistance for Indians and Eskimos in Northern Labrador, the group that made decisions about how to spend federal funding. Jack demanded that the committee include Indigenous representatives, in addition to the usual representatives from the federal and provincial governments.[23] Federal representatives had been pushing for the same goal, and the committee finally agreed to involve Indigenous participants at the next meeting.[24] In November 1973, Sam Andersen, the president of the Labrador Inuit Association, and Bart Jack, the president of the Native Association of Newfoundland and Labrador, attended as full committee members. Other Indigenous representatives from communities across Labrador, as well as from the Mi'kmaq community of Conne River in Newfoundland, also attended as guests.[25]

For the first time, Indigenous leaders were able to help decide how to spend federal funds in a number of areas, including education. By the next year, Inuit committee members were raising concerns about funding an education system that required their children to go to North West River for high school. Bill Edmunds, the second president of the Labrador Inuit Association, questioned the need for children to leave home after Grade 7 or 8. Minutes of the meeting record him arguing that "children are forced to go away while they are too young," and that he "felt that Grade 9 should be taught locally."[26]

In 1974, the provincial Department of Education hired a Curriculum Consultant for Native Schools to examine how to improve the school system for Indigenous peoples in the province. Rose Pamak Jeddore of Nain started the job in a tiny windowless office in the Vocational School in Happy Valley.[27] Jeddore was an outspoken advocate for changes in the educational system, and she wrote compelling reports about the situation. She argued that the lack of a high school in north coast communities created a situation that many had decided to boycott:

> The central high school at North West River has been a long standing grievance for native and settler alike. The high drop out rate and the failure of this system should be ample indicators for change. For many decades, students have been boycotting this system by dropping out of school. We cannot ignore this protest. There is no motivation for education beyond grade eight because the penalty for such education is too high. High school education has meant estrangement from one's own culture, language, family, friends and community. Instead of producing people caught between two cultures, we would like to see persons with a secure footing within their own culture and community, not in spite of education, but because of it.[28]

Instead of making North West River the only workable choice for students who wanted to go to high school, Jeddore recommended an alternative: either give all coastal communities enough resources to offer up to Grade 11 or build a central high school in Nain. She also advocated for Inuktitut language and culturally relevant material in the curriculum.[29]

Jeddore also questioned why so much federal and provincial funding had been directed at maintaining the dormitory system, instead of supporting schools on the coast. "There has been a great deal of government money invested in the new high school and dormitory at North West River," she wrote in an early draft of her final report. "If the government had consulted the people instead of the International Grenfell Association, this mistake could have been avoided."[30] She argued that political interests had driven the decision-making process, to the exclusion of Indigenous communities. As she saw it, the IGA was unconcerned by the alienation and loss of language that Inuit children experienced at North West River. She therefore recommended that the funding be redirected towards schools in Inuit communities.

> I do not believe that Dr. Paddon is aware of the problems or that he is sympathetic to the problems of the native community. His main concern is keeping alive North West River as a centre for the coast. In this way, the IGA can maintain control over us. We have no right to make decisions concerning our own affairs.[31]

Jeddore's work articulated the frustration that many Inuit felt about the dormitory system. In 1976, people in Nain co-ordinated their efforts again to press the Labrador East Integrated School Board for higher grades at their school.[32] Local control over educational matters had expanded in 1974 when school board representatives were elected for the first time instead of being appointed by the Moravian missionary.[33] In February 1976, the school board committee met with parents to discuss their dissatisfaction with the school and dormitory in North West River. According to a report in the local newspaper, *kinatuinamot illengajuk*:

> There have been a lot of complaints from the students who attend the North West River High School. The students don't seem to be happy with the food, teachers, the Dormitory, and they don't seem to get along with the residents of North West River. . . . All the parents attending the meeting here in Nain preferred to have a high school here because if the students aren't happy in North West River, they won't get anywhere, but if they were going to high school here, they would go to school during the day and help their parents in the evenings. Also, the boys would be able to go hunting on weekends, and the girls would learn to sew or help around the house. This way, the culture wouldn't disappear so fast. Some kids don't want to talk in eskimo anymore; even if their parents speak to them in eskimo, they just turn away, so they all think it would be much better if there was a high school here.[34]

Finally, the momentum towards a high school on the north coast shifted. In September 1976, the Labrador East Integrated School Board hired teachers for Grade 9 in Nain and Makkovik for a trial period of two years. The school board agreed to bring Grades 10 and 11 to Nain if the project proved successful.[35] Schools in Hopedale, Postville, and Rigolet eventually offered high school education to their children as well, although the difficulties in recruiting and keeping teachers in all communities persisted.[36]

By the late 1970s, encouraged by their victory, the Inuit in northern Labrador turned their attention to gaining more control over their children's education. Providing a high school in their home communities was one goal, but the overhaul of a provincial curriculum and education system that did not reflect Inuit culture and language was another. In 1977, the Labrador Inuit Association organized the first Labrador Inuit Education Conference in Nain. They invited participants from Labrador communities, the Labrador East Integrated School Board, the Department of Education, school officials, and Inuit from other parts of the Arctic.[37] The conference provided a forum for northern Inuit to discuss their concerns with government officials. It also gave them the chance to discuss educational programs for Inuit.

The five-day meeting was a contentious affair. Many of the provincial government officials in attendance denied any wrong-doing on the part of the province.[38] They attempted to redirect the blame onto the Inuit. But the local people's message was clear: "The educational system had suffered through two systems of control," as Amos Maggo of Nain put it. "First the Moravian missionaries, and then the provincial system. The Inuit were now awakening and didn't want any interference in the future."[39] Inuit wanted more authority over the curriculum, the location of the schools, and the funding. "The current system teaches only the values of white society," argued Sam Metcalfe, a prominent Inuk leader and translator. "The Inuit could do the best job of teaching their children the values of their own unique society."[40] Conference attendees outlined a number of Inuit education goals. These included promoting a strong sense of Inuit identity, developing Inuit skills, teaching Inuktitut, and laying the foundation for Inuit self-government and self-reliance.[41] Participants agreed that they wanted schools in their own communities to promote these goals and to provide instruction in Inuktitut.

During the meeting, some asked pointed questions about the federal funding being allocated to the dormitory in North West River. The community was not a designated Aboriginal community under the Federal–Provincial Agreement, yet it received significant funds. Tim Borlase of the Labrador East Integrated School Board suggested that funding to North West River be redirected to coastal schools instead. He thought the money could be put to good use developing Grade 11 programs in all the coastal communities, thereby ensuring the money is "kept at home."[42]

The meeting concluded with resolutions on curriculum development, adult education, vocational training, traditional skills, financing, and qualified teachers. One particular resolution summarized the conference:

> In the past, we educated our own children to survive in the special, and often hostile environment of Labrador. We believe we are more capable of educating today's children for survival in modern Labrador than all people from outside, no matter how well intentioned they might be.
>
> Be it resolved that the Labrador Inuit Association calls upon this Conference to affirm and uphold the right of parents to control their children's education, and the right of native people to control native education.[43]

The movement to provide high schools in coastal communities and to regain Inuit authority over their children's education spelled the end for the Grenfell dormitories in North West River. Internal discussions among IGA staff and board members in the late 1970s outline their concerns about continuing with the effort.[44] The Senior Dormitory, the Junior Dormitory, and the Infants' Home were very expensive to run. At the same time, the demand for accommodations from out-of-town students was decreasing since more students could attend high school in their home communities. The provincial government's approach to child welfare issues was also shifting towards family foster care instead of institutional care.[45] This meant that social services needed to accommodate fewer children who had been removed from their homes in dormitories. Tony Paddon, the long-time champion of the IGA dormitories, retired in 1978.[46] In 1979, the IGA's Executive Committee authorized its senior staff "to discuss with the Government of Newfoundland ways and means of withdrawing from this field of service, possibly before the commencement of the next school year."[47] In April 1980 the IGA withdrew its involvement from the Junior and Infants' dormitories.[48] The Senior Dormitory closed at the end of June 1980.[49]

The closures dealt a blow to the community and economy of North West River. The Senior Dormitory had employed 15 people from the community, and the Junior Dormitory and Infants' Home had also hired a number of workers.[50] Other changes at North West River also contributed to the diminishing role of the IGA. The provincial government built a bridge to connect North West River with Goose Bay in 1979 in anticipation of the construction of a road to a proposed uranium mine near Makkovik.[51] Road access to the larger centre called into question the need for a hospital in North West River. Just as with its dormitories, the IGA had been moving towards transferring authority for health care to the provincial government for some time. By April 1981 the IGA had handed over all health-care services and properties to the newly formed Grenfell Regional Health Services Board.[52]

With the transferral of its health-care responsibilities, the IGA's evolution was complete. From the sole medical provider and a prominent educational leader in the region, the IGA had evolved into a charitable organization that continues to fund educational, health, and community initiatives in Labrador and northern Newfoundland. As Dr. Gordon Thomas, superintendent of the International Grenfell Association between 1959 and 1979, put it: "The IGA was benevolent and efficient, but inherently paternalistic. Its contribution over the years had been magnificent, but it was run by outsiders and this would no longer do."[53]

Inuit in northern Labrador continued along their path to self-governance. The Labrador Inuit Association submitted a land claim to the federal and provincial governments in 1977.[54] Twenty-eight years later, in 2005, the Canadian and Newfoundland and Labrador governments recognized the Inuit right to self-government by finalizing a land claim agreement.[55] The agreement created the Nunatsiavut government and granted the Nunatsiavut Assembly the power to pass laws on many matters, including education, health, and justice. Inuit-controlled education and the preservation of the Inuktitut language remain as fundamental goals for the people of Nunatsiavut.

PART FOUR

The Innu Experience

CHAPTER THIRTEEN

Labrador Innu, Roman Catholic Schooling, and the IGA Boarding Schools

"The school, the agency now most engaged in influencing the Indians of tomorrow at North West River, must also hasten cultural change as much as possible."
— Our Lady of the Snows School principal, Sheshatshiu, 1967

"The best way to destroy a culture is to train its children in another culture."
— Pien Penashue (Innu Elder), Sheshatshiu, 1999

The Innu of Labrador have had a difficult relationship with schooling. They lived in *nutshimit* (on the land) until the 1960s, when Catholic priests and the provincial government forced them to settle in communities, partly by requiring that their children attend school. Instead of building boarding schools, the authorities built day schools in Sheshatshiu and Davis Inlet. When they made schooling mandatory, Innu families had to move into the villages. Although the Catholic Church did not establish any residential schools in Labrador, some Innu moved away to go to boarding schools. Some attended IGA boarding schools in North West River and St. Anthony, and some attended Catholic schools in Newfoundland, including the Mount Cashel Orphanage in St. John's. Innu children did not attend boarding schools to the same extent as Inuit children in Labrador, but the day schools that Catholic

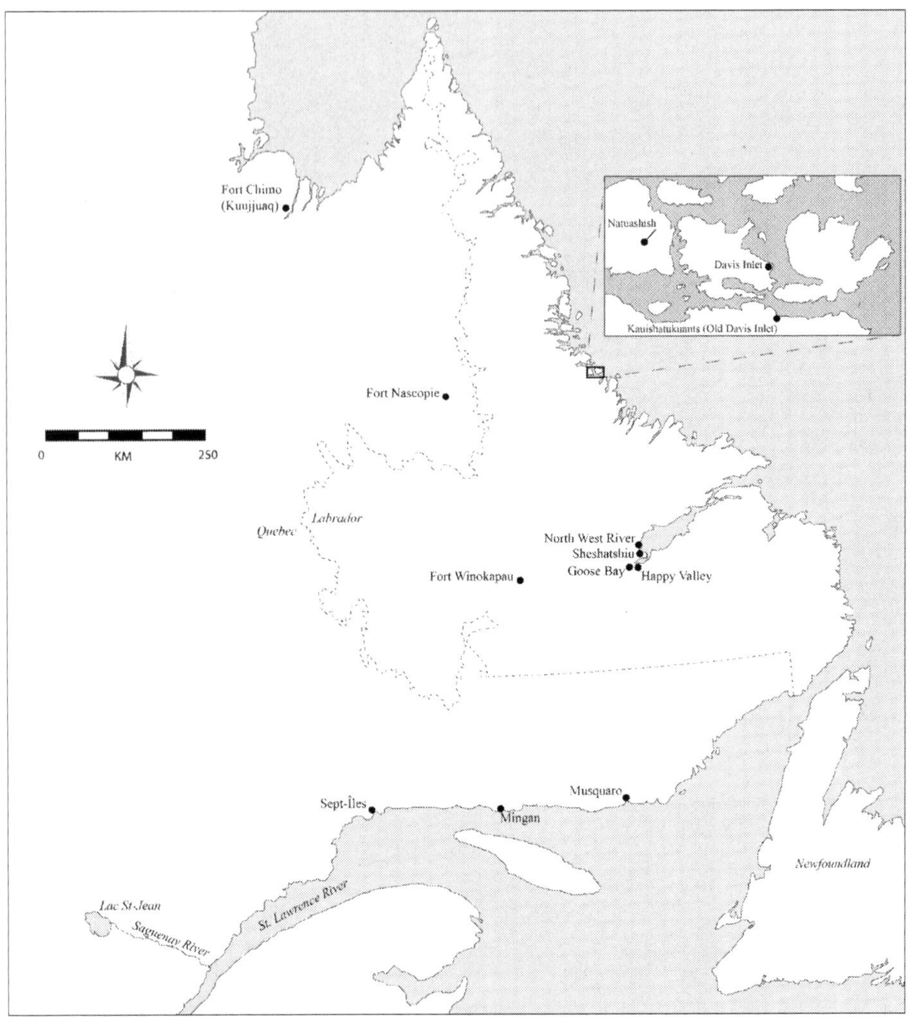

Map 4: Selected Innu communities and trading posts in Quebec and Labrador (map by Peter Ramsden).

priests established for Innu students have had a huge impact on the people of Sheshatshiu and Davis Inlet (now moved to Natuashish). This chapter briefly explores the history of Innu schooling in Labrador and includes the experiences of former students who lived at a boarding school.

The Innu and the Roman Catholic Church

Nitassinan — Innu territory — extends from Labrador to Quebec's North Shore of the St. Lawrence River to the Lac St-Jean and Saguenay region. As noted in Chapter One, Innu in Labrador largely adopted Roman Catholicism through their connections with their cousins in Quebec and with the Oblate missions along the St. Lawrence River. The Oblates of Mary Immaculate came to Canada from Europe in 1844 to convert Indigenous peoples to the Roman Catholic faith. The missionaries based themselves in the Ottawa region at first and then expanded into western Canada and east into Quebec.[1] By the mid-1850s, Innu living in Labrador often travelled to the Lower North Shore of the St. Lawrence River, where Oblate priests had built chapels at the Hudson's Bay Company trading posts. The Innu visited the posts at Musquaro and Mingan, east of Sept-Îles, where they traded their furs for better prices than they could get in Labrador. The Oblate missionaries conducted Mass, married couples, and baptized children.[2]

After the Hudson's Bay Company established posts at North West River and Davis Inlet in 1831, the traders hoped that having an itinerant priest stationed there might convince Innu in the region not to go to the Lower North Shore to trade.[3] In 1867, they invited an Oblate priest to visit their posts at North West River, Fort Winokapau on the Grand River, and Fort Nascopie in the interior of Labrador.[4] Over the next 30 years, Oblates maintained missions for Innu at North West River and as far north as Fort Chimo on Ungava Bay (present-day Kuujjuaq, Nunavik, the Inuit homeland in northern Quebec). The endeavour was expensive, however, and after 1896 the Oblates abandoned their activities in Labrador.[5] The Diocese of Newfoundland revived a Catholic presence in Labrador in the 1920s, when Father Edward O'Brien visited the region. He travelled to North West River each summer, starting in 1921. From 1927 on, he also travelled to Davis Inlet, where Innu came to the coast to trade at the Hudson's Bay Company post.[6]

By the mid-1920s, more non-Innu families were living at North West

River. Many were Inuit and the families of former Hudson's Bay Company employees who had married Inuit women, while others were from Newfoundland or elsewhere. The International Grenfell Association opened a new hospital and school in the village, and both the Hudson's Bay Company and the Revillon Frères trading company operated trading posts.[7] Trapping in the area was good. But with more people, it became harder to find areas to trap. Settler and Inuit trappers moved deeper into the interior and pushed Innu families farther inland.[8]

Non-Innu residents of North West River also pressured the Catholic Church to push Innu from the community site itself. In 1930, Father O'Brien convinced the Innu to relocate from their traditional camping grounds on the north side of North West River to the south side of the river (current-day Sheshatshiu).[9] As anthropologist John McGee wrote in 1961, "In order to avoid trouble with white settlers who had moved into land near the trading post, a Catholic missionary thirty years ago persuaded the Indians to move to their present site."[10] The Innu were pushed out of both their summer home and their trapping grounds, and many still feel frustrated that their land was taken from them.[11]

Father O'Brien continued his mission with the Labrador Innu until 1946, when the Catholic Church transferred the mission to the Oblates once again.[12] In 1949, Father Joseph Cyr arrived to live in Davis Inlet, and in 1952, Father Joseph Pirson from Belgium moved to Sheshatshiu.[13] Like Father O'Brien, both Oblate priests learned to speak Innu-aimun. Both also acted as the primary agent between the government and the Innu.[14]

Several factors forced changes to the Innu semi-nomadic way of life. At North West River, other trappers pushed the Innu deeper into the interior to hunt and trap.[15] Caribou, the main source of food for the Innu, were decreasing in number. The fur trade was also declining, resulting in the Hudson's Bay Company closing its posts in the Labrador interior. With little food and few ways to make a living, many Innu faced hunger and poor health. Instead of protecting Innu land rights, however, the government simply provided ration relief.[16] But it was not enough. Given the poor conditions, the priests and the provincial government thought it best to pressure Innu to stay in communities longer and to spend less time on the land hunting.[17] As Walter Rockwood of the provincial government argued in 1955:

> The Indian may be an excellent hunter, and more inclined when game resources permit to live off in the country, [but] . . . in view of the scarcity of game and the low prices for produce, these occupations alone can no longer provide even a bare existence. . . . The needs of the Indian are the same as for the Eskimo, namely a vigorous Health, Education, and Welfare programme to fit him for the Society of the future.[18]

Education Promotes Settlement

Preparing the Innu for the "Society of the future" proved complicated. Few provincial government officials lived in Labrador, and fewer still had even met any Innu. So the government relied on the missionaries to achieve their goals. Catholic priests played a major role in encouraging the Innu to settle in villages and to transform their way of life, just as the International Grenfell Association and the Moravian missionaries had done with the Inuit. The Catholic Church and the government believed that Labrador's Indigenous peoples should modernize. The priests discouraged the Innu lifestyle of hunting caribou, trapping fur-bearing animals, and travelling throughout Nitassinan. Instead, they promoted a sedentary life in communities with wage-paying jobs and schooling.

North West River

When Father Joseph Pirson arrived in Sheshatshiu (then known as the Innu side of North West River) in 1952, he tried to get families to live in the village. "The priest would come to visit us where we were camped," recalled Iskuess Pasteen, a woman from Sheshatshiu. "He would ask the families to come and reside in the community. . . . [He] got really angry because there was no one living in the community."[19]

Pirson taught school from the priest's house until the Catholic Church built a small schoolhouse two years later.[20] He promised housing and jobs if families stayed in the village and sent their children to school, as one Innu woman remembers:

> The Innu were told that houses would be built for them and they had to school their children in return. It's like bribing the Innu. The Innu were not to leave the community when their children were schooled. Not even to go into the country while their land was being destroyed through exploitation. That was the idea the governments must have had. And many Innu were led to believe all this. We were told the children would eventually find proper jobs once they finished school. It was never like that. All those promises.[21]

Father Pirson made promises, but he also made threats. Elizabeth Penashue of Sheshatshiu describes how the priest used his position of authority to pressure families to settle in the community:

> The priest would go to my mother and sit close by her, talking for a long time. He lectured her on how to bring up her children. He would say to her, "If you take your children into the country they will be hungry and cold, it's better for you to stay in the community year-round, your children will be schooled." And of course he was obeyed because he was treated like Jesus. Many Innu thought it was wrong not to obey the priest. I guess we never knew or foresaw how the future would be for us once we lived permanently in the community.[22]

Many Innu describe the schooling as harsh and humiliating. Their priest teachers aimed to change them fundamentally. Father Pirson considered the Innu to be "backward," and he called Innu beliefs "devil worship."[23] He believed that, in order to become "civilized," students needed

Sheshatshiu, ca. 1967 (courtesy of Them Days Archive).

discipline. They needed to learn to arrive on time, conform with his rules, and respect authority. Teachers followed this approach for years. As Anna Hammond, the principal of the Sheshatshiu school in 1967, wrote, Innu have a "primitive personality" and a culture that must be changed through schooling. "These people have their own methods of bringing up children. It is often done by the grandparents. . . . Thus, in school, they must often unlearn the patterns of responses learned in another culture."[24]

Although Father Pirson spoke Innu-aimun, he taught the Newfoundland school curriculum mainly in English. He made students memorize passages from the Bible, read and write in English, and study European history and math.[25] School schedules likewise followed non-Innu priorities. The school year ran from September to June, when Innu were usually hunting in *nutshimit*, rather than in the summer, when Innu usually gathered in Sheshatshiu.[26]

Discipline at school often took the form of corporal punishment.

Interior of classroom, Sheshatshiu, ca. 1967 (courtesy of Them Days Archive).

Father Pirson beat students with a stick, ruler, or leather belt for not paying attention, arriving late, or not knowing an answer.[27] Elizabeth Penashue remembers being punished at school one day in the 1950s when she asked another girl for help: "Father Pirson hit me over the face with a ruler and blood came down my face. I went home to tell my mother and she went to speak to the priest. But this happened to a lot of kids."[28]

Between the 1950s and the 1990s, several priests and teachers also sexually abused Innu children in Sheshatshiu. By 2001, Labrador Innu had filed almost 50 charges of sexual abuse and complaints against individual priests, the local diocese, and the Roman Catholic Church.[29] Many more victims likely did not press charges, as people deferred to the authority of priests and teachers.

Some Innu rejected the attempts by the priest and the provincial government to control their lives. Napess Ashini, a respected Innu leader from Sheshatshiu, was a child in the 1960s when his family refused to be intimidated by the authorities:

> Me and my sister didn't go to school. We went to the country in the spring of 1966, returning to Sheshatshiu in September. Then the priest came to the house telling us we had to go to school to become doctors or lawyers even though my father didn't like the priest or accept the non-Innu religion. He thought the priest was brainwashing the Innu kids. My grandfather knew that something would come wrong out of it. When we didn't go to school again, the priest hired a truant officer from Goose Bay to chase us all around the community and take us to school.[30]

The priest used any means he could to force children to come to school. One strategy was to threaten to cancel Family Allowance payments if parents refused to send their children. As Father Pirson explained to the Newfoundland Superintendent of Schools in 1959, fewer than half of the Innu children in the area were attending school. Writing in poor English, the French-speaking priest described his plans: "I think that I have to do something. I told the parents many time I am afraid to do that but I will suggest in inform Family Allowances Department and ask them to discontinue allowances to parents who are careless."[31]

As more families moved into the community, the Catholic Church in 1959 built a larger facility, Our Lady of the Snows School, to accommodate the new students.[32] Provincial government officials argued that a school dormitory should also be built so that children could attend school if their parents went to the country.[33] However, federal officials were reluctant to commit funding for a boarding school because federal policy at the time favoured day schools over residential schools for Indigenous students.[34] In the end, no boarding school was built in Sheshatshiu. The provincial government focused its efforts instead on convincing Innu families to live in the community permanently. Between 1962 and 1968, the provincial

Department of Public Welfare accessed federal funding to build more than 30 houses in Sheshatshiu.[35] The houses were poorly built, however, with no running water and inadequate insulation for the cold Labrador winter.[36]

In 1965, with the old Sheshatshiu school overflowing with students, the Roman Catholic School Board for Labrador North (formed in 1960) requested and received federal funding for a new eight-room school.[37] However, federal government representatives on the Federal–Provincial Committee on Financial Assistance for Indians and Eskimos in Northern Labrador questioned the plan's practicality. The school board at North West River was also asking for money to fund a new high school on the other side of the river. Federal representatives asked whether it made sense for the committee to fund two new schools so close to each other.[38] Instead of having two schools, they suggested that all students attend one of the schools. But provincial representatives held to their conviction that combining students in one school would not work.[39] The province's denominational education system divided schools between Protestant and Catholic school boards. The system ensured that students at the Catholic school in Sheshatshiu and at the Protestant school (run by the Central Labrador Amalgamated School Board) in North West River were kept separate. The churches involved in education in Labrador — Catholic, United, Moravian, and Anglican — did not want to expose their students to other religious teachings.

In addition to religious grounds, other officials also argued against combining the students for social reasons. Some believed that the "Eskimo and White" children attending school in North West River should not go to the school in Sheshatshiu, where they would be exposed to Innu language and culture.[40] Dr. Tony Paddon, the head of the International Grenfell Association at North West River and superintendent of the local school board, argued that the school in North West River did a better job of assimilating Indigenous children into the dominant culture. He recommended against North West River students going to the Innu school in Sheshatshiu; he thought the Innu children should come to the North West River school instead:

> If the Indian could be integrated into the general school system instead of being educated in the Indian School he would learn much from his white and Eskimo classmates and could put the new language to work and become fluent in it and he would probably raise his sights and prepare himself for a career, or at least make a reasonable adjustment to Canadian life.[41]

In spite of Paddon's hopes for integrating Innu students into the North West River school, however, the river continued to separate the students, the schools, and the communities of Sheshatshiu and North West River. In 1967, the Catholic School Board built the Peenamin McKenzie School for Innu students in Sheshatshiu, naming it after a devoutly Catholic and prominent Innu Elder.[42]

Davis Inlet

In Davis Inlet, Oblate Father Joseph Cyr arrived in 1949 as the first priest to live at the trading post year-round. Starting in 1953, he organized classes to teach children how to read and write in Innu-aimun.[43] Children attended for short periods of time, while their families camped at the post. Like Father Pirson in North West River, Father Cyr was determined to make attendance in the classes obligatory. He used threats to convince families to send their children to school:

> He told the people the children should stay behind to go to school while the parents went in the country. He told us if we didn't send our children to school, they would be taken away and placed where they could attend school. He also told us our social assistance would be cut off. When the children didn't go to school, he would go look for them in the tents.[44]

After a few years, Father Frank Peters from Belgium replaced Father Cyr as the village Oblate priest. He continued with teaching, although he realized that the curriculum was unsuited for life in northern Labrador, where there was no real alternative to a life of hunting. School was preparing Innu children "for a way of life that does not exist," he wrote.[45]

Despite the obvious problems with the curriculum, the priest and the provincial government remained convinced that education was the best way to transform Innu into wage labourers. W.G. Rockwood, the director of the provincial Northern Labrador Affairs, argued in 1960 that Innu were not hired at military construction projects in Labrador because "the adults had no formal education and could not speak or write English."[46] The solution was schooling:

> The Indians must be taught the 3 R's, and will also need vocational training, but it would be naive to think that this will automatically solve all the problems overnight. As with the Indians elsewhere there are deeply rooted psychological attitudes to be overcome before the process of integration is complete.[47]

According to the authorities, the Innu needed to be integrated into Canadian society and their "deeply rooted psychological attitudes" conquered. The government and the priests saw Innu culture and independence as a problem and something to be corrected. As Bishop Scheffer, the senior Catholic official in Labrador, stated in a letter to the Deputy Minister of Education in 1956, "They need more education if they want to enter into normal communities and live a regular life."[48]

The Catholic Church, the provincial government, and the federal government worked together to create what they saw as a "normal community" and a "regular life" for the Innu. The first requirement was that Innu abandon life in *nutshimit* and instead live in the village permanently. The provincial government built about 30 houses and the Mushuau Innu School in 1967 and 1968, with funds from the federal government.[49] For the first time, the school offered classes higher than Grade 5. Catholic priests and nuns taught the students in both Innu-aimun and English until trained English-speaking teachers were hired to teach the higher grades in 1968.[50] Under threat and coercion from the priests and government officials, more families moved into the village, and more children attended the schools.

Innu Students at Boarding Schools

Throughout the 1950s and 1960s, more Innu settled in the communities of Davis Inlet and Sheshatshiu. But sedentary life meant that people had to rely on poor relief and social welfare payments to buy store-bought food, which did not provide enough nutrition for good health. Moreover, community life created new challenges. Hunting for food was difficult, and diseases such as tuberculosis spread easily in poor and crowded housing conditions. As a result, doctors sent more and more Innu patients to Grenfell hospitals in North West River and St. Anthony for medical treatment.

In some cases, IGA officials placed the children of patients or sick children themselves in Grenfell dormitories at either North West River or St. Anthony, where they attended school. Caroline Andrew, for instance, was taken to the dormitory in North West River from her home in Kauishatukuants (Old Davis Inlet) in 1952. She went to school there while medical staff treated her for pneumonia. She describes having to learn English, and going once to a Protestant church in North West River with the Grenfell dormitory staff and children. The priest in Sheshatshiu became angry when he learned that she and her brother had attended a non-Catholic church:

> We didn't say anything because we were so scared. He told us he was going to tell the priest in Kauishatukuants. The priest would then tell our parents. He said he was also going to tell the kamituatshet (bishop) when he came. I didn't know what my parents were going to think when they heard this. We weren't allowed to go back to the dorm after this and there was no place to continue our schooling. The priest did not want us to go to a non-Catholic school anymore and there was no school in Sheshatshiu yet.[51]

Elizabeth Penashue was another child who was sent to the hospital in North West River when she was sick with tuberculosis:

> First when I went to school, I was shy and nervous because my English was very slow. I was a bit happy when I found out there was Natuashish people there, three of them. There was two Innu ladies and one young man, Sam Nui. I stayed a couple of months in the school and I started to get friends with the akeneshau [white people]. . . . I was very very happy when I went home. I was tired of eating akeneshau food every day. I wanted duck, fish, goose, meat, not sardines and beets. My mother brought lots of dried caribou and pemmican from the bush, and fish, and that's what I wanted to eat.[52]

As Caroline Andrew's story shows, the Oblate priests were keen to maintain religious divisions between the Catholic Innu and the Protestant residents of Labrador. In co-ordination with the provincial government, the priests sent Innu students from Sheshatshiu or Davis Inlet to Catholic high schools in Newfoundland or western Labrador instead of the much closer Protestant high schools at North West River or Happy Valley.

In the 1950s, for example, Father Pirson selected Francis Penashue and another younger boy to go to school at Mount Cashel Orphanage in St. John's. Mount Cashel was a Catholic institution run by the Congregation of Christian Brothers. The school is infamous for one of the largest sexual and physical abuse scandals in Canada. Francis described the rigid routine and the severe discipline at Mount Cashel during a Truth and Reconciliation Commission sharing panel in Goose Bay in 2011: "[It was a] very strict school. We had long hours. You had to get up 6:30 every morning, go to church, grab breakfast, go to classroom, 15 minute break."[53] One day, Francis forgot to do some chores, and a Christian Brother strapped him 15 times on his palms. He was then ordered to write two thousand lines of "I did not do what I was told." Francis and the other boy returned to Sheshatshiu after the school year, but both ran away when it came time to go back to St. John's in September. Neither boy returned to Mount Cashel.[54]

In 1969, the provincial government and the Roman Catholic School Board used federal funds to sponsor Innu students in getting higher education. Two Innu boys travelled to St. John's to attend a Catholic high school, while three Innu girls trained at the General Hospital in St. John's as nursing assistants.[55] A few years later, two Innu boys moved to Labrador West to complete high school under the same program.[56] In the 1970s, about 20 Innu students attended Catholic high schools in St. John's, where they boarded with families. The majority did not return to St. John's after the first year because they were unhappy with their experiences at the schools.[57]

Taking Back Control

An abrupt immersion into an English-language curriculum and the regimented system of education at the Peenamin McKenzie and Mushuau Innu schools was a traumatic experience for many Innu children. Students suffered abuse from teachers and priests. Yet these figures wielded such authority in the villages that children found it difficult to report the abuse or gain support in questioning their teachers' power.[58] School administrators in the 1960s were dismissive of Innu culture and spoke openly of "the school's function in the acculturation of a primitive race."[59] Many Innu believe that the formal education system caused widespread harm to their society:

> Most problems are because of the school. Like us, we went to school. That's when our problems started. When we were in school, just like today, we never learned anything about our own culture. That is why we don't live like our forefathers lived. We really blame the school for what has happened to our children.[60]

But as Innu families saw their children expected to submit to the conditioning of the school, they demanded more control of education. Their calls for increased authority gained momentum in the 1970s and 1980s. Young and articulate Innu leaders such as Bart Jack, Tony Penashue, and Etienne Andrew argued for more Indigenous participation in government decision-making about education.[61] They demanded that government recognize Innu land and governance rights, and that the federal government provide them with the same services as it gave their Innu relatives in Quebec. The Innu Nation, the governing organization of the Labrador Innu, eventually regained authority over education in Sheshatshiu and in the new northern community of Natuashish. Today, Innu children attend schools that champion Innu-aimun and Innu culture.[62]

CONCLUSION

Moving towards Respectful Relationships

We've come a long journey.
— Sarah Anala (Nunatsiavut Elder), 2017

The prime minister's apology to former boarding school students in November 2017 acknowledged some aspects of the complex and challenging stories we have seen in this book. For many who attended the apology ceremony, it was a difficult day. Toby Obed, a former student who lived in the North West River dormitories and the main driver behind the court case, accepted Trudeau's apology on behalf of the other plaintiffs. "This apology has been a long time in the making," Toby told the gathering. "Too long."[1] Former students in the audience cheered and cried. Choking back tears, Toby welcomed the prime minister's words:

> Because I come from a patient and forgiving culture, I think it's proper for us to accept the apology from the Government of Canada. This apology is an important part of the healing. The survivors of Newfoundland and Labrador can finally feel a part of the family of survivors nationwide, across Canada. We have connected with the rest of Canada. I accept your apology on behalf of the residential school survivors, even though some may not want me to.[2]

Like Toby, many in the audience accepted Trudeau's apology as genuine and welcomed his statement as part of their healing journey. For Josie Curl Penny, a Lockwood student in the 1950s, the ceremony helped to ease her pain.

> I found that the apology did me very well in terms of my mental and emotional well-being. . . . I don't know if it helped out a lot of other people, but it did for me. . . . My husband was with me and we cried together, and it was a good healing experience for me.[3]

Beatrice Winters Hope of Happy Valley–Goose Bay also believed that Trudeau's words would help repair some of the hurt caused by the schools. "I'm really pleased that the apology happened because for those students who really needed to hear it, it is healing for them."[4]

For Natan Obed, Toby's cousin and the president of the national Inuit organization, Inuit Tapiriit Kanatami, the apology also addressed

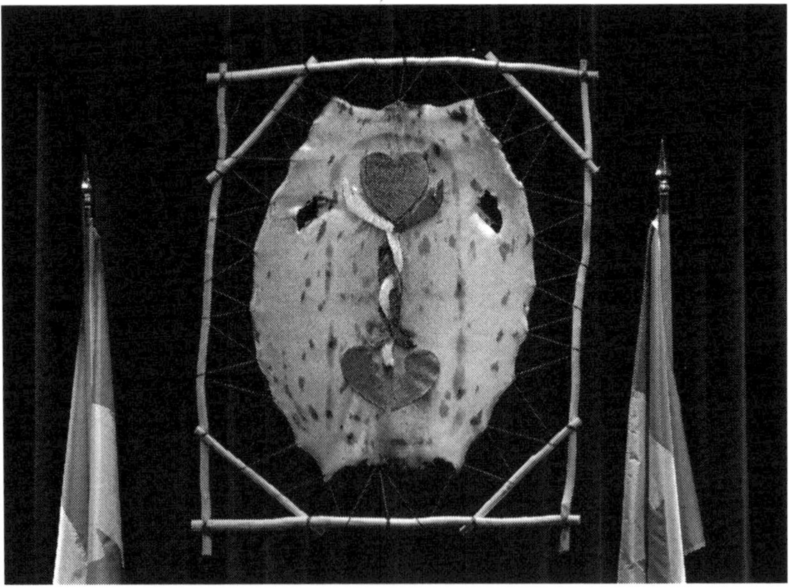

"The Healing" — sealskin artwork by Inez, Jack, and Jane Shiwak of Rigolet created for the apology ceremony (courtesy of the Department of Crown–Indigenous Relations and Northern Affairs Canada).

the political and structural issues behind the boarding schools. As he told a CBC interviewer afterwards, Trudeau's statement recognized the pain, suffering, and social inequity that still exist in Inuit communities because of how authorities once regarded Indigenous peoples. "It was an acknowledgment of the way in which Canada, the province, the church, and other health organizations like the International Grenfell Association, thought of Inuit, as if we were sub-human, or that we didn't have self-determination, we didn't have rights."[5] But, as Natan explained, Trudeau's words also signalled a change in the way the government views Inuit today, "as partners moving forward."[6] He therefore welcomed the apology and the opportunity to establish a renewed respectful relationship between Inuit and the government of Canada.

But not everyone was open to the government's offering. The Innu Nation, representing Labrador Innu from both Sheshatshiu and Natuashish, refused to accept Trudeau's apology. Innu leaders and Elders argued that the current child welfare system, which uproots many Innu children from their communities, is based on the same colonial mindset that led to the boarding schools. To them, it makes little sense to accept an apology for one system of child removal when a very similar system is still in operation.[7] They maintain that government policies and attitudes have caused multiple generations of Innu to lose their language, culture, and identity. So before entertaining any kind of apology, Innu leaders want to see governments change their approach.

In other cases, some former boarding school students found the apology unnecessary. Solomon Davis, for one, attended the Lockwood School in the 1950s. In a 2017 letter to the editor of *The Telegram* newspaper in St. John's, he wrote that, in his time at Lockwood, he "certainly did not see or hear any reason for Trudeau or anybody else to apologize."[8] He added that, "In my opinion, the prime minister should be honouring Sir Wilfred's great work, instead of apologizing for it."[9] As this book has shown, the experience of each student at the boarding schools could vary widely, often depending on why the child was there and how she or he was treated. Some felt no need for an apology.

For others, however, Trudeau's words were simply not enough. Former students and the families of those who had attended the boarding schools before Confederation found themselves once again excluded. For the many who had lived in the institutions before 1949 and for their families, the apology was a reminder that their experiences had not been officially recognized. Others felt that the other parties involved in running the boarding schools — the Moravian Church, the International Grenfell Association, and the provincial government — should also have acknowledged their role and should have apologized for the harm done.[10]

The Other Parties: The Moravian Church, the International Grenfell Association, and the Provincial Government

The federal government took responsibility for settling the court case, but many former students had hoped for an apology from the other three organizations involved in the boarding schools. The Moravian Church, the IGA, and the Newfoundland and Labrador government all played central roles in establishing and running the institutions, well before the federal government was involved.

The Moravian Church, which continues to serve a central spiritual role for the communities of Nain, Hopedale, and Makkovik, as well as for a Moravian congregation in Happy Valley, has not responded publicly about the court case or its settlement. Labradorians now run the local churches without the involvement of European or American ministers. Inuit lay ministers and chapel servants provide church services, and the board for the Moravian Church of Newfoundland and Labrador (MCNL) consists entirely of Labradorians. Some of the board members are also former boarding school students themselves, which leads to many conflicting loyalties and emotions when they discuss the role and responsibility of the Church in dealing with the boarding school legacy.[11]

While some MCNL board members feel that an apology would be helpful to former students, others do not feel that it should be the board that makes the apology. In February 2019, the board issued a statement to the Healing and Commemoration project that expresses its perspective on the history of the boarding schools:

> MCNL Board members do not feel it is their place to apologize on behalf of the Moravian Mission for the way in which residential schools were run. The Board understands that the policies the Unitas Fratrum had in place were good ones, especially the practice that its missionaries learn the language of the people they served. Perhaps the Inuktitut language may even have died out by now, if not for the efforts and accomplishments of the Moravian Mission.
>
> Bringing schooling to a place where no education system existed is not a bad move. The positive attributes of the Moravian Missionaries cannot go unnoticed. They started the educational system; missionaries were also the only nurse/doctor/dentist people had to go to when they were ill. They started some of the first gardens in Labrador, to provide vegetables, rhubarb, kept hens for eggs, and pigs. They worked side by side with store keepers, Rangers. They were a liaison between the government and the people. Discipline in schools went beyond the era of the missionaries; the ruler or the strap was still used in the 70s.
>
> There have been instances of abuse and unwanted outcomes in the residential school system. However, it is the failing of humans which brought this about. Human failure is not specific to any one organization.[12]

Like the Moravian Church, the International Grenfell Association has not issued an official statement about the court case or its settlement. However, in a 2018 statement to APTN (the Aboriginal Peoples' Television Network), the chair of the IGA board, Keating Hagmann, expressed the board's regret for causing any harm to children who lived at its institutions. "The IGA offers its sincere apology for in any way not sheltering these individuals from the suffering they endured," Hagmann wrote. "In the spirit of reconciliation, IGA looks forward to walking into the future with all peoples of Newfoundland and Labrador."[13]

After the IGA closed the North West River dormitories and transferred responsibility for medical services to the provincial government in the early 1980s, the organization transformed itself into a charitable entity. The endowment funds set up during Wilfred Grenfell's time and controlled by its Grenfell associations in Boston, New York, and London continue to support community efforts.[14] The IGA Board of Directors distributes money from these endowment funds to community organizations, schools, and medical facilities in Labrador and northern Newfoundland in the form of scholarships, grants, and project funding. Since 1997, this financial support has contributed more than $35 million to the region.[15] Several Newfoundlanders and Labradorians are also members of the IGA Board of Directors and help make the decisions about which projects and initiatives to support.[16]

The premier of Newfoundland and Labrador, Dwight Ball, has signalled that the provincial government will apologize for its involvement in the boarding schools. The premier called Trudeau's apology "an important step, and one of many our respective governments are taking to advance reconciliation with Indigenous people in Newfoundland and Labrador."[17] As of the time of writing (spring 2019), the provincial government had yet to issue an apology.[18]

Colonial Ways of Thinking

The federal government's apology marks the beginning of a new relationship with Indigenous peoples. Both Indigenous and non-Indigenous Canadians have a responsibility to acknowledge and learn more about the "shameful part[s] of Canada's history," as Trudeau said. The apology calls for all Canadians to understand how the decisions and attitudes that led to the boarding schools have impacted Indigenous lives and communities.[19] As the prime minister told the country, "We must recognize the colonial way of thinking that fuelled these practices."[20]

The stories of the boarding schools in Labrador and northern Newfoundland are complex and diverse. But the schools shared a common goal: to transform Indigenous people through educating their children. In their own ways, both the Moravian Church and the IGA saw the Inuit and Innu of Labrador as culturally inferior. Relying on this assumption, they used their institutions to separate children from the influence of their families and their communities, and tried to influence students to adopt new ideas and attitudes. They hoped the children would spread these new values and practices to their families and communities when they returned home. As we have seen, the Moravian schools aimed to make the children into Christians who respected Church authority and beliefs. The Inuktitut-language school at Nain and the English-language school in Makkovik taught students how to read and write, while also training them in what the missionaries regarded as the civilizing habits of industry and cleanliness. The IGA schools, in similar fashion, offered an education to the children of southern Labrador and northern Newfoundland. IGA officials also sometimes removed children from home situations they deemed to be unfit and housed them in the IGA institutions. In the early days, Grenfell "collected" poor children from homes where poverty and, often, the loss of a parent made living conditions difficult. In later years, the IGA co-operated with the provincial government to house children who had become wards of the state in its dormitories. Like the Moravian schools, the IGA schools placed a heavy emphasis on their Euro-Christian values of work discipline and respect for authority. They aimed to assimilate the children into "Canadian mainstream society" and make them into good "citizens." But in doing so, they conveyed the idea that Indigenous cultures were primitive and that Indigenous people could not survive in modern society without changing. As a result, many students felt inadequate and ashamed of their families' Indigenous culture.

Over the decades, the boarding schools and dormitories had mixed impacts on their students. As we have seen, they had many positive outcomes, and some children attained an education that allowed them to live prosperous lives. But the boarding schools also caused widespread damage to multiple generations of Indigenous families, communities, and languages. Children were vulnerable to abuse and bullying while they lived in the dormitories. As schooling became offered only in English, far fewer children learned how to speak Inuktitut. Families suffered the ill effects of social disconnection between generations. Parents raised their children with the institutional discipline and rigid style of parenting that they had learned at the boarding schools. Indeed, in this regard they may have mirrored the behaviours and attitudes of those who founded and ran the schools, who commonly sent their own children to boarding schools in England, Germany, and, later, North America, a regular practice among the middle and upper classes of the time. Bullying and abuse were not uncommon in such settings, and bullying certainly continues today. The difference, however, is that Indigenous boarders in Labrador — and across Canada — at the same time were often denied their own language, culture, and autonomy. They were forced to live in institutions premised on their cultural "deficiencies" and designed to radically transform them. As a result, shame, guilt, and memories of racism and abuse caused deep pain and sometimes fuelled addictive or self-destructive behaviours.

But at the time, most of the teachers and administrators of the boarding schools firmly believed in the superiority of the Euro-Canadian culture and way of life, and thought that they were doing the best thing for the children. They did not doubt that taking them away from their families was for their own good. And they thought that teaching the children new skills and different cultural values would help them grow into productive members of the dominant Canadian society. So how could such seemingly good intentions cause so much harm?

The answer rests largely on the impact of colonial assumptions and attitudes. Upon arriving in Labrador, the Moravian missionaries and Wilfred Grenfell's IGA staff saw Indigenous society as deficient and concluded that they should reform the region. They did not recognize the ways in which Indigenous peoples governed themselves. They dismissed many Indigenous cultural practices, including child-rearing, as flawed.

They saw themselves as racially or culturally superior to Indigenous peoples, and as therefore responsible for bringing "civilization" to Labrador.

Accordingly, both the Moravian Church and the IGA stepped into what they perceived to be an absence of governance, and assumed control themselves. They intervened to make decisions about other people's lives, and, prompted by a desire to reshape the region, established schools, trading posts or co-operative stores, and hospitals and churches. But their efforts were paternalistic and were carried out without the full involvement of local people. Because they assumed they were culturally superior, they felt justified in coercing people to abide by their new authority. This could mean forcibly removing children from their families or threatening parents into allowing their children to live at their institutions. It could also mean withdrawing services and closing stores to force entire communities to relocate.

When the provincial and federal governments later became involved in Labrador, their officials also joined this elite group of decision-makers. By the 1950s, this clique of authorities — Moravian, IGA, and provincial and federal officials — assumed control and agreed that the Indigenous population needed to become wage-earning citizens and abandon their hunting and fishing way of life if they were to succeed in Canadian society.

Of course, the history of the Indigenous–colonizer relationship is not always this simplistic. Indigenous families and communities in Labrador constantly asserted their own interests in the face of outside interference. The Moravian Church and the IGA quickly learned that they needed to negotiate with local people in order to attract them to their projects. Over time, the lines that separated each group were not always distinct. Many Indigenous men and women worked closely with the organizations to become Moravian or IGA leaders themselves and, in turn, helped to adapt the governance and educational systems to Indigenous interests.

From the 1950s onward, as Inuit and Innu communities found themselves increasingly alienated from the schooling system, Indigenous leaders demanded more say in their children's education. Hopedale parents, upset at the Makkovik boarding school, organized a local day school for their children. Spotted Island families, angry at the religious education imposed on their children at Lockwood, pressured the Anglican Church to reopen a school in their home community. Nain students boycotted the North West River dormitory, forcing changes to education on the coast. In these and many other cases, Indigenous families transformed and ultimately helped to shut down the boarding school system.

Since then, Indigenous communities have continued to fight for their right to make their own decisions — their right to self-determination. The Moravian Church and the IGA both responded by withdrawing from active involvement and adopting a more community-driven approach. The provincial and federal governments responded by acknowledging Indigenous rights through land claims negotiations and dialogue. Yet, while much has changed, the Innu Nation's statement about the parallels between the boarding school system and the current child welfare system suggests that vestiges of colonial ways of thinking endure.

Indigenous communities are leading the way in creating new governance and educational systems, in questioning assumptions behind government policies, and in encouraging healing. As the Inuit board members of the Moravian Church in Newfoundland and Labrador suggest, "the way to move forward now is to strive to build a better future and learn from mistakes of the past. We are strong. We are resilient."[21]

Education in Labrador Today

The educational system in Labrador has changed drastically since the last boarding school closed in 1980. All communities now have local schools, even if the number of students is low. High school students can stay at home to finish their schooling. If classes are too small to justify hiring a specialist teacher, students can complete their classes online. Teachers have easier access to housing, and they receive financial incentives for teaching in isolated communities.[22] The provincial curriculum also now includes some recognition of the Indigenous peoples in the province and their history and cultures. But more work remains to be done.

The schools face many of the same challenges they faced in the past — difficulty in finding and keeping qualified teachers, a curriculum ill-suited for Labrador, and noticeably high student dropout rates.[23] However, all three Indigenous governments in Labrador — Nunatsiavut, NunatuKavut, and the Innu Nation — have assumed more control over their children's education and their own affairs. All three are working to make their schools better reflect their cultural identity and needs, and to create a positive schooling experience for their youth. All three governments also offer scholarships and funding for post-secondary education and training programs.[24]

The NunatuKavut Community Council, representing the NunatuKavut Inuit throughout central and southern Labrador, is pursuing self-determination through a land claim with the federal government. While the Newfoundland and Labrador English School District still administers the schools in its territory, education staff at the NunatuKavut Community Council are developing programs to make schooling more relevant to their children. These programs help teachers in schools between Cartwright and Mary's Harbour to incorporate NunatuKavut Inuit cultural knowledge into the curriculum. Taught by community Elders, students learn traditional skills, including how to build *Kamutet* (sleds pulled by snowmobiles or dogs), make snowshoes, and survive on the land.[25]

The Nunatsiavut government is also working within the existing provincial school system to make it better suit Nunatsiavut. Under its land claim agreement, the Nunatsiavut government has the right to take over primary and secondary education in Nunatsiavut communities, although it has not yet done so.[26] For now, the Newfoundland and Labrador English School District still runs all the schools. As a first step towards taking over the education system, Nunatsiavut is working on improving the existing curriculum. In 2018, it developed a new high school course on Nunatsiavut Inuit culture and history. Students also take Inuktitut-language classes and *Ilusivut* ("our customs") courses in Inuit skills, such as constructing tools and equipment and learning traditional Inuit games.[27]

The Nunatsiavut government has also tried to increase the number of teachers who come from Nunatsiavut. By doing so, it hopes to attract teachers who have a deep understanding of the region and a strong commitment to living there long term. Between 2014 and 2018 it funded an Inuit Bachelor of Education program to train Nunatsiavummiut as teachers.[28] Many of these new Inuit teachers are now teaching in Labrador.

The Labrador Innu have taken a more direct route to decolonizing education, having taken over control of their children's education. The Mamu Tshishkutamashutau Innu Education School Board, established in 2008, now runs the schools in Sheshatshiu and Natuashish. The Chief and Council of Sheshatshiu and Natuashish appoint six people from their communities to sit on the Board of Trustees, which hires all the teachers and school staff.[29] The schools have Innu-aimun classes from kindergarten to Grade 9, and they aim to help children succeed by celebrating Innu culture. Elders visit the classrooms to share stories, history, and geography, and they take students on trips to *nutshimit*. The schools have also created Innu teaching modules based on the provincial curriculum, and try to include Innu content in all teaching.[30]

Healing from the Boarding School Legacy

The Healing and Commemoration project for the Labrador and northern Newfoundland boarding schools is part of the federal government's efforts at reconciling and rebuilding its relationship with Indigenous peoples. In addition to this historical account, the project includes several other commemoration activities. Federal officials are working with communities at each of the five boarding school locations to install commemorative plaques that honour the memory of former students. The provincial archive at The Rooms in St. John's will preserve the collection of interviews with former students, which were recorded as part of the Healing and Commemoration community events. Eventually, archivists will transfer this collection to Them Days Archive in Labrador. Two Labradorians are also developing a travelling exhibit on the boarding school experience. This exhibit will visit Labrador communities before travelling across the country to educate other Canadians about the Labrador and northern Newfoundland story.[31]

All of those involved in these commemoration activities hope that these various ways of telling the boarding school story and of sharing experiences will help to heal the wounds of the past. As Indigenous and non-Indigenous Canadians, listening to different experiences and perspectives on the boarding schools and reflecting on our relationships with one another is the first step towards reconciliation.

The Healing and Commemoration project offers all Canadians a chance to move along this path, started years ago by the first former students brave enough to speak out about their experiences. As Inuk Elder Sarah Anala told the gathering at Trudeau's apology:

> We've come a long journey. I am honoured and privileged to be here with my fellow survivors, who survived hunger, who survived ugly words, who had the strength to stay alive today. And maybe today, our younger people, our grown children, our grandchildren will finally understand what happened to us.[32]

As we have seen, the colonial mentality of those in power harmed many of the people their institutions intended to help. But recognizing colonial attitudes can help to ensure that these stories will not be repeated. Building respectful relationships is our next step, as Toby Obed stated when he accepted the government's apology: "There is so much work left to be done. But now, together — now, together — we can start."[33]

APPENDIX 1

Record of Children at the Children's Home, 1929

The following children are identified in *Among the Deep Sea Fishers* (Apr. 1930) as living at the Children's Home in St. Anthony as of 31 December 1929.

Clara Barrett
Eleanor Bird
Milicent Bird
Milicent Blake
Gertrude Bownes
Jessie May Bownes
Lydia Bownes
Bill Burden
Peter Burden
Priscilla Burden
Rhoda Burden
Bertha Cadwell
Elsie Clark
Martha Clark
Mary Clark
Frank Cove
John Dyson
Ethel Fequet
Margaret Fequet
Elsie Ford
George Ford
Robert Gray
Triffie Gray
Nancy Hillier
Betty Humber
Katie Humber
Phyllis Humber
Raymond Johnson
Clayton Laing
Violet Learning
Elizabeth Lucy
John Thomas Lucy
George Mangrove
Mary Martin
Hubert Michelmore
Julia Nicholas
Amy Noseworthy
Nora Noseworthy
Alice Parsons
Chessley Patey
Fred Patey
Gertie Reid
Nellie Reid
Randolph Reid
Edith Roberts
Flossie Roberts
Rubena Roberts
Eli Rumboldt
Henry Rumboldt
Ina Rumboldt
Israel Rumboldt
Eva Shiwak
Mary Spurrel
Beatrice St. Johns
Everton Strangemore
Maitland Strangemore
Seaton Strangemore
Jimmy Turnbull
Truman Turnbull
Harry Ward
Joey Ward
Martha Ann Ward
Edward Webb

APPENDIX 2

Record of Children at Lockwood Boarding School, 1935–36

The students registered at Lockwood School for the 1935–36 school year are listed in the Lockwood School log written by the principal, Ewart Young (APL 3/3, File 2, Them Days Archive).

Elsie Dyson
Clarice Hamel
Effie McDonald
Howard Martin (day scholar)
Thomas Moores (day scholar)
Hilda Bird (day scholar)
Florence Elson
Flora Dyson
Joyce Pardy
Minnie Williams
Hayward Holwell
Rachel Dyson
Gerald Dyson
Alvina Dyson
Bobby Bird (day scholar)
Bertha Mesher
Charlotte Dyson
Solomon Elson
Johnny Webber
Abe Webber
Stuart Dyson
Edward Elson
Emily Dyson
Robert John Mesher
Samuel Elson

APPENDIX 3

Record of Children at St. Mary's River Boarding School, 1935–36

The school register for the 1935–36 school year listed the following students at the boarding school at St. Mary's River (*Among the Deep Sea Fishers* 33, no. 4 [Jan. 1936]: 158d).

Olive Doane
Charlie Samson
Sarah Rose
Paul Poole
Mabel Rumboldt
Joe Thoms
Gordon Acreman
Angus Clarke
Judson Morris
Irene Morris
Jimmie Samson
Dorothy Greene
Frank Grant
Violet Burden
Joe Chubbs
Mary Russell
Hughlett Acreman
Wilfred Burden
Rita Ward
John Russell
Dulcie Clarke
Amos Roberts
Muriel Clarke
Arthur Hopkins
Mary Ann Clarke
Hayward Roberts
Elma Clarke
Herbert Russell
Mary Grant
Sam Kippenhuck
Walter Rumboldt
John Kippenhuck

NOTES

Introduction

1 A note on terminology: In Labrador and St. Anthony, the residential schools were called "boarding schools" or "dormitories." Although some people who attended these boarding schools refer to themselves as "survivors," the more commonly used term in Labrador is "former students." I will use these terms in this account as well.

2 Prime Minister Justin Trudeau, "Statement of Apology on Behalf of the Government of Canada to Former Students of the Newfoundland and Labrador Residential Schools, 24 November 2017" (Ottawa: Government of Canada, 2017).

3 Charlotte Wolfrey, 27 Oct. 2011, National Centre for Truth and Reconciliation Archives, Sharing Panel (Atlantic National Event): ANE205, Halifax, Truth and Reconciliation Commission of Canada (TRC).

4 Danny Pottle, 30 June 2011, National Centre for Truth and Reconciliation Archives, Sharing Panel (Northern National Event): SP150, Inuvik, TRC.

5 "Strapped, Bullied, and Sexually Assaulted at Residential School, Ex-Student Testifies," *CBC News*, 5 Oct. 2015, https://www.cbc.ca/news/canada/newfoundland-labrador/residential-school-lawsuit-toby-obed-1.3256895.

6 Newfoundland and Labrador residential schools healing and commemoration website: https://www.rcaanc-cirnac.gc.ca/eng/1511531626107/1539962009489.

7 "N.L. Residential School Survivors' Lawyers Reach $50M Settlement with Ottawa," *CBC News*, 10 May 2016, https://www.cbc.ca/news/canada/newfoundland-labrador/residential-school-case-update-1.3574080.

8 Newfoundland and Labrador residential schools healing and commemoration website: https://www.rcaanc-cirnac.gc.ca/eng/1511531626107/1539962009489.

9 Trudeau, "Statement of Apology."

10 Ronald Niezen, *Truth and Indignation: Canada's Truth and Reconciliation Commission on Indian Residential Schools,* 2nd ed. (Toronto: University of Toronto Press, 2017).

11 Truth and Reconciliation Commission of Canada (TRC), *Canada's Residential Schools: The Final Report for the Truth and Reconciliation Commission of Canada* (Montreal and Kingston: McGill-Queen's University Press, 2015).

12 Shirley Flowers, 20 Sept. 2011, National Centre for Truth and Reconciliation Archives, Sharing Panel (Goose Bay Hearing): SP025, TRC.

13 Trudeau, "Statement of Apology."

14 TRC, *Final Report.*

15 James Hiller, "The Foundation and Early Years of the Moravian Missionaries in Labrador, 1752–1805," MA thesis, (Memorial University of Newfoundland, 1967).

16 Ronald Rompkey, *Grenfell of Labrador: A Biography* (Montreal and Kingston: McGill-Queen's University Press, 2009).

17 John C. Kennedy, *Encounters: An Anthropological History of Southeastern Labrador* (Montreal and Kingston: McGill-Queen's University Press, 2015).

18 Hans Rollmann, "Moravian Education in Labrador: A Legacy of Literacy," In *Conference Proceedings*, ed. Gerald Galway and David Dibbon (St. John's: Memorial University of Newfoundland, 2008), 227–36.

19 Rompkey, *Grenfell of Labrador.*

20 Frederick Rowe, *The Development of Education in Newfoundland* (Toronto: Ryerson Press, 1964).

21 Dianne Grant, "Nain's Silenced Majority: An Anthropological Examination of Schooling in Northern Labrador," MA thesis (Memorial University of Newfoundland, 2003); Rompkey, *Grenfell of Labrador.*

22 *Among the Deep Sea Fishers* (Oct. 1942): 81.

23 Rowe, *Development of Education*, 71.

24 Patrick Flanagan, "Schooling, Souls, and Social Class: The Labrador Inuit," MA thesis (University of New Brunswick, 1984).

25 Maura Hanrahan, *The Lasting Breach: The Omission of Aboriginal People from the Terms of Union between Newfoundland and Canada and Its Ongoing Impacts* (St. John's: Royal Commission on Renewing and Strengthening Our Place in Canada, 2003).

26 Rowe, *Development of Education.*

27 Adrian Tanner, John Kennedy, Susan McCorquodale, and Gordon Inglis, *Aboriginal Peoples and Governance in Newfoundland and Labrador: A Report for the Governance Project* (St. John's: Royal Commission on Aboriginal Peoples, 1994), 31.

28 Hanrahan, "Lasting Breach"; Prime Minister Pearson to Premier Smallwood, 25 May 1965, PRC 35, Box #46 (location: 52-1-5-3), File 75, Vol. 1, Federal–Provincial Committee Appointments/Minutes of Meetings — Native Education,

PANL; Minutes of 6th meeting of Federal–Provincial Committee on Financial Assistance for Indians and Eskimos in Northern Labrador, 28 Nov. 1967; Minutes of 14th meeting of Federal–Provincial Committee on Financial Assistance for Indians and Eskimos in Northern Labrador, 21 June 1972; Minutes of 19th meeting of Federal–Provincial Committee on Financial Assistance for Indians and Eskimos in Northern Labrador, 10 Dec. 1974, PRC 35, Box #46 (location: 52-1-5-3), File 75, Vol. 2, Federal–Provincial Committee Appointments/Minutes of Meetings — Native Education, PANL.

29 Prime Minister Pearson to Premier Smallwood, 25 May 1965, PRC 35, Box #46 (location: 52-1-5-3), File 75, Vol. 1, Federal–Provincial Committee Appointments/Minutes of Meetings — Native Education, PANL.

30 Minutes of 17th meeting of Federal–Provincial Committee on Financial Assistance for Indians and Eskimos in Northern Labrador, 28–29 Nov. 1973, PRC 35, Box #46 (location: 52-1-5-3), File 75, Vol. 2, Federal–Provincial Committee Appointments/Minutes of Meetings — Native Education, PANL.

31 See Minutes of meetings of Federal–Provincial Committee on Financial Assistance for Indians and Eskimos in Northern Labrador, 1965–79, PRC, Box #46 (location: 52-1-5-3), F75, Vol. 1-3, PANL.

32 Labrador Inuit Association, "Labrador Inuit Education Conference" (St. John's: MUN Extension Service, 1977).

33 Kennedy, *Encounters*.

34 Minutes of IGA meeting, 7 Mar. 1979, MG 63.3035, Dr. Linwood Brown (folder 2), PANL.

35 Geoff Bartlett, "Residential Schools Settlement: Retired Judge James Igloliorte to Lead Healing Portion," *CBC News*, 14 June 2017, https://www.cbc.ca/news/canada/newfoundland-labrador/residential-schools-settlement-newfoundland-labrador-healing-1.4158176.

Chapter One

1 Marianne Stopp, *Thule Inuit and Greenlandic Norse in the Eastern Canadian Arctic: A Discussion*, Historic Sites and Monuments Board of Canada, Report Number 2011-27 (Ottawa: Government of Canada, 2011).

2 Peter Ramsden and Lisa Rankin, "Thule Radiocarbon Chronology and Its Implications for Early Inuit–European Interaction in Labrador," in *Exploring Atlantic Transitions: Archeologies of Transience and Permanence in New Found Lands*, ed. Peter Pope with Shannon Lewis-Simpson. Society for Post-Medieval

Archaeology Monograph 8 (Woodbridge, Suffolk: Boydell Press, 2013), 299–309.

3 Brad Loewen and Vincent Delmas, "The Basques in the Gulf of St. Lawrence and Adjacent Shores," *Canadian Journal of Archaeology* 36, no. 2 (2012): 213–66.

4 Jean-Pierre Proulx, *Basque Whaling in Labrador in the 16th Century* (Ottawa: Environment Canada, Parks Service, 1993), 70.

5 Gerald Sider, *Skin for Skin: Death and Life for Inuit and Innu* (Durham, NC: Duke University Press, 2014), 42.

6 Sider, *Skin for Skin.*

7 Helge Kleivan, *The Eskimos of North-East Labrador: A History of Eskimo-White Relations 1771–1955* (Oslo: Norsk Polar-Institut, 1966), 146–47, 154–55.

8 Peter Pope, "Bretons, Basques, and Inuit in Labrador and Northern Newfoundland: The Control of Maritime Resources in the 16th and 17th Centuries," *Études/Inuit/Studies* 39, no. 1 (2015): 15–36.

9 Natalie Brewster, "The Inuit in Southern Labrador: A View from Snack Cove" (MA thesis, Memorial University of Newfoundland, 2005), 100–01.

10 William Gilbert Gosling, *Labrador: Its Discovery, Exploration, and Development* (London: A. Rivers, 1910).

11 NunatuKavut Community Council, *Unveiling NunatuKavut: Describing the Lands and People of South/Central Labrador* (Goose Bay, NL: NunatuKavut Community Council, 2010), 31.

12 Greg Mitchell, "The Inuit of Southern Labrador and their Conflicts with Europeans, to 1767," in *Exploring Atlantic Transitions: Archeologies of Transience and Permanence in New Found Lands*, ed. Peter Pope with Shannon Lewis-Simpson. Society for Post-Medieval Archaeology Monograph 8 (Woodbridge, Suffolk: Boydell Press, 2013), 320–30.

13 Susan Kaplan, "Labrador Inuit Ingenuity and Resourcefulness: Adapting to a Complex Environmental, Social, and Spiritual Environment," in *Settlement, Subsistence, and Change among the Labrador Inuit: The Nunatsiavummiut Experience*, ed. David Natcher, Lawrence Felt, and Andrea Procter (Winnipeg: University of Manitoba Press, 2012), 15–42.

14 Mitchell, "The Inuit of Southern Labrador."

15 Carol Brice-Bennett, "Land Use in the Nain and Hopedale Regions," in *Our Footprints are Everywhere: Inuit Land Use and Occupancy in Labrador*, ed. Carol Brice-Bennett (Nain, NL: Labrador Inuit Association, 1977), 97–203.

16 Amelia Fay, "Big Men, Big Women, or Both? Examining the Coastal Trading System of the Eighteenth-Century Labrador Inuit," in *History and Renewal of Labrador's Inuit-Métis*, ed. John C. Kennedy (St. John's: ISER Books, 2014), 75–93.

17 Pauktuutit Inuit Women of Canada, *The Inuit Way: A Guide to Inuit Culture* (Ottawa: Pauktuutit, 2006).

18 Ibid.

19 Ibid.

20 Hugh Brody, *The Other Side of Eden: Hunters, Farmers, and the Shaping of the World* (Vancouver: Douglas & McIntyre, 2000), 31; Pauktuutit Inuit Women of Canada, *The Inuit Way*, 34–35.

21 James Hiller, "Early Patrons of the Labrador Eskimos: The Moravian Mission in Labrador, 1764–1805," in *Patrons and Brokers in the East Arctic*, ed. Robert Paine (St. John's: ISER Books, 1971), 78.

22 Brody, *The Other Side of Eden.*

23 Colin Samson, *A World You Do Not Know: Settler Societies, Indigenous Peoples and the Attack on Cultural Diversity* (London: University of London, 2013).

24 Pauktuutit Inuit Women of Canada, *The Inuit Way.*

25 Ibid.

26 Jean Briggs, "'Qallunaat Run on Rails; Inuit Do What They Want to Do.' Autonomies in Camp and Town," *Études/Inuit/Studies* 25, nos. 1–2 (2001): 229–47.

27 Pauktuutit Inuit Women of Canada, *The Inuit Way.*

28 Jean Briggs, *Inuit Morality Play: The Emotional Education of a Three Year Old* (St. John's: ISER Books, 1998); Jean Briggs, *Childrearing Practices: Interviewing Inuit Elders*, vol. 3 (Iqaluit, NU: Nunavut Arctic College, 2017).

29 Jean Briggs, *Never in Anger: Portrait of an Eskimo Family* (Cambridge, MA: Harvard University Press, 1970).

30 Pauktuutit, *The Inuit Way.*

31 José Mailhot, *The People of Sheshatshit: In the Land of the Innu*, trans. Axel Harvey (St. John's: ISER Books, 1997), 8.

32 Sider, *Skin for Skin*, 79.

33 Sider, *Skin for Skin*; Georg Henriksen, *Hunters in the Barrens: The Naskapi on the Edge of the White Man's World* (St. John's: ISER Books, 1973).

34 Marie Wadden, *Nitassinan: The Innu Struggle to Reclaim their Homeland* (Toronto: Douglas & McIntrye, 1991), 60.

35 Ibid, 61.

36 Henriksen, *Hunters in the Barrens.*

37 George Gregoire, *Walk with My Shadow: The Life of an Innu Man* (St. John's: Creative Publishers, 2012).

38 Ibid.

39 Innu Nation and Mushuau Innu Band Council, *Gathering Voices: Finding*

Strength to Help Our Children, ed. Camille Fouillard (Toronto: Douglas & McIntrye, 1995).

40 Tuamish, quoted in Innu Nation, *Gathering Voices*, 67.

41 Meneskuesh and Tshenish, quoted in Innu Nation, *Gathering Voices*, 65.

42 Nishet Penashue, "Learning from My Mother," *Them Days* 30, no. 2 (2006): 169.

43 Ibid., 170.

44 Kaniuekutat, quoted in Innu Nation, *Gathering Voices*, 65.

45 Innu Nation, *Gathering Voices*.

46 Stephen Howe, *Empire: A Very Short Introduction* (Oxford: Oxford University Press, 2002).

47 Sider, *Skin for Skin*.

48 Rompkey, *Grenfell of Labrador*.

Chapter Two

1 Hiller, "Foundation and Early Years."

2 Ibid., 1–2.

3 J.E. Hutton, *A History of Moravian Missions* (London: Moravian Publication Office, 1922), 9–10.

4 Hiller, "Foundation and Early Years."

5 Hutton, *History of Moravian Missions*; Hans Rollmann, "Introduction," in *Moravian Beginnings in Labrador: Papers from a Symposium held in Makkovik and Hopedale*, ed. Hans Rollmann (St. John's: Newfoundland and Labrador Studies Occasional Publications No. 2, 2009), 13–22.

6 Garth Taylor, "In the Wake of the *Hope*: Jens Haven's 1764 Reconnaissance Journey in Northern Newfoundland and Southern Labrador," in *Moravian Beginnings in Labrador: Papers from a Symposium held in Makkovik and Hopedale*, ed. Hans Rollmann (St. John's: Newfoundland and Labrador Studies Occasional Publications No. 2, 2009), 87–103.

7 Palliser to the Board of Trade, 9 Oct. 1764, Labrador Boundary Dispute Documents, No. 214.

8 Remarks, &c., by Palliser, made in Obedience to the Several Articles of his Majesty's Instructions to Him, 1764, Labrador Boundary Dispute Documents, No. 215.

9 Hans Rollmann, "The Labrador Land Grants of 1769 and 1774," in *Moravian Beginnings in Labrador: Papers from a Symposium held in Makkovik and Hopedale*, ed. Hans Rollmann (St. John's: Newfoundland and Labrador

Occasional Publications No. 2, 2009), 104–31.

10 17 Apr. 1765 letter from James Hutton, Secretary of the SFG, to Lord Hillsborough, First Lord of the Board of Trade, cited in James Hiller, "Moravian Land Holdings on the Labrador Coast: A Brief History," in *Our Footprints Are Everywhere: Inuit Land Use and Occupancy in Labrador*, ed. Carol Brice-Bennett (Nain, NL: Labrador Inuit Association, 1977), 83.

11 Hans Rollmann, "Johann Christian Erhardt and the First Moravian Exploration of Labrador in 1752," in *Moravian Beginnings in Labrador: Papers from a Symposium held in Makkovik and Hopedale*, ed. Hans Rollmann (St. John's: Newfoundland and Labrador Occasional Publications No. 2, 2009), 53–68.

12 Hiller, "Foundation and Early Years," 70–71, 86.

13 Ibid.

14 James Hiller, "Early Patrons of the Labrador Eskimos: The Moravian Mission in Labrador, 1764–1805," in *Patrons and Brokers in the East Arctic*, ed. Robert Paine (St. John's: ISER Books, 1971), 83–93.

15 Carol Brice-Bennett, "Missionaries as Traders: Moravians and Labrador Inuit, 1771–1860," in *Merchant Credit and Labour Strategies in Historical Perspective*, ed. Rosemary E. Ommer (Fredericton, NB: Acadiensis, 1990), 223–46.

16 Amelia Fay, "Missionaries, Merchants, and Inuit Entrepreneurs: An Examination of Trade Relations along the Labrador Coast," *Études/Inuit/Studies* 39, no. 1 (2015): 144.

17 Hans Rollmann, "'So fond of the pleasure to shoot': The Sale of Firearms to Inuit on Labrador's North Coast in the Late Eighteenth Century," *Newfoundland and Labrador Studies* 26, no. 1 (2011): 5–24.

18 Brice-Bennett, "Missionaries as Traders," 224–25, 246.

19 Ibid.

20 Hiller, "Foundation and Early Years."

21 NunatuKavut Community Council, *Unveiling NunatuKavut: Describing the Lands and People of South/Central Labrador* (Goose Bay, NL: NunatuKavut Community Council, 2010), 184–85.

22 Proclamation by Governor Shuldham to Keep Esquimaux within Moravian Settlement, 4 May 1772, Labrador Boundary Dispute Documents, No. 423.

23 Rollmann, "'So fond of the pleasure to shoot.'"

24 NunatuKavut Community Council, *Unveiling NunatuKavut.*

25 Linda Sabathy-Judd, "Winning Souls for Jesus: Moravians in Nain, Labrador, 1771–1781," in *Moravian Beginnings in Labrador: Papers from a Symposium held in Makkovik and Hopedale*, ed. Hans Rollmann (St. John's: Newfoundland and Labrador Occasional Publications No. 2, 2009), 135.

26 Hiller, "Moravian Land Holdings," 86–87.

27 Carol Brice-Bennett, "Two Opinions: Inuit and Moravian Missionaries in Labrador 1804–1860," MA thesis (Memorial University of Newfoundland, 1981).

28 Ibid.

29 Kleivan, *The Eskimos.*

30 Brice-Bennett, "Missionaries as Traders."

31 Brice-Bennett, "Two Opinions."

32 Society for the Furtherance of the Gospel, 1772, "Concerning Labrador" [pamphlet], cited in J.W. Davey, *The Fall of Torngak, or The Moravian Mission on the Coast of Labrador* (London: Partridge, 1905), 140.

33 Anthony Williamson, "The Moravian Mission and Its Impact on the Labrador Eskimo," *Arctic Anthropology* 2, no. 2 (1964): 35.

34 Brice-Bennett, "Two Opinions."

35 Brice-Bennett, "Two Opinions"; Hiller, "Foundation and Early Years."

36 *Periodical Accounts of the Moravian Missions* 1 (1790): 12.

37 Brice-Bennett, "Missionaries as Traders."

38 Rollmann, "'So fond of the pleasure to shoot.'"

39 Brice-Bennett, "Two Opinions."

40 Brice-Bennett, "Missionaries as Traders."

41 Brice-Bennett, "Two Opinions."

42 Ibid.

43 Anonymous. *Moravians in Labrador* (Edinburgh: J. Ritchie, 1833), 103.

44 Melanie Cabak, "Inuit Women as Catalysts of Change: An Archaeological Study of 19th Century Northern Labrador," MA thesis (University of South Carolina, 1991).

45 Brother Freitag, 1840, as cited in Brice-Bennett, "Two Opinions," 339.

46 Cabak, "Inuit Women."

47 *Periodical Accounts of the Moravian Missions* 17 (1844–45): 108–09.

48 Kleivan, *The Eskimos.*

49 Cabak, "Inuit Women."

50 Hiller, "Foundation and Early Years."

51 Carol Brice-Bennett, "Land Use in the Nain and Hopedale Regions," in *Our Footprints Are Everywhere: Inuit Land Use and Occupancy in Labrador*, ed. Carol Brice-Bennett (Nain, NL: Labrador Inuit Association, 1977), 97–203.

52 Carol Brice-Bennett, "Renewable Resource Use and Wage Employment in the Economy of Northern Labrador" (St. John's: Background Report for the Royal Commission on Employment and Unemployment, 1986).

53 Brice-Bennett, "Two Opinions"; Cabak, "Inuit Women."

Chapter Three

1 Grant, "Nain's Silenced Majority."
2 Rollmann, "Moravian Education."
3 Ibid.
4 Labrador differs from other Inuit regions in Canada in its use of Roman orthography instead of syllabics for Inuktitut.
5 Brigitte Schloss, "The Development of Nain School: 1771–1963" (Research Paper, Memorial University of Newfoundland, 1964), 8.
6 *Periodical Accounts of the Moravian Missions* 27 (1868): 57.
7 Rollmann, ""Moravian Education."
8 *Periodical Accounts of the Moravian Missions* 9 (1824): 237–38.
9 Rollmann, "Moravian Education."
10 *Periodical Accounts of the Moravian Missions* 14 (1838): 426.
11 Ibid. 9 (1824): 236.
12 Rollmann, "Moravian Education."
13 Grant, "Nain's Silenced Majority"; Rollmann, "Moravian Education."
14 *Periodical Accounts of the Moravian Missions* 9 (1824): 238–39.
15 Hans Rollmann, "Moravians in Central Labrador: The Indigenous Inuit Mission of Jacobus and Salome at Snooks Cove," *Journal of Moravian Studies* 9 (Fall 2010): 7–40.
16 Grant, "Nain's Silenced Majority."
17 Kleivan, *The Eskimos.*
18 Wilfred Grenfell, *Labrador: The Country and Its People* (New York: Macmillan, 1922), 175.
19 Grant, "Nain's Silenced Majority."
20 Rollmann, "Moravian Education."
21 Rowe, *Development of Education in Newfoundland.*
22 Brice-Bennett, "Two Opinions," 334.
23 *Periodical Accounts of the Moravian Missions* 13 (1834–36): 161.
24 Ibid., 355.
25 Ibid. 14 (1838): 426.
26 Ibid. 25 (1865): 487.
27 Ibid.
28 Ibid. 26 (1866): 99.
29 Ibid.
30 Ibid., 163.
31 Ibid., 99.

32 Ibid. 28 (1872): 349.

33 Samuel Liebisch to the Unity Elders Conference, 7 Oct. 1782, R15Kb17b44, Unity Archives, Herrnhut, Germany, as quoted in Rollmann, "Moravian Education," 229.

34 Hans Rollmann, "The First Moravian Schools in Labrador," *Them Days* 27, no. 2 (Winter 2001): 8–12.

35 *Periodical Accounts of the Moravian Missions* 4 (1806–10): 323.

36 Rollmann, "Moravian Education."

37 *Periodical Accounts of the Moravian Missions* 4 (1806–10): 459.

38 Ibid. 14 (1836): 214.

39 Ibid. 3 (1802): 112–13.

40 Ibid. 10 (1826): 57.

41 Ibid. 12 (1831): 451.

42 Ibid., 67.

43 Ibid. 20 (1851): 282; Andrea Procter, "The Prospects of Culture: Resource Management and the Production of Difference in Nunatsiavut, Labrador," PhD diss. (Memorial University of Newfoundland, 2012).

44 Brice-Bennett, "Two Opinions."

45 Ibid.

46 John Kennedy, *Encounters: An Anthropological History of Southeastern Labrador* (Montreal and Kingston: McGill-Queen's University Press, 2015), 60, 86.

47 Patricia Way, "The Story of William Phippard." in *History and Renewal of Labrador's Inuit-Métis*, ed. John C. Kennedy (St. John's: ISER Books, 2014), 136.

48 Kennedy, *Encounters,* 91.

49 Kennedy, *Encounters,* 64–73.

50 Brice-Bennett, "Two Opinions," 427–28.

51 Kleivan, *The Eskimos.*

52 Hans Rollmann, "'. . . That Between Their Church and Ours There Is Hardly Any Difference': Settler Families on Labrador's North Coast Join the Moravian Church," in *History and Renewal of Labrador's Inuit-Métis*, ed. John C. Kennedy (St. John's: ISER Books, 2014), 180–214.

53 Kleivan, *The Eskimos.*

54 Settlers were later called Kablunângajuit/Kallunângajuit ("partly white"), and the families of those who lived in the Nunatsiavut land settlement area, as defined by the 2005 Labrador Inuit Land Claims Agreement, are recognized as Nunatsiavut beneficiaries. See Indian and Northern Affairs Canada (INAC), "Labrador Inuit Land Claims Agreement" (Ottawa: Government of Canada, 2005).

55 Rollmann, ". . . That Between Their Church and Ours."

56 Kleivan, *The Eskimos.*
57 Rollmann, "... That Between Their Church and Ours."
58 Kleivan, *The Eskimos.*
59 *Periodical Accounts of the Moravian Missions* 31 (1878–81): 236.
60 Kleivan, *The Eskimos.*
61 *Periodical Accounts of the Moravian Missions* 25 (1863–66): 489.
62 Kleivan, *The Eskimos.*
63 Hiller, "The Foundation and Early Years," iii.
64 *Periodical Accounts of the Moravian Missions* 32 (1881): 194.
65 Ibid.
66 Grant, "Nain's Silenced Majority."
67 *Periodical Accounts of the Moravian Missions* 31 (1878–81): 245.
68 Joan Andersen, *Makkovik: 100 Years Plus* (Makkovik, NL: Robinson-Blackmore, 1996); Rollmann, "... That Between Their Church and Ours."
69 *Periodical Accounts of the Moravian Missions* 31 (1878–81): 246.
70 Ibid., 342.
71 Ibid. 32 (1881): 119–20.
72 Ibid. 31 (1878–81): 341–42.
73 Rollmann, "Moravian Education in Labrador."
74 *Periodical Accounts of the Moravian Missions* 7, no. 79 (1909): 428.
75 Ibid., 428–29.
76 Ibid.
77 Rev. Peacock, "Education among the Eskimos of Northern Labrador," 1952, 193.6.07.001, Education in Labrador, 1949–1955, MUN Archives.
78 *Periodical Accounts of the Moravian Missions* 31 (1878–81): 341.
79 Ibid. 2, no. 17 (1894): 247.
80 Grant, "Nain's Silenced Majority."
81 Kleivan, *The Eskimos.*
82 *Periodical Accounts of the Moravian Missions* 8, no. 85 (1911): 15; ibid. 8, no. 92 (1912): 397.
83 Ibid. 8, no. 92 (1912): 398.
84 Kleivan, *The Eskimos.*
85 *Periodical Accounts of the Moravian Missions* 9, no. 108 (1916): 536.
86 Ibid.
87 Ibid.
88 Ibid.

Chapter Four

1 *Periodical Accounts of the Moravian Missions* 2, no. 17 (1894): 247.

2 Ibid. 4, no. 41 (1900): 243; ibid. 5, no. 52 (1902): 162.

3 Andersen, *Makkovik*.

4 *Periodical Accounts of the Moravian Missions* 9, no. 99 (1914): 114.

5 Ibid. 9, no. 100 (1914): 185.

6 Ibid.

7 Joan Andersen, *Celebrating the 100th Anniversary of the White Elephant* (Makkovik, NL: White Elephant Museum, 2015), 5.

8 *Periodical Accounts of the Moravian Missions* 10, no. 112 (1917): 120.

9 Ibid. 10, no. 124 (1920): 496.

10 Ibid., 500.

11 Ibid., 496.

12 Andersen, *Celebrating*, 7.

13 Hilda Dicker, Them Days interview F116, 1977.

14 *Periodical Accounts of the Moravian Missions* 11, no. 4 (1922): 146.

15 Alice Perrault, *Them Days* 3, no. 1 (Sept 1977): 4; Edna Perrett, Them Days interview F044, 1976.

16 Kate Hettasch, 1977, interview F202, Them Days Archive.

17 Samuel King Hutton to Paul Hettasch, 9 Mar. 1936, Moravian Church records, box 37, Them Days Archive.

18 Peacock to employment office in Nova Scotia, 6 Sept. 1947, Moravian Church records, box 37, Them Days Archive.

19 Peacock to Miss May, 8 Mar. 1948, Moravian Church records, box 37, Them Days Archive.

20 The £30 that remained would have been worth the equivalent of about £1430 today, or $2,440 in today's money. Correspondence 1936 - 1938 in Moravian Church House Archives, Muswell Hill, London.

21 *Viewpoint from Distant Lands* [replaced the *Periodical Accounts*] (1962): 51.

22 Rowe, *Development of Education*.

23 Letter to Samuel Hutton from Evelyn Shaw, 11 Feb. 1932, Correspondence 1930–32, Moravian Church House Archives, Muswell Hill, London.

24 Alice Andersen, Them Days interview F293, 1977.

25 Mary Oliver Clarke, *Them Days* 9, no. 1 (Sept. 1983): 5.

26 Muriel Andersen, Healing and Commemoration project, Happy Valley–Goose Bay, NL, 10 Mar. 2018.

27 Muriel Andersen, *Them Days* 11, no. 1 (Sept. 1985): 54.

28 Ruth Flowers, 23 Sept. 2011, National Centre for Truth and Reconciliation Archives, Sharing Panel (Hopedale Hearing): SP027, TRC.

29 Sybilla Nitsman, Them Days interview F299, 1977.

30 Manasse Pijogge, *Them Days* 3, no. 1 (Sept 1977): 7.

31 "Inuttitut" and "Inuttut" are Labrador dialectical ways of spelling "Inuktitut," the name of the Inuit language.

32 Silpa Edmunds, Them Days interview, 2009.

33 *Periodical Accounts of the Moravian Missions* 11, no. 8 (1924): 324.

34 Alice Perrault, Them Days interview F111, 1977.

35 Jim Voisey, Them Days interview F089, 1977.

36 Hilda Dicker, Them Days interview F116, 1977.

37 *Periodical Accounts of the Moravian Missions* 11, no. 6 (1923): 222–23.

38 Joan Andersen, personal communication, 2018.

39 Sach to Shawe, 15 Oct. 1942, Correspondence 1939–42, Moravian Church House Archives, Muswell Hill, London.

40 1937 timetables from teachers, Makkovik, Correspondence 1936–38, Moravian Church House Archives, Muswell Hill, London.

41 Jim Voisey, Them Days interview F089, 1977.

42 Annie Evans, Healing and Commemoration project, Makkovik, 24 Apr. 2018.

43 *Periodical Accounts of the Moravian Missions* 12, no. 2 (1927): 84.

44 George and Linda Harp to Dear Friends, Makkovik, 1947, in PRC 9, Box 7433, File 75, Vol. III, Moravian Mission and Northern Labrador, Provincial Archives of Newfoundland and Labrador (PANL).

45 Rev. George Harp, Makkovik School Report, 1951, Annual Reports, Makkovik 1949–55, Makkovik White Elephant Museum Archive.

46 Siegfried Hettasch to Peacock, 24 Jan. 1944, Moravian Church records, Box 37, Them Days Archive.

47 Ruth Flowers, 23 Sept. 2011, National Centre for Truth and Reconciliation Archives, Sharing Panel (Hopedale Hearing): SP027, TRC.

48 Annie Evans, Healing and Commemoration project, Makkovik, 24 Apr. 2018.

49 Jim Voisey, Them Days interview F089, 1977.

50 Gladys Chard Burdett, Them Days interview F220, 1978.

51 Nurse M.E. Tatterson came to Makkovik in 1920 with Reverend R.S. Callander to attend to his wife, who was pregnant. Concerns within the Mission over the Callanders' harsh treatment of the school teachers, especially, forced them to resign. They returned to England in 1922 with Nurse Tatterson (Andersen, *Makkovik*; Charles Uglow, *The Seafaring Jacksons* (UK: Privately printed, 2009).

52 Gladys Chard Burdett, Them Days interview F220, 1978.

53 Ibid.

54 Muriel Andersen, Them Days interview, 2012.

55 *Periodical Accounts of the Moravian Missions* no. 149 (1941): 54–55.

56 Annie Evans, Healing and Commemoration project, Makkovik, 24 Apr. 2018.

57 Ruth Flowers, 23 Sept. 2011, National Centre for Truth and Reconciliation Archives, Sharing Panel (Hopedale Hearing): SP027, TRC.

58 Annie Evans, Healing and Commemoration project, Makkovik, 24 Apr. 2018.

59 Ruth Flowers, 23 Sept. 2011, National Centre for Truth and Reconciliation Archives, Sharing Panel (Hopedale Hearing): SP027, TRC.

60 Ibid.

61 *Among the Deep Sea Fishers* (Oct. 1942); Peacock to Birtill, 7 Oct. 1950, Correspondence Sept. 1950 to Dec. 1951, Moravian Church House Archives, Muswell Hill, London.

62 Uglow, *The Seafaring Jacksons*, 76.

63 *Periodical Accounts of the Moravian Missions* no. 137 (1929): 321.

64 Ibid., 322.

65 Ibid. no. 138 (1930): 406.

66 Paul Hettasch to Hutton, 26 Jan. 1934, Correspondence 1933–35, Foreign Missions: LABRADOR, Moravian Church House Archives, Muswell Hill, London.

67 Clara Voisey, Them Days interview F027.

68 Rhoda Dawson to ND, 20 Apr. 1932, Rhoda Dawson Bickerdike Collection, 198.5.04.002, MUN Archives.

69 *Periodical Accounts of the Moravian Missions* no. 138 (1930): 406.

70 Ibid. no. 136 (1928): 238.

71 Ibid. no. 138 (1930): 406.

72 Alice Perrault, Them Days interview F111, 1977.

73 Brice-Bennett, "Renewable Resource Use."

74 *Periodical Accounts of the Moravian Missions* 11, no. 4 (1922): 146.

75 Ibid. no. 138 (1930): 406.

76 W. Mullaly, Ranger report re: School attendance in Hopedale, Mar. 1949, PRC 9, Box 7433, File 75, Vol. V: Moravian Mission, PANL; Andersen, *Makkovik*.

77 See Appendix in Kleivan, *The Eskimos*, for a listing of epidemics and health at Moravian stations between 1773 and 1955.

78 Alice Perrault, Them Days interview F111, 1977; Millicent Harriet Olive Flowers (1929–39) came from Nuertorarvik, or Flowers' Bay, near Davis Inlet; Amos

Manuel Voisey (1913–27) may have died of a ruptured appendix (Register of Deaths, Labrador, 1939; Patty Way, personal communication, 2018).

79 *Periodical Accounts of the Moravian Missions* no. 136 (1928): 247.

80 Ibid. 158 (1950): 55.

81 Memorandum on the Eskimos of Northern Labrador, presented by the Moravian Mission Board to the Commission of Government, Newfoundland. PRC 9, Box 7433, File 75, Vol. I: Moravian Mission, PANL.

82 Rev. Birtill, BMB, to L.W. Shaw, Department of Education, 13 Jan. 1943, Box 37, Moravian Church records, Them Days Archive.

83 L.W. Shaw, Secretary for Education, to Rev. Birtill, BMB, 21 May 1941, PRC 9, Box 7433, File 75, Vol. I: Moravian Mission, PANL.

84 Peacock to Samson, 6 Sept. 1943, Box 37, Moravian Church records, Them Days Archive.

85 Peacock to Minister of Mines and Resources (Ottawa), 21 May 1941, Box 37, Moravian Church records, Them Days Archive. No response to Peacock's letter has been located.

86 Memorandum on the Eskimos of Northern Labrador, presented by the Moravian Mission Board to the Commission of Government, Newfoundland. PRC 9, Box 7433, File 75, Vol. I: Moravian Mission, PANL.

87 Ibid.

88 *Periodical Accounts of the Moravian Missions* no. 154 (1946): 43.

89 Hettasch to Shawe, 6 July 1941, Moravian Church records, Box 37, Them Days Archive.

90 Br. Wilson to Alice Perrett, 16 Jan. 1936, Moravian Church records, box 37, Them Days Archive; Paul Hettasch to Shawe, 8 Mar. 1939, Moravian Church House Archives, Muswell Hill, London; Paul Hettasch to Birtill, 24 Aug. 1940, Moravian Church records, Box 37, Them Days Archive.

91 Shawe to Hettasch, 8 June 1938, Moravian Church House Archives, Muswell Hill, London.

92 Birtill to Hettasch, 31 Dec. 1940, Moravian Church records, Box 37, Them Days Archive.

93 Hettasch to Birtill, 21 July 1941, Moravian Church records, Box 37, Them Days Archive.

94 Fred Grubb to Bill Peacock, 3 Aug. 1945, Moravian Church records, Box 37, Them Days Archive.

95 Peacock to Harp, 22 Feb. 1945, Moravian Church records, Box 37, Them Days Archive.

96 Bertie Lane, Register of Girls — St. Anthony Children's Home, MG 63.4233, PANL; Hudson's Bay Company Archives biographical sheets: George Ford, https://www.gov.mb.ca/chc/archives/hbca/biographical/f/ford_george.pdf.; Register of Children — St. Anthony Children's Home, MG 63.4235, PANL.

97 *Among the Deep Sea Fishers* (Apr. 1930): 24; Register of Children — St. Anthony Children's Home, MG 63.4235, PANL. Another boy, William John Piercy, was brought to the orphanage on the IGA medical ship in 1914. According to the records, his father was dead and his mother was left with five small children. Two of the family were adopted by William Ford of Ford's Harbour, and William was sent to St. Anthony (Register of Boys, St. Anthony Children's Home, MG 63.4234, PANL).

98 British Mission Board Minutes, 24 Oct. 1941, Book #9, Moravian Church House Archives, Muswell Hill, London.

99 Ibid.

100 Sach to Shawe, 18 Mar. 1941, Correspondence 1939–42, Moravian Church House Archives, Muswell Hill, London.

101 Peacock to Harp, 22 Feb. 1945, Moravian Church records, Box 37, Them Days Archive.

102 Frecker: Visit to northern Labrador report, 1948, PRC 9, Box 7433, File 75, Vol. IV: Moravian Mission, PANL.

103 Walter Rockwood, memo to Deputy Minister of Public Welfare, 28 Jan. 1953, Education in Northern Labrador, 1953–61, GN 56/2, Department of Labrador Affairs, Box 10, PANL.

104 Harp to British Mission Board, 31 Jan. 1948, Moravian Church records, Box 37, Them Days Archive.

105 Joan Andersen, personal communication, 2018, based on discussions that Joan had with Ted Andersen of Makkovik about his memories of the fire.

106 Millie Mitsuk Martin, Them Days interview, 2014.

107 Peacock to Harp, 1 Feb. 1948, Moravian Church records, Box 37, Them Days Archive.

108 *Periodical Accounts of the Moravian Missions* no. 156 (1948): 53–54.

109 Makkovik Annual Report (George Harp), 1948, Makkovik White Elephant Museum.

110 Makkovik Annual Report (George Harp), 1949, Makkovik White Elephant Museum.

111 Ibid.

112 Harp to Peacock, 19 Mar. 1948, Moravian Church records, Box 37, Them Days Archive.

113 Ibid.

114 W. Mullaly, Ranger report re: School attendance in Hopedale, Mar. 1949, PRC 9, Box 7433, File 75, Vol. V: Moravian Mission, PANL.

115 Ibid.

116 J.C. Parsons, Regional Director of Family Allowances, Newfoundland, to Peacock, 14 Aug. 1950, 075.1.23.004, MUN Archives.

117 Peacock to Parsons, Regional Director of Family Allowances, Newfoundland, 7 Oct. 1950, 075.1.23.004, MUN Archives.

118 Peacock to Premier Smallwood, 9 Oct. 1950, 075.1.23.004, MUN Archives.

119 William Wall, *The Wall Report: A Survey of Educational Problems in Selected Study Areas in Northern Newfoundland and Labrador*, A Report to the Board of Directors of the International Grenfell Association (1960), 39.

120 Birtill to Secretary, Department of Education, 28 Feb. 1950, PRC 9, Box 7433, File 75, Vol. V: Moravian Mission, PANL.

121 23 Nov. 1949: 34, British Minute Book #13, Moravian Church House Archives, Muswell Hill, London.

122 W.G. Rockwood, Director of Northern Labrador Affairs, 1959 Annual Report for Department of Public Welfare: 123. HV 109 N11, PANL

123 Statistics for Makkovik Station, 1948–53, Makkovik White Elephant Museum Archive.

124 Doris Peacock, 1951 Annual Education Report, PRC 9, Box 7433, File 75, Vol. X: Moravian Mission, PANL.

125 Rev. George Harp to R.L. Andrews, Department of Education, July 1949, Miscellaneous correspondence, Makkovik White Elephant Museum Archive.

126 Harp to J.G. Parsons, 25 Jan. 1951, Correspondence 1950–52, Makkovik White Elephant Museum Archive.

127 [Anonymous] to Rev. Harp, 10 Apr. 1951, Correspondence 1950–52, Makkovik White Elephant Museum Archive.

128 Telegram, Harp to Parsons, n.d., Correspondence 1950–52, Makkovik White Elephant Museum Archive.

129 *Periodical Accounts of the Moravian Missions* no. 158 (1950): 55

130 Harp to Birtill, 16 May 1951, Correspondence 1950–51, Moravian Church House Archives, Muswell Hill, London. Rev. Harp provided an outline of Makkovik school expenses and income with his letter to Birtill in 1951. School expenses amounted to $2,475.53, and $1,675 was collected in school fees.

131 Birtill to Peacock, 21 Nov. 1951, Correspondence 1950–51, Moravian Church House Archives, Muswell Hill, London.

132 *Periodical Accounts of the Moravian Missions* no. 162 (1954): 17.

133 British Mission Board Minute Book #14, 17 Aug. 1953, Moravian Church House Archives, Muswell Hill, London.

134 1953 Makkovik Annual Report, Makkovik White Elephant Museum.

135 1955 Makkovik Annual Report (Inga and G.J. Vollprecht), Makkovik White Elephant Museum.

136 J.R. Chalker, Minister of Education, Memorandum to Executive Council: Northern Labrador Education, 11 Aug. 1955, PRC 9, Box 7433, File 75, Vol. XIII: Moravian Mission, PANL.

137 Brice-Bennett, "Renewable Resource Use," 28.

138 Northern Labrador Affairs, Annual Report for Department of Public Welfare for Year ending March 31, 1959.

139 Carol Brice-Bennett, "Dispossessed: The Eviction of Inuit from Hebron, Labrador," Submitted to Royal Commission on Aboriginal Peoples (Happy Valley–Goose Bay, NL: Labrador Institute, 1994).

140 The federal government paid two-thirds of the costs for the school retroactively in 1965, when the Federal–Provincial Agreement on funding for Indigenous communities was implemented. First meeting of the Federal–Provincial Committee on Financial Assistance for Indians and Eskimos of Northern Labrador, 6–7 July 1965. Appendix A: Capital Expenditure Period 1959–1964. PRC, Box #46 (location: 52-1-5-3), File 75, Vol. 1, PANL.

141 Andersen, *Makkovik.*

Chapter Five

1 Paul Hettasch to Hutton, 18 Jan. 1930, Correspondence 1930–32, Moravian Church House Archives, Muswell Hill, London.

2 Kleivan, *The Eskimos*, 128–29.

3 Brice-Bennett, "Renewable Resource Use."

4 *Periodical Accounts of the Moravian Missions* no. 137 (1929): 325.

5 Ibid., 328.

6 Ibid. no. 136 (1928): 247–48.

7 Ibid. no. 137 (1929): 329.

8 Ibid. no. 138 (1930): 414.

9 Miriam MacMillan, *Green Seas and White Ice* (New York: Dodd, Mead and Company, 1948), 60; *Periodical Accounts of the Moravian Missions* no. 137 (1929): 323.

10 *Periodical Accounts of the Moravian Missions* no. 139 (1931): 62.

11 MacMillan, *Green Seas and White Ice,* 60.
12 Paul Hettasch to Hutton, 16 Jan. 1931, Correspondence 1930–32, Moravian Church House Archives, Muswell Hill, London.
13 *Periodical Accounts of the Moravian Missions* no. 139 (1931): 64.
14 Kate Hettasch, Them Days interview F202, 1977.
15 Kate Hettasch, Diary of Nain Moravian Mission School, 14 Jan. 1931, Moravian Archives, Bethlehem, PA.
16 Kate Hettasch to "My Dear True Friend," 31 Dec. 1931, Correspondence 1930–32, Moravian Church House Archives, Muswell Hill, London.
17 Kate Hettasch, 5 Mar. 1931, Diary of Nain School, Apr.–July 1931, HeK30, Moravian Archives, Bethlehem, PA.
18 Kate Hettasch, 11 Apr. 1931, ibid.
19 Paul Hettasch to Hutton, 25 July 1930, Correspondence 1930–32, Moravian Church House Archives, Muswell Hill, London.
20 Secretary of BMB to Captain MacMillan, 26 July 1930, ibid.
21 *Periodical Accounts of the Moravian Missions* no. 141 (1933): 271.
22 Kate Hettasch, 24 Oct. 1931, Diary of Nain School, Oct.–Dec. 1931, HeK30, Moravian Archives, Bethlehem, PA.
23 Interview with Beatrice Watts, 2003, in Martha MacDonald, "Inside Stories: Agency and Identity through Language Loss Narratives in Nunatsiavut," PhD diss. (Memorial University of Newfoundland, 2015), 269.
24 John Igloliorte, *An Inuk Boy Becomes a Hunter* (Halifax: Nimbus Publishing, 1994), 14.
25 Betty Ford Koch, Them Days interview F254.
26 Rose Voisey Ford Spurvey, *Them Days* 34, no. 4 (2010): 41.
27 Sylvia Potter, 27 Oct. 1931, Diary of Nain School, Oct.–Dec. 1931, HeK30, Moravian Archives, Bethlehem, PA.
28 *Periodical Accounts of the Moravian Missions* no. 141 (1933): 85.
29 Lucas Ittulak, Them Days interview, 2010.
30 Paul Hettasch to Hutton, 21 Apr. 1931, Correspondence 1930–32, Moravian Church House Archives, Muswell Hill, London.
31 Kate Hettasch to Dear Friends, 31 Dec. 1931, Correspondence 1930–32, Moravian Church House Archives, Muswell Hill, London.
32 Kate Hettasch to My Dear True Friend, 6 July 1931, Correspondence 1930–32, Moravian Church House Archives, Muswell Hill, London.
33 Rev. Paul Hettasch, *Periodical Accounts of the Moravian Missions* no. 150 (1942): 40.

34 Hettasch to Shawe, 8 Mar. 1937, Correspondence 1936–38, Moravian Church House Archives, Muswell Hill, London.

35 Paul Hettasch to Shawe, 16 Jan. 1937, Correspondence 1936–38, Moravian Church House Archives, Muswell Hill, London.

36 Rev. Paul Hettasch, *Periodical Accounts of the Moravian Missions* 142 (1934): 85.

37 Hutton to Sir John Hope Simpson, 31 Dec. 1934, Correspondence 1933–35, Moravian Church House Archives, Muswell Hill, London.

38 Hutton to Hon. Alderdice, 16 Feb. 1934, Correspondence 1933–35, Moravian Church House Archives, Muswell Hill, London.

39 British Mission Board Minute Book #7, 16 Sept. 1933; Paul Hettasch to Hutton, 28 July 1933, Correspondence 1933–35, Moravian Church House Archives, Muswell Hill, London.

40 Paul Hettasch to Hutton, 28 July 1933, Correspondence 1933–35, Moravian Church House Archives, Muswell Hill, London.

41 Paul Hettasch to Hutton, 16 Jan. 1931, Correspondence 1930–32, Moravian Church House Archives, Muswell Hill, London.

42 1933 Conference Minutes, Correspondence 1933–35, Moravian Church House Archives, Muswell Hill, London.

43 Ibid.

44 Hutton to Paul Hettasch, 23 Dec. 1931, Moravian Church records, Box 37, Them Days Archive.

45 Paul Hettasch to Br. Wilson, 16 Jan. 1936, Moravian Church records, Box 37, Them Days Archive.

46 Peacock: Education in Northern Labrador 1946, PRC 9.7433.75, Vol. III, PANL.

47 Paul Hettasch to Br. Wilson, 11 Apr. 1936, Correspondence 1936–38, Moravian Church House Archives, Muswell Hill, London.

48 Hettasch to Br. Wilson, 14 Jan. 1937, Moravian Church records, Box 37, Them Days Archive.

49 The building is also known as the OKâlaKatiget Society building as it housed the local TV and radio station in the 1990s and 2000s. It stands near the Illusuak Cultural Centre on the Nain shoreline.

50 *Periodical Accounts of the Moravian Missions* no. 148 (1940): 60.

51 Nain School Diaries, HeK29, HeK30, HeK31, Moravian Archives, Bethlehem, PA.

52 *Periodical Accounts of the Moravian Missions* no. 151 (1943): 39.

53 Patrick Flanagan, "Schooling, Souls, and Social Class: The Labrador Inuit," MA thesis (University of New Brunswick, 1984), 69.

54 Igloliorte, *An Inuk Boy*, 13, 16.

55 Kate Hettasch to Br. Shawe (London), 18 Sept. 1938, Correspondence 1936–38, Moravian Church House Archives, Muswell Hill, London.

56 Julius Ikkusek, 2010, Them Days interview (with John Jararuse interpreting).

57 Tabea Murphy, 2010, Them Days interview.

58 Paul Hettasch to Br. Wilson, 14 Jan. 1937, Correspondence 1937, Box 37, Moravian Church records, Them Days Archive.

59 Nain School Diary, 1931, HeK30, Moravian Archives, Bethlehem, PA.

60 Ibid.

61 Macmillan Moravian Mission School, List of Dinners and Suppers — 1936, HeK28, Moravian Archives, Bethlehem, PA. "Bl berries" are either blackberries (crowberries) or blueberries; "Doughboys" are fried dough; "Pipse" is dried char; and "Brewis" is a dish made of salt cod and hardtack.

62 In Labrador, a "lunch" is a snack, not a meal.

63 Abe Flowers, 22 Sept. 2011, National Centre for Truth and Reconciliation Archives, Sharing Panel (Hopedale Hearing): SP026, TRC.

64 Julius Ikkusek, 2010, Them Days interview (with John Jararuse interpreting).

65 Ibid. Pitsik is dried char, and nikku is dried caribou meat.

66 Flanagan, "Schooling," 62.

67 Julius Ikkusek, 2010, Them Days interview (with John Jararuse interpreting).

68 Tabea Murphy, 2010, Them Days interview.

69 Flanagan, "Schooling," 70.

70 Julius Ikkusek, 2010, Them Days interview (with John Jararuse interpreting).

71 Tabea Murphy, Them Days interview, 2010.

72 Tabea Murphy, 28 Oct. 2011, National Centre for Truth and Reconciliation Archives, Sharing Panel (Atlantic National Event): SP132B, Halifax, TRC. The tradition of remaining in the church porch until the missionaries had entered was also practised in Nain in the 1930s, when Miriam MacMillan visited. She wrote, "When the church bell rang, every home emptied. En masse they came — old, young, blind, coughing, with crying babies in arms and hoods. All respectfully waited outside for Dr. and Mrs. Hettasch to enter. Two by two, the young girls followed" (MacMillan, *Green Seas*, 50).

73 Schloss, "The Development of Nain School: 1771–1963," 6.

74 Tabea Murphy, 2010, Them Days interview.

75 Rev. Peacock, 1946, Education in Northern Labrador, PRC 9.7433.75, Vol. III, PANL.

76 Kate Hettasch, Nain School diary 1941–42, PP HeK36, Moravian Archives, Bethlehem, PA.

77 Peacock and Harp, History and Geography Curriculum, PRC 9.7433.75, Vol. II,

PANL; Peacock to Samson, 6 Sept. 1943, Moravian Church records, Box 37, Them Days Archive.

78 Peacock to British Mission Board, May 1936, 069.3.01.002, MUN Archives.

79 Walter Rockwood, "Educational Problem in Northern Labrador," memo for Department of Education, 2 Mar. 1945, PRC 9.7433.75, Vol. II, PANL.

80 Peacock to Shaw, Secretary for Education, 12 Sept. 1941, PRC 9.7433.75, Vol. I, PANL.

81 Peacock to Birtill, 10 Aug. 1940, Moravian Church records, Box 37, Them Days Archive.

82 British Mission Board to the Congregations of Labrador, 17 July 1939, Correspondence 1939–42, Moravian Church House Archives, Muswell Hill, London.

83 Secretary of Education to Rev. Birtill (BMB), 21 May 1941, PRC 9.7433.75, Vol. I, PANL.

84 Memo from Commissioner for Finance to Hon. Commissioner for Home Affairs and Education, 27 Oct 1945, PRC 9.7433.75, Vol. III; Peacock: Education in Northern Labrador, 1952, PRC 9.7433.75, Vol. VIII, PANL.

85 Commissioner of Finance to A.J. Walsh, Commissioner for Home Affairs and Education, 27 Oct. 1945, PRC 9, Box 7433, File 75, Vol. III, PANL; Peacock to Frecker, 11 Sept. 1946, PRC 9, Box 7433, File 75, Vol. III, PANL.

86 Anne Brantenberg, "The Marginal School and the Children of Nain," in *The White Arctic: Anthropological Essays on Tutelage and Ethnicity*, ed. Robert Paine (St. John's: ISER Books, 1977), 344–58.

87 Ted McNeill, the grandson of Torsten and Mary Andersen, was taught by Moravian missionaries in Makkovik before attending the Grenfell school in St. Anthony and then Pratt Institute in New York. He later designed and built many of the International Grenfell Association buildings in St. Anthony and Labrador. (Patty Way, personal communication, 2018.)

88 Inuk woman from Nain, as quoted in Flanagan, "Schooling," 60.

89 Rockwood to Peacock, 25 Sept. 1943, Correspondence in Moravian Church records, Box 37, Them Days Archive.

90 Silpa Barbour interview (1976), translated by Rose Pamak, *Them Days* 11, no. 1 (Sept. 1985): 53.

91 Peacock to Carter, Department of Natural Resources, 9 Oct. 1949, photocopies from Them Days Archive in White Elephant Museum.

92 Rev. Peacock, *Viewpoint from Distant Lands* (1963): 48.

93 Sam Andersen, Them Days interview F723.

94 Shaw, Department of Education, to Peacock, 4 Oct. 1941, Moravian Church records, Box 37, Them Days Archive.

95 27 Feb 1950, Peacock to Frecker, PRC 9.7433.75 Vol. V, Provincial Archives of NL.
96 Rev. Peacock, "Education among the Eskimos of Northern Labrador," 1952, 3–4. PRC 9.7433.75, Vol. VIII, PANL.
97 Peacock to Shaw, Department of Education, 10 Apr. 1943, PRC 9.7433.75, Vol. I, PANL.
98 Abel Leo in Labrador Inuit Association, "Labrador Inuit Education Conference" (St. John's: MUN Extension Service, 1977), 20. See also Martha McDonald's exploration of the transition to English in Nunatsiavut in "Inside Stories: Agency and Identity through Language Loss Narratives in Nunatsiavut," PhD diss. (Memorial University of Newfoundland, 2015).
99 Julius Ikkusek, 2010, Them Days interview (with John Jararuse interpreting).
100 Tabea Murphy, 28 Oct. 2011, National Centre for Truth and Reconciliation Archives, Sharing Panel (Atlantic National Event): SP132B, Halifax, TRC. Sam Andersen later became the first president of the Labrador Inuit Association.
101 2 Feb 1944, Peacock to Siegfried Hettasch, Moravian Church records, Box 37, Them Days Archive.
102 *Periodical Accounts of the Moravian Missions* no. 161 (1953): 7.
103 Shmuel Ben-Dor, *Makkovik: Eskimos and Settlers in a Labrador Community* (St. John's: ISER Books, 1966), 190.
104 Tabea Murphy, 28 Oct. 2011, National Centre for Truth and Reconciliation Archives, Sharing Panel (Atlantic National Event): SP132B, Halifax, TRC.
105 Doris Peacock, Report on Nain school, 1950–51, Correspondence Sept. 1950 to Dec. 1951, Moravian Church House Archives, Muswell Hill, London.
106 Scale of Wages paid in Nain School, Correspondence Sept. 1950–Dec. 1951, Moravian Church House Archives, Muswell Hill, London. The housemother at the Grenfell dormitory in North West River was paid $950 for the 10-month school year in 1954–55, a salary which Grenfell officials felt was low, given her qualifications (16 Nov. 1955, Dr. Paddon to Frecker and summary of expenses; PRC 10, Temp Box 21(B), File 77/25, Vol. II, Grenfell Public School Board, PANL.
107 Peacock: Education in Northern Labrador, 1952, PRC 9.7433.75, Vol. VIII, PANL.
108 *Periodical Accounts of the Moravian Missions* no. 163 (1955): 163.
109 Telegram from Peacock to Rev. Redberger, Alberta, 1946, in Moravian Church records, Box 37, Them Days Archive.
110 Contract for Beatrice Ford, 6 Sept. 1946, and contract for Robert Lyall, 26 Aug, 1946, Moravian Church records, Box 37, Them Days Archive.
111 Beatrice Ford to Rev. Birtill, 6 Mar. 1951, Correspondence Sept. 1950–Dec. 1951, Moravian Church House Archives, Muswell Hill, London.
112 Julie Green, "Sunday Best: Portrait of Beatrice Watts" (Happy Valley–Goose

Bay, NL: CBC, 1997); "Beatrice Watts of North West River," *kinatuinamot illengajuk* (Summer 1992): 19–23.

113 "Beatrice Watts of North West River."

114 *Among the Deep Sea Fishers* 40, no. 3 (Oct. 1942): 81.

115 Rowe, *The Development of Education*, 71.

116 Peacock to Ranger Tilley, 12 Nov. 1943, Moravian Church records, Box 37, Them Days Archive.

117 Peacock, "The Labrador Mission Field," 1 Feb. 1950, in White Elephant Archive, Makkovik.

118 *Encyclopedia of Newfoundland and Labrador*, vol. 4, s.v. "Ranger Force, Newfoundland."

119 British Mission Board Minute Book #13, 6 Feb. 1951, Moravian Church House Archives, Muswell Hill, London.

120 British Mission Board to Peacock, 7 Feb. 1951, Correspondence Sept. 1950–Dec. 1951, Moravian Church House Archives, Muswell Hill, London.

121 Peacock to Frecker, 26 July 1955, PRC 9, Box 7433, File 75, Vol. XIII: Moravian Mission, PANL.

122 Ibid.

123 F.W. Peacock, "The Erosion of the Inuit Culture," St. John's, unpublished manuscript, 1984, 15: Peacock Collection, 069.2.01.018, MUN Archives.

124 *Periodical Accounts of the Moravian Missions* no. 152 (1944): 50.

125 *Them Days* 26, no. 3 (Spring 2001): 31–32.

126 Bertha Holeiter, 20 Sept. 2011, National Centre for Truth and Reconciliation Archives, Sharing Panel (Goose Bay Hearing): SP025, TRC.

127 Peacock to Frecker, 7 Mar. 1956, PRC 9, Box 7433, File 75, Vol. XIV Moravian Mission and Northern Labrador, PANL.

128 J.R. Chalker, Minister of Education, Memorandum to Executive Council, n.d. (1956), PRC 9, Box 7433, File 75, Vol. XIV, Moravian Mission and Northern Labrador, PANL.

129 Peacock to Shaw, Department of Education, 10 Apr. 1943, PRC 9.7433.75.1; *Periodical Accounts of the Moravian Missions* no. 157 (1949): 40.

130 *Periodical Accounts of the Moravian Missions* no. 160 (1952): 160.

131 Doris Peacock, Annual Report for Moravian Schools, 1952–53, 193.6.07.001, MUN Archive; Doris Peacock to Frecker, 3 Jan. 1956, PRC 9.7433.75.13; *Periodical Accounts of the Moravian Missions* no. 163 (1955): 50.

132 Katie Merkuratsuk, personal communication, 2018.

133 Paul Jararuse, Healing and Commemoration session, Rigolet, 16 May 2018.

134 Sarah Webb, Healing and Commemoration session, Nain, 14 Apr. 2018.

135 Ibid.
136 Paul Jararuse, Healing and Commemoration session, Rigolet, 16 May 2018.
137 David J. Dickinson to C.J. Grant, Director of Administration, Department of Education, 9 Mar. 1973, PRC 35, Box #6 (location: 51-1-1-3), File 75, Vol. 25, Moravian Mission and Northern Labrador, PANL.
138 David J. Dickinson to C.F. Fury, Director of Administration, Department of Education, 20 Sept. 1974, PRC 35, Box #6 (location: 51-1-1-3), File 75, Vol. 27, Moravian Mission and Northern Labrador; C.F. Fury to David J. Dickinson, 30 Sept. 1974, ibid.
139 "'Labrador Kate,' the Life of Kate Hettasch (1905–1987)," *This Month in Moravian History* 72 (Mar. 2012), Moravian Archives, Bethlehem, PA.

Chapter Six

1 The Newfoundland government's Northern Labrador Trading Operations (NLTO) established a store at Nutak after the Hudson's Bay Company closed its trading post there in 1942.
2 *Periodical Accounts of the Moravian Missions* no. 147 (1939): 121.
3 George Harp to Bishop Shawe, Feb. 1938, Correspondence 1936–38, Moravian Church House Archives, Muswell Hill, London.
4 Peacock to Carter, 17 Aug. 1943, Moravian Church records, Box 37, Them Days Archive; Brice-Bennett, "Renewable Resource Use," xxv.
5 Memorandum to Honourable Minister of Education from Deputy Minister of Education, 16 Dec. 1949, 193.6.07.001 Education in Labrador, 1949–55, MUN Archives; British Mission Board Minute Book #10, 11 Aug. 1944, Moravian Church House Archives, Muswell Hill, London.
6 British Mission Board Minute Book #13, 23 Nov. 1950, Moravian Church House Archives, Muswell Hill, London.
7 1951 Superintendent's visit to Hebron, 25 Aug. 1951, Correspondence Sept. 1950–Dec. 1951, Moravian Church House Archives, Muswell Hill, London.
8 *Periodical Accounts of the Moravian Missions* no. 159 (1951): 30.
9 Nellie Winters, interview with Andrea Procter in Nain, 23 Sept. 2015.
10 *Periodical Accounts of the Moravian Missions* no. 158 (1950): 50.
11 Nellie Winters, Healing and Commemoration project, Makkovik, 24 Apr. 2018.
12 Walter Rockwood, Draft confidential memo to the Deputy Minister for Public Welfare 1953, MG 902, Rockwood Collection, PANL.

13 Walter Rockwood, "Visit to Northern Labrador, July 4th to August 3rd, 1953," 077.1.01.036, MUN Archives.
14 Dr. Paddon, "Community Aspects of Health and Welfare in Northern Labrador," 27 Feb. 1955, 077.1.01.020, MUN Archives.
15 Ibid.
16 Ibid.
17 Peacock to Rowe, 22 Aug. 1955, 077.1.01.035, MUN Archives.
18 Ibid.
19 Peacock to Rowe, 6 Sept. 1955, 077.1.01.035, MUN Archives.
20 Curtis to Dr. Leonard Miller (Deputy Minister of Health, NL), 23 Aug. 1955, 077.1.01.022 Correspondence Housing Conditions 1955, Rowe Collection, MUN Archives.
21 Ibid.
22 Walter Rockwood, Memorandum on General Policy in Respect to the Indians and Eskimos of Northern Labrador, 1955, GN 56.2, PANL.
23 "Petition of the Hebron People to the Government in St. John's, Hebron," to Dr. F.W. Rowe, Minister of Mines and Resources (translated by Rev. Siegfried Hettasch), 9 Aug. 1956, 077.1.01.020, MUN Archives.
24 Brice-Bennett, "Dispossessed."
25 British Mission Board Minute Book #15, 27 Sept. 1955, Moravian Church House Archives, Muswell Hill, London.
26 Frecker, Deputy Minister of Education, Memorandum to the Deputy Minister of Public Works: Boarding School at Nain, 19 Oct. 1955, PRC 9.7433.75.13, PANL.
27 Peacock to Frecker, 20 Dec. 1955, PRC 9.7433.75.13, PANL.
28 Paddon to Frecker, 18 Oct. 1955, PRC 10, Temp Box 21(B), File 77/25, Vol. II Grenfell Public School Board, PANL.
29 Ibid.
30 Frecker to Peacock, 1 Nov. 1955, PRC 9.7433.75.13, PANL.
31 Government of Newfoundland, "Labrador Conference, February 13th–16th, 1956," Dr. F.W. Rowe, Chairman, PRC 9, Box 7433, File 75, Vol. XIII, PANL.
32 Ibid.
33 Brice-Bennett, "Dispossessed," 3–4.
34 Ben-Dor, *Makkovik*, 161; Brice-Bennett, "Dispossessed," 151.
35 Siegfried Hettasch in *Labrador North* [film], National Film Board, 1973.

Chapter Seven

1 NunatuKavut, *Unveiling.*
2 William Gilbert Gosling, *Labrador: Its Discovery, Exploration, and Development* (London: A. Rivers, 1910).
3 Kennedy, *Encounters*, 111.
4 Ibid.
5 Ibid.
6 The NunatuKavut Inuit have been called various names, including "liveyers," "planters," "settlers," and, by the Moravian missionaries, "Southlanders." Many of these labels carried racist or derogatory connotations. So when asked to define themselves, NunatuKavut Inuit often focused on their relationship with the land, calling themselves "Labradorians." See NunatuKavut, *Unveiling*, 249–51, for more discussion on this topic.
7 Kennedy, *Encounters*, 154.
8 Ibid.
9 NunatuKavut, *Unveiling.*
10 Kennedy, *Encounters.*
11 Gosling, *Labrador.*
12 Ronald Rompkey, *Grenfell of Labrador: A Biography* (Montreal and Kingston: McGill-Queen's University Press, 2009), 38.
13 Letter by Francis Hopwood in *Toilers of the Deep*, quoted in James Lennox Kerr, *Wilfred Grenfell: His Life and Work* (New York: Dodd, Mead & Company, 1959), 51.
14 Rompkey, *Grenfell of Labrador.*
15 Ibid., ix.
16 Ibid.
17 Kennedy, *Encounters.*
18 Rompkey, *Grenfell of Labrador*, 179.
19 Ibid.; Ronald Rompkey, ed., *The Labrador Memoir of Dr Harry Paddon, 1912–1938* (Montreal and Kingston: McGill-Queen's University Press, 2003).
20 Rompkey, *Grenfell of Labrador*; xvi.
21 "Dr Grenfell's Heroic Work," *Among the Deep Sea Fishers* 1, no. 1 (April 1903): 5.
22 Evelyn Plaice, *The Native Game: Settler Perceptions of Indian/Settler Relations in Central Labrador* (St. John's: ISER Books, 1990).
23 Kennedy, *Encounters*, 231–33.
24 Rompkey, *Grenfell of Labrador*; Kerr, *Wilfred Grenfell*; Kennedy, *Encounters.*

25 Rompkey, *Grenfell of Labrador*, 175.
26 Gordon Thomas, *From Sled to Satellite: My Years with the Grenfell Mission* (Toronto: Irwin Publishing, 1987), 105.
27 Rompkey, *Grenfell of Labrador.*
28 Rompkey, *Labrador Memoir.*
29 Rompkey, *Grenfell of Labrador.*
30 In his biography of Wilfred Grenfell, Rompkey describes the origin of the "wop" term. In the early years of the Grenfell Mission, a spoiled young American complained that the manual work he was expected to do was only fit for "wops" — a derogatory term used at the time for Italian-American labourers. Grenfell replied that all Mission workers in Labrador were "wops," and that everyone was expected to do manual labour. He continued to use the term, but created the antecedent "without pay." Rompkey, *Grenfell of Labrador*, 243.
31 Kennedy, *Encounters.*
32 Kennedy, *Encounters*; Plaice, *Native Game.*
33 Rompkey, *Grenfell of Labrador,* 195.
34 *Periodical Accounts of the Moravian Missions* 3, no. 28 (1896): 175–76; Kerr, *Wilfred Grenfell.*
35 Wilfred Grenfell, *Forty Years for Labrador* (Boston: Houghton Mifflin, 1919), 157.
36 Ibid.
37 Ibid.
38 *Among the Deep Sea Fishers* 1, no. 4 (Jan. 1904): 31.
39 Francis Buckle, ed., *Labrador Diary, 1915–1925: The Gordon Journals* (St. John's: Print Atlantic, 2003), 209–12.
40 *Among the Deep Sea Fishers* 1, no. 4 (Jan. 1904): 22.
41 Ibid., 25.
42 Personal communication, Patty Way, 2018. As a child, Patty knew Kirkina in Happy Valley–Goose Bay.
43 Wilfred Grenfell, *A Labrador Doctor: The Autobiography of Wilfred Thomason Grenfell* (Boston: Houghton-Mifflin, 1919), 243.
44 Grenfell, *Forty Years for Labrador,* 156.
45 Ibid.
46 *Among the Deep Sea Fishers* 1, no. 2 (July 1903): 13–14.
47 Ibid. 1, no. 1 (Apr. 1903): 8.
48 Ibid. 1, no. 4 (Jan. 1904): 25.
49 Ibid.
50 Grenfell, *A Labrador Doctor*, 255.
51 Ibid.

52 *Among the Deep Sea Fishers* 56, no. 1 (Apr. 1958): 5.
53 Helen Woodrow, "Education at the Grenfell Mission in the 1920s," in *The Grenfell Medical Mission and American Support in Newfoundland and Labrador, 1890s–1940s*, ed. Jennifer Connor and Katherine Side (Montreal and Kingston: McGill-Queen's University Press, 2019), 180–219.
54 *Among the Deep Sea Fishers* 56, no. 1 (Apr. 1958).
55 Woodrow, "Education at the Grenfell Mission," 198.
56 Anne Grenfell quoted in Woodrow, "Education at the Grenfell Mission in the 1920s," 197.
57 Grenfell, *A Labrador Doctor*, 172–73.
58 The Register of Children for the St. Anthony orphanage lists James Shugalo [Shuglo] (born 1901) and William Shugalo [Shuglo] (born 1898) from Hamilton Inlet, admitted in September 1908 and only their mother as living (James Shugalo and William Shugalo, Register of Children, St. Anthony Children's Home, MG 63.4235, PANL).
59 Rompkey, *Grenfell of Labrador*, 234.
60 Rompkey, *Grenfell of Labrador*.
61 Grenfell, *Forty Years*, 160.
62 Grenfell, *A Labrador Doctor*, 176.

Chapter Eight

1 *Among the Deep Sea Fishers* 9, no. 2 (July 1911): 25.
2 Ibid. 3, no. 1 (Apr. 1905): 11.
3 Ibid. 3, no. 3 (Oct. 1905): 3.
4 Ronald Rompkey, ed., *Jessie Luther at the Grenfell Mission* (Montreal and Kingston: McGill-Queen's University Press, 2001), maps.
5 *Among the Deep Sea Fishers* 3, no. 3 (Oct. 1905): 4.
6 Ibid.
7 Emmeline "Emmie" Roberts, Register of Girls — St. Anthony Children's Home, MG 63.4233, PANL.
8 David Gill, St. Anthony Children's Home records, MG 63.4237, PANL; John Newell, Register of Boys — St. Anthony Children's Home, MG 63.4234, PANL.
9 Emmeline "Emmie" Roberts, Register of Girls — St. Anthony Children's Home, MG 63.4233, PANL.
10 Ibid.
11 After a year at the orphanage, John left to work for the Mission and fish with a

St. Anthony fisherman in the summer. In 1910, he started to work for and live with Wilfred Grenfell as his "boy," as he was "turning into quite a bright useful lad" (John Newell, Register of Boys — St. Anthony Children's Home, MG 63.4234, PANL). John later was sent to study at the Pratt Institute in New York and then returned to St. Anthony to run the IGA's St. Anthony Inn with his wife, Louisa Simms, until he died in 1959 (Rachel Brown, Horace McNeill, and Lincoln Brown, *Inasmuch: The Grenfell Mission — St. Anthony* [Winslow, ME: n.p., 1992], 36).

12 David Gill, Register of Boys — St. Anthony Children's Home, MG 63.4234, PANL. See Wilfred Grenfell's description of taking Davy Gill from his father later in this chapter (*Among the Deep Sea Fishers* 3, no. 4 [Jan. 1906]: 16).

13 Lizzie and her brother returned home at Christmas 1907 after their mother had remarried. Elizabeth "Lizzie" Hedderson, Register of Girls — St. Anthony Children's Home, MG 63.4233, PANL.

14 Hayward Patey, Register of Boys — St. Anthony Children's Home, MG 63.4234, PANL.

15 Grenfell, *A Labrador Doctor*, 250.

16 James Johnston, *Grenfell of Labrador* (London: S.W. Partridge & Co., 1908), 122. When she left the orphanage seven years later, Eleanor Storr helped to organize the London office of the International Grenfell Association, enlisting the help of Canon Storr and her cousin, Col. Otter-Barry (*Among the Deep Sea Fishers* 56, no. 4 (Jan. 1959): 116.

17 *Among the Deep Sea Fishers* 4, no. 2 (July 1906): 3.

18 Rompkey, *Jessie Luther*, 22. Eleanor Storr and Ethel Bayley had worked together at the Bermondsey Medical Mission for girls and women in East London before coming to St. Anthony.

19 Ibid., 24. Emmie later was sent to study dressmaking at the Pratt Institute in New York. She married Wilfred Mesher, another Grenfell graduate of the Pratt Institute from Labrador and the IGA's electrician, and settled in St. Anthony (Emmeline "Emmie" Roberts, Register of Girls — St. Anthony Children's Home, MG 63.4233, PANL).

20 Mae left the orphanage at 17 to study at a home economics school, MacDonald Institute in Guelph, Ontario (Lydia May Martin, Register of Girls — St. Anthony Children's Home, MG 63.4233, PANL).

21 *Them Days* 9, no. 1 (Sept. 1983): 20–21.

22 Grenfell, *A Labrador Doctor.*

23 Rompkey, *Jessie Luther*, 314 n. 146.

24 *Among the Deep Sea Fishers* 61, no. 1 (Apr. 1963): 6–7; ibid., 8, no. 4 (Jan. 1911): 6.

25 Report of Children's Home, 1917, Reports — St. Anthony Children's Home, MG 63.4238, PANL.

26 James Lennox Kerr, *Wilfred Grenfell: His Life and Work* (New York: Dodd, Mead & Company, 1959), 236.

27 Dr. Charles Curtis in Rompkey, *Grenfell of Labrador,* 194.

28 *Among the Deep Sea Fishers* 3, no. 4 (Jan. 1906): 16; David Gill, St. Anthony Children's Home Records, MG 63.4237, PANL.

29 *Among the Deep Sea Fishers* 3, no. 4 (Jan. 1906): 16.

30 Ibid.

31 Register of Girls — St. Anthony Children's Home, MG 63.4233; Register of Boys — St. Anthony Children's Home, MG 63.4234; St. Anthony Children's Home Records, MG 63.4237; Records St. Anthony Children's Home, MG 63.4239, PANL.

32 Ibid.

33 Elizabeth "Bessie" Blake, Register of Children — St. Anthony Children's Home, MG 63.4235, PANL.

34 Noah Karle, St. Anthony Children's Home records, MG 63.4237, PANL.

35 *Among the Deep Sea Fishers* 17, no. 4 (Jan. 1920): 140.

36 Anne Budgell, *We All Expected to Die: Spanish Influenza in Labrador, 1918–1919* (St. John's: ISER Books. 2018).

37 Ibid., 162, 271.

38 Edward Pardy interview, 1976, Them Days F056. Edward's interview and the IGA records for the Children's Home give conflicting information about which of the Pardy children were sent to St. Anthony. Edward said that Dr. Grenfell took Jim and Alvina, while the IGA records list Jim (James Levi) and Henry (Silas Henry) (Levi Pardy, Register of Boys — St. Anthony Children's Home, MG 63.4234, PANL). The IGA records also state that "there were 7 children in all. Eldest (girl) was with Sister Bailey. One girl with the grandmother, one with an aunt" (Silas Pardy, Register of Boys — St. Anthony Children's Home, MG 63.4234, PANL).

39 Register of Children — St. Anthony Children's Home, MG 63.4235, PANL; Budgell, *We All Expected to Die,* 141–42.

40 Katie and William left the orphanage the following summer (William Lethbridge, Register of Boys — St. Anthony Children's Home, MG 63.4234, PANL). Jim and Henry were sent to the Labrador Public School in Muddy Bay after three years at the orphanage (Register of Boys — St. Anthony Children's Home, MG 63.4234, PANL).

41 Budgell, *We All Expected to Die.*

42 Wilfred Grenfell to J.R. Bennett, 22 Aug. 1919, as quoted in Budgell, *We All Expected to Die*, 272.

43 *Among the Deep Sea Fishers* 20, no. 1 (July 1922): 52.

44 Katie Spalding and Anne Grenfell, *Le Petit Nord, or Annals of a Labrador Harbour* (Boston: Houghton Mifflin, 1920), 147.

45 *The Congregationalist and Advance* 103 (1918).

46 Ibid.

47 *Among the Deep Sea Fishers* 18, no. 4 (Jan. 1921): 166.

48 Ibid. 20, no. 2 (Oct. 1922): 79; see also ibid. 23, no. 3 (Oct. 1925): 113.

49 Ibid. 18, no. 3 (Oct. 1920): 131.

50 Ibid., 120.

51 Ibid. 20, no. 2 (Oct. 1922): 59.

52 Harriot Houghteling became a leader in children's education in St. Anthony and later married Dr. Charles Curtis, an American doctor and the superintendent of the IGA from 1936 to 1959. Harriot Curtis Collegiate, opened in 1964 in St. Anthony, was named in her honour.

53 *Among the Deep Sea Fishers* 21, no. 1 (Apr. 1923).

54 Millicent Blake Loder, *Daughter of Labrador* (St. John's: Harry Cuff Publications, 1989), 32–33.

55 *Among the Deep Sea Fishers* 32, no. 1 (Apr. 1934); ibid. 33, no. 1 (Apr. 1935); ibid. 45, no. 4 (Jan. 1948); Dr. Charles Curtis, Report to the Board of Directors, 1944, MG 63.2184, PANL; Dr. Charles Curtis, Report of Activities on the Coast, 1946 to the Board of Directors, MG 63.2184, PANL.

56 *Among the Deep Sea Fishers* 36, no. 1 (Apr. 1938): 10.

57 Brown, McNeill, and Brown, *Inasmuch*; *Them Days* 18, no. 1 (Oct. 1992): 28–33.

58 Brown, McNeill, and Brown, *Inasmuch*, 38–41.

59 *Among the Deep Sea Fishers* 43, no. 2 (July 1945).

60 Wall, *Wall Report*, 34, 42.

61 Grenfell, *A Labrador Doctor*, 178.

62 *Among the Deep Sea Fishers* 61, no. 1 (Apr. 1963): 6.

63 The school was named the Wilfred T. Grenfell School after 1917.

64 Grenfell, *A Labrador Doctor*, 181.

65 *Among the Deep Sea Fishers* 5, no. 3 (Oct. 1907): 5; Rompkey, *Jessie Luther*, 308 n. 69.

66 Rompkey, *Jessie Luther*, 99, 308 n. 69.

67 *Among the Deep Sea Fishers* 9, no. 2 (July 1911): 18.

68 Ibid., 5.

69 Ibid. 15, no. 4 (Jan. 1918): 160.

70 Ibid. 9, no. 2 (July 1911): 18.

71 Ibid. 18, no. 4 (Jan. 1921): 166.

72 Ibid. 17, no. 4 (Jan. 1920): 126.

73 Wilfred Grenfell quoted in Theodore L. Badger, "Why Sir Wilfred Grenfell?" *The North American Review* 226, no. 11 (July 1928): 14–21.

74 Grenfell, *Forty Years,* 167.

75 *Among the Deep Sea Fishers* 61, no. 1 (Apr. 1963): 6.

76 Grenfell, *A Labrador Doctor,* 261.

77 Ibid.

78 *Among the Deep Sea Fishers* 9, no. 2 (July 1911): 14.

79 Grenfell, *A Labrador Doctor,* 261.

80 *Among the Deep Seas Fishers* 20, no. 2 (Oct. 1922): 79.

81 Ibid. 20, no. 2 (Oct. 1922): 82.

82 Ibid.

83 Ibid. 61, no. 1 (Apr. 1963): 6.

84 Ibid. 30, no. 3 (Oct. 1932): 103.

85 Ibid., 102.

86 Ibid., 101.

87 Ibid. 40, no. 2 (July 1942): 36.

88 Ibid.

89 Ibid.

90 Ibid., 37.

91 Ibid. 55, no. 2 (July 1957): 40–41.

92 Stanley Hodge also grew up in the orphanage with his siblings. His widowed mother had moved the family from Savage Cove, Newfoundland, to St. Anthony so she could work at the orphanage (Brown, McNeill, and Brown, *Inasmuch*, 96).

93 *Among the Deep Sea Fishers* 54, no. 4 (Jan. 1957): 102.

94 *Periodical Accounts of the Moravian Missions* no. 166 (1958): 31–32.

95 Wall, *Wall Report,* 37.

96 Grenfell, *A Labrador Doctor,* 250. The boy from Cape Chidley was Bertie Lane, whose adoptive father, George Ford, a retired clerk at the HBC post in Nachvak, brought him to the Children's Home in 1910 after his wife had died (Bertie Lane, Register of Girls — St. Anthony Children's Home, MG 63.4233, PANL).

97 The IGA records for the Children's Home are housed at the Provincial Archives of Newfoundland and Labrador (The Rooms): Restricted Records: Children's Home, Educational Fund, Admissions and Case Books, MG 63.4233-4242, PANL.

98 Register of Children — St. Anthony Children's Home, MG 63.4235, PANL.

99 Ibid.

100 Ibid.

101 Ibid.

102 Ibid.

103 Register of Children — St. Anthony Children's Home, MG 63.4235, PANL.

104 The International Grenfell Association stipulates that the personal details in its records more than 100 years old at PANL can be disclosed, but not those in records less than 100 years old. No records less than 50 years old are available (Restricted Records: Children's Home, Educational Fund, Admissions and Case Books, MG 63.4233-4242, PANL).

105 *Among the Deep Sea Fishers* 28, no. 1 (Apr. 1930): 24. Complete lists of children who lived at the institutions explored in this book are rare.

106 The area between Batteau and Mary's Harbour was home to the Burden, Clarke, Cove, Dyson, Fequet, Lucy, Roberts, Rumboldt, Turnbull, and Ward families; Sandwich Bay names include Bird, Martin, and Learning; Hamilton Inlet and Groswater Bay names include Blake and Shiwak; and Nain area names are Ford and Webb.

107 Register of Girls — St. Anthony Children's Home, MG 63.4233; Register of Boys — St. Anthony Children's Home, MG 63.4234, PANL. The "quadred" term appears to describe someone with one Indigenous grandparent or a "quarter" Indigenous ancestry.

108 George Warren Morris (admitted 1919), Register of Boys — St. Anthony Children's Home, MG 63.4234, PANL.

109 Ibid.

110 Ibid. These average figures are based on incomplete records; although they are not exact, they can offer an idea of general trends.

111 Wall, *Wall Report.*

112 This percentage represents 103 of the 276 children admitted into the three IGA dormitories in 1959–60. The Cartwright dormitory heavily tilted this number. There, 90 per cent of the children (or 56 of the 62) came from the communities of Spotted Island, Batteau, and Seal Islands, which did not have schools (Wall, *Wall Report*, 40).

113 Sixty children of the 276 in the three IGA dormitories in 1959–60 (Wall, *Wall Report*, 40).

114 Of the 276 children, 41 had one deceased parent, "generally mother," and 28 came from "poor home condition[s]" (Wall, *Wall Report*, 40).

115 Twenty-seven of the 276 children (Wall, *Wall Report*, 40.)

116 These two groups consisted of nine children with medical needs and eight

children with special circumstances (Wall, *Wall Report*, 40).

117 *Among the Deep Sea Fishers* 28, no. 1 (Apr. 1930): 21–22.

118 St. Anthony Children's Home Records (D-K), MG 63.4237, PANL.

119 St. Anthony Children's Home Records (R-W), MG 63.4239, PANL.

120 Ibid.

121 *Among the Deep Sea Fishers* 49, no. 3 (Oct. 1951): 74.

122 Grenfell, *Forty Years*, 167.

123 *Among the Deep Sea Fishers* 20, no. 1 (July 1922): 45.

124 *Them Days* 9, no. 1 (Sept. 1983): 12–13.

125 Redgeway Snook in Battle Harbour Literary Council, *Linking the Generations: A Collection of Oral Histories. Excerpts from the Battle Harbour Region* (Mary's Harbour, NL: Battle Harbour Literacy Council, 1998), 62.

126 *Them Days* 19, no. 4 (1994): 33.

127 Ibid., 38, no. 4 (2014): 22–26.

128 Ibid., 26.

129 Ibid. 18, no. 1 (Oct. 1992): 28.

130 Ibid.

131 Ibid., 31.

132 Ibid. 23, no. 3 (Spring 1998): 34.

133 Ibid. 24, no. 4 (Summer 1999): 59–60. Bella returned to Labrador and worked as a housemother at the Grenfell dormitory in North West River for years.

134 Ibid. 20, no. 3 (Spring 1995): 36.

135 Joan Holmes & Associates, "Newfoundland and Labrador Schools — St. Anthony," Report for Andersen class action court case (St. John's, n.d.), 12, 18–19; *Among the Deep Sea Fishers* 51, no. 1 (Apr. 1953).

136 *Among the Deep Sea Fishers* 53, no. 4 (Jan. 1956): 101.

137 Fran Williams, Healing and Commemoration project, Nain, 13 Apr. 2018.

138 Laura Millie, Healing and Commemoration project, Nain, 13 Apr. 2018.

139 William Palliser, Healing and Commemoration project, North West River, 13 Mar. 2018.

140 Department of Public Welfare, *Annual Report* (St. John's: Government of Newfoundland, 1951), 41, PANL.

141 Gordon Thomas, Superintendents' Report to IGA Board of Directors for 1963, MG 63.2028, folder 2, Reports, surveys, etc., PANL; Department of Public Welfare, *Annual Report* (St. John's: Government of Newfoundland, 1959), PANL.

142 Rosina Holwell, Healing and Commemoration project, Nain, 14 Apr. 2018.

143 Ibid.

144 Ibid.

145 Ibid.

146 Enoch Obed, "From Nutak to Now," *kinatuinamot illengajuk* (Fall 1999): 44–47.

147 K. Naeme Merkuratsuk, Healing and Commemoration project, Nain, 12 Apr. 2018.

148 Ibid.

149 Register of Children — St. Anthony Children's Home, MG 63.4235, PANL.

150 Kerr, *Wilfred Grenfell*, 210.

151 Rompkey, *Grenfell of Labrador*, 208. 217.

152 *Among the Deep Sea Fishers* 17, no. 4 (Jan. 1920): 126.

153 St. Anthony Orphanage — Support of Children, n.d. [1930s], MG 63.232, St. Anthony, Nfld. (orphanage — endorsements, support, etc.), PANL.

154 *Among the Deep Sea Fishers* 36, no. 1 (Apr. 1938): 33.

155 Ibid. 31, no. 1 (Apr. 1933): 8; Brown, McNeill, and Brown, *Inasmuch*. When Elizabeth "Lizzie" Lucy Morrison was sent to the orphanage at St. Anthony, her mother had died and her father lived in northern Labrador (Patty Way, personal communication, 2018).

156 Brown, McNeill, and Brown, *Inasmuch*.

157 Register of Children — St. Anthony Children's Home, MG 63.4235, PANL.

158 Curtis: Supplementary and Final Report, MG 62.113; Curtis, Report of Activities on the Coast, 1946 to the Board of Directors, MG 63.2184, Reports of the coast: 1930, 1938–47, PANL.

159 Curtis, 1938 Report, MG 63.2184, Reports of the coast: 1930, 1938–47, PANL.

160 St. Anthony Children's Home records 1910–56, MG 63.4239, PANL.

161 St. Anthony Children's Home records, MG 63.4237, PANL.

162 Ibid.

163 Curtis: Supplementary and Final Report, MG 62.113, PANL.

164 Curtis: Report to the Board of Directors, IGA, 1945, MG 63.2184, Reports of the coast: 1930, 1938–47, PANL.

165 Curtis: Report to the Board of Directors, IGA, 1946, MG 63.2184, Reports of the coast: 1930, 1938–47, PANL.

166 Ibid.

167 Horace McNeill in Brown, McNeill, and Brown, *Inasmuch*, 51.

168 Curtis, 1950 Confidential Report to the Board of Directors, MG 62.113, PANL.

169 *Among the Deep Sea Fishers* 49, no. 3 (Oct. 1951): 74.

170 Dr. Gordon Thomas, Report to the Board of Directors, 1960, MG 63.113, PANL.

171 Annual Report of the Department of Public Welfare, 1960, PANL.

172 Wall, *Wall Report*; Gordon Thomas, "International Grenfell Association," in

Some Briefs submitted to the Royal Commission on Education and Youth (St. John's: Royal Commission on Education and Youth, 1967).

173 Smallwood, Erection and Equipment Regional and Central H Schools, Feb. 1958, 193.7.03.002, MUN Archives.

174 Dr. Thomas to Hefferton, Minister of Education, 20 June 1952, PRC 10, Box 21B, File 77/25, Vol. I, PANL; Dr. Thomas to Rowe, 2 May 1953, 077.1.01.025, Correspondence International Grenfell Association 1952–55, MUN Archives.

175 As Dr. Paddon wrote in his 1963 Report to the Superintendents, "The Province cannot and will not involve itself in running a dormitory" (MG 63.2028, folder 2, Reports, surveys, etc., PANL).

176 Gordon Thomas to Alain Frecker, 8 June 1961, PRC 10, Temp Box 21(B), File 77/25 Vol. V, PANL.

177 Wall, *Wall Report*, 48.

178 Minutes of a Meeting of the Executive and Finance Committees of the International Grenfell Association, 7 Dec. 1962, 3, MG 63.2881, PANL.

179 Superintendents' Report to Board of Directors, 1963, MG 63.2028, folder 2, Reports, surveys, etc., PANL.

180 Houghton to Dr. Frecker, 30 June 1964, PRC 10, Temp Box 21(B), File 77/25, Vol. V, PANL.

181 Dr. Thomas to Paddon, 30 May 1964, MG 63.3066, North West River — folder 6, PANL.

182 *Them Days* 41, no. 3 (2017): 10–11.

183 International Grenfell Association Meeting of the Executive Committee Held in the Rideau Club, Ottawa, Canada on February 3rd, 1969, MG 63.2881, PANL.

184 *Among the Deep Sea Fishers* 75, no. 3 (Oct. 1978): 6–12.

185 Gordon Thomas, "The International Grenfell Association: Its Role in Northern Newfoundland and Labrador, Part 1: The Early Days," *Canadian Medical Association Journal* 118 (4 Feb. 1978): 308.

Chapter Nine

1 Bishop of Newfoundland to Earl Grey, St. John's, Newfoundland, 26 Oct. 1848, Privy Council, Labrador Boundary Dispute Documents, no. 361.

2 Ibid.

3 B. Sweetland, "Report of Judge Sweetland of Proceedings of Labrador Court during the summer of 1864, etc., together with census returns of resident

population Blanc Sablon to Indian Harbor, 1864," Privy Council, Labrador Boundary Dispute Documents, no. 529; Robert John Pinsent, "Report of Robert J. Pinsent, Esq., Judge of the Court of Labrador to his Excellency the Governor, December 31th, 1868," Privy Council, Labrador Boundary Dispute Documents, no. 534.

4 Kennedy, *Encounters*.

5 Ibid.

6 R.J. Pinsent, "Report of Robert J. Pinsent, Esq., Judge of the Court of Labrador to his Excellency Steven John Hill, Esq., C.B., Governor of Newfoundland, etc., 27 November 1869," Privy Council, Labrador Boundary Dispute Documents, no. 535.

7 *Among the Deep Sea Fishers* 20, no. 4 (Jan. 1922): 117. One teacher, Helen Coffin, who taught in Batteau, describes how she found only four nine-year-old children to teach. She started with kindergarten work, but soon found that there was a greater demand for her first aid skills in the community, so she gave up teaching regular hours (*Among the Deep Sea Fishers* 21, no. 1 [Apr. 1923]: 22).

8 Ibid. 56, no. 1 (Apr. 1958): 7.

9 Francis Buckle, ed., *Labrador Teacher: Clara Gordon's Journal* (St. John's: Anglican Parish of Cartwright, 2005), x.

10 Henry Gordon, *The Labrador Parson: Journal of the Reverend Henry Gordon, 1915–1925*, ed. F. Burnham Gill (St. John's: Provincial Archives of Newfoundland, 1972).

11 Gordon, *The Labrador Parson*, 51.

12 Ibid.

13 Ibid., 139.

14 *Among the Deep Sea Fishers* 16, no. 2 (July 1918): 48; Gordon, *The Labrador Parson*; Francis Buckle, ed., *Labrador Diary, 1915–1925: The Gordon Journals* (St. John's: Print Atlantic, 2003).

15 Henry Gordon to A. Mews, Deputy Colonial Secretary, 15 Nov. 1920, GN 2.5.396, Box 57, Special File: Labrador Public Schools Inc., PANL.

16 Gordon, *The Labrador Parson*.

17 Ibid., 122.

18 Henry Gordon to Clara Ashall, 1918, in Buckle, *Labrador Teacher*, ix.

19 Maria Montessori was an Italian doctor who developed a child-centred approach to education that encourages creativity and child-driven inquiry. Her methods were popular in the 1910s, and were later revived in the 1950s (Canadian Council of Montessori Administrators: http://www.ccma.ca/).

20 Buckle, ed., *Labrador Teacher*, 1.

21 Gordon, *The Labrador Parson*, 117.

22 Budgell, *We All Expected to Die*, 162, 271.

23 Ibid., 248–54.

24 Gordon, *The Labrador Parson*, 144–45.

25 Ibid., 152.

26 Harry Paddon in Rompkey, *Labrador Memoir*, xxvi–xxvii.

27 Henry Gordon, *A Winter in Labrador 1918–1919: Journal of the Rev. Henry Gordon, Cartwright, Labrador* (New York: Published by the author, 1919), 68–69.

28 *Among the Deep Sea Fishers* 17, no. 3 (Oct. 1919): 95.

29 Ibid.

30 Gordon, *The Labrador Parson*, 149.

31 Ibid.

32 Budgell, *We All Expected to Die*, 272.

33 Rev. Henry Gordon, 1919, quoted in Budgell, *We All Expected to Die*, 249.

34 Gordon, *The Labrador Parson*, 251.

35 Ibid.; Buckle, ed., *Labrador Diary*.

36 Registration of Labrador Public Schools under the Newfoundland Companies Act, 17 July 1920, GN 2.5.396, Box 57, Special File: Labrador Public Schools Inc., PANL; Gordon, *The Labrador Parson*, 165.

37 Gordon, *The Labrador Parson*, 151.

38 Birdseye famously went on to develop the multi-million dollar frozen food industry, based on his observations of how NunatuKavut Inuit froze country food for storage in the winter (Buckle, ed., *Labrador Diary*).

39 Gordon, *The Labrador Parson*, 162.

40 Buckle, ed., *Labrador Teacher*, 30.

41 Ibid., 31.

42 Gordon, *The Labrador Parson*, 170–71.

43 Ibid., 173.

44 Buckle, ed., *Labrador Teacher*.

45 Gordon, *The Labrador Parson*, 173.

46 *Among the Deep Sea Fishers* 19, no. 1 (Apr. 1921): 24.

47 Buckle, ed., *Labrador Diary*. "Part orphan" means that the child has lost one parent.

48 *Among the Deep Sea Fishers* 20, no. 1 (July 1922): 48.

49 Gordon, *The Labrador Parson*, 161.

50 Buckle, ed., *Labrador Teacher*, 41.

51 Ibid.

52 *Among the Deep Sea Fishers* 19, no. 1 (Apr. 1921): 25.

53 Buckle, ed., *Labrador Teacher*, 42.

54 Buckle, ed., *Labrador Diary*, 142.

55 *Among the Deep Sea Fishers* 19, no. 1 (Apr. 1921): 25.

56 Buckle, ed., *Labrador Teacher.*

57 Gordon, *The Labrador Parson*, 185.

58 *Among the Deep Sea Fishers* 19, no. 1 (Apr. 1921): 25.

59 Ibid. 19, no. 4 (Jan. 1922): 137.

60 Ibid. 19, no. 1 (Apr. 1921): 25–26.

61 Gordon, *The Labrador Parson*, 206.

62 *Among the Deep Sea Fishers* 21, no. 1 (Apr. 1923): 18.

63 Ibid. 20, no. 2 (Oct. 1922): 83.

64 Ibid. 23, no. 2 (July 1925): 71.

65 Buckle, ed., *Labrador Teacher*, 40.

66 *Among the Deep Sea Fishers* 19, no. 1 (Apr. 1921): 26.

67 Mews, Deputy Colonial Secretary, to O'Dwyer, Commissioner of Public Charities, 1 Nov. 1920, GN 2.5.396, Box 57, Special File: Labrador Public Schools Inc., PANL.

68 *Among the Deep Sea Fishers* 19, no. 2 (July 1921): 55.

69 Gordon, *The Labrador Parson*, 199–200.

70 Ibid., 200.

71 Buckle, ed., *Labrador Teacher*, 109.

72 *Among the Deep Sea Fishers* 32, no. 3 (Oct. 1934): 115; ibid. 34, no. 3 (Oct. 1936): 92.

73 Ibid. 35, no. 1 (Apr. 1937): 18.

74 Ibid. 19, no. 1 (Apr. 1921): 25.

75 Gordon, *The Labrador Parson*, 110.

76 *Among the Deep Sea Fishers* 25, no. 3 (Oct. 1927): 112.

77 Buckle, ed., *Labrador Diary*, vi.

78 Miriam Hamel, Them Days interview F074, Mar. 1975.

79 Ida Sheppard, Them Days interview F039, 1976.

80 *Among the Deep Sea Fishers* 24, no. 3 (Oct. 1926): 102.

81 Ibid. 20, no. 1 (July 1922): 45; ibid. 18, no. 2 (July 1920); 21, ibid. no. 1 (Apr. 1923).

82 Ibid. 24, no. 2 (July 1926): 71.

83 Harry Paddon quoted in Rompkey, *The Labrador Memoir*, 191.

84 Harry Paddon quoted ibid., 172.

85 Millicent Loder, *Them Days* 5, no. 1 (1979): 39.

86 Miriam Hamel, Them Days interview F074, 1975.

87 Millicent Loder, *Them Days* 5, no. 1 (1979): 39–40.

88 Patty Way, personal communication, 2019.

89 *Among the Deep Sea Fishers* 26, no. 1 (Apr. 1928).

90 Ibid. 26, no. 2 (July 1928): 96.

91 Mrs. Lockwood had previously donated $5,000 to the Grenfell Mission in 1915, which was used to build a cottage hospital in North West River named the Emily Beaver Chamberlin Memorial Hospital as a memorial to her mother (ibid. 27, no. 4 (Jan. 1930): 162; ibid. 38, no. 3 (Oct. 1940): 81).

92 Ibid. 27, no. 4 (Jan. 1930): 150.

93 Harry Paddon in Rompkey, *The Labrador Memoir*, 216.

94 *Among the Deep Sea Fishers* 27, no. 3 (Oct. 1929): 105.

95 Ibid., 108.

96 Ibid. 27, no. 4 (Jan. 1930): 150.

97 Ibid. 29, no. 4 (Jan. 1932): 172.

98 Ibid. 30, no. 3 (Oct. 1932); ibid. 31, no. 4 (Jan. 1934).

99 Ibid. 29, no. 1 (Apr. 1931): 23.

100 Ibid. 28, no. 1 (Apr. 1930).

101 Millicent Loder, *Them Days* 5, no. 1 (1979): 40.

102 *Among the Deep Sea Fishers* 28, no. 2 (July 1930): 92.

103 Ibid.

104 Ibid. 29, no. 1 (Apr. 1931): 14; ibid. 30, no. 2 (July 1932): 81.

105 Ibid. 29, no. 3 (Oct. 1931): 111.

106 Lewis Brown, *Them Days* 25, no. 1 (Fall 1999): 24.

107 *Among the Deep Sea Fishers* 32, no. 2 (July 1934): 71.

108 Chesley Lethbridge, Them Days interview F725, 1999.

109 Lockwood School log written by Ewart Young, principal, 1935–36, APL 3/3, File 2, Them Days Archive.

110 Ibid.

111 Ibid.

112 *Among the Deep Sea Fishers* 37, no. 4 (Jan. 1940): 128.

113 Gary Elson, *Them Days* 25, no. 1 (Fall 1999): 27.

114 *Among the Deep Sea Fishers* 37, no. 4 (Jan. 1940).

115 Kennedy, *Encounters*.

116 Wall, *Wall Report*, 40.

117 Ibid.

118 *Among the Deep Sea Fishers* (Oct. 1942).

119 Gerald Day, Report on visit to Southern Labrador, Nov. 1952, PRC 10, Temp Box 21(B), File 77/25, Vol. I, p. 5, PANL.

120 Kennedy, *Encounters*, 277.
121 Millicent Blake Loder, *Daughter of Labrador* (St. John's: Harry Cuff Publications, 1989), 27.
122 Ethel Campbell, Healing and Commemoration project, Rigolet, 15 May 2018.
123 Betti Mesher Broomfield, *Them Days* 25, no. 1 (Fall 1999): 26.
124 Chesley Lethbridge, Them Days interview F725, 1999.
125 Anonymous interview, Healing and Commemoration project, Cartwright, 14 Feb. 2018.
126 Ibid.
127 Ibid.
128 Jane Dyson Light, Healing and Commemoration project, Cartwright, 14 Feb. 2018.
129 Ibid.
130 Hazel Williams Beaulac, Healing and Commemoration project, Happy Valley–Goose Bay, 10 Mar. 2018.
131 Bertha Chaulk, "Coombs Family History," *Them Days* 33, no. 1 (2009): 28–31.
132 John Webber, Them Days interview F730, 1999.
133 Ibid.
134 *Among the Deep Sea Fishers* 28, no. 3 (Oct. 1930): 111.
135 Victor Mesher, *Them Days* 25, no. 1 (Fall 1999): 32.
136 Bella Learning Gear, *Them Days* 25, no. 1 (Fall 1999): 34.
137 Bill Pardy, *Them Days* 25, no. 1 (Fall 1999): 33.
138 John Webber, *Them Days* 25, no. 1 (Fall 1999): 51.
139 Chesley Lethbridge, *Them Days* 25, no. 1 (Fall 1999): 51.
140 Bill Pardy, *Them Days* 25, no. 1 (Fall 1999): 51.
141 Chesley Lethbridge, Them Days interview F725, 1999.
142 Anonymous, Healing and Commemoration project, Cartwright, 14 Feb. 2018.
143 Jane Shiwak, Healing and Commemoration project, Rigolet, 15 May 2018.
144 Ibid.
145 Forsyth in Curtis: Annual report and comments on the activities of the coast, 1938–39, MG 63.2184, PANL.
146 Charles Curtis, Supplementary and Final Report, 1943, MG 63.113, PANL.
147 Chesley Lethbridge, Them Days interview F725, 1999.
148 Gary Elson, *Them Days* 25, no. 1 (Fall 1999): 31.
149 Loder, *Daughter of Labrador*, 30.
150 Avis Lethbridge Kremer, *Them Days* 25, no. 1 (Fall 1999): 37.
151 Emily Bird, Them Days interview F739, 1999.
152 Victor Mesher, Them Days interview F728, 1996.

153 Josie Curl Penny, *So Few on Earth: A Labrador Métis Woman Remembers* (Toronto: Dundurn Press, 2010), 307.
154 Jane Dyson Light, Healing and Commemoration project, Cartwright, 14 Feb. 2018.
155 Clayre Forsyth, "Lockwood at Play," *Lockwood Magazine* (Nov. 1943), APL 3/3 File 1, Them Days Archive.
156 Chesley Lethbridge, *Them Days* 25, no. 1 (Fall 1999): 58.
157 Raymond Mesher, *Them Days* 25, no. 1 (Fall 1999): 60.
158 Jane Dyson Light, Healing and Commemoration project, Cartwright, 14 Feb. 2018.
159 William Max Clarke, Healing and Commemoration project, St. John's, 28 Apr. 2018.
160 Chesley Lethbridge, Them Days interview F725, 1999.
161 *Among the Deep Sea Fishers* 31, no. 4 (Jan. 1934): 167.
162 Ibid. 37, no. 4 (Jan. 1940): 131.
163 Betty Lloyd Chatham, *Them Days* 25, no. 1 (Fall 1999): 11.
164 Martha Davis Compton, Them Days interview F732, 1996.
165 Penny, *So Few on Earth*, 114.
166 Josie Curl Penny, Healing and Commemoration project, Ottawa, 3 Mar. 2018.
167 Jane Dyson Light, Healing and Commemoration project, Cartwright, 14 Feb. 2018.
168 Raymond Dyson, Healing and Commemoration project, Cartwright, 15 Feb. 2018.
169 *Among the Deep Sea Fishers* 31, no. 4 (Jan. 1934): 177.
170 Rompkey, *Grenfell of Labrador*.
171 Grenfell Mission Report of Activities on the Coast, 1946, to the Board of Directors, MG 63.2184, PANL.
172 *Among the Deep Sea Fishers* 37, no. 4 (Jan. 1940).
173 Forsyth in Curtis: Annual report and comments on the activities of the coast, 1938–39. MG 63.2184, PANL.
174 Curtis: Annual report and comments on the activities of the coast, 1938–39.
175 *Among the Deep Sea Fishers* 40, no. 3 (Oct. 1942).
176 Martha Davis Compton, *Them Days* 25, no. 1 (Fall 1999): 22.
177 Chesley Lethbridge, Them Days interview F725, 1999.
178 Emily Bird, Them Days interview F739, 1999.
179 Penny, *So Few on Earth*, 106–07.
180 Charles Curtis, Supplementary and Final Report, 1943, MG 63.113, PANL.
181 Sarah Elson Holwell, *Them Days* 25, no. 1 (Fall 1999): 3.

182 Chesley Lethbridge, Them Days interview F725.

183 Charles Curtis, Supplementary and Final Report to the Board of Directors, IGA, MG 63.113, Charles Curtis, Superintendent, PANL; Charles Curtis, "The Superintendent Reports," *Among the Deep Sea Fishers* 45, no. 4 (Jan. 1948): 110.

184 W.A. Paddon, "Some Educational Problems in Labrador," 1953, PRC 10, Temp Box 21(B), File 77/25, Vol. I, Grenfell Public School Board, PANL.

185 Ibid.

186 Gerald Day, Report on visit to Southern Labrador, November 1952, PRC 10, Temp Box 21(B), File 77/25, Vol. I, PANL.

187 Ibid., p. 5.

188 Ibid., p. 4.

189 Order-in-Council #87-'52, Newfoundland Executive Council, 26 Jan. 1952, PRC 10, Temp Box 21(B), File 77/25, Vol. I, PANL.

190 Charles Curtis to Hon. J.L. Chalker, Minister of Education, 7 May 1956, PRC 10, Temp Box 21(B), File 77/25, Vol. III, Grenfell Public School Board, PANL.

191 Telegram from Paddon to Frecker, Deputy Minister of Education, 26 Aug. 1957, PRC 10, Temp Box 21(B), File 77/25, Vol. III, Grenfell Public School Board, PANL.

192 Deputy Minister, Education, to Accountant, IGA, 21 Oct. 1958, PRC 10, Temp Box 21(B), File 77/25, Vol. IV, Grenfell Public School Board, PANL.

193 Unidentified speaker, Healing and Commemoration project, Cartwright, 14 Feb. 2018.

194 Ibid.

195 Tony Paddon to Gordon Thomas, 20 Nov. 1959, MG 63.3066.1, PANL.

196 Ibid.

197 Tony Paddon to Gordon Thomas, 10 July 1959, MG 63.3066.1, PANL.

198 Telegram from Dr. Thomas to Paddon, 16 June 1960; Paddon to Curtis, 11 May 1960, MG 63.3066.2, PANL.

199 Francis Buckle, *The Anglican Church in Labrador, 1848–1998* (Labrador City, NL: Archdeaconry of Labrador, 1998), 114–15.

200 Paddon to Curtis, 24 Mar. 1962, MG 63.3066.3, PANL.

201 John Newfoundland, Bishop's Court, St. John's, to Justice D.C. Abbott, Chairman, Grenfell Labrador Medical Mission, Ottawa, 30 Nov. 1961, MG 63.1881, PANL.

202 Buckle, *The Anglican Church*, 115.

203 Gordon Thomas, Superintendent's Report, April 1963 for 1962, MG 63.2028, folder 2, Reports, surveys, etc., PANL.

204 Gordon Thomas, Superintendent's Report, Dec. 1964, MG 63.2028.2, PANL.

205 Ibid.

206 Frank Houghton, IGA, to Department of Education, 12 Dec. 1965, PRC 10, Temp Box 21(B), File 77/25, Vol. 5, PANL.

207 Correspondence re: Cartwright Dormitory library: 28 Mar. 1963–16 Feb. 1966, MG 63.24, PANL.

208 Letter from Millicent J. Davis (Mrs.), Cartwright, to Premier Smallwood, 1966, 075.1.25.009, Memorial University Archives.

Chapter Ten

1 Kennedy, *Encounters.*

2 Ibid., 238.

3 Ibid.

4 Ibid.

5 International Grenfell Association Act 1932, APL 3/17, Them Days Archive.

6 *Among the Deep Sea Fishers* 29, no. 3 (Oct. 1931); ibid. 31, no. 4 (Jan. 1934).

7 Ibid. 28, no. 2 (July 1930): 54.

8 Ibid. 28, no. 4 (Jan. 1931): 183. Frances Conrow later married Hayward Pye from Cape St. Charles/Lodge Bay (Eva and Bert Coish, Them Days interview F442, 1982).

9 *Among the Deep Sea Fishers* 29, no. 3 (Oct. 1931): 123–24.

10 Ibid. 31, no. 2 (July 1933): 79.

11 Gerald Day, Report on visit to Southern Labrador, Nov. 1952, PRC 10, Temp Box 21(B), File 77/25, Vol. I, PANL.

12 *Among the Deep Sea Fishers* 31, no. 2 (July 1933): 81.

13 Ibid.

14 Ibid.

15 Ibid. 29, no. 1 (Apr. 1931): 14.

16 Ibid. 31, no. 2 (July 1933): 83.

17 Eva Coish, "School Days," *Them Days* 10, no. 3 (Mar. 1985): 52–53.

18 *Among the Deep Sea Fishers* 31, no. 4 (Jan. 1934).

19 Ibid., 177e.

20 Ibid.

21 Ibid. 31, no. 2 (July 1933): 83.

22 Ibid.

23 Eva Coish, "School Day Memories," in *Linking the Generations: A Collection of Oral Histories. Excerpts from the Battle Harbour Region* (Mary's Harbour, NL:

Battle Harbour Literary Council, 1998), 58.

24 *Among the Deep Sea Fishers* 31, no. 4 (Jan. 1934); ibid. 32, no. 4 (Jan. 1935); ibid. 35, no. 1 (Apr. 1937); ibid. 36, no. 3 (Oct. 1938).

25 Ibid. 30, no. 3 (Oct. 1934); ibid. 34, no. 3 (Oct. 1936).

26 Ibid. 30, no. 3 (Oct. 1934); ibid. 34, no. 2 (July 1936): 67; ibid. 35, no. 2 (July 1937): 68.

27 Ibid. 31, no. 2 (July 1933): 84.

28 Kennedy, *Encounters*, 233.

29 Ibid.

30 *Among the Deep Sea Fishers* 36, no. 2 (July 1938): 60; Dr. Charles Curtis, Annual Report and Comment on the Activities on the Coast, 1938–39, MG 63.2184, Reports of the coast: 1930, 1938–47, PANL.

31 *The Lockwood Magazine* (Nov. 1938), APL 3/3, File 1, Them Days Archive; *Among the Deep Sea Fishers* 37, no. 4 (Jan. 1940).

32 Dr. Charles Curtis, Annual Report of the Superintendent to the Board of Directors, International Grenfell Association, 1942, MG 63.311, Charles Curtis, Superintendent, PANL.

33 Ibid.

34 *Among the Deep Sea Fishers* 56, no. 1 (Apr. 1958): 8.

35 Kennedy, *Encounters.*

36 Mary Acreman, "Teaching in the Early Years," in *Linking the Generations: A Collection of Oral Histories. Excerpts from the Battle Harbour Region* (Mary's Harbour, NL: Battle Harbour Literary Council, 1998), 55–58.

Chapter Eleven

1 Labrador Circuit Judge Pinsent reported in 1867 that many people of Eskimo Bay (Lake Melville) could read: "They are very docile and well behaved, and in their simple way, fond of learning; most of them can read, and some can write — taught by the fathers and by each other" (P.C. No. 533:1454, quoted in David Zimmerly, *Cain's Land Revisited: Culture Change in Central Labrador, 1775–1972* (St. John's: ISER Books, 1975), 122.

2 Zimmerly, *Cain's Land.*

3 John Montague, Them Days interview F076, 12 Dec. 1965.

4 Edna Campbell, Them Days interview F143, 1977.

5 Bella McLean Shouse in Labrador Institute, "Court House Mug-Up (Justice Theme)" (Happy Valley–Goose Bay, NL: Labrador Institute, 2005), 13.

6 *Among the Deep Sea Fishers* 12, no. 4 (Jan. 1915): 139.

7 Ibid. 10, no. 4 (Jan. 1913): 5.

8 Ibid. 12, no. 2 (July 1914): 55.

9 Ibid. 14, no. 3 (Oct. 1916): 105.

10 Ibid.

11 Ibid. 10, no. 4 (Jan. 1913): 5.

12 Ibid. 13, no. 4 (Jan. 1916): 152.

13 Ibid. 14, no. 3 (Oct. 1916): 104; ibid. 24, no. 4 (Jan. 1927): 145.

14 Shouse in Labrador Institute, "Court House Mug-Up," 13.

15 Rompkey, *The Labrador Memoir*, 192.

16 Ibid.

17 Wilfred Grenfell wrote afterwards, "I want to thank every wop and wopess, as these magnificent workers have labeled themselves, for their contribution to progress while our people are so discouraged. Wherever they go they bring in that irrepressible joie de vivre which is infinitely valuable but apt to be underrated. . . . Metaphorically I stand bareheaded before those who dug the Cartwright waterway, those who built the Yale School at Northwest River" (*Among the Deep Sea Fishers* 31, no. 4 [Jan. 1934]: 155–56).

18 Ibid. 24, no. 4 (Jan. 1927): 145.

19 Shouse in Labrador Institute, "Court House Mug-Up," 13.

20 Alfreda Davis Blake, *Them Days* 9, no. 1 (Sept. 1983): 8–10.

21 Ibid.

22 *Among the Deep Sea Fishers* 26, no. 4 (Jan. 1929): 181.

23 Ibid. 32, no. 2 (July 1934): 77; ibid. 26, no. 4 (Jan. 1929): 181.

24 Ibid. 37, no. 4 (Jan. 1940): 127; Curtis and Paddon, 9 Dec. 1950, Confidential Report to the Board of Directors, MG 63.113, PANL.

25 In 1927–28, Yale School had 14 boarders of the total 47 pupils (*Among the Deep Sea Fishers* 25, no. 3 [Oct. 1927]); in 1930–31, it had 34 boarders of the total 69 students (ibid. 29, no. 4 [Jan. 1932]); in 1940–41, 35 boarders were part of the 63 total students at the school (ibid. 38, no. 3 [Oct. 1940]).

26 Rompkey, *The Labrador Memoir*, 195.

27 Ibid.

28 Rompkey, *The Labrador Memoir*, 195–96.

29 Charles Curtis, "Annual Report of the Superintendent," 1942, MG 63.113, Charles Curtis, Superintendent, PANL.

30 Harry Paddon, North West River in 1934. MG 63.2184, PANL. The July 1934 issue of *Among the Deep Sea Fishers* reports that the staff at the school consisted of Blanche Davis (Sandwich Bay), teacher; Bella Butt (East St

Modeste) and Ethel Pye (Cape Charles), housemothers; Sarah Sharpe (Newfoundland), teacher; and Marjorie Beard (Connecticut), principal.

31 Woodrow, "Education at the Grenfell Mission in the 1920s."

32 *Among the Deep Sea Fishers* 25, no. 1 (Apr. 1927): 32.

33 Ibid. 29, no. 4 (Jan. 1932): 160.

34 Elizabeth Blake Osmond, in Healing Journey Team, "Gathering the Stories" (Happy Valley–Goose Bay, NL: Labrador Aboriginal Legal Services, 2010).

35 Jean Blake Crane, ibid.

36 Rompkey, *The Labrador Memoir*, 82.

37 *Among the Deep Sea Fishers* 41, no. 2 (July 1943): 41; ibid. 40, no. 4 (Jan. 1943): 104.

38 Ibid. 46, no. 4 (Jan. 1949): 107.

39 Ibid. 45, no. 3 (Oct. 1947): 87.

40 Ibid. 46, no. 4 (Jan. 1949): 107. The Department of Education contributed $30,000 for the school and the IGA contributed $8,000.

41 Ibid. 46, no. 4 (Jan. 1949): 107.

42 Dr. Anthony Paddon in 1950 (9 Dec.) Confidential Report to the Board of Directors (Curtis with info from Paddon), MG 63.113, PANL.

43 Polly Taylor to her father, Herbert W. Taylor, Haverford, PA, 9 Dec. 1952, MG 166, PANL.

44 Wall, *Wall Report*, 60.

45 *Among the Deep Sea Fishers* 46, no. 4 (Jan. 1949): 107; ibid. 38, no. 3 (Oct. 1940); S.J. Hefferton, Minister of Education, Memorandum to Executive Council of Provincial Government: Request from North West River, Labrador, for Extra Teacher, 13 Mar. 1952, PRC 10, Temp Box 21(B), File 77/25, Vol. IV, PANL; Wall, *Wall Report*, 42.

46 *Among the Deep Sea Fishers* 40, no. 3 (Oct. 1942): 81.

47 Rompkey, *The Labrador Memoir*, 230.

48 Ibid., 128.

49 Ibid., 230.

50 *Among the Deep Sea Fishers* 40, no. 3 (Oct. 1942): 81.

51 Andrews, Superintendent, to Minister of Education, 7 Mar. 1951, PRC 10, Temp Box 21(B), File 77/25, Vol. I, Grenfell Public School Board, PANL.

52 Rowe, *Development of Education;* Hector Swain, *Lester Leeland Burry: Labrador Parson and Father of Confederation* (St. John's: Harry Cuff Publications, 1983), 34.

53 W.A. Paddon, Some Educational Problems in Labrador, 1953, PRC 10, Temp Box 21(B), File 77/25, Vol. I, Grenfell Public School Board, PANL.

54 Ibid., p. 7.

55 Guy Fowlow, Report on the Educational Setup of the Sandwich Bay Mission, Labrador, in the Diocese of Newfoundland, 29 Sept. 1951, PRC 9, Box 7433, File 75, Vol. VI, Moravian Mission and Northern Labrador, PANL.

56 Paddon, Some Educational Problems in Labrador, 1953, p. 7.

57 Dr. Anthony Paddon, in Confidential Report to the Board of Directors (Curtis with info from Paddon), 9 Dec. 1950, MG 63.113, PANL.

58 Paddon to P.J. Hanley, Deputy Minister of Education, 20 Jan. 1965, PRC 10, Temp Box 21(B), File 77/25, Vol. V, PANL.

59 Ibid.

60 Paddon to Frecker, 18 Oct. 1955, PRC 10, Temp Box 21(B), File 77/25, Vol. II, PANL.

61 Anthony Paddon, *Labrador Doctor* (Toronto: J. Lorimer, 1989), 176.

62 Wall, *Wall Report.*

63 Polly Taylor to her father, Herbert W. Taylor, Haverford, PA, 9 Nov. 1952.

64 Rompkey, *Grenfell of Labrador.*

65 See *North Wind* 2, no. 1: 2, in *Among the Deep Sea Fishers* 34, no. 3 (Oct. 1936), for letters by Charlie Rich (age 16), Hayward Groves (age 12), Arthur Williams (age 14), and Leonard Shepherd (age 11).

66 Paddon, in Confidential Report to the Board of Directors, 9 Dec. 1950.

67 Rompkey, *Grenfell of Labrador.*

68 Kevin Bell, "Lake Melville High School: Developments in North West River's Education System from 1925–1979" (North West River, n.d.), Centre for Newfoundland Studies, MUN.

69 Paddon, *Labrador Doctor.*

70 Ibid., 176.

71 In 1953, Dr. Paddon described how "several children spent a total of nearly forty months at Mission expense at North West River and attended no classes" because the teachers had refused to take any more children into their classrooms. W.A. Paddon, Some Educational Problems in Labrador, 1953, p. 3, PRC 10, Temp Box 21(B), File 77/25, Vol. I, PANL.

72 Wall, *Wall Report*, 38; Charles Curtis, Report to the IGA Board of Directors, 1961, PRC 10, Temp Box 21(B), File 77/25, Vol. V, Grenfell Public School Board, PANL.

73 Report on visit to Southern Labrador, Gerald Day, Nov. 1952, p. 2, PRC 10, Temp Box 21(B), File 77/25, Vol. I, PANL.

74 Annual Report of the Department of Education, 1953–54, MUN Archives.

75 In 1950, for example, the dormitories cost $9,358.42 (gross), while the IGA received $1,587.48 in fees for children's board. Curtis to Hefferton, 4 Oct. 1951,

PRC 10, Temp Box 21(B), File 77/25, Vol. I. In 1953–54, the gross cost of running the dormitory was $25,259.94, while the IGA received $2,350.24 in boarding fees. Paddon to Frecker, 16 Nov. 1955, PRC 10, Temp Box 21(B), File 77/25, Vol. II. In 1959 (January to December), gross cost of running the dormitory was $35,467.51 and the net cost was $29,330.89. Wall, *Wall Report*, 39.

76 In 1966, for example, the provincial government initiated a bursary of $50/month for all boarding students at the North West River school from Grade 7 and up to cover boarding fees and clothes (Peacock, Royal Commission on Education and Youth, 1967).

77 Beginning in September 1953, the Department of Public Welfare paid a grant of $5 per month to the parents of children at the IGA dormitories at Cartwright and North West River, as well as to children in the Moravian boarding schools at Makkovik and Nain. When passed along to the boarding schools, the payments enabled the parents to qualify for the Family Allowance (Wall, *Wall Report*, 39).

78 Wall, *Wall Report*, 58.

79 Ibid.

80 Charles Curtis to Dr. Frecker, 29 Feb. 1960, Minister of Education, PRC 10, Temp Box 21(B), File 77/25, Vol. IV, Grenfell Public School Board, PANL.

81 Wall, *Wall Report*.

82 Ibid, 46.

83 Ibid., 25–29.

84 Ibid., 46–47.

85 Ibid.

86 Charles Curtis, Report to IGA Board of Directors 1961, PRC 10, Temp Box 21(B), File 77/25, Vol. V, Grenfell Public School Board, PANL.

87 Harry Paddon died of peritonitis, an inflammation in the abdominal wall, caused by a bacterial infection. As his son, Tony, wrote, "There was no treatment for this infection — penicillin was still four years away." Harry was 59. (Paddon, *Labrador Doctor*, 42.)

88 Rompkey, *Grenfell of Labrador*, 293.

89 Paddon, *Labrador Doctor*.

90 Charles Curtis, "Report to the Board of Directors, 1944," MG 63.2184, Reports of the coast: 1930, 1938–47, PANL.

91 Bill Rompkey, *The Story of Labrador* (Montreal and Kingston: McGill-Queen's University Press, 2003), 97.

92 In 1959, the two schools in North West River had 167 students, and the three schools in Happy Valley had 586 students (Wall, *Wall Report*, 35).

93 Ibid., 56–57.

94 Ibid., 57.

95 Gordon Thomas, "Superintendents' Report, December 1964," MG 63.2028, folder 2, Reports, surveys, etc., PANL.

96 Tony Paddon to Gordon Thomas, 6 Aug. 1962, MG 63.3066, North West River — folder 4, PANL.

97 Ibid.

98 Minutes of Meeting of Council of Education, 3 Apr. 1962, 193.14.7.02.003, MUN Archives.

99 Yale School brief to the Royal Commission on Education and Youth, 1967, 3.

100 Diamond Jenness, *Eskimo Administration III: Labrador* (Montreal: Arctic Institute of North America, 1965), 90.

101 Brief #26 by Rev. Peacock to the Royal Commission on Education and Youth, 1967.

102 Paddon, Educational Problems in Labrador, for the Royal Commission on Education and Youth, 1967, 9.

103 Telegram from Paddon to Smallwood, 21 Nov. 1963, 075.1.24.006, MUN Archives.

104 Prime Minister Pearson to Premier Smallwood, 25 May 1965, PRC 35, Box #46 (location: 52-1-5-3), File 75, Vol. 1, Federal–Provincial Committee Appointments/Minutes of Meetings — Native Education, PANL.

105 Minutes of 1st meeting of Federal–Provincial Committee on Financial Assistance for Indians and Eskimos in Northern Labrador, 6–7 July 1965, PRC 35, Box #46 (location: 52-1-5-3), File 75, Vol. 1, Federal–Provincial Committee Appointments/Minutes of Meetings — Native Education, PANL.

106 Minutes of 3rd meeting of Federal–Provincial Committee on Financial Assistance for Indians and Eskimos in Northern Labrador, 21 June 1966, PRC 35, Box #46 (location: 52-1-5-3), File 75, Vol. 1, Federal–Provincial Committee Appointments/Minutes of Meetings — Native Education, PANL.

107 C.M. Bolger, Assistant Director, [Department of Northern Affairs and National Resources], to Mr. Gordon, 27 June 1966, Library and Archives Canada (LAC), RG 85, Acc. 1997-98/076, Box 158, File 1006-5, Vol. 9 [Restricted], as referenced in Joan Holmes & Associates, "Newfoundland and Labrador Schools — North West River," Report for Andersen class action court case (St. John's, n.d.) 60.

108 Holmes, "Newfoundland and Labrador Schools — North West River."

109 The International Grenfell Association paid $100,000, while the provincial government (with federal government funding) paid $200,000 for the dormitory: Frank Houghton — Memorandum to IGA executive committee re: dormitory

project in NWR, 21 Oct. 1966, MG 63.3066.9, PANL. The federal government agreed to pay 90 per cent of two-thirds of the costs because about two-thirds of the new students would be Inuit or partly Inuit (Paddon to Ed Schreyer, MP for Selkirk District, 26 Aug. 1968, MG 63.3066, North West River — folder 11, PANL).

110 Paddon, *Labrador Doctor*; Minutes of 23rd meeting of Federal–Provincial Committee on Financial Assistance for Indians and Eskimos, 9–11 Dec. 1975, PRC, Box #46 (location: 52-1-5-3), File 75, Vol. 3, 9 Feb. 1976 — Federal–Provincial Committee Appointments/Minutes of Meetings — Native Education, PANL.

111 Paddon, Educational Problems in Labrador in light of the Grenfell Mission's experience in education, Royal Commission on Education and Youth, 1967, 19.

112 Ibid.

113 Frederick William Rowe, ed., *Proceedings of the Conference on Labrador Affairs, held Feb. 13th–16th, 1956* (St. John's: Government of Newfoundland, 1956).

114 Annual Reports of the Department of Public Welfare: Annual Report for Year ending March 31, 1956, Division of Northern Labrador Affairs, p. 73, HV 109, N11, PANL.

115 Paddon to Ed Schreyer, MP for Selkirk District, 26 Aug. 1968, MG 63.3066, North West River — folder 11, PANL.

116 Brief #55 from Yale School teachers to the Royal Commission on Education and Youth, 1967, 2.

117 W.A. Paddon to Edward Roberts, 17 June 1966, MG 63.3066.8, PANL.

118 In the early 1950s, the school lobbied the provincial government for additional teachers because of the number of Indigenous students. W.A. Paddon, Some Educational Problems in Labrador, 1953, PRC 10, Temp Box 21(B), File 77/25, Vol. I, PANL; Paddon to Frecker, 20 July 1956, PRC 10, Temp Box 21(B), File 77/25, Vol. III, PANL; Paddon to Dept. of Education, 10 July 1957, PRC 10, Temp Box 21(B), File 77/25, Vol. III, PANL.

119 Sean Cadigan, *Newfoundland and Labrador: A History* (Toronto: University of Toronto Press, 2009), 241.

120 Paddon to Roberts, 21 Feb. 1968, 075.1.24.011, MUN Archives.

121 H.B. Hawthorn, ed., *A Survey of the Contemporary Indians of Canada: Economic, Political, Educational Needs and Policies* (Hawthorn Report), vol. 2 (Ottawa: Indian Affairs Branch, 1967), 88.

122 Paddon to Ed Schreyer, MP for Selkirk District, 26 Aug. 1968, PRC 10, Temp Box 21(B), File 77/25, Vol. I, PANL.

123 Bella Shouse, *Them Days* 13, no. 1 (Sept. 1987): 9.

124 Anonymous writer in Healing Journey Team, "Gathering the Stories."

125 Patricia Kemuksigak in Navarana Igloliorte and Shirley Flowers (directors), *The*

Courage to Remember: Stories of Our Labrador Residential School Experience [film], (Happy Valley, NL: Nunatsiavut Government, 2010).

126 Newfoundland and Labrador Healing and Commemoration sharing panel transcripts, 2018, PANL; TRC sharing panel transcripts for Hopedale, Happy Valley–Goose Bay, Halifax, and Inuvik sessions, 2011, National Centre for Truth and Reconciliation, University of Manitoba.

127 Kitora Abel, in *Courage to Remember* film.

128 Rosie Mitsuk, in *Courage to Remember* film.

129 Abe Flowers, 22 Sept. 2011, National Centre for Truth and Reconciliation Archives, Sharing Panel (Hopedale Hearing): SP026, TRC.

130 Jim Tuttauk, Healing and Commemoration project, Hopedale, 21 Feb. 2018.

131 Ivy Andersen Strangemore, Healing and Commemoration project, Makkovik, 24 Apr. 2018.

132 Philip Abel, 22 Sept. 2011, National Centre for Truth and Reconciliation Archives, Sharing Panel (Hopedale Hearing): SP026, TRC.

133 Hulda Nochasak, in *Courage to Remember* film.

134 Philip Abel, in *Courage to Remember* film.

135 Evelyn Winters, Healing and Commemoration project, Happy Valley–Goose Bay, 11 Mar. 2018.

136 Laura Palliser Pardy, Healing and Commemoration project, Rigolet, 15 May 2018.

137 Irene Voisey, Healing and Commemoration project, Makkovik, 24 Apr. 2018.

138 Dr. Paddon to Edward Roberts, 16 June 1966, 075.3.22.002, MUN Archives.

139 Wanda Lucy, in *Courage to Remember* film.

140 Emma Ford Reelis, Healing and Commemoration project, St. John's, 28 Apr. 2018.

141 Kitora Abel, in *Courage to Remember* film.

142 Kitora Abel, 22 Sept. 2011, National Centre for Truth and Reconciliation Archives, Sharing Panel (Hopedale Hearing): SP026, TRC.

143 Natan Obed is the current president of Inuit Tapiriit Kanatami.

144 Jim Tuttauk, Healing and Commemoration project, Hopedale, 21 Feb. 2018.

145 Edna McLean, in Healing Journey Team, "Gathering the Stories."

146 Philip Abel, in *Courage to Remember* film.

147 Sybella Tuglavina, Healing and Commemoration project, Hopedale, 21 Feb. 2018.

148 Jim Tuttauk, Healing and Commemoration project, Hopedale, 21 Feb. 2018.

149 Marjorie Flowers, Healing and Commemoration project, Hopedale, 21 Feb. 2018.

150 Hulda Pijogge, in *Courage to Remember* film.

151 Rose Oliver, Healing and Commemoration project, written submission, Happy Valley–Goose Bay, 8 May 2018.

152 Kitora Abel, 22 Sept. 2011, National Centre for Truth and Reconciliation Archives, Sharing Panel (Hopedale Hearing): SP026, TRC.

153 Marjorie Flowers in Legacy of Hope Foundation, *We Were So Far Away: The Inuit Experience of Residential Schools*, curated by Heather Igloliorte (Ottawa: Legacy of Hope Foundation, 2010), 69–70.

154 Elaine Lane, Healing and Commemoration project, Postville, 26 Feb. 2018.

155 Richard Rich, Healing and Commemoration project, Rigolet, 15 May 2018.

156 Maria Brown Brazeau, Healing and Commemoration project, Ottawa, 3 Mar. 2018.

157 Sybella Tuglavina, Healing and Commemoration project, Hopedale, 21 Feb. 2018.

158 Katherine Baikie-Pottle, Letter to the editor, *The Labradorian*, 23 June 2008, A2.

159 Department of Public Welfare, Annual Report for Year ending March 31, 1951, HV 109, N11, Annual Reports of the Department of Public Welfare, PANL.

160 Ibid.

161 Department of Public Welfare, Annual Report for Year ending March 31, 1954, HV 109, N11, Annual Reports of the Department of Public Welfare, PANL; Wall, *Wall Report*.

162 Rosina Holwell, Healing and Commemoration project, Nain, 14 Apr. 2018.

163 Ibid.

164 Arie Molema, "'National Memory' and Its Remainders: Labrador Inuit Counter-histories of Residential Schooling," in *Power through Testimony: Reframing Residential Schools in the Age of Reconciliation*, ed. Brieg Captaine and Karine Vanthuyne (Vancouver: University of British Columbia Press, 2017), 144.

165 Toby Obed, Healing and Commemoration project, Hopedale, 21 Feb. 2018.

Chapter Twelve

1 Flanagan, "Schooling," 121.

2 Nain Moravian Mission Diaries for 1962: "August 30: Teachers arrived and considerable trouble about grades X and XI. Children do not want to return to NWR but want to stay here to do high school. September 2: High school children refuse to go out to school. Can be taught here they say. September 6: MV Hopedale arrived. Mr. Peacock on board. Air ambulance arrived with Dr. Paddon. Both had talk with high school. Fees will be taken care of. Most children going. Dr. Paddon here overnight. Trying to procure enough high school students to establish regional high school for coastal area." (Newsletters, White Elephant Museum Archive, Makkovik.)

3 Flanagan, "Schooling," 122.

4 Peacock to Rowe, 20 Feb. 1963, 077.6.01.011, MUN Archives.
5 Flanagan, "Schooling," 118–19.
6 Ibid., 156, 163, 168.
7 Ibid., 169.
8 Anonymous woman quoted ibid., 126.
9 Flanagan illustrates how class divisions impacted access to education. He provides details of the 56 students who did go to North West River during this period: two were sent there for medical reasons, two were social services placements, while the other 52 were bursary students, most of whom had connections with the Moravian schools or were from elite families. Of the 149 children (73 per cent) who did not go, more than half were from relocated families from Hebron or Nutak. Although only 10 had received high school diplomas, this is an incomplete number, as 13 were still in school in 1978–79 (ibid., 167–68).
10 Susanna Webb, Healing and Commemoration project, Nain, 13 Apr. 2018.
11 *kinatuinamot illengajuk* 1, no. 2 (26 Feb. 1975): 7.
12 Angus Andersen, St. John's, 2018.
13 Faculty Council, "Education in Labrador: A Brief submitted to the Royal Commission on Labrador" (St. John's: Memorial University, 1973).
14 Rowe, *The Development of Education*, 161.
15 Joan Holmes & Associates, "Newfoundland and Labrador Schools — Nain," Report for Andersen class action court case (St. John's, n.d.), 43.
16 Minutes of 4th meeting of Federal–Provincial Committee on Financial Assistance for Indians and Eskimos in Northern Labrador, 13–14 Dec. 1966; Minutes of 6th meeting of Federal–Provincial Committee on Financial Assistance for Indians and Eskimos in Northern Labrador, 28 Nov. 1967; Minutes of 11th meeting of Federal–Provincial Committee on Financial Assistance for Indians and Eskimos in Northern Labrador, 3 Dec. 1970, PRC 35, Box #46 (location: 52-1-5-3), File 75, Vol. 1, Federal–Provincial Committee Appointments/Minutes of Meetings — Native Education, PANL.
17 Royal Commission on Labrador, *Report of the Royal Commission on Labrador* (St. John's: Royal Commission on Labrador, 1974), 219.
18 Ibid.
19 *kinatuinamot illengajuk* published a public notice from the Nain School Committee stating: "We are glad to let you know that we will have a teacher here next September to teach grade 9. We hope that those who thought they would have to go to Northwest River will be glad of this chance to stay home in Nain" (*kinatuinamot illengajuk*, no. 20 [26 July 1972]: 6, Centre for Newfoundland Studies, MUN).

20 *kinatuinamot illengajuk*, no. 52 (13 Aug. 1973): 64: "Will we have grade 8 this year? Hopedale. What we don't understand is why some communities here on the coast have grade eight while other communities have to send their grade eight school children to North West River." (Centre for Newfoundland Studies, MUN.)

21 Terje Brantenberg, "Ethnic Commitments and Local Government in Nain, 1969–76," in *The White Arctic: Anthropological Essays on Tutelage and Ethnicity*, ed. Robert Paine (St. John's: ISER Books, 1977), 392–94.

22 Brice-Bennett, *Our Footprints Are Everywhere*; Andrea Procter, Lawrence Felt, and David Natcher, "Introduction," in *Settlement, Subsistence, and Change among the Labrador Inuit: The Nunatsiavummiut Experience*, ed. David Natcher, Lawrence Felt, and Andrea Procter (Winnipeg: University of Manitoba Press, 2012), 3–13.

23 Minutes of 14th meeting of Federal–Provincial Committee on Financial Assistance for Indians and Eskimos in Northern Labrador, 21 June 1972.

24 Minutes of 3rd meeting of Federal–Provincial Committee on Financial Assistance for Indians and Eskimos in Northern Labrador, 21 June 1966; Minutes of 11th meeting of Federal–Provincial Committee on Financial Assistance for Indians and Eskimos in Northern Labrador, 3 Dec. 1970; Minutes of 14th meeting of Federal–Provincial Committee on Financial Assistance for Indians and Eskimos in Northern Labrador, 21 June 1972.

25 Minutes of 17th meeting of Federal–Provincial Committee on Financial Assistance for Indians and Eskimos in Northern Labrador, 28–29 Nov. 1973.

26 Minutes of 19th meeting of Federal–Provincial Committee on Financial Assistance for Indians and Eskimos, 10 Dec. 1974, p. 13.

27 Rosina Jeddore to C. Roebothan, Deputy Minister of Education, 7 Oct. 1974, PRC 35, Box #6 (location: 51-1-1-3), File 75, Vol. 27, Native Education, PANL.

28 Rose Jeddore, "Report on Native Schools at Nain, Hopedale, and Makkovik, 1975," APL 100/12, Them Days Archive.

29 Ibid.

30 Rose Jeddore, "Draft Report on High School Education," 2, PRC 35, Box #6 (location: 51-1-1-3), File 75, Vol. 28, Native Education, PANL.

31 Rose Jeddore, "Draft Report on Native Schools, 1975," 3–4, PRC 35, Box #6 (location: 51-1-1-3), File 75, Vol. 28, Native Education, PANL

32 "School Board Committee Holds Meeting," *kinatuinamot illengajuk* 1, no. 24 (Feb. 1976): 1.

33 Flanagan, "Schooling," 157.

34 "School Board Committee Holds Meeting."

35 "From the School," *kinatuinamot illengajuk* 1, no. 39 (23 Oct. 1976): 5.

36 Labrador Inuit Association, "Labrador Inuit Education Conference" (Nain, NL: Labrador Inuit Association, 1987).

37 Beatrice Ford Watts, who had been one of the first students from Nain to go to North West River for high school, attended in her position as School Board Supervisor with special duties in the Inuit language (Labrador Inuit Association, "Labrador Inuit Education Conference," St. John's: MUN Extension Service, 1977).

38 See ibid., 32–34, for comments and debates between provincial officials and Inuit.

39 Ibid., 91.

40 Ibid.

41 Ibid., Appendix: Resolutions, 1.

42 Ibid., 76.

43 Ibid., 89.

44 Minutes of IGA meeting, 7 Mar. 1979, MG 63.3035, Dr. Linwood Brown (folder 2), PANL.

45 Ibid.

46 The provincial government recognized Tony Paddon's lifetime of leadership in Labrador by appointing him Lieutenant-Governor of Newfoundland and Labrador between 1981 and 1986.

47 Minutes of the Combined Executive and Finance Committees of the IGA meeting, 7 Mar. 1979, 5, MG 63.3035.2, PANL.

48 Minutes of the 104th Meeting of the Board of Directors of the IGA, 21 Sept. 1979, MG 63.2880, PANL.

49 R.H. Mack, Financial Advisor, IGA, "Current Developments in the Grenfell Work," 16 Oct. 1980, MG 63.28, PANL.

50 Resolutions for the Combined Councils of Labrador, 25–30 Mar. 1979. *kinatuinamot illengajuk* 3, no. 24 (29 June 1979): 5.

51 Town Council of Northwest River, "Presentation to the Environmental Hearings Board: Kitts/Michelin Uranium Project" (Northwest River, 1979), Centre for Newfoundland Studies, MUN.

52 *Among the Deep Sea Fishers* 78, no. 2 (July 1981): 35; Gordon Thomas, From Sled to Satellite: My Years with the Grenfell Mission (Toronto: Irwin Publishing, 1987), 110.

53 Thomas, From *Sled to Satellite*, 107.

54 Brice-Bennett, *Our Footprints Are Everywhere.*

55 Government of Canada, "Labrador Inuit Land Claims Agreement" (Ottawa: Indian and Northern Affairs Canada, 2005).

Chapter Thirteen

1 Mailhot, *The People of Sheshatshit*, 16.
2 Ibid., 17.
3 Henriksen, *Hunters in the Barrens*; Mailhot, *The People of Sheshatshit*.
4 Mailhot, *The People of Sheshatshit*, 19.
5 Ibid., 20.
6 Ibid., 22.
7 Zimmerly, *Cain's Land Revisited*.
8 Wadden, *Nitassinan*.
9 Ibid., 61.
10 John McGee, *Cultural Stability and Change among the Montagnais Indians of the Lake Melville Region of Labrador* (Washington, DC: Catholic University of America Press, 1961), 29.
11 Wadden, *Nitassinan*, 61.
12 Mailhot, *The People of Sheshatshit*, 23.
13 Anna Hammond, principal of Our Lady of the Snows School, "Brief to the Royal Commission on Education and Youth" (St. John's, 1967); Colin Samson, *A Way of Life That Does Not Exist: Canada and the Extinguishment of the Innu* (St. John's: ISER Books, 2003).
14 Samson, *A Way of Life*; Wadden, *Nitassinan*.
15 Zimmerly, *Cain's Land Revisited*.
16 Wadden, *Nitassinan*, 61.
17 Samson, *A Way of Life*; Wadden, *Nitassinan*.
18 Walter Rockwood, Memorandum on General Policy in Respect to Indians and Eskimos of Northern Labrador, 1955, MG 908, Box 2, Staff Correspondence, PANL.
19 Innu Nation and Mushuau Innu Band Council, *Gathering Voices*, 27.
20 Hammond, "Brief to the Royal Commission on Education and Youth."
21 Maniaten in Wadden, *Nitassinan*, 65.
22 Tshaukuesh (Elizabeth Penashue) in Wadden, *Nitassinan*, 64–65.
23 Samson, *A Way of Life*, 168.
24 Hammond, "Brief to the Royal Commission on Education and Youth," 3.
25 Ibid.
26 Roman Catholic School Board for Labrador North, "Notes on the Education for the Labrador Indians: Brief to the Royal Commission on Education and Youth" (St. John's, 1967).

27 Samson, *A Way of Life*.
28 Elizabeth Penashue in Samson, *A Way of Life*, 174.
29 Samson, *A Way of Life*, 179.
30 Napess Jean-Pierre Ashini in Samson, *A Way of Life*, 177.
31 Father Pirson in James Roche, *Resettlement of the Mushuau Innu 1948 and 1967: A Collection of Documents from the Provincial Archives of Newfoundland and Labrador and the Centre for Newfoundland Studies* (Sheshatshiu, NL: Innu Nation, 1992).
32 Hammond, "Brief to the Royal Commission on Education and Youth"; Wadden, *Nitassinan*.
33 Annual Reports of the Department of Public Welfare, Annual Reports for Years ending March 31, 1959 and 1960, HV 109, N11, PANL.
34 Government of Newfoundland, *Labrador Conference* (St. John's, 13–16 Feb. 1956), 16.
35 Minutes of 1st meeting of Federal–Provincial Committee on Financial Assistance for Indians and Eskimos in Northern Labrador, 6–7 July 1965; Minutes of 2nd meeting of Federal–Provincial Committee on Financial Assistance for Indians and Eskimos in Northern Labrador, 30 Nov.–1 Dec. 1965, PRC 35, Box #46 (location: 52-1-5-3), File 75, Vol. 1, PANL; Minutes of 3rd meeting of Federal–Provincial Committee on Financial Assistance for Indians and Eskimos in Northern Labrador, 21 June 1966.
36 Wadden, *Nitassinan*.
37 Minutes of 2nd meeting of Federal–Provincial Committee on Financial Assistance for Indians and Eskimos in Northern Labrador, 30 Nov.–1 Dec. 1965.
38 Ibid.
39 Minutes of 18th meeting of Federal–Provincial Committee on Financial Assistance for Indians and Eskimos in Northern Labrador, 3 July 1974, PRC 35, Box #46 (location: 52-1-5-3), File 75, Vol. 1, PANL.
40 Minutes of 3rd meeting of Federal–Provincial Committee on Financial Assistance for Indians and Eskimos in Northern Labrador, 21 June 1966.
41 Dr. W.A. Paddon, "Brief to the Royal Commission on Labrador, on behalf of the International Grenfell Association," 1 June 1973, 16, GN 142.39, PANL.
42 Annual Reports of the Department of Public Welfare. Annual Report for Year ending March 31, 1968, HV 109, N11, PANL.
43 Kaniuekutat with Georg Henriksen, *I Dreamed the Animals. Kaniuekutat: The Life of an Innu Hunter* (New York: Berghahn Books, 2009), 210.
44 Innu Nation and Mushuau Innu Band Council, *Gathering Voices*, 57.
45 Samson, *A Way of Life*, 173.

46 Rockwood, Northern Labrador Affairs, Annual Report for Year ending March 31, 1960, Annual Reports of the Department of Public Welfare, HV 109, N11, PANL.

47 Ibid.

48 Bishop Lionel Scheffer to Frecker, 12 May 1956, PRC 9.7433.75.14, PANL.

49 Etuetish and Akatis in Innu Nation and Mushuau Innu Band Council, *Gathering Voices*, 67; Minutes of 5th meeting of Federal–Provincial Committee on Financial Assistance for Indians and Eskimos in Northern Labrador, 7 June 1967, PRC 35, Box #46 (location: 52-1-5-3), File 75, Vol. 1, PANL.

50 Henriksen, *Hunters in the Barrens.*

51 Caroline Andrew, "Early Childhood Education," in *It's Like the Legend: Innu Women's Voices*, ed. Nympha Byrne and Camille Fouillard (Charlottetown, PEI: Gynergy Books, 2000), 124–25.

52 Elizabeth Penashue, *Them Days* 32, no. 1 (2008): 10.

53 Francis Penashue, Sept. 20, 2011, National Centre for Truth and Reconciliation Archives, Sharing Panel (Goose Bay Hearing): SP025, TRC.

54 Ibid.

55 Annual Reports of the Department of Public Welfare. Annual Report for Year ending March 31, 1969, HV 109, N11, PANL.

56 Annual Reports of the Department of Public Welfare. Annual Report for Year ending March 31, 1971, HV 109, N11, PANL.

57 Minutes of 16th meeting of Federal–Provincial Committee on Financial Assistance for Indians and Eskimos in Northern Labrador, 26 June 1973, PRC 35, Box 46, PANL.

58 Innu Nation and Mushuau Innu Band Council, *Gathering Voices*; Samson, *A Way of Life*.

59 Hammond, "Brief to the Royal Commission on Education and Youth" (St. John's, 1967).

60 Etuetish and Akatis in Innu Nation and Mushuau Innu Band Council, *Gathering Voices*, 67.

61 Minutes of 17th meeting of Federal–Provincial Committee on Financial Assistance for Indians and Eskimos in Northern Labrador, 28–29 Nov. 1973; Minutes of 19th meeting of Federal–Provincial Committee on Financial Assistance for Indians and Eskimos in Northern Labrador, 10 Dec. 1974.

62 Mamu Tshishkutamashutau Innu Education, https://www.innueducation.ca.

Conclusion

1 Toby Obed, acceptance of apology speech, 24 Nov. 2018, Happy Valley–Goose Bay, NL.
2 Ibid.
3 Josie Curl Penny, Healing and Commemoration project, Ottawa, 3 Mar. 2018.
4 Beatrice Winters Hope, Healing and Commemoration project, Happy Valley–Goose Bay, 10 Mar. 2018.
5 Natan Obed, "Power and Politics," CBC TV, 24 Nov. 2018, https://www.cbc.ca/player/play/1103191107627.
6 Ibid.
7 Justin Brake, "Innu Nation Says It Will Refuse Trudeau's Labrador Residential School Apology," *APTN News*, 23 Nov. 2017, https://aptnnews.ca/2017/11/23/innu-nation-says-it-will-refuse-trudeaus-labrador-residential-school-apology/.
8 Solomon Davis, "Letter to the Editor: My Residential School Experience Was Positive," *The Telegram*, 25 Nov. 2017, B3.
9 Ibid.
10 The Catholic Church is not included in this list because it did not establish or operate boarding schools in Labrador.
11 Personal communication, Bertha Holeiter and Beatrice Hope, Happy Valley–Goose Bay, NL, 2019.
12 Statement by the Moravian Church of Newfoundland and Labrador, Healing and Commemoration Project, Feb. 2019.
13 "Labrador Residential School Survivors Left Out of Federal Apology and Settlement," *APTN News*, 19 Mar. 2018, https://aptnnews.ca/2018/03/19/labrador-residential-school-survivors-left-federal-apology-settlement/.
14 As of December 2017, the New England Grenfell Association reported assets of $11,043,547 (ledger value) and income of $798,552: http://www.bigdatabase.com/Big-DB/USFoundation-profiles/NEW%20ENGLAND%20GRENFELL%20ASSOCIATION-042192696.HTML.
15 From International Grenfell Association website: http://www.grenfellassociation.org/grants/completed-grants/.
16 See IGA website: http://www.grenfellassociation.org/who-we-are/leadership/.
17 Statement by the Premier on Residential Schools, Government of Newfoundland and Labrador, 23 Nov. 2018, https://www.releases.gov.nl.ca/releases/2017/exec/1123n02.aspx.

18 Mark Quinn, "Dwight Ball's 'Broken Promise': Residential School Survivors Await Apology," *CBC News*, 14 May 2019, https://www.cbc.ca/news/canada/newfoundland-labrador/ball-residential-school-apology-1.5135406.

19 Trudeau, "Statement of Apology."

20 Ibid.

21 Statement by the Moravian Church of Newfoundland and Labrador, Healing and Commemoration Project, Feb. 2019.

22 For example, see Labrador Benefits Agreement for teachers: https://www.nlta.nl.ca/lba/.

23 Grant, "Nain's Silenced Majority."

24 For more information, see https://nunatukavut.ca/programs/employment-and-skills-development/; https://www.nunatsiavut.com/beneficiary-information/education-employment/; and https://www.innueducation.ca/post-secondary.html.

25 NunatuKavut Inuit Education Program: https://nunatukavut.ca/programs/nunatukavut-inuit-education-program/.

26 Government of Canada, "Labrador Inuit Land Claims Agreement."

27 Department of Education and Economic Development, Nunatsiavut Government, https://www.nunatsiavut.com/government/departments/.

28 Inuit Bachelor of Education program: https://www.nunatsiavut.com/article/students-graduate-from-inuit-bachelor-of-education-program/.

29 Mamu Tshishkutamashutau Innu Education: https://www.innueducation.ca/trustees.html.

30 Mamu Tshishkutamashutau Innu Education: https://www.innueducation.ca.

31 Newfoundland and Labrador Residential Schools Healing and Commemoration: https://www.rcaanc-cirnac.gc.ca/eng/1511531626107/1539962009489.

32 Sarah Anala, Nunatsiavut Elder for apology gathering, 24 Nov. 2017, Happy Valley–Goose Bay, NL.

33 Toby Obed, acceptance of apology speech.

BIBLIOGRAPHY

Archival Sources

Archives and Special Collections, Memorial University of Newfoundland, St. John's, NL.

Frecker Collection.

Rhoda Dawson Bickerdike Collection.

Rowe Collection.

Smallwood Collection.

Makkovik White Elephant Museum, Makkovik, NL.

Moravian Church annual reports, correspondence and newsletters.

Moravian Church House Archives, Muswell Hill, London, UK.

Foreign Missions: Labrador Collection.

British Mission Board minute books.

Moravian Church Archives, Bethlehem, Pennsylvania, USA.

Kate Hettasch Collection.

National Centre for Truth and Reconciliation, Winnipeg, MB.

Truth and Reconciliation Archives, Sharing Panel: Northern National Event, Atlantic National Event, Goose Bay Hearing, and Hopedale Hearing.

Newfoundland and Labrador Heritage, St. John's, NL.

Labrador Boundary Dispute Documents (Judicial Committee of the Privy Council): https://www.heritage.nf.ca/articles/politics/privy-council-introduction.php

Provincial Archives Division, The Rooms, St. John's, NL.

Department of Labrador Affairs.

Department of Public Welfare annual reports.

Education Collections: PRC 9, PRC 10, and PRC 35.

International Grenfell Association Collection.

Office of the Colonial Secretary Fonds.

Polly Taylor Fonds.

Walter Rockwood Collection.

Them Days Archive, Happy Valley–Goose Bay, NL.
International Grenfell Association Collection.
Interview transcripts.
Moravian Church records.

Periodicals

Among the Deep Sea Fishers
kinatuinamot illengajuk
Periodical Accounts of the Moravian Missions (Series 1: 1790–1889, volumes 1–34; Series 2: 1890–1961, volumes and numbers starting at 1 until the year 1928, when only numbers, beginning with 136, are used)
Them Days

Published Sources

Andersen, Joan. *Celebrating the 100th Anniversary of the White Elephant.* Makkovik, NL: White Elephant Museum, 2015.

———. *Makkovik: 100 Years Plus.* Makkovik, NL: Robinson-Blackmore, 1996.

Andrew, Caroline. "Early Childhood Education." In *It's Like the Legend: Innu Women's Voices*, edited by Nympha Byrne and Camille Fouillard. Charlottetown, PEI: Gynergy Books, 2000.

Anonymous. *Moravians in Labrador.* Edinburgh: J. Ritchie, 1833.

Badger, Theodore L. "Why Sir Wilfred Grenfell?" *The North American Review* 226, no. 11 (July 1928): 14–21.

Baikie-Pottle, Katherine. Letter to the editor, *The Labradorian*, 23 June 2008, A2.

Battle Harbour Literary Council. *Linking the Generations: A Collection of Oral Histories, Excerpts from the Battle Harbour Region.* Mary's Harbour, NL: Battle Harbour Literacy Council, 1998.

Ben-Dor, Shmuel. *Makkovik: Eskimos and Settlers in a Labrador Community.* St. John's: ISER Books, 1966.

Brantenberg, Anne. "The Marginal School and the Children of Nain." In *The White Arctic: Anthropological Essays on Tutelage and Ethnicity*, edited by Robert Paine, 344–58. St. John's: ISER Books, 1977.

Brantenberg, Terje. "Ethnic Commitments and Local Government in Nain, 1969–76." In *The White Arctic: Anthropological Essays on Tutelage and Ethnicity*, edited by Robert Paine, 376–410. St. John's: ISER Books, 1977.

Brewster, Natalie. "The Inuit in Southern Labrador: A View from Snack Cove." MA thesis, Memorial University of Newfoundland, 2005.

Brice-Bennett, Carol. "Land Use in the Nain and Hopedale Regions." In *Our Footprints Are Everywhere: Inuit Land Use and Occupancy in Labrador,* edited by Carol Brice-Bennett, 97–203. Nain, NL: Labrador Inuit Association, 1977.

———. "Two Opinions: Inuit and Moravian Missionaries in Labrador 1804–1860." MA thesis, Memorial University of Newfoundland, 1981.

———. "Renewable Resource Use and Wage Employment in the Economy of Northern Labrador." St. John's: Background Report for the Royal Commission on Employment and Unemployment, 1986.

———. "Missionaries as Traders: Moravians and Labrador Inuit, 1771–1860." In *Merchant Credit and Labour Strategies in Historical Perspective,* edited by Rosemary E. Ommer, 223–46. Fredericton, NB: Acadiensis, 1990.

———. "Dispossessed: The Eviction of Inuit from Hebron, Labrador." Submitted to Royal Commission on Aboriginal Peoples. Happy Valley–Goose Bay: Labrador Institute, 1994.

Briggs, Jean. *Never in Anger: Portrait of an Eskimo Family.* Cambridge, MA: Harvard University Press, 1970.

———. *Inuit Morality Play: The Emotional Education of a Three Year Old.* St. John's: ISER Books, 1998.

———. "'Qallunaat Run on Rails; Inuit Do What They Want to Do.' Autonomies in Camp and Town." *Études/Inuit/Studies* 25, nos. 1-2 (2001): 229–47.

———. *Childrearing Practices: Interviewing Inuit Elders*, Vol. 3. Iqaluit, NU: Nunavut Arctic College, 2017.

Brody, Hugh. *The Other Side of Eden: Hunters, Farmers, and the Shaping of the World.* Vancouver: Douglas & McIntyre, 2000.

Brown, Rachel, Horace McNeill, and Lincoln Brown. *Inasmuch: The Grenfell Mission — St. Anthony.* Winslow, ME: n.p., 1992.

Buckle, Francis. *The Anglican Church in Labrador, 1848–1998,* Labrador City, NL: Archdeaconry of Labrador, 1998.

———. ed. *Labrador Diary, 1915–1925: The Gordon Journals.* St. John's: Print Atlantic, 2003.

———, ed. *Labrador Teacher: Clara Gordon's Journal.* St. John's: Anglican Parish of Cartwright, 2005.

Budgell, Anne. *We All Expected to Die: Spanish Influenza in Labrador, 1918–1919.* St. John"s: ISER Books, 2018.

Cabak, Melanie. "Inuit Women as Catalysts of Change: An Archaeological Study of 19th Century Northern Labrador." MA thesis, University of South Carolina, 1991.

Cadigan, Sean. *Newfoundland and Labrador: A History.* Toronto: University of Toronto Press, 2009.

Canada, Truth and Reconciliation Commission of Canada. *Canada's Residential Schools: The Final Report for the Truth and Reconciliation Commission of Canada.* Montreal and Kingston: McGill-Queen's University Press, 2015.

Davey, J.W. *The Fall of Torngak, or The Moravian Mission on the Coast of Labrador.* London: Partridge, 1905.

Davis, Solomon. "Letter: My Residential School Experience Was Positive." *The Telegram,* 23 Nov. 2017.

Faculty Council. "Education in Labrador: A Brief submitted to the Royal Commission on Labrador." St. John's: Memorial University, 1973.

Fay, Amelia. "Big Men, Big Women, or Both? Examining the Coastal Trading System of the Eighteenth-Century Labrador Inuit." In *History and Renewal of Labrador's Inuit-Metis,* edited by John C. Kennedy, 75–93. St. John's: ISER Books, 2014.

———. "Missionaries, Merchants, and Inuit Entrepreneurs: An Examination of Trade Relations along the Labrador Coast." *Études/Inuit/Studies* 39, no. 1 (2015): 141–64.

Flanagan, Patrick. "Schooling, Souls, and Social Class: The Labrador Inuit." MA thesis, University of New Brunswick, 1984.

Gordon, Henry. *A Winter in Labrador 1918–1919: Journal of the Rev. Henry Gordon, Cartwright, Labrador.* New York: Published by the author, 1919.

———. *The Labrador Parson: Journal of the Reverend Henry Gordon, 1915–1925,* edited by F. Burnham Gill. St. John's: Provincial Archives of Newfoundland, 1972.

Gosling, William Gilbert. *Labrador: Its Discovery, Exploration, and Development.* London: A. Rivers, 1910.

Government of Canada. *Labrador Inuit Land Claims Agreement.* Ottawa: Indian and Northern Affairs Canada, 2005.

Grant, Dianne. "Nain's Silenced Majority: An Anthropological Examination of Schooling in Northern Labrador." MA thesis, Memorial University of Newfoundland, 2003.

Green, Julie. "Sunday Best: Portrait of Beatrice Watts." Happy Valley–Goose Bay: CBC, 1997.

Gregoire, George. *Walk with My Shadow: The Life of an Innu Man.* St. John's: Creative Publishers, 2012.

Grenfell, Wilfred. *A Labrador Doctor: The Autobiography of Wilfred Thomason Grenfell.* Boston: Houghton Mifflin, 1919.

———. *Forty Years for Labrador.* Boston: Houghton Mifflin, 1919.

———. *Labrador: The Country and Its People.* New York: Macmillan, 1922.

Hanrahan, Maura. *The Lasting Breach: The Omission of Aboriginal People from the Terms of Union between Newfoundland and Canada and Its Ongoing Impacts.*

St. John's: Royal Commission on Renewing and Strengthening Our Place in Canada, 2003.

Hawthorn, H.B., ed. *A Survey of the Contemporary Indians of Canada: Economic, Political, Educational Needs and Policies* (Hawthorn Report), vol. 2. Ottawa: Indian Affairs Branch, 1967.

Healing Journey Team. "Gathering the Stories." Happy Valley-Goose Bay, NL: Labrador Aboriginal Legal Services, 2010.

Henriksen, Georg. *Hunters in the Barrens: The Naskapi on the Edge of the White Man's World*. St. John's: ISER Books, 1973.

Hiller, James. "The Foundation and Early Years of the Moravian Missionaries in Labrador, 1752–1805." MA thesis, Memorial University of Newfoundland, 1967.

———. "Early Patrons of the Labrador Eskimos: The Moravian Mission in Labrador, 1764–1805." In *Patrons and Brokers in the East Arctic*, edited by Robert Paine, 74–97. St. John's: ISER Books, 1971.

———. "Moravian Land Holdings on the Labrador Coast: A Brief History." In *Our Footprints Are Everywhere: Inuit Land Use and Occupancy in Labrador*, edited by Carol Brice-Bennett, 83–95. Nain, NL: Labrador Inuit Association, 1977.

Holmes, Joan, & Associates. "Newfoundland and Labrador Schools — Nain." Report for Andersen class action court case. St. John's, n.d.

———. "Newfoundland and Labrador Schools — North West River." Report for Andersen class action court case. St. John's, n.d.

———. "Newfoundland and Labrador Schools — St. Anthony." Report for Andersen class action court case. St. John's, n.d.

Howe, Stephen. *Empire: A Very Short Introduction*. Oxford: Oxford University Press, 2002.

Hutton, J.E. *A History of Moravian Missions*. London: Moravian Publication Office, 1922.

Igloliorte, John. *An Inuk Boy Becomes a Hunter*. Halifax: Nimbus Publishing, 1994.

Igloliorte, Navarana, and Shirley Flowers, directors. *The Courage to Remember: Stories of Our Labrador Residential School Experience* [film]. Happy Valley, NL: Nunatsiavut Government, 2010.

Indian and Northern Affairs Canada. "Labrador Inuit Land Claims Agreement." Ottawa: Government of Canada, 2005.

Innu Nation and Mushuau Innu Band Council. *Gathering Voices: Finding Strength to Help Our Children*, edited by Camille Fouillard. Toronto: Douglas & McIntyre, 1995.

Jackson, Lawrence. *Bounty of a Barren Coast: Resource Harvest and Settlement in Southern Labrador.* Happy Valley–Goose Bay: Memorial University of Newfoundland, 1982.

Jenness, Diamond. *Eskimo Administration III: Labrador*. Montreal: Arctic Institute of North America, 1965.

Johnston, James. *Grenfell of Labrador.* London: S.W. Partridge & Co., 1908.

Kaniuekutat with Georg Henriksen. *I Dreamed the Animals. Kaniuekutat: The Life of an Innu Hunter.* New York: Berghahn Books, 2009.

Kaplan, Susan. "Labrador Inuit Ingenuity and Resourcefulness: Adapting to a Complex Environmental, Social, and Spiritual Environment." In *Settlement, Subsistence, and Change among the Labrador Inuit: The Nunatsiavummiut Experience*, edited by David Natcher, Lawrence Felt, and Andrea Procter, 15–42. Winnipeg: University of Manitoba Press, 2012.

Kennedy, John. *Encounters: An Anthropological History of Southeastern Labrador.* Montreal and Kingston: McGill-Queen's University Press, 2015.

Kerr, James Lennox. *Wilfred Grenfell: His Life and Work.* New York: Dodd, Mead & Company, 1959.

Kleivan, Helge. *The Eskimos of North-East Labrador: A History of Eskimo–White Relations 1771–1955*. Oslo: Norsk Polar-Institut, 1966.

Labrador Institute. "Court House Mug-Up (Justice Theme)." Happy Valley–Goose Bay, NL: Labrador Institute, 2005.

Labrador Inuit Association. "Labrador Inuit Education Conference." St. John's: MUN Extension Service, 1977.

———. "Labrador Inuit Education Conference." Nain, NL: Labrador Inuit Association, 1987.

Legacy of Hope Foundation. *We Were So Far Away: The Inuit Experience of Residential Schools*, curated by Heather Igloliorte. Ottawa: Legacy of Hope Foundation, 2010.

Loder, Millicent Blake. *Daughter of Labrador.* St. John's: Harry Cuff Publications, 1989.

Loewen, Brad, and Vincent Delmas. "The Basques in the Gulf of St. Lawrence and Adjacent Shores." *Canadian Journal of Archaeology* 36, no. 2 (2012): 213–66.

MacDonald, Martha. "Inside Stories: Agency and Identity through Language Loss Narratives in Nunatsiavut." PhD diss., Memorial University of Newfoundland, 2015.

MacMillan, Miriam. *Green Seas and White Ice.* New York: Dodd, Mead and Company, 1948.

Mailhot, José. *The People of Sheshatshit: In the Land of the Innu*, translated by Axel Harvey. St. John's: ISER Books, 1997.

McGee, John. *Cultural Stability and Change among the Montagnais Indians of the Lake Melville Region of Labrador*. Washington: Catholic University of America Press, 1961.

Mitchell, Greg. "The Inuit of Southern Labrador and Their Conflicts with Europeans, to 1767." In *Exploring Atlantic Transitions: Archeologies of Transience and Permanence in New Found Lands*, edited by Peter Pope with Shannon Lewis-Simpson, 320–30. Society for Post-Medieval Archaeology Monograph 8. Woodbridge, Suffolk: Boydell Press, 2013.

Molema, Arie. "'National Memory' and Its Remainders: Labrador Inuit Counterhistories of Residential Schooling." In *Power through Testimony: Reframing Residential Schools in the Age of Reconciliation*, edited by Brieg Captaine and Karine Vanthuyne, 135–54. Vancouver: University of British Columbia Press, 2017.

National Film Board. *Labrador North* [film]. Ottawa: National Film Board, 1973.

Niezen, Ronald. *Truth and Indignation: Canada's Truth and Reconciliation Commission on Indian Residential Schools*, 2nd ed. Toronto: University of Toronto Press, 2017.

NunatuKavut Community Council. *Unveiling NunatuKavut: Describing the Lands and People of South/Central Labrador.* Goose Bay, NL: NunatuKavut Community Council, 2010.

Obed, Enoch. "From Nutak to Now." *kinatuinamot illengajuk* (Fall 1999): 44–47.

Paddon, Anthony. *Labrador Doctor.* Toronto: J. Lorimer, 1989.

Pauktuutit Inuit Women of Canada. *The Inuit Way: A Guide to Inuit Culture.* Ottawa: Pauktuutit, 2006.

Penny, Josie Curl. *So Few on Earth: A Labrador Métis Woman Remembers.* Toronto: Dundurn Press, 2010.

Plaice, Evelyn. *The Native Game: Settler Perceptions of Indian/Settler Relations in Central Labrador.* St. John's: ISER Books, 1990.

Pope, Peter. "Bretons, Basques, and Inuit in Labrador and Northern Newfoundland: The Control of Maritime Resources in the 16th and 17th Centuries." *Études/Inuit/Studies* 39, no 1 (2015): 15–36.

Procter, Andrea. "The Prospects of Culture: Resource Management and the Production of Difference in Nunatsiavut, Labrador." PhD diss., Memorial University of Newfoundland, 2012.

———, Lawrence Felt, and David Natcher. "Introduction." In *Settlement, Subsistence, and Change among the Labrador Inuit: The Nunatsiavummiut Experience*, edited by David Natcher, Lawrence Felt, and Andrea Procter, 3–13. Winnipeg: University of Manitoba Press, 2012.

Proulx, Jean-Pierre. *Basque Whaling in Labrador in the 16th Century.* Ottawa: Environment Canada, Parks Service, 1993.

Ramsden, Peter, and Lisa Rankin. "Thule Radiocarbon Chronology and Its Implications for Early Inuit–European Interaction in Labrador." In *Exploring Atlantic Transitions: Archeologies of Transience and Permanence in New Found Lands*, edited by Peter Pope with Shannon Lewis-Simpson, 299–309. Society for Post-Medieval Archaeology Monograph 8. Woodbridge, Suffolk: Boydell Press, 2013.

Roche, James. *Resettlement of the Mushuau Innu 1948 and 1967: A Collection of Documents from the Provincial Archives of Newfoundland and Labrador and the Centre for Newfoundland Studies.* Sheshatshiu, NL: Innu Nation, 1992.

Rollmann, Hans. "Moravian Education in Labrador: A Legacy of Literacy." In *Conference Proceedings*, edited by Gerald Galway and David Dibbon, 227–36. St. John's: Memorial University of Newfoundland, 2008.

———. "Johann Christian Erhardt and the First Moravian Exploration of Labrador in 1752." In *Moravian Beginnings in Labrador: Papers from a Symposium held in Makkovik and Hopedale*, edited by Hans Rollmann, 53–68. St. John's: Newfoundland and Labrador Occasional Publications No. 2, 2009.

———. "The Labrador Land Grants of 1769 and 1774." In *Moravian Beginnings in Labrador: Papers from a Symposium held in Makkovik and Hopedale*, edited by Hans Rollmann, 104–31. St. John's: Newfoundland and Labrador Occasional Publications No. 2, 2009.

———. "Moravians in Central Labrador: The Indigenous Inuit Mission of Jacobus and Salome at Snooks Cove." *Journal of Moravian Studies* 9 (Fall 2010): 7–40.

———. "'So fond of the pleasure to shoot': The Sale of Firearms to Inuit on Labrador's North Coast in the Late Eighteenth Century." *Newfoundland and Labrador Studies* 26, no. 1 (2011): 5–24.

———. ". . . That Between Their Church and Ours There Is Hardly Any Difference: Settler Families on Labrador's North Coast Join the Moravian Church." In *History and Renewal of Labrador's Inuit-Métis*, edited by John C. Kennedy, 180–214. St. John's: ISER Books, 2014.

Rompkey, Bill. *The Story of Labrador.* Montreal and Kingston: McGill-Queen's University Press, 2003.

Rompkey, Ronald, ed. *Jessie Luther at the Grenfell Mission.* Montreal and Kingston: McGill-Queen's University Press, 2001.

———, ed. *The Labrador Memoir of Dr Harry Paddon, 1912–1938.* Montreal and Kingston: McGill-Queen's University Press, 2003.

———. *Grenfell of Labrador: A Biography.* Montreal and Kingston: McGill-Queen's Press, 2009.

Rowe, Frederick William, ed. *Proceedings of the Conference on Labrador Affairs, held Feb. 13th–16th, 1956.* St. John's: Government of Newfoundland, 1956.

———. *The Development of Education in Newfoundland.* Toronto: Ryerson Press, 1964.

Royal Commission on Labrador. *Report of the Royal Commission on Labrador.* St. John's: Royal Commission on Labrador, 1974.

Sabathy-Judd, Linda. "Winning Souls for Jesus: Moravians in Nain, Labrador, 1771–1781." In *Moravian Beginnings in Labrador: Papers from a Symposium held in Makkovik and Hopedale*, edited by Hans Rollmann, 132–42. St. John's: Newfoundland and Labrador Occasional Publications No. 2, 2009.

Samson, Colin. *A Way of Life That Does Not Exist: Canada and the Extinguishment of the Innu.* St. John's: ISER Books, 2003.

———. *A World You Do Not Know: Settler Societies, Indigenous Peoples and the Attack on Cultural Diversity.* London: University of London, 2013.

Schloss, Brigitte. "The Development of Nain School: 1771–1963." Research paper, Memorial University of Newfoundland, 1964.

Schneider, Robert. "The Formation of Attitudes towards Development in Labrador." PhD thesis, McGill University, 1984.

Sider, Gerald. *Skin for Skin: Death and Life for Inuit and Innu.* Durham, NC: Duke University Press, 2014.

Spalding, Katie, and Anne Grenfell. *Le Petit Nord, or Annals of a Labrador Harbour.* Boston: Houghton Mifflin, 1920.

Stopp, Marianne. *Thule Inuit and Greenlandic Norse in the Eastern Canadian Arctic: A Discussion.* Historic Sites and Monuments Board of Canada, Report Number 2011-27. Ottawa: Government of Canada, 2011.

Swain, Hector. *Lester Leeland Burry: Labrador Parson and Father of Confederation.* St. John's: Harry Cuff Publications, 1983.

Tanner, Adrian, John Kennedy, Susan McCorquodale, and Gordon Inglis. *Aboriginal Peoples and Governance in Newfoundland and Labrador: A Report for the Governance Project.* St. John's: Royal Commission on Aboriginal Peoples, 1994.

Taylor, Garth. "In the Wake of the *Hope*: Jens Haven's 1764 Reconnaissance Journey in Northern Newfoundland and Southern Labrador." In *Moravian Beginnings in Labrador: Papers from a Symposium held in Makkovik and Hopedale*, edited by Hans Rollmann, 87–103. St. John's: Newfoundland and Labrador Studies Occasional Publications No. 2, 2009.

Thomas, Gordon. "The International Grenfell Association: Its Role in Northern Newfoundland and Labrador, Part 1: The Early Days." *Canadian Medical Association Journal* 118 (4 Feb. 1978): 308–10, 326.

———. *From Sled to Satellite: My Years with the Grenfell Mission.* Toronto: Irwin Publishing, 1987.

Trudeau, Justin. "Statement of Apology on Behalf of the Government of Canada to Former Students of the Newfoundland and Labrador Residential Schools, 24 November 2017." Ottawa: Government of Canada, 2017.

Truth and Reconciliation Commission of Canada. *They Came for the Children: Canada, Aboriginal Peoples, and Residential Schools.* Ottawa: Truth and Reconciliation Commission of Canada, 2012.

Uglow, Charles. *The Seafaring Jacksons.* UK: Privately printed, 2009.

Wadden, Marie. *Nitassinan: The Innu Struggle to Reclaim Their Homeland.* Toronto: Douglas & McIntyre, 1991.

Wall, William. *The Wall Report: A Survey of Educational Problems in Selected Study Areas in Northern Newfoundland and Labrador.* A Report to the Board of Directors of the International Grenfell Association, 1960.

Way, Patricia. "The Story of William Phippard." In *History and Renewal of Labrador's Inuit-Métis,* edited by John C. Kennedy, 135–54. St. John's: ISER Books, 2014.

Williamson, Anthony. "The Moravian Mission and Its Impact on the Labrador Eskimo." *Arctic Anthropology* 2, no. 2 (1964): 32–36.

Woodrow, Helen. "Education at the Grenfell Mission in the 1920s." In *The Grenfell Medical Mission and American Support in Newfoundland and Labrador, 1890s–1940s,* edited by Jennifer Connor and Katherine Side, 180–219. Montreal and Kingston: McGill-Queen's University Press, 2019.

Zimmerly, David. *Cain's Land Revisited: Culture Change in Central Labrador, 1775–1972.* St. John's: ISER Books, 1975.

INDEX

Children and local staff at the Makkovik boarding school mentioned in this book

Alice Voisey Andersen
Bertha Andersen
Bill Andersen
Inga Andersen
Jim Andersen
Muriel Lucy Andersen
Violet Andersen
Gladys Broomfield
Gladys Chard Burdett
Mary Oliver Clarke
Rachel Daniels
Sophia Daniels
Hilda Broomfield Dicker
Lavinia Edmunds
Silpa Sillitt Edmunds
Annie Andersen Evans
Margaret Evans
Millicent Harriet Olive Flowers (*1929–1939; died of meningitis at the Makkovik boarding school*)
Ruth Andersen Flowers
Emily Gear
Susie Lucy
Millie Mitsuk Martin
Susie Mitsuk
Sybilla Pamak Nitsman
Manasse Pijogge
Amos Manuel Voisey (*1913–1927; died of a ruptured appendix at the Makkovik boarding school*)
Clara Voisey
Edward Voisey
Jim Voisey

Children and local staff at the Nain boarding school mentioned in this book

Sam Andersen
Melena Barbour
Silpa Sillitt Barbour
Miriam Flowers Brown
Joan Martin Dicker
Katie Sillitt Dicker
Mary Sillitt Dicker
Abe Flowers
Garfield Flowers
Millie Flowers
Elsie Ford
Amos Fox
Josasi Fox
Oma Freitag
Huldah Green
Bertha Kairtok Holeiter
Hulda "Hilda" Hunter
Marcus Hunter
John Igloliorte
Julius Ikkusek
Lucas Ittulak
Maggie Ittulak Jararuse
Paul Jararuse
Betty Ford Koch
Bella Winters Voisey Leo
Regina Maggo
Susan Martin
Juliana Merkuratsuk
Tabea Murphy
Eva Okkuatsiak Nochasak
Edward Sillitt
Kristianna Sillitt
Sibilla Sillitt
Rosie Voisey Ford Spurvey
Minnie Voisey
Beatrice Ford Watts
Bill Webb
Chesley Webb
Eliza Webb
Jim Webb
Joe Webb
Rose Nukappiak Webb
Sarah Webb
Nellie Andersen Winters

Children and local staff at the St. Anthony Children's Home / Orphanage mentioned in this book

Silpa Sillitt Barbour
Clara Barrett
Eleanor Bird
Millicent Bird
Mina Bird
Elizabeth "Bessie" Blake (*1902–1918; died of Spanish flu while at the orphanage*)
Millicent Blake
Phyllis Blake
Gertrude Bownes
Jessie May Bownes
Lydia Bownes
Bella Butt Brown
Bill Burden
Peter Burden
Priscilla Burden
Rhoda Burden
Mary "Mae" Bird Burton
Bertha Cadwell
Elsie Clark
Martha Clark
Mary Clark
Frank Cove
Blanche Davis
Frank Davis
John Dyson
John "Jack" Edmunds
Albert Elson
Gladys Elson
Ethel Fequet
Margaret Fequet
Elsie Ford
George Ford
Audrey Frieda
Davy Gill
Robert Gray
Triffie Gray
James Hedderson
Lizzie Hedderson
Nancy Hillier
Stanley Hodge
Rosina Kalleo Holwell
Betty Humber
Katie Humber
Phyllis Humber
Hulda "Hilda" Hunter
Raymond Johnson
William Kalleo
Noah Karle (*1897–1918; died of tuberculosis while at the orphanage*)
Clayton Laing
Bertie Lane
Violet Learning
Katie Lethbridge
William Lethbridge
Millicent Blake Loder
Elizabeth "Lizzie" Lucy
John Thomas Lucy
Eva Elson Luther
George Mangrove
Mary Martin
K. Naeme Merkuratsuk
Florence Goudie Michelin
Hubert Michelmore
Laura Millie
David Mitsuk
George Warren Morris
John Newell
Julia Nicolas
Amy Noseworthy
Nora Noseworthy
Enoch Obed
William Palliser
Levi James "Jim" Pardy
Silas Henry Pardy
Alice Parsons
Chesley Patey
Fred Patey
Hayward Patey
William John Piercy
Gertie Reid
Nellie Reid
Randolph Reid
Edith Roberts
Emmie Roberts
Flossie Roberts
Priscie Roberts
Rubena Roberts
Tommy Roberts
Eli Rumboldt
Henry Rumboldt
Ina Rumboldt
Alice Rumbolt
Israel Rumbolt
Lillian Rumbolt
Eva Shiwak
Redgeway Snook
Beth Green Solis
Mary Spurrell

Children and local staff at Muddy Bay boarding school (Labrador Public School) and Lockwood School mentioned in this book

Children and local staff in dormitories at St. Mary's River boarding school (Mary's Harbour) mentioned in this book

Children and local staff in dormitories at North West River mentioned in this book